The *Other* Evangelicals

The ~~Other~~ Evangelicals

A Story of Liberal, Black, Progressive,
Feminist, and Gay Christians—
and the Movement That Pushed Them Out

Isaac B. Sharp

WILLIAM B. EERDMANS PUBLISHING COMPANY
GRAND RAPIDS, MICHIGAN

Wm. B. Eerdmans Publishing Co.
4035 Park East Court SE, Grand Rapids, Michigan 49546
www.eerdmans.com

Published 2023
Printed in the United States of America

29 28 27 26 25 24 23   1 2 3 4 5 6 7

ISBN 978-0-8028-8175-5

Library of Congress Cataloging-in-Publication Data

A catalog record for this book is available from the Library of Congress.

For my three mentors:

Ross Brummett
David P. Gushee
Gary Dorrien

You showed me a better way.

Contents

Foreword

This book makes an indispensable contribution to the understanding of American evangelicalism. It is a work that should reshape the discussion of the identity and history of the American evangelical movement. It has profound implications for today. And it might just make you mad.

While recounting the "canonical" account of evangelicalism that can be found in the scholarly literature, which has focused on supposed evangelical doctrinal distinctives, Isaac Sharp offers here a groundbreaking historical study of "the other evangelicals"—that is, some of the most important groups and individuals that lost major internal battles within evangelicalism and were defined out of the community.

The groups whose losing struggles Sharp tells here are (theologically) liberal evangelicals, Black evangelicals, politically progressive evangelicals, feminist evangelicals, and gay evangelicals. Each group emerged from within the evangelical community and firmly claimed evangelical identity. Each group, however, held certain exegetical, theological, political, or moral views that fell outside the convictions of the evangelical power brokers. Some within each group raised critiques about dominant forms of evangelicalism and asked that these critiques be engaged seriously. Each group sought space to remain within the evangelical community while holding firm to its distinctive beliefs in this or that area.

In each case, the evangelical "big tent" proved not big enough. High-profile individuals within each group were singled out for attack by evangelical authority structures. The convictions of the group were eventually rejected as "unevangelical." Another way to say it is that each group was defeated by the straight-white-male-conservative evangelical power structure in bruising conflicts, with the groups and key individuals within them flushed out of evangelicalism altogether.

The result of several generations of such battles has been to reinforce and make all but definitive for US evangelicalism the characteristics of anti-liberalism, whiteness, hard-right politics, anti-feminism, and anti-LGBTQ rejectionism. Rather than being known for, say, personal devotion to Christ, missions to the world, or radical love of neighbor, evangelicalism gradually hardened into this unholy other thing.

While Isaac Sharp does not write in emotional terms, I will add some emotion by saying this: a post–World War II neo-evangelical movement that had wanted to be defined by its winsome gospel spirit instead became known for what it was against and whose voices must be excluded. A movement self-defined as focused on the gospel of the Crucified One became a movement that often crucified those who challenged its boundaries, biases, and injustices.

The details of the battles the leaders of these "other evangelicals" fought and lost are told in a riveting, detailed, authoritative way in this book. There will be little need for other accounts of these particular struggles. This is it. It's all right here.

Many fine thinkers these days—including numerous refugees from US evangelicalism—are asking what exactly happened to this once-promising religious movement. Isaac Sharp offers an answer to that question from the perspective of those who have been ground under evangelicalism's wheels. Sharp shows how most evangelical historiography has been written from above, from an elite and insider perspective. This is history from below, in the bruising spaces where exclusion and dispossession have happened, featuring the voices of those who vainly fought for a more inclusive evangelicalism. That is where new truth is to be found.

Reading this book will give you a clearer sense of what has happened to evangelicalism. Its tragic devolution will make much more sense after you read this book. What you do with the information that Isaac Sharp offers so powerfully here will be up to you.

David P. Gushee

Acknowledgments

My debts are many and my word-limit looming, so without further ado: for their willingness to serve as the committee for such a sprawling dissertation, my thanks go first to Gary Dorrien, David Gushee, and Andrea White.

For taking a chance on this book, I am forever grateful to James Ernest, Jenny Hoffman, Justin Howell, and the entire Eerdmans team. But I'm especially grateful to my now former acquisitions editor David Bratt, whose editorial guidance, invaluable input, and enthusiastic support were utterly indispensable. For crucial title and subtitle input, special thanks also go to Laura Bardolph Hubers.

I would thank all of my many teachers by name if I could. But in this case, Sarah Azaransky, the late James H. Cone, Kelly Brown Douglas, Marvin Ellison, Roger Haight, Jan Rehmann, Josef Sorett, John Thatamanil, and Cornel West deserve special mention. Some piece of this project took shape in each of their classrooms, and for that I'm forever grateful.

For their encouragement, solidarity, and support, thanks as well to Nkosi DuBois Anderson, Jamall Calloway, Eddie Escalón, Chris Fici, Evan Goldstein, Mary Julia Jett, Carolyn Klaasen, Kelly Maeshiro, Amy Meverden, Wesley Morris, Esther Parajuli, Jorge Juan Rodríguez V, Anthony Jermaine Ross-Allam, Aaron Stauffer, Joe Strife, Stanley Talbert, AJ Turner, Colleen Wessel-McCoy, Jason Wyman, and all the rest of my Union colleagues and friends. Learning from and with them was and is one of my greatest joys.

Thanks also to Fred Davie. His support and friendship have been an incredible gift, and each chance we have had to collaborate a real honor.

Special thanks also go to the students in my spring 2021 RS210: Evangelicalism class at Union Theological Seminary. Rachel Beaver, Jim Benson, Shelley Burtt, Hannah Ervin, Luke Estrada, Prisca Juyoung Lee-Pae, Jon Mehlhaus, Mehmet M. Ozalp, and Matt Puckett were a delight to learn with, and I'm humbled by the generosity and grace they all brought to the subject.

For helpful suggestions, insightful commentary, and rich discussions, my thanks go as well to William Stell. There are pieces of this puzzle that he knows better than anyone else; his forthcoming dissertation will be indispensable, and I'm very grateful our paths have crossed.

I am also immensely grateful for Greg Given. Growing up together and ultimately winding up in the same line of work has been a rare treat. Our often uncannily parallel journeys mean there are times when only he could possibly understand what I'm feeling, and I'm unbelievably lucky to count one of my oldest friends among my closest to this day.

My life has been richer thanks to Arianna Grande Flat White, my pub trivia team. The friendship, fellowship, and community offered by Richie Allen, Lesley-Ann Hix Tommey, and Blake Tommey during our weekly outings was a gift and a refuge—even when we lost, which was often.

A special word of thanks goes to Jameson McGregor. Throughout the entire journey, he patiently listened to every new idea, direction change, and progress update no matter how convoluted, insignificant, or boring. Although he never seemed to get around to reading any of the drafts, he has heard every piece of the argument a dozen times over and undoubtedly knows its ins and outs by heart. Our near-weekly phone calls are often a lifeline when I am drowning, and his friendship has been a torch in the darkness too many times to count.

For the mere gift of their presence, I owe a debt of gratitude to Lucy, Gracie, and Harvey, my ever-faithful animal companions.

For their steadfast love, I'm forever grateful for my parents, Stan Sharp and Ginger Sharp, and my siblings, Jordan and Jillian.

For journeying alongside me on this preposterous path, for supporting my academic habit, and for providing her patients the kind of compassionate care that every person deserves, above all else I am thankful for and oh so very proud of Katie. She's the best women's health nurse practitioner in New York City. None of this would have been possible without her, and it wouldn't have been worth it even if it were.

Finally, I would be remiss in failing to state as clearly as possible that my dissertation was the direct result of a doctoral program that fully funds every admitted student, and this book is the direct result of the fact that I was fortunate enough to secure full-time academic work after graduating. Both factors were essential preconditions, both are tragically and vanishingly rare, and it is impossible to overstate the degree to which both depend more on luck than perhaps anything else. If my academic career ends as quickly as it began, which it might, at least I got the chance to write this one. Fewer and fewer young scholars get such a chance, and that makes me almost unbearably sad.

Prologue

Based on the doctrinal statement of one US American evangelical organization, an evangelical is someone who believes that "the Bible alone, and the Bible in its entirety, is the Word of God written and is therefore inerrant in the autographs." According to another major evangelical group, anyone who "takes the Bible seriously and believes in Jesus Christ as Savior and Lord" is an evangelical. In some contexts, an evangelical is a born-again Christian; in others, an evangelical is an orthodox Protestant. One of the nation's premiere evangelical seminaries puts it this way: "to be evangelical has always meant, along with a personal commitment to Jesus Christ as Lord and Savior, affirming a cluster of doctrines"—including "the person and work of Jesus Christ, including his deity, virgin birth, true humanity, substitutionary death, bodily resurrection, and ascension to heaven." In the judgment of one sociologist of religion, actually, an evangelical is someone who practices a certain distinctive style of religious devotion, which has become so popular in the contemporary United States that "there is also a sense in which we are all evangelicals now."[1]

Originally, the Greek word *euangelion* meant simply "good news." In German, *evangelisch* essentially means Protestant or even just non-Catholic. In the circles where people laugh about such things, there is an old joke that the best definition of an evangelical is simply "anyone who likes Billy Graham." Unfortunately, jokes are not nearly as funny when explained. But they aren't funny at all unless you understand the reference, and in this case, getting the joke requires knowing something about its main character. For the uninitiated, a little background is likely in order.

William Franklin "Billy" Graham was a powerfully persuasive and widely popular twentieth-century preacher. He was as theologically conservative as any fundamentalist when he thought it mattered and willing to let dogmatic minutiae and the finer points of doctrinal debate take a back seat when it didn't. Driven by the goal of preaching the gospel throughout the entire world, he was a lifelong Baptist who was also devoted to the kind of interdenominational cooperation necessary for effectively reaching as many people as possible. Despite a carefully constructed public image as a figure above the fray of politics, Graham was socially and politically conservative in every imaginable way, with a track record of partisan involvement that belied his apolitical self-image. The close friend and personal pastor of several successive US presidents, he was also white, a native southerner, and a husband and father dutifully committed to strictly traditional ideals of both. Among the most famous preachers of all time, over the course of his life, Graham invited millions of people to accept Jesus Christ as their personal Savior, calling countless thousands to conversion during his services.

Understanding who Graham was gets us halfway there. But the riddle only fully unfolds when his story is properly situated in a particular time and place. To see why defining an evangelical as "someone who likes Billy Graham" is both funny and not so far from the truth, one must also have a sense of his twentieth-century US context—one in which *evangelicalism* became known as an enormously popular, transdenominational movement of born-again Christians, organized and led by successive generations of dynamic leaders who successfully built a religious subculture known for its consistent social, political, and theological conservatism. Although evangelicals never completely cornered the market on liking Graham, and even if Graham-appreciation did not necessarily an evangelical make, in *this* context, Graham's status as a pivotal figurehead, the affinity for whom did indeed represent a rough and ready barometer for gauging evangelicalness, meant that the old joke was not so far from the mark.

But in many ways, Graham's role in twentieth-century American evangelical history was actually even larger than that. He was undoubtedly *both* the most powerfully symbolic evangelical figurehead *and* the popularly designated representative of the evangelical masses. But he also was—and perhaps still is—at once the prototypical version, the archetypical example, and the platonic ideal of what it meant to be a capital-E Evangelical. And so, with one minor tweak, perhaps the joke reveals even a bit more: if twentieth-century American evangelicals could humorously (and not inaccurately) be defined as "those who liked Billy Graham," they might also be described as "those who *were like* Billy Graham"–or, if not Graham, someone who believed, thought, acted, voted, and looked an awful lot like him.

By focusing primarily on the emergence of the post-World War II neo-evangelical coalition and its subsequent proliferation into an extensive interdenominational network of schools, publishing houses, parachurch ministries, and organizations, for decades, historians, journalists, political scientists, and theologians have told and retold the story of twentieth-century American evangelicalism as roughly *this* story, the story of *these* evangelicals, the story of the liking and being-like-Graham kind. Flagship institutions like *Christianity Today*, Fuller Theological Seminary, and the National Association of Evangelicals, as well as major evangelical figureheads such as Harold Ockenga, Carl F. H. Henry, and Billy Graham, are the stars of this story and justifiably so: the rise to predominance of the midcentury evangelical movement is undeniably the main event in the twentieth-century history of what became contemporary mainstream US American evangelicalism.

Conventional narratives rightly emphasize the outsized influence of major evangelical leaders and powerful evangelical organizations in the development of a mainstream evangelical movement–one that would eventually become known for its theological, social, and, most of all, political conservatism, as well as its high degree of racial and cultural homogeneity. This is a true story. Over the course of the twentieth century, mainstream American evangelicalism did indeed become increasingly associated with an ever-narrower range of ideological, cultural, theological, and political possibilities. *The* Evangelicals do indeed look, believe, and think like this, and conventional accounts of their history have helped us understand why.

But standard portraits also tend to overlook the fact that the process of specifying what precisely it should mean to be an evangelical was neither quick nor inevitable for at least two reasons: (1) American evangelicals have often been more diverse than their representation in popular and scholarly discourses, and (2) the conservative, white men who have always been in charge of the twentieth-century US American version of the movement have often been simultaneously ill-equipped to deal with that fact. By failing to seriously consider the role that those in power played in shaping what counted as mainstream—a process that regularly involved offering ad hoc rulings about what was in bounds and out of bounds for "true" evangelicals when it came to a host of theological, social, and political questions—most standard histories gloss over the question of how it is that the mainstream version *became* mainstream.

The post-World War II neoevangelical coalition was undeniably remarkably successful at building and growing a big-tent movement of generally conservative Protestants that became known as mainstream evangelicalism. But along with this success came a host of particular kinds of conservative Protestants with a variety of competing and often contradictory theological, social, and political views, who regularly struggled to find their place inside the evangelical gates. When forced to face the uncomfortable reality of evangelicalism's internal pluralism, twentieth-century evangelical leaders frequently responded by sidelining minority groups and excommunicating dissenters in an ongoing series of efforts to define and police the boundaries of evangelical identity. In so doing, a succession of powerful evangelical gatekeepers thereby defined themselves and their followers—who, not coincidentally, thought, believed, voted, and looked like them—as *the* evangelicals, claiming the evangelical label as their proprietary trademark in the process. These twentieth-century guardians of the evangelical mainstream successfully shaped a religious identity in their own image, thereby contributing to popular (and scholarly) perceptions of a monolithically conservative, mostly white evangelicalism predominated by fundamentalistic, Reformed, or Calvinistic theologians—an evangelicalism that, crucially, seems to have come ready-made with these particular characteristics baked in as intrinsic features.

In order to begin recognizing how it was that these evangelicals became the official evangelicals, how it is that their story became the canonical history of evangelicalism, we need to look again at twentieth-century evangelical history for traces of those who were left behind—which is an evangelical joke, by the way—pushed out, excommunicated, or defined out, those who labored for years on the margins of an evangelical mainstream in which they were never quite welcome, or those who simply threw up their hands and left in despair.

This book tells the story of some of those who did just that: those who for one reason or another did not subscribe to the de facto evangelical orthodoxy on a particular issue, or who literally could not fit within the prevailing cultural expectations of the mainstream evangelical world, or who lost their argument for a different kind of evangelicalism, or who believed, thought, acted, voted, or simply looked a bit different from the predominant picture of what an evangelical was supposed to be, who nonetheless defended the legitimacy of their evangelicalness in the face of an evangelical mainstream that told them they didn't belong, and who have been all but forgotten in the evangelical history books.

This is the story of the *other* evangelicals.

Introduction

The Evangelicals?

Given the contemporary obsession with all things evangelical, it may come as a surprise that much of the broader US American public spent the better part of the twentieth century thoroughly disinterested in something called evangelicalism. Until at least the early years of the 1970s in fact, popular and scholarly observers were mostly content to ignore evangelicalism, and those who did happen to consider it largely viewed it as an insignificant aspect of contemporary religious life. All things considered, in other words, the current picture of evangelicalism as an immensely popular historical version of American religiosity that lived on in an enormously influential contemporary movement was a relatively late development in both academic and popular discussions of the twentieth century.

So too was the idea that the country might actually be chock-full of evangelicals. Other than a few major evangelical organizations, for the better part of the twentieth century, almost no one was particularly interested in even so simple a consideration as an approximate estimate of the total number of evangelical Christians in the United States. When some evangelical leaders had hazarded a guess, their numbers furthermore had varied considerably. Since its founding in the early 1940s, for its part, the National Association of Evangelicals (NAE) had variously suggested that the country's population included anywhere from two to ten million evangelicals. If based solely on the membership of the NAE's constituent denominations, through the late 1960s, the number of "official" evangelicals would indeed have been right around two million. But in those years, the members of a number of the nation's largest Protestant groups—the Southern Baptist Convention, for instance—were increasingly being counted as among the evangelicals for the first time, even though they had not yet officially joined the ranks of evangelical organizations like the NAE. When the traditionally but not yet officially evangelical groups were added to the mix, some estimates at the time thus put the number of evangelicals closer to twenty million and even as high as twenty-five million.[1]

Not that it would have mattered all that much though. Whether their numbers were closer to two or twenty million, in those years, evangelicals were still mostly off the radar in US public life. But not for long.

Introducing the Evangelicals: The Year of the Evangelical and the Rediscovery of Evangelicalism

The earliest signs that change was afoot came in the form of two men. The first was Jimmy Carter. Following a 1976 Democratic primary in which he shocked political pundits by clinching his party's nomination, Carter surprised much of the nation when he candidly highlighted his personal evangelical faith in the ensuing campaign. By reintroducing the broader American public to a form of religiosity that many scholars and historians at the time believed had long since been relegated to the dustbin of history, the Carter campaign sent the national media on a harried search both for an explanation for what exactly an evangelical Christian was and for a better grasp of the likelihood that there might be a portion of the country's citizenry that actually shared Carter's faith. In the lead-up to Carter's election as the country's first officially by that name born-again president, journalists and commentators baffled by the prospects of a larger-than-imagined evangelical electorate increasingly turned to a second major harbinger of change for American evangelicalism: George Gallup Jr.[2]

Gallup the younger was a public opinion pollster and Episcopalian like his father before him—though, in contrast to George Gallup Sr., Gallup the son also considered himself an evangelical. Over time, in sociologist Robert Wuthnow's expert judgment, it would become clear that Gallup Jr. "was to religious polling what his father had been to political polling." And not just any religious polling either. By the time that the Carter campaign was making the word "evangelical" famous, Gallup Jr.'s increasingly popular and widely referenced polling statistics on the state of the nation's faith were fast making him famous as the go-to source of objective data on the mysterious phenomenon known as evangelicalism. In 1976, one set of survey data in particular helped fast-track both Gallup and evangelicals into the national spotlight like never before.[3]

The bombshell came in late September, six weeks or so before the 1976 election, when Gallup announced the surprising results of his newest poll while attending the Episcopal Church's annual convention in Minneapolis as a lay delegate. According to a recent survey by his organization, Gallup explained, an astounding 34 percent of voting-age Americans suggested that they had in fact been "born-again" or "had a 'born-again' experience" akin to Jimmy Carter's. Even more of the country's citizens, around 38 percent, believed that the Bible was "the actual word of God and is to be taken literally, word for word," he reported, and the percentage of those who claimed to have "ever tried to encourage someone to believe in Jesus Christ or to accept Him as his or her Savior" was higher still at 47 percent. When it came to the implications of such astonishing numbers, Gallup left nothing to the imagination. Not only did evangelicals represent a "built-in power base" for Jimmy Carter, evangelicalism was clearly "currently the hot movement in the church." The numbers simply could not lie. In light of the survey's results, Gallup confidently proclaimed that "1976 can be considered the year of the evangelical."[4]

The press had a field day. In the days and weeks following Gallup's announcement, journalists breathlessly reported both the numbers *and* the official interpretation of the man behind them. In a September 25 article, a *Los Angeles Times* reporter described how "Gallup's new survey of 1,500 persons, scientifically selected and polled in late August, probes the born-again phenomenon," demonstrating that "more than one-third of those who are old enough to vote, have experienced 'born-again' religious conversions like that of Democratic presidential candidate Jimmy Carter," and explaining that "a born-again Christian, for poll purposes, was generally defined as one who has had a dramatic conversion, accepts Jesus as his or her personal savior, believes that the Bible is the authority for all doctrine and feels 'an urgent duty to spread the faith.'"[5]

The following month, *Time* magazine amplified the signal with an article that similarly featured both the results of the survey and quotations from Gallup's speech announcing the findings.[6] In late October, *Newsweek* did Gallup one better, giving front page billing to a story, "Born Again! The Evangelicals," which prominently featured the survey results along with an explanation that "evangelical spokesmen have long argued that they represent the silent majority of Protestants in the pew. . . . This year polltakers are providing evidence to support that claim."[7] In each case, the articles repeated Gallup's straightforward announcement that it was clearly the year of the evangelical.

It would thus be difficult either to overstate the role that Carter's election played in reintroducing the broader American citizenry to their born-again neighbors or to overplay the massive influence that pollsters in general and George Gallup Jr. in particular had on the public's understanding of evangelicalism. As Wuthnow points out in *Inventing American Religion*, for instance, for all intents and purposes, "the scope of evangelicalism remained indeterminate" throughout much of the 1960s, and, "against that backdrop the polling that took place in connection with Carter's election dramatically redefined the face of American evangelicalism."[8] Year of the evangelical indeed.

But the year of the evangelical represented more than just the dramatic reappearance of evangelicals into the public eye. In Wuthnow's persuasive telling, it also marked the beginning of a new era in which polling took on an increasingly prominent role in informing popular interpretations of religion in America. For weal or woe, from that point forward, pollsters like Gallup became one of if not *the* primary sources of information about the faith of the nation in general and one of if not *the* go-to authorities on evangelicals in particular.[9]

In the wake of the watershed that was the year of the evangelical, the newly rekindled interest in evangelicalism quickly spread to other forums as well. Pollsters, it turned out, were not the only ones equipped to interpret and describe evangelicalism. By the early 1980s, a discussion among interpreters of an entirely different sort would begin shaping both scholarly and popular perceptions of evangelicalism too.

Contextualizing the Evangelicals:
The Evangelical Historians and the Birth of Evangelical Studies

It is no coincidence that the person responsible for the old joke about evangelicals and Billy Graham, the eminent historian of evangelicalism George

Marsden, is also the person who deserves a lion's share of the credit for kick-starting a now decades-long conversation—and, among those who care about such things, ongoing debate—about where the evangelicals came from, what exactly the evangelicals believe, and what precisely it is that makes someone an evangelical. As one of the twentieth century's most influential evangelical historians, Marsden knew better than most that what was meant as a tongue-in-cheek example of the inherent difficulty of precisely delineating what makes evangelical Christians different from, well, other kinds of Christians contained more than a bit of truth.[10]

Marsden fully recognized that, as a transdenominational, decentralized, and popular tradition of Protestant Christianity without an agreed-upon authority structure or official magisterium, evangelicalism was and *is* a tricky thing to define. Absent an official roster of legitimately vetted card-carrying members, he furthermore knew that identifying the evangelicals and distinguishing them from the nonevangelicals posed an inherent difficulty both for evangelicals and for those who studied them. When it came to pinning down the essence of evangelicalism and the precise details of what it is that made someone an evangelical, in other words, *connotation* is often easier than *denotation*.

He was also among the first to call attention to an unusual evangelical-sized hole in the extant literature of US American religious history. In his first book, published in 1970 as *The Evangelical Mind and the New School Presbyterian Experience*, Marsden hypothesized that the almost total lack of historical interest in evangelicalism at the time could be explained by "a quiet prejudice against evangelical Protestantism in nineteenth-century American life," which had long pervaded twentieth-century American historiography for one simple reason. The problem could be traced to an earlier generation of historians who "in the midst of their own emancipation from Protestant intellectual and moral dogmatism, emphasized the tolerant and the progressive in America's national tradition. Evangelicalism, which in the opening decades of this century was usually masked in the robes of militant fundamentalism, appeared retrograde and obscurantist. Its heritage seemed best forgotten."[11]

For a while, it seemed as though things were going to stay that way too: Marsden's first book didn't make much of a splash. But by the time that he was ready to publish his second book, the winds of scholarly and popular conversations about American religion had shifted dramatically and fortuitously. A newly awakened interest in evangelicals had set the stage perfectly for another look at the history of evangelicalism, the public was hungry for a better understanding of evangelicals and their origins, and Marsden was perfectly suited to deliver. In 1980, with the publication of *Fundamentalism and American Culture*, he gave it to them in spades.[12]

To understand contemporary evangelicalism, Marsden explained, one must first understand the early twentieth-century movement known as fundamentalism, and in order to understand fundamentalism, one must first zoom out for a wider look at the longer arc of American evangelical history. Evangelicalism, in his telling, had been the dominant manifestation of American religion until at least the early 1870s, and the vast majority of American Christians throughout the nation's history had therefore been the kind "professing complete confidence in the Bible and preoccupied with the message of God's salvation of sinners through the death of Jesus Christ. Evangelicals were convinced that sincere acceptance of this 'Gospel' message was the key to virtue in this life and to eternal life in heaven; its rejection meant following the broad path that ended with the tortures of hell."[13]

Such beliefs represented a broadly evangelical consensus, long shared among and across the various historical streams of US Protestantism, that only began to crack in Marsden's view with the post-Civil War rise of modernism—a label most closely associated with the emergence of Darwinian evolution and higher biblical criticism on the American theological scene. Although some nineteenth-century Christians concluded that these modernist intellectual developments were perfectly compatible with their faith, others viewed them as direct assaults on the very essence of evangelical belief. Further still, some evangelicals eventually became so alarmed that they set out to eradicate any and all traces of modernism from their churches. Early in the twentieth century, Marsden explained, these militantly antimodernist crusaders became known as fundamentalists. Their subsequent development into "a loose, diverse, and changing federation of co-belligerents united by their fierce opposition to modernist attempts to bring Christianity into line with modern thought" gave rise to the evangelical submovement known as fundamentalism.[14]

Respectable intellectuals and secular historians had spent decades maligning evangelical fundamentalism, dismissing it as an old-fashioned movement destined for irrelevance. In so doing, Marsden judged that they had thereby confused the part for the whole while simultaneously missing the forest for the trees. Reducing all of historical evangelicalism to fundamentalism and thereby dismissing it was a mistake. But so too was overlooking fundamentalism's lasting influence among later generations of American evangelicals. In addition to tracing the historical transformation of a particular subgroup of early twentieth-century evangelicals into militantly antimodernist crusaders, Marsden's landmark 1980 book thus also aimed to demonstrate that, as "the background of the wider coalition of contemporary American evangelicals whose common identity is substantially grounded in the fundamentalist experience of an earlier era," fundamentalism's legacy was anything but dead.[15]

His timing could not have been more perfect. Published the same year that the newly ascendant evangelical political forces of the Religious Right helped send Ronald Reagan to the White House, *Fundamentalism and American Culture* quickly became indispensable reading. Expertly supplying a newly rising demand for more information about evangelicals and where they came from with the first extensive, contemporary historical reconsideration of fundamentalism and its lasting legacy among twentieth-century evangelicals, Marsden effectively established what became the paradigmatic understanding of American evangelicalism and its history, thereby laying the groundwork for everything that followed. As another evangelical historian would eventually recount, Marsden's work was so groundbreaking in fact that it almost single-handedly defined fundamentalism and evangelicalism, catapulted discussions of evangelical history into mainstream discourse, and inaugurated an entirely new subfield of evangelical-studies research all in one fell swoop. It is no small wonder then that Marsden would go on to earn the unofficial but undisputed title "dean of American evangelical historians." *Fundamentalism and American Culture* represented a watershed moment in the study of evangelicalism, with Marsden's framing of evangelical history quickly becoming near canonical.[16]

In the wake of Marsden's groundbreaking account, the emergence during the 1980s of a new generation of historians of evangelicalism soon proved that evangelical studies was here to stay. This new breed of historians did more than just demonstrate the ongoing relevance of the conversation Marsden started, however. They also gave rise to what another religious historian described as "one of the most arresting" academic developments of the era.[17] Like their unofficial dean, the group of new historians of evangelicalism that swam in his wake were not merely scholars of evangelicalism. Almost without exception, they were also *evangelicals themselves*. During the first generation of contemporary evangelical studies, the conversation was dominated by a group of pioneering historians who were interpreters of an evangelical tradition that they called home—or, in a couple of instances, that they had once called home. By describing, explaining, and defining their tradition for outside observers who often knew next to nothing about it, for the rest of the decade, historians like Joel Carpenter, Nathan Hatch, Mark Noll, and Grant Wacker began filling the evangelical-sized hole in the literature on American religious history with an increasingly detailed and nuanced portrait of evangelicalism. By offering persuasive and compelling historical accounts that were often well regarded by the broader public and secular historians alike, over time, many of the first-generation evangelical historians increasingly became the foremost authorities on and go-to interpreters of American evangelicalism—whether because or in spite of their insider status.

The narratives developed during the new era of "evangelical historiography on evangelicalism" fast became the paradigmatic pictures of evangelicalism and for good reason: they were robust critical histories of a tradition that their authors clearly understood. But as the nonevangelical historian Leonard Sweet soon pointed out, there was often more at stake in this most arresting development than merely the disinterested writing of exemplary histories. In a 1988 essay on the "new evangelical historiography," Sweet perceptively identified an overriding existential concern that was already jumping off the pages of the evangelical historians' work, thereby anticipating a dynamic that would become a permanent feature of much subsequent work on evangelicalism and its history.[18]

As a primarily participant-observer attempt to interpret an ever-evolving tradition that perennially struggled with determining, guarding, and occasionally redrawing its borders, Sweet explained that, for the new evangelical historiography of evangelicalism, "issues of identity are writ large." He observed, for instance, that many of the new evangelical historians were clearly motivated in part by a need to come to terms with the lasting legacy of fundamentalism among contemporary evangelicals. Further still, he noted that almost all of them found the lingering accretions of fundamentalism an

8

utter embarrassment for evangelicalism, highlighting Marsden and Noll as particularly willing to put fundamentalism's dangerous anti-intellectualism and bellicosity on display in their work as a not-so-subtle argument for jettisoning it in favor of an older, better form of evangelical faith.[19]

As appreciative as he was of the considerable strengths of the evangelical historians' work, Sweet nonetheless felt that it thus had its limits. The tendency to hold up one stream of the historical evangelical tradition as the sine qua non of true evangelicalism was a prime example. In their search for a halcyon, prefundamentalist evangelical past, he judged, some of the evangelical historians wound up emphasizing one kind of evangelical faith at the expense of a variety of other, equally evangelical versions of Christianity. As insiders writing contemporary histories of "an unforgiving religious group," Sweet surmised that the new evangelical historians had furthermore been compelled to offer kid-glove treatment in their accounts of some of the nastier evangelical boundary battles and border wars. Such limitations, in Sweet's view, were by no means disqualifying though. By deeply engaging their own tradition, warts and all, he concluded, evangelical historians were rendering an invaluable service to the scholarly community because "critical history of a tradition presupposes inside-out immersion in that tradition. Or, put differently, the best attacks are inside jobs."[20]

As Sweet's analysis helped demonstrate, over the course of the 1980s, the groundbreaking work of the new evangelical historians had begun pulling back the curtain on a variety of intraevangelical debates over the essential nature of the historic evangelical faith and consequently over the limits of contemporary evangelicalism. But as twentieth-century evangelicals themselves, many of the first-generation evangelical historians had more than a little at stake in the very debates that they were helping outsiders understand. Many were indeed convinced, for instance, that contemporary evangelicals were in real danger of letting the worst legacies of fundamentalism become the dominant expression of evangelical faith, thereby obscuring a broader, richer, older, and better evangelical tradition. Like the evangelical and fundamentalist leaders featured in their narratives, many of the first-generation evangelical historians of the 1980s themselves were not merely concerned with but also deeply invested in answering the crucial question: What should it mean to be an evangelical in the twentieth-century American context?

By contextualizing contemporary evangelicalism against its own historical background, the new evangelical historians were thus doing more than just helping insiders and outsiders alike better understand where it is that evangelicals came from and how evangelicalism had changed over time. By offering their takes on various aspects of the evangelical story, they were thereby shaping normative understandings of evangelicalism that were developing in both popular and scholarly discourses at the time. They were also affording evangelical theologians and evangelical leaders the chance to claim that history was on their side in some of the era's most contentious debates over the limits of evangelical identity. After all, what better way to support one's own interpretation of what it meant to be evangelical than to point to precedents throughout the historic evangelical tradition?

The foremost example of the era's existentially inflected historiographical debates over the true nature of evangelicalism came in the form of an extended dialogue between the ascendant dean of evangelical historians, George Marsden, and one of his earliest interlocutors and most frequent critics, Donald W. Dayton. Beginning as early as the late 1970s and reaching its peak more than a decade later in the early 1990s, the Marsden-Dayton debate went something like this.

With *Fundamentalism and American Culture* and his follow-up 1987 book *Reforming Fundamentalism: Fuller Seminary and the New Evangelicalism*, Marsden established what became the authoritative paradigm for understanding recent fundamentalist and evangelical history. The only problem in Dayton's view was that Marsden had gotten it all wrong. Viewing evangelical history through a "Presbyterian paradigm," which interpreted evangelicalism primarily as a conservative, dogmatic, defense of orthodoxy in the face of liberalism, in Dayton's telling, Marsden painted a skewed picture that cast the evangelical tradition in an almost exclusively Reformed-Calvinistic light. In so doing, he had furthermore undergirded the authority of the contemporary evangelical establishment—which was dominated by Reformed and Calvinist thinkers and leaders—lent credence to their mythos about "true evangelicalism," and bolstered their claims as the rightful heirs and guardians of the evangelical tradition. For years, Dayton had tried to argue that the kind of needlessly fundamentalist, overwhelmingly Calvinist, unhelpfully doctrinaire, and maddeningly conservative evangelicalism embodied in contemporary mainstream evangelical culture was neither the only nor the best version. In his mind, Marsden's account of evangelical history implied that it was.[21]

For his part, Dayton proposed what he believed was a far better framework that more faithfully captured the essence of evangelicalism and its relationship to the broader scope of Christian history. In place of Marsden's Presbyterian paradigm, Dayton pressed for a "Pentecostal paradigm," viewing evangelicalism *not* as a rationalistic response to liberalism but instead as an innovative, Spirit-filled disruption to the stodgy conservatism of the traditional churches. The evangelical tradition, in his telling, had always been the current that carried Christianity's more populist, radical, experiential, and antidoctrinaire elements, not its orthodox, antisecular, antimodern, fundamentalist, and conservative elements. With a Pentecostal paradigm, you could properly see that the former was indeed the case. With a Presbyterian paradigm, you could see only a one-sided evangelical tradition that began with the magisterial Reformers, traced its way down through the likes of the Puritans and Congregationalists, and eventually wound up with the fundamentalists and their predominantly Calvinistic contemporary American evangelical offspring. With a Pentecostal paradigm, you could see evangelicalism from below, emerging from the people. With a Presbyterian paradigm, you could see it only from the top-down view of the elites.[22]

In 1993, *Christian Scholar's Review* played host to the Marsden-versus-Dayton debate, featuring the latter's review of the former's *Reforming Fundamentalism* and devoting an entire issue to responses and reactions from a veritable who's who of evangelical historians, including Marsden himself. Acknowledging the importance of Dayton's work as an expert interpreter of the holiness and Pentecostal traditions, Marsden nonetheless judged that his friend and critic had misread his book in some fundamental ways. Most crucially, Marsden argued, Dayton mistakenly interpreted his historical descriptions of midcentury evangelical leaders' theological understandings of evangelicalism—which did indeed include preoccupations with antimodernism, antiliberalism, inerrancy, and highly rationalistic defenses of orthodoxy—as normative judgments about their validity. There was indeed something like a Presbyterian paradigm at work among the prescriptive definitions of evangelicalism offered by some of the most powerful twentieth-century evangelical leaders, but Marsden protested that he was by no means endorsing it by describing it.[23]

Joel Carpenter concurred. If anything, he suggested, Marsden's work did just the opposite. By methodically outlining midcentury evangelical leaders' normative assumptions about the limits of evangelicalism while explicitly highlighting their inaccuracy, Marsden's most recent book actually *both* gave the lie to the idea that evangelicalism was as narrow as some of its recent guardians suggested *and* demonstrated that he had learned from Dayton's critiques. In Carpenter's judgment, Dayton's vehement criticisms of any picture of evangelicalism in which the fundamentalist, Reformed-Calvinist, inerrantist, "Presbyterian" concerns of the evangelical elite were considered essential or normative were simply misplaced. Marsden wasn't his real enemy; the midcentury evangelical figures Marsden wrote about were.[24]

Like Marsden, Carpenter nonetheless appreciated the importance of Dayton's work as a helpful corrective to a couple of undeniable imbalances that had already emerged in the burgeoning field of evangelical studies. For one thing, Dayton's concern with evangelicalism's populist flavor and appeal to the masses rightfully brought attention to the underside of evangelical history in a field predominated by intellectual and institutional histories. Antielite dynamics were an undeniably important part of evangelical history, and the field was only beginning to flesh out this story. Greater still was the importance of Dayton's personal, existential interest in the various non-Calvinist groups throughout evangelical history. For whatever reason, Carpenter judged, the Reformed tradition simply produced more historians, whose legitimate interest in their own heritage meant that Presbyterians, Baptists, Calvinists, and fundamentalists really did receive more attention in histories of evangelicalism than Wesleyan, Methodist, Pietist, Holiness, and Pentecostal groups. Marsden and Noll were the prime example, and their prolific work and massive influence really had made the picture look a bit distorted. Dayton's work on the other, non-Reformed streams of evangelical history was helping to mitigate the distortion. But in Carpenter's analysis, Dayton's insistence on replacing the Presbyterian paradigm with his Pentecostal paradigm was just as distorting. Rather than forcing evangelical historians to choose one or the other, he concluded, what was needed was a *both-and* approach to evangelical history—a point with which Marsden heartily agreed, stressing that his and Dayton's work should be seen as complementary rather than oppositional.[25]

In a follow-up response, Douglas Sweeney echoed Marsden and Carpenter's judgment about the necessity of a complementary approach, stressing the importance of acknowledging both evangelicalism's Reformed-Calvinist-Presbyterian heritage and its Wesleyan-Methodist-Pentecostal-Holiness legacy. In fact, Sweeney argued, the "observer-participant dilemma" at work in the debates between evangelical historians like Marsden and Dayton were an apt demonstration of a dialectic functioning within both evangelical historiography and within the "inner logic of evangelical history" itself. In light of its appropriateness to the "essential evangelicalism dialectic," Sweeney expressed hope that the point-counterpoint relationship between Marsden's "Reformed thesis" and Dayton's "Holiness antithesis" might indeed give rise to a richer *synthesis*, offering a fuller and more comprehensive picture that better reflected the reality of the complex and competing dynamics within the history of evangelicalism.[26]

*

The widely respected work of the new evangelical historians went a long way toward securing a commonly, though by no means universally accepted understanding of the scope of the historical evangelical tradition. But from the earliest days of the new era of evangelical studies, it also quickly became apparent that evangelicalism was harder to pin down than one might expect—especially when it came to internal debates between evangelical historians over the true nature of their own tradition. Good historiography could never fully hide the existential stakes involved in delimiting the boundaries of historic evangelicalism, and competing interpretations of the essence and limits of the evangelical tradition meant that even appeals to historical precedent would ultimately be unable to fully resolve the problem. If contemporary evangelicalism was best understood as that which met the criteria of faithfulness to evangelical history, then the question soon became this: Which version or, more appropriately, whose interpretation of evangelical history are we talking about?

Counting the Evangelicals:
Moral Majority or Beleaguered Remnant

Disagreements over what evangelicalism actually was and what exactly made someone an evangelical were by no means confined to discussions among evangelical historians either. By the time that the new evangelical historiography was in full swing, even the putatively more scientifically objective approaches offered by pollsters were already becoming plagued by

a perennial difficulty for anyone interested in evangelicals and evangelicalism: there are multiple ways of deciding who goes in the column marked
evangelical, determining the best way depends on who you ask, and the
resulting pictures of evangelicalism look dramatically different based on
the chosen method. Try though they might to overcome them with data
and figures, definitional debates among pollsters and sociologists were no
less fraught with existential stakes and participant-observer dynamics than
among the evangelical historians either.

Gallup's work was a prime example. Were *all* of the "50 million 'Born-
again'" that his organization discovered during the "Year of the Evangelical"
really evangelicals? Or were the *real* evangelicals actually a smaller subset of
the born-again who *also* believed that the Bible was the actual word of God,
and who had ever tried to convert someone else to the Christian faith? As
early as their 1976 study, the Gallup organization began regularly using the
latter, threefold criterion as their operative definition of what it meant to
be an evangelical, while simultaneously giving the undeniable impression
in public announcements that *all* of the born-again should be considered as
within the evangelical fold.[27]

Things only got thornier from there. In 1978, Gallup partnered with the
editors of *Christianity Today* (*CT*)—twentieth-century evangelicalism's most
important publication by a mile—to develop and conduct a new, comprehensive study of US American evangelical Christianity. Setting out to answer
questions like "Who are the evangelicals?" and "How pervasive are evangelical beliefs in American life?" under *CT*'s direction, Gallup began designing a
far more specific poll aimed at delivering a clearer picture of evangelicalism
and its contours. There was just one problem: even the editors of the flagship evangelical periodical admitted that determining precisely who was and
wasn't an evangelical was not so easy to do. As one anonymous member of
the editorial staff later confessed, for instance, "After several weeks of serious consideration as to how this matter should be handled in the poll, the
editor took the resulting definition home to his wife and discovered that by
that definition she wasn't an evangelical."[28]

The *CT* team eventually decided on a definition that would separate the
evangelical wheat from the unevangelical chaff via a list of specifically evangelical beliefs and practices. Real evangelicals, they suggested, were those
who attended church and read the Bible at least once each month, and who

also *either* believed that Jesus was divine, that faith in him offered the only path to salvation, and that the Bible was the inerrant word of God—a subset they called the "orthodox evangelicals"—*or* who could at least identify a specific point when they had asked Jesus to become their personal Savior—a group they labeled the "conversionist evangelicals." Armed with a battery of questions handcrafted by the *CT* team, Gallup conducted the newly designed survey of evangelicalism in late 1978.[29]

For a religious tradition that had only recently been viewed as an insignificant factor in the nation's religious life, the results were impressive and more than a bit surprising. Even with a definition of evangelical identity far narrower than mere self-affiliation, in late 1979, *CT* confidently and excitedly reported their survey's discovery that no less than one in five adults, some thirty-one million Americans, were actually, truly evangelicals. To the editorial team, the implications were clear: evangelicalism was a significant and potent religious force that was poised to expand its influence in the coming years.[30]

Their polling partner agreed. Along with the findings, the magazine ran an interview with Gallup, which wasted exactly no time getting directly to the point. Emphasizing the study's unprecedented comprehensiveness and assuring readers of the trustworthiness of the results, Gallup forthrightly judged, "I really feel that from the variety of survey evidence, the 1980s could be described as the decade of the evangelicals, because that is where the action is. . . . If evangelical ministers are able to mobilize the large number of evangelicals, their effect on the shape of the 1980s could be profound."[31]

The *CT*-Gallup dream team wasn't alone in their assessment. Nor would they remain the only game in town. With the 1984 establishment of the Barna Research Group, George Barna and his organization soon began challenging Gallup's pride of place as the authoritative source of information for all things evangelical. Although both Gallup and Barna were self-identified evangelicals who worked closely with the evangelical establishment, Barna targeted evangelical leaders as his primary audience in a way that Gallup never would. He found his mark too: for evangelical leaders curious about what the laity actually believed or interested in finding out how to more effectively evangelize and impact the surrounding culture, Barna increasingly became the go-to consultant.[32]

Throughout the 1980s, Barna's analysis of contemporary evangelicalism and its place in the broader culture consistently included a twofold emphasis. On the one hand, like Gallup and *CT*, he regularly stressed that evangelicalism was a formidable force, which in fact offered the last best hope in an increasingly godless, materialistic, self-centered, and shallow society. But on the other hand, Barna simultaneously judged that the evangelical church had proven time and again that it was falling woefully short of its true potential. According to his research, for instance, there were indeed a considerable number of born-again Christians in the country. But not nearly as many as one might expect at first blush. Recent data showing that 64 percent of the 1983 population claimed to have made a personal commitment to Jesus Christ, for example, seemed like an impressive bump from the 53 percent who claimed as much in 1980. Skewering the idea that this increase somehow indicated a time of unprecedented evangelical revival, Barna nonetheless explained, "Deeper digging, however, reveals that among the 64 percent who claim to have made such a commitment, only half believe that they will obtain eternal salvation because Jesus Christ died for their sins. The other half—who cannot truly be considered born again—cite various works that they are performing as their ticket to heaven." The only really born-again evangelicals, in other words, were those who believed that faith in Jesus was the only way to heaven. And by that definition, in Barna's estimation, the truly born-again percentage of the population had in fact remained essentially unchanged, hovering right around 31 percent from 1976 through 1984, which actually meant that there had been next to no significant growth in the evangelical share of the religious market.[33]

Other than one small surge to a high of 40 percent in 1992, which Barna attributed to turbulent current events rather than any increase in the effectiveness of evangelization efforts, for the rest of the 1980s and into the early 1990s, Barna consistently found that the proportion of the American populace that were true born-again evangelical Christians remained virtually unchanged. Though their total numbers had grown to nearly sixty million by 1990, as a relative percentage of a growing population, Barna's evangelicals were about where they were in 1976. In his judgment, it was likely to stay that way too. Surrounded by a broader culture in an ongoing process of "spiritual decay," Barna predicted that "'the remnant' (i.e., the portion of the population dedicated to following Christ)" would continue holding steady within the range of 30 to 35 percent.[34]

But once again, things only got thornier from there. In 1992, the Barna organization debuted a new, far more detailed metric for sorting the evangelical sheep from the unevangelical goats that forced them to revise their estimates of the total number of actual evangelicals dramatically downward. Although numerous groups were purportedly identifying and describing the evangelicals, Barna explained that almost no one—other than God—really knew what the label actually meant, warning readers to be wary of accepting the conclusions of any study without first understanding how the researchers were defining evangelicals. Until that time when God chose to reveal who the true evangelicals actually were, Barna set forth nine provisional criteria that might be used in the interim to estimate about how many real evangelicals were out there. According to the organization's survey, along with the standard conversion experience and belief that accepting Jesus was the only way to heaven, the true evangelicals were Christians who *also* held in high regard a totally accurate Bible that they read at least once a week, felt that prayer could affect one's circumstances, shared their faith with another person at least once a month, and believed in a perfect, all-powerful, and all-knowing God who created the universe. Perhaps unsurprisingly, the results were bleak. Despite all of the media hype, Barna noted that only 12 percent, "a very select segment of the population," met all of the evangelical criteria in their 1992 study. It only got worse from there: by 1993, the truly evangelical percentage of the population had already fallen from 12 to 9 percent. The remnant, it seemed, was an even smaller slice of the American population than many had believed, and it was growing smaller by the year.[35]

Describing the Evangelicals:
Antimodern Conservatives or Embattled and Thriving

Competing understandings of the essential nature of the evangelical tradition have thus resulted in dramatically different pictures of evangelical history. Competing understandings of what it is that makes someone a true evangelical, which are often based on contested accounts of that same history, likewise have given rise to drastically divergent portraits of the true scope of contemporary evangelicalism. Definitional variations and discrepancies in rubrics have affected more than just the telling of evangelical history and the tallying of current evangelical numbers, however. The differences between, say, the truly evangelical 9 percent that Barna found in 1993 and the self-identified evangelical 42 percent that Gallup found that same year, for instance, undoubtedly encompassed far more than just numbers. Since the advent of contemporary evangelical studies in the early 1980s, sociological profiles of the evangelicals indeed have delivered wildly inconsistent and often flatly contradictory profiles of who they are, what they are like, where they live, and what they think. The various theoretical explanations of the evangelical phenomenon unsurprisingly have varied right along with them.[36]

James Davison Hunter's classic 1983 study, *American Evangelicalism: Conservative Religion and the Quandary of Modernity*, is a prime example. In his sociological analysis of the 1979 *CT*-Gallup research, Hunter found that evangelicals were statistically overrepresented among older, lower- to middle-class, relatively uneducated, married, white women who lived in the rural South and who more likely than not voted Democrat. This particular demographic profile, he theorized, helped explain how it was that the traditionally conservative evangelical worldview was able to survive in the context of a pluralistic contemporary US society dominated by the forces of modernity. The cultural isolation that placed evangelicals at a "greater demographic distance from the institutional structures and processes of modernity than any other religious group" was precisely what made evangelicalism "cognitively plausible and behaviorally viable." By the time he published his follow-up 1987 book *Evangelicalism: The Coming Generation*, Hunter nonetheless went on to argue that evangelicalism's ability to remain distinct and apart from the forces of modernity was already slipping. Drawing on his study of younger evangelicals, he concluded that a new generation far less devoted to evangelical orthodoxy was showing signs of accommodation that would likely transform evangelicalism into something unrecognizable to its elders.[37]

That was one picture. Within a few short years, Christian Smith had another. In 1995, Smith and his colleagues conducted a national survey that defined evangelicals as the subset of "churchgoing Protestants" who considered themselves evangelical. In contrast to both the yes-no, evangelical/born-again or not, self-identification method that Gallup sometimes used, and the theological-behavioral rubric developed in the *CT*-Gallup study, Smith's team presented respondents with four options of religious identification—evangelical, fundamentalist, mainline Protestant, and theologically liberal

Protestant—which they believed best corresponded with the four major traditions of US American Protestantism. By allowing churchgoing Protestants to self-select their preferred identity category, Smith and his colleagues estimated that only about 7 percent of the population should be considered evangelical. Presented in the 1998 book *American Evangelicalism: Embattled and Thriving*, the study's conclusions offered a snapshot of the evangelicals distinctly different from the one Hunter had developed. On a purely demographic level, for instance, Smith's team discovered that evangelicals were not nearly as heavily concentrated in the South, that they were far more upwardly mobile, and that they were actually among the most well-educated groups in the nation. Far from withering away under the pressures of modernity, Smith furthermore argued, evangelicalism was actually *thriving*. In fact, judging by religious strength—an assessment based on characteristics like faithfulness to, confidence in, and the salience of essential Christian beliefs in people's lives, as well as commitment to and participation in the religious group—evangelicalism was the strongest and most vital religious tradition on the contemporary US scene.[38]

Smith's theoretical explanation for why a theologically conservative tradition like evangelicalism was doing so well in a modern society with which it was seemingly so at odds was perhaps even more surprising. Twentieth-century evangelical leaders, he explained, had successfully built a movement that effectively restructured the field of American religious identity. By claiming the religious terrain between fundamentalism and liberalism, naming that territory evangelical, developing and promoting their vision of what evangelical identity would mean, and inviting a range of like-minded Christians to join them in the space, the figureheads of twentieth-century American evangelicalism had thereby "created a distinct, publicly recognizable collective identity, in relation to which individuals, congregations, denominations, and para-church organizations were thereafter able to recognize and form their own faith identities and action-commitments."[39]

Smith's interpretation of the evangelical relationship to pluralism was perhaps most surprising of all. Within the pluralistic context of contemporary US society, evangelicals had been forced to construct and regularly reinforce a "subcultural identity" that was particularly distinct and therefore needed to be especially strong. Twentieth-century evangelical leaders had done just that and in spades. The new evangelical identity that they built had furthermore equipped the contemporary evangelicals who inhabited it with the cultural tools necessary "to create both clear distinction from and significant engagement and tension with other relevant outgroups." At least in part, in other words, evangelicalism was thriving *because* it was embattled.[40]

Reifying the Evangelicals: Establishing (and Deconstructing?) the Conventional Story

Since the late 1970s, the ongoing popular and scholarly fascination with evangelicals has thus given rise to an ever-proliferating series of portraits of evangelicals and their corresponding ism, shot through the disciplinary lenses of a host of subfields. Sociologists, historians, political scientists, theologians, and journalists (among others) have all joined the party, each offering a fresh reinterpretation or subtle clarification of one or more pieces of the evangelical story. Over time, as the roster of commentators and chroniclers has grown ever longer, the picture of evangelicalism in general and its twentieth-century history in particular has undeniably become more nuanced and increasingly complex. But a problem still remains. Whether the picture is larger or smaller, includes all of the self-identified or just the multipoint theological evangelicals, focuses primarily on the evangelical masses or looks instead at the evangelical elite, or picks up on one or another arc of the historical evangelical tradition, the story of twentieth-century evangelicalism is almost always sketched in a fairly limited range of hues. The details and shading may be different, but the broad lines are all there. Once securely fastened in mind, the image becomes incredibly hard to shake. With few notable exceptions, standard accounts of the twentieth-century history of mainstream evangelicalism still generally follow a recipe that goes something like this:

- Begin with the turn-of-the-century fundamentalist movement, which was a militant subset of an older evangelical tradition;
- continue with a post–World War II neoevangelical coalition that tried to differentiate itself from its fundamentalist forebearers by rallying conservative Protestants around both orthodoxy and a kinder, gentler cultural reengagement;

- move next to midcentury evangelicals' successful development of a massive network of interdenominational schools, publishing outfits, institutional associations, and parachurch organizations;
- emphasize the emergence of the evangelical political forces of the Religious Right;
- and conclude, depending on who is telling the story, with some reflection on either the waxing or waning of evangelicalism's influence on US public life at century's end.

Even though the standard recipe has never been totally replaced, there have been occasional attempts to shake things up along the way. Some observers have done so by emphasizing the ongoing presence of other flavors of evangelical religion that were either only tangentially related to the evangelical mainstream or that had little contact with the rest of mainstream evangelicalism in the first place. Others (evangelical historians, usually) have qualified the conventional picture by attempting to distinguish between the contemporary, transdenominational, US American evangelical coalition and a broader, older evangelical tradition that included a variety of revivalist and theologically orthodox strands of Protestantism. In some such retellings, evangelicalism is the historic *tradition* out of which one particular version, the twentieth-century US evangelical *movement*, arose. But for the most part, such distinctions have done little to shake the predominant narrative, and the overall picture remains largely unchanged.

The very fact that conventional accounts exist is perhaps unremarkable. The more interesting question, which most scholars of evangelicalism and evangelical leaders alike often fail to consider, is *how* the conventional story became conventional. For the last four decades, scholars involved in the contemporary evangelical studies project have spent most of their time either reinforcing or nuancing the standard accounts, and precious little energy interrogating either how the standard narratives came about or why they gained so much power.

There have been clues along the way, however. The evolution of religious polling measures, for example, offers one major piece of the puzzle. As Robert Wuthnow compellingly argues, by the late twentieth century, polling about religion in general and about evangelicals in particular had increasingly become more than mere descriptions of the world, transforming into a force that actually *defined* reality as well. The idea that evangelicalism was the liveliest and most interesting force in US American religious life, that evangelicals comprised somewhere between 25 and 40 percent of the total population, and that they overwhelmingly took conservative stances on nearly every social issue, for instance, became an increasingly foregone conclusion as time went on. But where exactly did this common knowledge come from? "The way a casual observer would have known this," he argues, "is that polls overwhelmingly, consistently, and repeatedly said so. . . . Pollsters could report confidently that this or that many evangelicals existed and that these evangelicals believed such and such. Journalists and political operatives could take that information to the bank. Or so it seemed."[41]

On the one hand, Wuthnow explains, polling played an undeniably powerful role in the transformation of evangelicals from a ragtag group of Christians representing a range of denominational, theological, and ecclesial backgrounds into a singular, definable group. In this sense, polling was crucial for the establishment of conventional accounts about evangelicalism. But then, on the other hand, Wuthnow points out, evangelicals simultaneously tested the limits of polling's ability to impose a coherent narrative on what was a far messier reality than many observers grasped. Evangelical insiders, for instance, were by no means in agreement about either what evangelicalism actually was or how it should be defined. The evangelical reaction to Gallup's sensational 1976 announcement was a prime example: although many evangelical leaders had responded with barely contained excitement, others soon began reconsidering both the implications of and assumptions behind the data. Pollsters, in other words, taught the public several major lessons about this thing called evangelicalism. But what they didn't tell them was anything about the ongoing, behind-the-scenes disagreements among evangelical leaders over what evangelicalism actually was and what it should mean to count someone as among the evangelicals.[42]

Christian Smith's subcultural identity theory offers yet another clue that helps explain not only how such debates over the nature of evangelical identity wound up being settled but also how the conventional portraits of evangelicalism became so powerful. Because if Smith is right, then one of the primary ways that evangelicalism became such a strong and vital contemporary religious tradition was through the remarkable ability of mid-twentieth-century evangelical leaders to carve out a new religious identity space called evangelical. Regardless of whether the post–World War II evangelical movement was wholly representative of either contemporary evangelicalism or the historic evangelical tradition, the neoevangelical coalition was undeniably successful in at least this sense: they invented an evangelical identity that caught on in the twentieth-century American context in a major way. In Smith's judgment, midcentury evangelical leaders were so successful in fact that their version of evangelical identity effectively restructured the entire field of twentieth-century American religious belonging—in which case, it would be thoroughly unsurprising that this version of evangelicalism became associated in the popular and scholarly consciousness with evangelicalism writ large.

Because by staking a claim for a new identity space called evangelical, such leaders were simultaneously claiming the power to define evangelical identity however they saw fit. And if being an evangelical meant what they said it meant, then it is no small wonder that standard accounts, be they statistical, historical, sociological, or otherwise, have indeed consistently looked like the relatively small group of theologically and politically conservative power brokers behind flagship institutions like *Christianity Today* and the National Association of Evangelicals. By positioning themselves as the rightful heirs of the evangelical *tradition*, in other words, the leaders of the twentieth-century evangelical *movement* were able to secure their understanding of evangelicalism as the mainstream version. In so doing, their definition of evangelical identity became canonical.

But whether the version of evangelical identity established by midcentury evangelical leaders was a good one, and whether the ism propagated along with it was a coherent one, is another question altogether. Although few and far between, over the years, a handful of (again, mostly evangelical) scholars have challenged the conventional picture of twentieth-century evangelicalism on precisely this point.

With his persistent argument that the predominance of mostly Reformed or Calvinist, essentially fundamentalist, overwhelmingly conservative thinking in what became known as mainstream evangelicalism was both an unfortunate and unnecessary historical development, Donald Dayton was among the earliest and most infamous challengers. In his view, the version of evangelical identity that existed by the latter half of the twentieth century had swallowed up smaller, older, more coherent denominational traditions—like his own Wesleyan-Holiness tradition—extinguished their important theological distinctives, imposed a generically conservative, lowest-common-denominator viewpoint on everything labeled evangelical, and thereby ruined everything it touched. Initially arguing that there were other (better) versions of evangelical faith that offered remedies to some of contemporary mainstream evangelicalism's worst characteristics, over time, Dayton increasingly concluded that the very concept of an identifiable thing called evangelicalism was hopelessly incoherent. In light of the vast array of often contradictory meanings associated with the word "evangelical," he noted, the category should be understood as an "essentially contested concept," which indeed had outlived its usefulness. Eventually deciding that any and all efforts to make the diverse theological traditions subsumed under the evangelical umbrella fit together consistently ended up doing more harm than good, Dayton ultimately called for a moratorium on the usage of the label. By the end of his career, Dayton believed that the word had in fact become so woefully irredeemable that he had admittedly begun describing himself as "Holiness" rather than evangelical. The reason? So as to avoid any association "with the name of my theological enemies."[43]

To date, the most thoroughgoing attempt to demythologize the evangelical mythos is also the most recent. In his 2004 book *Deconstructing Evangelicalism*, D. G. Hart makes an extended argument that twentieth-century evangelicalism was at best an unstable and amorphous coalition and at worst a dangerous chimera. The story of twentieth-century American evangelicalism, in Hart's telling, is not a story about the emergence of a particular evangelical movement from within a broader history of conservative Protestantism known as the "evangelical tradition." The *real* story is about how a group of post–World War II neoevangelical leaders constructed a new religious identity for conservative Christians who were disaffected with liberal Protestant leaders, called it evangelical, defined evangelicalism as a nicer, gentler form of culturally reengaged fundamentalism, and conjured from thin air the idea of an evangelical tradition to go along with it. For Hart, the only problem was that the version of evangelical identity dreamed up by the midcentury evangelical leaders represented "a constructed ideal without any real substance," and the corresponding ism they invented to go along with it was never anything more than an incoherent abstraction. For the purposes of movement building, Hart concedes, the abstraction was remarkably useful, and it *did* function as a way of rallying conservative Protestants into a coalition that could compete for influence on the American religious scene.[44]

Evangelical leaders weren't the only ones to find it useful either, and the construction of evangelicalism required more than just the vision cast by the neoevangelicals. According to Hart's analysis, for evangelicalism to truly catch on, a second phase of construction, in which a team of subcontractors employed the category in a range of new venues and thereby put flesh on the skeleton erected by the post-World War II evangelical leaders, had also been necessary. In his judgment, pollsters like Gallup and Barna, historians like Marsden and Noll, and sociologists like Hunter and Smith had risen to the occasion, thereby shoring up "evangelicalism as one of the more forceful tools of analysis within the contemporary academic study of religion."[45]

Demonstrating that what became known as mainstream evangelicalism was actually an invention developed by midcentury evangelical leaders and reinforced by the evangelical studies project is among *Deconstructing Evangelicalism*'s primary tasks. But for Hart, the novelty of the concept is never really the main point. Neither how, nor why, nor even who invented evangelicalism is as important to him as *what the invention did*. The most serious problem with the category evangelical, he argues, is its fundamental and inherent insufficiency as either an academic tool or a version of the Christian faith. Evangelicalism needed deconstructing, in other words, because of the havoc its construction has wreaked on *both* the study *and* practice of Christianity. In the former case, he points out, evangelical studies had eclipsed the older kind of denominational and church histories that were able to capture important distinctions among Protestants in a way that the newer histories of evangelicalism could not. For decades, the study of evangelicalism had obscured the importance of the institutional church as the true site of Christian identity formation and thereby glossed over crucial divergences within various streams of Protestantism. Historians would be better off, Hart surmises, if they opted for more precise categories of analysis.

But for Hart, the historiographical imprecision of the category is not nearly as serious a problem as its implications for Christian faith. The success of the abstraction in mobilizing huge numbers of generally conservative Protestants around some common goals was undeniable. But that success, in Hart's mind, had come at too high a cost. Evangelicalism had reduced the real stuff of historic Christian traditions—which needed dogma, and church discipline, and institutional structures for accountability and succession—down to a minimal consensus of sentiments, practices, and convictions that were unenforceable. At best, he judged, evangelicalism was a pseudotradition that prompted churches and congregations to sacrifice some of the most historic structures of Christian life in favor of du jour kinds of "lowest common denominator theology" and "pop-culture-inspired devotion." Having thereby become "something of a parasite on historic Christian communions," evangelicalism had time and again demonstrated that it was fatally hollow, formless, and shallow. In light of the fact that the Christian church in the United States would be much healthier without it, in Hart's view, evangelicalism thus desperately needed deconstruction.[46]

The *Other* Evangelicals: The Problem of Diversity, The Marginalization of Difference, and the Shaping of Evangelical Identity

I, too, am convinced that the midcentury evangelical movement constructed a religious identity that was incredibly effective at rallying conservative Protestants beneath the evangelical banner, thereby opening up a new religious space that millions of people would eventually find themselves within. Over time, the evangelicals who built this space and the evangelicals that later filled it in really did become *the* evangelicals. In the process, the twentieth-century evangelical leaders behind this project furthermore established what became the most widely accepted understanding of what contemporary evangelicalism actually was: an interdenominational movement of generally conservative Protestants united around a set of theological commitments that were, at least initially, necessarily bare bones for coalition-building's sake. Whatever else it would mean, to be a capital-E Evangelical in the twentieth-century US context would eventually come to mean some level of participation with, involvement in, or connection to this version of evangelicalism, which unquestionably became the mainstream kind.

But I am also convinced that the coalition of generally conservative Protestants that became known as *the* evangelicals were faced with a profound identity crisis from the outset. The problem, which Douglas Sweeney has argued represents the "essential evangelicalism dialectic," could be found in the uncomfortable discrepancy between the ideological (or at least rhetori-

26

cal) unity of the early evangelical establishment, on the one hand, and the significant internal diversity of their growing evangelical constituency, on the other. Further still, in Sweeney's judgment, the foundational tension of mainstream twentieth-century evangelicalism—between unity at the top and diversity at the bottom—was often transmuted into and repeated within the competing narratives of its history. Where some historians saw "the doctrinal unity of early neo-evangelicalism," another side saw only "the definitional trouble latent in the multifarious constituency," when the reality is that both things were true at the same time. Midcentury evangelical leaders really did cast an undeniably decisive vision of evangelical identity that blended an essentially fundamentalist theology with what was supposed to be a culturally reengaged social agenda. The architects of this new evangelical religious territory were also unbelievably successful at convincing a host of various kinds of Protestants to set up camp inside their borders.[47]

But along with this success came a fundamental and perennial problem that would bedevil the capital-E Evangelicals for the rest of the twentieth century: post–World War II evangelical leaders' rhetorical consensus on the question of what it meant to be a real, true evangelical consistently belied the fragility of a coalition built upon an evangelical identity pragmatically constructed to allow for significant internal diversity. Twentieth-century evangelical leaders wanted a lot of evangelicals, they found a lot of evangelicals, and the way they found them was through defining the capital-E Evangelical territory as just wide enough to include all sorts of Calvinists, Arminians, Pietists, Charismatics, Fundamentalists, Baptists, Presbyterians, Methodists, Dutch Reformed, Lutherans, Brethren, Vineyard, Covenant, nondenominationalists, and Jesus People, to name a few. The diversity—indeed, the *pluralism*—inside the evangelical gates made the newly inaugurated twentieth-century mainstream form of evangelical identity an inherently tricky project prone to the kind of definitional problems that evangelical leaders, historians, insiders, and outsiders alike have been wrestling with ever since.

I am less convinced however that either the constructed nature or the foundational tension within what became contemporary US evangelicalism necessarily prefigured its eventual collapse into nothingness, spelled its eventual downfall, made it impossible to maintain, or somehow means that it never really existed. Capital-E evangelical identity was invented and mainstream twentieth-century evangelicalism constructed right along with it, but they were (and are) no less real for that fact. Although some have questioned its coherence, judged it ultimately to have been a disastrous failure, or concluded that it was nebulous and unstable—all legitimate and true enough points—the version of evangelical identity invented by the mid-century transdenominational evangelical coalition never fully unraveled. If anything, it became more influential, more clearly defined, and even more secure in its position as the unrivaled definition of what it meant to be an evangelical in the twentieth-century US context as time marched on.

But I also believe that how that happened—how it is that *the* evangelicals became *the* evangelicals and defined what it would mean to be one of *the* evangelicals along the way—is a story that is still mostly untold. This book is one attempt at telling one part of that story, and the argument that I am making herein goes something like this:

The history of mainstream twentieth-century evangelicalism is best understood as a story about how a group of mostly self-appointed evangelical leaders—including theologians, historians, ethicists, famous pastors, popular authors, and political activists—transformed the generally conservative version of evangelical identity invented by the midcentury evangelical coalition into a proprietary religious identity marker with an increasingly specific set of explicit criteria and implicit connotations. The most determinative characteristic was the first: when a group of kinder, gentler fundamentalists rallied the generally conservative but uncomfortably diverse set of Protestants around a new identity called evangelical, they thereby successfully drew a circle around *the* evangelicals that distinguished those on the inside from the more liberal varieties of Protestants who were now on the outside. But that was only the beginning.

From that point forward and for the rest of the century, evangelical leaders would be continuously forced to deal with the ongoing problem of border clarification and boundary maintenance. Without an official evangelical magisterium that could provide authoritative rulings on the limits of the newly secured evangelical territory, evangelical thought-leaders resorted to a never-ending cycle of debate over the very nature of the circle itself. The resulting decisions were often ad hoc and provisional, occasionally ending in a stalemate with one side begrudgingly acknowledging that the other was dubiously evangelical but still in bounds. Other times, like when the clarification resulted in job loss or membership revocation, the judgment was decisive and binding. Occasionally, there were those who *thought* they were still in only to find that they had been ruled out. Sometimes, those who realized they had lost simply surrendered the field and saw themselves out. Some decisions became clear quickly. Others resurfaced and were readjudicated time and again over the years. But over time, the sum total of the various clarifications over the specifics of evangelicalness nonetheless added up to an increasingly detailed and commonly (if never universally) accepted understanding of what it meant to be a real evangelical.

What I am suggesting, in other words, is that *the* evangelicals became *the* evangelicals by effectively promoting, popularizing, and disseminating their understanding of evangelical identity—precisely as a number of scholars have now argued. But for that identity to truly catch on with large numbers of the nation's Christians, it needed to be generic enough to avoid excluding too many of the generally conservative, born-again, or essentially orthodox Protestants that the post–World War II evangelical leaders believed were out there. When it was indeed well suited for such purposes, the various kinds of evangelicals that it brought into the camp brought their own specific doctrinal quirks, alternative social-ethical and political views, divergent cultural practices, pet theological emphases, and competing interpretations with them. The next step, which was harder and took much longer, thus involved fleshing out a fuller definition of evangelical identity by sorting out the border cases from the central examples, differentiating between the ideally evangelical and the questionably evangelical, distinguishing between the conservative-enough-to-count and the too-liberal-to-consider, and separating the sheep from the goats. After making the first crucial *external* differentiation, defining evangelicals as anyone securely on the theologically conservative Protestant spectrum and thereby excluding the liberals, came a long period of *internal* differentiation whereby the questions became far more specific.

This internal differentiation process often took the form of power struggles between (and among) members of the almost universally conservative, white, male evangelical establishment and a variety of upstart movements, minoritized groups, and dissenting voices that emerged from within the twentieth-century evangelical world. Time and again, the mostly white, male, evangelical power brokers in charge during any given controversy retained their power by serving as self-appointed gatekeepers who could rule those who challenged their interpretations out of bounds. These periodic struggles to distinguish between the real, true, card-carrying evangelicals and the subevangelical, unevangelical, and questionably evangelical furthermore became one of the primary ways that the evangelical establishment clarified the finer points of twentieth-century evangelical identity. They also left a trail of both winners and losers in their wake.

Most accounts of twentieth-century evangelicalism focus on the winners, *the* evangelicals, the ones who became mainstream by defining the mainstream, the evangelicals whose theological, political, and social-ethical views were ruled in bounds, those who thought, acted, worshiped, voted, or just looked like they fit within the acceptable range of soundly evangelical options, the kind who liked and were like Billy Graham.

In this book, I focus on the evangelical losers, the dissenters who were sidelined, those who tried to carve out space for an alternative kind of evangelicalism and were marginalized for doing so, those who were ruled out of bounds, or who left voluntarily, or who were excommunicated over a major or minor difference, those who were defined out of the category evangelical and were thereby forgotten by the historical record, the *other* evangelicals. Recovering their stories, I argue, sheds new light on how *the* evangelicals became *the* evangelicals, how contemporary, twenty-first-century US American evangelicalism took on some of its most distinguishing characteristics, and what was left behind in the process.

The story begins with the early neoevangelical leaders who struggled to distinguish themselves from their fundamentalist forebearers and began defining what became mainstream evangelical identity by institutionalizing twentieth-century evangelicalism in flagship organizations like the NAE for the first time. In so doing, they also effectively defined self-confessed liberal thinkers like Shailer Mathews and Harry Emerson Fosdick, as well as accused liberal theologians like Karl Barth, out of the evangelical tradition forever. Even though many such figures always maintained that they too were evangelical, in the wake of the rise of the post–World War II neoevangelical coalition, liberalism (or even the slightest hint thereof) and evangelicalism became an irreconcilable contradiction in terms for the first time. Chapter 1 recovers the stories of the evangelical liberals, demonstrating how evangelicals became reactionarily antiliberal from that point forward.

The decision that the evangelical circle would never again include liberal theology of any kind should not have precluded the involvement of the large proportion of Black Christians in the twentieth century who held theological beliefs strikingly similar to their white evangelical counterparts. But it did. Though the majority of the historically independent Black church traditions in the United States have subscribed to what can legitimately be described as a thoroughly evangelical kind of faith, Black Christians by and large have neither been included among *the* evangelicals nor been interested in the label whatsoever. But some were. Chapter 2 recovers the story of a little-known movement of radical Black evangelicals—led by figures like William Bentley, William Pannell, and Tom Skinner—who developed a radically Black-nationalist evangelical perspective that critiqued the racism of the majority white evangelical culture. Their struggles and eventual marginalization illustrate one of contemporary evangelicals' most enduring problems: the uninterrogated racism and de facto cultural whiteness of a mainstream evangelical world, which has alienated successive generations of Black and Brown Christians who have moved in its orbit.

With the rise of the Religious Right, mainstream evangelical identity took on what became its strongest connotation of all. From that point forward, theological conservatism would no longer be enough. Real evangelicals would need to be politically conservative as well. Countless books have tried to explain how and why evangelicalism became synonymous with contemporary US American Republicanism. But most such accounts fail to give as much as a footnote to the fact that a small but significant movement known as the evangelical left actually *predated* the appearance and ascendance of the evangelical political forces of the Religious Right. Chapter 3 recounts the stories of progressive evangelical figures like John Alexander, Jim Wallis, and Ron Sider who tirelessly tried to decouple twentieth-century evangelicalism from its close alignment with political conservatism, all to precious little avail.

Along with its close alignment with political conservatism, by the end of the twentieth century, evangelicalism had become infamous for its staunch defense of rigidly midcentury gender roles—an order maintained in no small part by its near universally male leadership. The fact that the eventual rise of the so-called biblical manhood, biblical womanhood movement began as a direct response to a burgeoning biblical equality, egalitarian, evangelical feminist movement is less frequently remembered, however. Chapter 4 recovers the story of the emergence, rise, and eventual marginalization of the kind of evangelical feminism pioneered and developed during the 1970s by women like Nancy Hardesty, Virginia R. Mollenkott, and Letha Scanzoni. While mainline Protestants spent the final decades of the twentieth century arguing about homosexuality, evangelicals by and large refused to even discuss the matter. As a result, mainstream evangelicalism entered the twenty-first century with a well-earned reputation as universally antigay. In recent years, a growing number of (mostly younger) evangelicals have increasingly called for reconsidering mainstream evangelicalism's default position of condemnation and rejection toward LGBTQ people. But such calls are by no means new, and the trail of dissent goes back further than most accounts of evangelicalism acknowledge or realize. Beginning with the woefully undertold story of Ralph Blair and his progay, explicitly evangelical organization Evangelicals Concerned, chapter 5 highlights the preposterously uphill battle faced by those who have dared to challenge evangelical orthodoxy by articulating an explicitly LGBTQ-affirming evangelical perspective.

By the time that the twenty-first century was in full swing, what it meant to be an evangelical had come to include an increasingly specific list of de facto orthodoxies on everything from theological method and political partisanship to race, sex, and gender. For contemporary evangelicals, deviation from any number of the reigning mainstream views often inevitably results in marginalization or excommunication. Insiders can become outsiders with frightening speed. In the conclusion, I therefore suggest that evangelical identity in the context of the contemporary United States has become a proprietary trademark reserved almost exclusively for its most fundamentalistic, theologically and politically conservative, white, straight, and male-headship-affirming claimants. For this reason, I furthermore argue that anyone looking for a more capacious and theologically nuanced, or less sectarian, homogenous, and insular kind of faith would do best to look beyond the heavily guarded evangelical gates.

one

The Liberals

The first chapter of the history of twentieth-century evangelicalism almost always begins something like this.

For most of the nineteenth century, the vast majority of Protestant Christianity in the United States was essentially evangelical in nature. But by the latter part of the century, this broad consensus of evangelical belief had begun cracking under the weight of controversy. The culprit? The creeping influence of a variety of modern ideas—Darwinian evolution and critical biblical scholarship in particular—that would soon introduce a deep and lasting divide in American Protestantism. On one side were those who were willing to accept one or more of these new ideas. On the other side were those who viewed most or all of these modern innovations as alien incursions that were fundamentally incompatible with true evangelical faith.

The dividing line between the two sides became clearer than ever before in the early decades of the twentieth century. Faced with the rising popularity of modernist beliefs in certain Protestant circles, a number of concerned Christians rose to the defense of what they believed were the long-standing, truly evangelical doctrines of the faith. The most zealously antimodernist of these defenders of orthodoxy eventually coalesced into a tenuous but increasingly militant alliance devoted primarily to the eradication of all traces of liberal modernism from the nation's churches. In light of their dogged commitment to preserving what they felt were the fundamentals of Christianity, the militant antimodernists eventually became known as fundamentalists. Fundamentalism, by extension, would eventually emerge as a moniker for the short list of essential beliefs that the fundamentalists so vehemently sought to defend.

But by the time that fundamentalism became an established phenomenon, its days were already numbered. After losing a number of important, high-profile battles against modernism, fundamentalism rapidly disappeared from the main stage of US history. In the aftermath of the so-called fundamentalist-modernist controversies, American Protestantism was effectively divided into two irreconcilable parties that would take two diverging paths for the rest of the twentieth century.

In one corner were the evangelicals. Until the late nineteenth century, *most* American Protestants had been evangelicals. When modernist ideas threatened the historic evangelical tradition, fundamentalism emerged as a militantly modernist subtradition of evangelicalism in response. Fundamentalists, in other words, were evangelicals zealously committed to driving out the modernist defectors in order to preserve the historic evangelical faith. Even though they were mostly unsuccessful in their efforts, and even though not all evangelicals had necessarily been fundamentalists, all fundamentalists were clearly evangelicals.

In the other corner were the modernists. By attempting to reconcile the new knowledge of modernism with the Christian faith, the modernists parted ways with the historic evangelical tradition and left the evangelical fold in the process. Whether the modernists could even be considered true Christians would remain a live debate, but by the end of the fundamentalist-modernist controversies of the early twentieth century, one crucial distinction had already become abundantly clear: whatever they were, modernists were *not* evangelicals.

*

In the wake of the evangelical historiography renaissance in the 1980s, roughly this version of the story of twentieth-century evangelicalism and fundamentalism became the mostly canonical account. Successive generations of historians would eventually add a variety of nuances and qualifications to the standard picture, but the main tenets of the conventional narrative have never been totally overridden, and the overall outlines of the story have remained durably fixed. The idea that the fundamentalist-modernist controversies set the stage for the rest of twentieth-century American Christian history furthermore gave rise to one of the most influential heuristics for interpreting historical and contemporary trends in US Protestantism: the two-party thesis. Ever since historians began reconsidering the history of evangelicalism, the fact that twentieth-century Protestants were always in either the modernist-liberal-mainline party or the fundamentalist-conservative-evangelical party has become one of the most widely accepted and frequently deployed taxonomies in American religious life.[1]

The popularity of the two-party categorization is due at least in part to the fact that it has proved remarkably helpful for distinguishing between competing trends in twentieth-century Protestant life. It caught on, in other words, because it works: there really was something different going on in the sector of US American Christian life called conservative-evangelical, on the one hand, and in the one called liberal-mainline, on the other. But commonly accepted taxonomies are also rarely as objectively descriptive as they seem. When labels like mainline and evangelical take on a mostly agreed upon set of connotations, it becomes all too easy to forget that categories have histories. Labels evolve over time. The early development of the evangelical label's twentieth-century connotations is a case in point.

Because despite what conventional narratives might suggest, there was a time when whether liberal-modernists were evangelicals was more of an open question than it would be in years to come. In the early decades of the twentieth century, in fact, the idea that accepting modernist ideas placed someone squarely beyond the pale of traditionally evangelical belief was less of a foregone conclusion than the usual story makes it seem. For a long while, whether the fundamentalists or the modernists were truer representatives of the historic evangelical tradition remained to be seen. Although the struggle to determine where exactly evangelical faith ended and un-evangelical faith began certainly became pivotal as never before during the height of the fundamentalist-modernist struggles, even in the aftermath of the controversies, the evangelical label remained up for grabs for far longer than most standard accounts of twentieth-century evangelical history commonly claim. The origin story of what became mainstream evangelicalism usually begins with the fundamentalists' battle with modernism, but the turning point came much later. Twentieth-century evangelicalism first took on its most determinative characteristics a generation later when a new kind of fundamentalist burst onto the scene.

The Neoevangelicals and the Institutionalization of Twentieth-Century Evangelical Identity

The story of the capital-E Evangelicals begins in the early 1940s with a group of second-generation fundamentalists who were fed up with their forebearers' unnecessary sectarianism and unhelpful militancy. In the years following World War II, these new fundamentalists set to work busily building the institutional superstructure necessary for establishing and sustaining an interdenominational movement that could vie for pride of place as the predominant version of American Christian religiosity. They began their crusade under the flag of a neoevangelical identity, which they believed could jettison the worst excesses and failures of the early fundamentalist movement while retaining the best of orthodox fundamentalist doctrine in a kinder, gentler, and culturally reengaged package. Soon enough, the architects of the midcentury, neofundamentalist, neoevangelical coalition dropped the "neo" and began staking their claim as simply *the* evangelicals instead. By building a network of institutions and organizations purposefully named and described as such, these evangelical leaders institutionalized an official explicitly evangelical identity for the first time in the twentieth century. From that point forward, their kinds of evangelicals would be the real, card-carrying kind, and evangelicalness would be adjudicated according to their standards. For the rest of the twentieth century, these evangelicals would be *the* evangelicals.

The National Association of Evangelicals

The first crucial step toward an officially institutionalized kind of evangelical identity began between late 1940 and early 1941 with a group of pastors who felt that the nation's evangelicals were no longer represented by the mainstream Protestant establishment. In their judgment, the millions of conservative evangelicals in the country represented an "unvoiced multitude" with beliefs that were fundamentally at odds with progressive organizations like the Federal Council of Churches, which had become so infected with the "great apostasy" of liberalism that it had compromised essential Christian doctrine. In the hopes of remedying the fact that the nation's soundly evangelical masses had no soundly evangelical vehicle for cooperation and organization, in 1941 the group of concerned pastors thus circulated a letter inviting evangelicals from throughout the country to come together for a meeting the following year to discuss a possible solution.[2]

In April 1942, those who heard and answered the call traveled to Saint Louis to lay the groundwork for a possible answer to their problem. During the first meeting of what became one of twentieth-century evangelicalism's most significant institutional bellwethers, the group of concerned evangelicals gathered in Saint Louis voted to affirm a provisional constitution for a new organization, the National Association of Evangelicals for United Action, designed to fill the gap. From the outset, the fledgling institution's founding document made it abundantly clear why a faithfully evangelical alternative had become so utterly necessary:

Whereas: there is no existing organization which adequately represents or acts for a very large proportion of our evangelical Protestant constituency:

and

Whereas: we realize that in many areas of Christian endeavor the organizations which now purport to be the representatives of Protestant Christianity have departed from the faith of Jesus Christ, we do now reaffirm our unqualified loyalty to this Gospel as herein set forth, declaring our unwillingness to be represented by organizations which do not have such loyalty to the Gospel of Christ; and we express our unqualified opposition to all such apostasy. And in this loyalty to the evangelical Christian faith and opposition to all apostasy, we do hereby unite our testimony.

We propose, therefore, to organize an Association which shall give articulation and united voice to our faith and purposes in Christ Jesus.[3]

The following year, "a thousand evangelical Protestants," representing "in one way or another some fifty denominations (with a potential constituency of 15,000,000)," gathered in Chicago for the constitutional convention of the newly minted National Association of Evangelicals (NAE).[4] While there, the representatives of the untold millions of conservative evangelicals unanimously voted to adopt a seven-point statement of faith that any prospective member—a status that would be offered to whole denominations, independent organizations, and individual congregations—would be required to sign both before joining and again each year prior to renewing their membership. At its founding, membership in the NAE thus required affirmation of a statement that read:

1. We believe the Bible to be the inspired, the only infallible, authoritative word of God.
2. We believe that there is one God, eternally existent in three persons, Father, Son and Holy Ghost.
3. We believe in the deity of our Lord Jesus Christ, in His virgin birth, in His sinless life, in His miracles, in His vicarious and atoning death through His shed blood, in His bodily resurrection, in His ascension to the right hand of the Father, and in His personal return in power and glory.
4. We believe that for the salvation of lost and sinful man regeneration by the Holy Spirit is absolutely essential.
5. We believe in the present ministry of the Holy Spirit by whose indwelling the Christian is enabled to live a godly life.
6. We believe in the resurrection of both the saved and the lost; they that are saved unto the resurrection of life and they that are lost unto the resurrection of damnation.
7. We believe in the spiritual unity of believers in our Lord Jesus Christ.[5]

With the 1942 formation of the NAE, the neoevangelical movement thereby established the first twentieth-century example of an institutional guardianship concretely and explicitly tied to the evangelical label. By developing a national-level institution with clear membership requirements, the NAE furthermore staked a proprietary claim on the name evangelical. By requiring the annual reaffirmation of its seven-point statement of faith, the group simultaneously positioned itself as an arbiter in perpetuity of potential claimants to the evangelical mantle. Even though nonmembers might still be able to claim that they were evangelical, from that point forward, they would no longer be able to say that they were National Association of Evangelicals evangelicals.

The founding of the NAE by no means marked the end of debates over who was and wasn't an official evangelical. In some ways, it merely focused them. But by establishing an official membership roll of credentialed evangelicals for the first time in the twentieth century, the organization instantly shifted the burden of proof in such arguments. From the outset, the architects of the NAE furthermore made their answer to one particular question about who could—and more importantly who could not—consider themselves real, true evangelicals absolutely clear. The organization's very raison d'être, after all, was in and of itself an argument about evangelical identity. In the eyes of the group's founders, the faithfully conservative Protestant masses who were no longer represented by the apostate liberal leadership of mainstream Protestant organizations like the Federal Council were the true evangelicals. Whatever else it might come to mean, in other words, the advent of the official, card-carrying, capital-E Evangelical kind of NAE evangelicals at least meant this: twentieth-century evangelical identity would no longer have any room for liberal Protestants.

Fuller Theological Seminary

Around the same time that the NAE began endeavoring to speak *for* the "unvoiced multitudes" of conservative Protestants, fundamentalist radio evangelist Charles Fuller was speaking *to* them. Like the NAE, he, too, offered the nation's evangelicals a conspicuously conservative alternative to what was currently available. Jockeying for position in a market dominated by Protestants of a decidedly *less* conservative bent, Fuller had his work particularly cut out for him. During the early to mid-1940s, time slots reserved for religious programming on the most widely known national radio networks were all but monopolized by the Federal Council of Churches, which regularly broadcasted antifundamentalist sermons from the kinds of liberal Protestant leaders the NAE set out to replace. Effectively locked out of the major networks, Fuller nonetheless managed to reach massive audiences by broadcasting his show *The Old Fashioned Revival Hour* on various independent radio stations. In 1942 and 1943, for instance, more Americans listened to his programming than to Bob Hope's. By 1944, as many as twenty million people from all over the world were tuning in to hear Fuller's messages about sin, hell, damnation, and redemption through belief in Jesus.[6]

After conquering the airwaves, in the latter half of the decade, Fuller's attention turned to the question of his ministerial legacy and the possibility of passing the torch in avenues beyond radio broadcasting. Increasingly convinced that what the country really needed in those "terrible days" was a school that could prepare ministers to boldly preach the gospel, he began envisioning an institution that would combine a strict commitment to the fundamentals of the Christian faith with high-caliber academics. Once the vision was firmly secured, Fuller set out in search of prospective professors who might be attracted by the prospects of such a school. He soon found a number of willing candidates, quickly assembling a crack team of founding faculty members who subsequently joined him in the process of recruiting an inaugural group of students. Charles Fuller's vision came to fruition in the fall of 1947, when the first admitted class of seminarians began their studies at the newly established Fuller Theological Seminary in Pasadena, California.[7]

From the outset, the team behind the new evangelical seminary made the school's raison d'être abundantly clear. In the lead-up to the inaugural class, Fuller's team had promoted their fledgling school in the pages of *United Evangelical Action*, a periodical published by the recently established NAE, specifically as "A Center for Evangelical Scholarship." In their own advertising material, the leaders behind this newly formed evangelical scholarly clearinghouse had furthermore identified their beliefs that "naturalist modernism had invaded many old line seminaries," that too many of the remaining soundly evangelical seminaries had become too narrowly focused on particular doctrinal emphases, and that the region was thus utterly devoid of an "interdenominational theological seminary of outstanding academic and evangelical qualifications" as among the institution's founding motivations. Like the NAE before it, Fuller Theological Seminary was therefore positioned from its birth as a remedy to the problem of the liberalization of US American Protestantism. In the NAE, the leaders of the emerging post–World War II evangelical coalition hoped for a soundly evangelical alternative to the apostate Federal Council of Churches. With Fuller, they envisioned a thoroughly evangelical answer to the ongoing problem of liberal drift among the nation's most prominent Protestant seminaries.[8]

At their inception, both projects were furthermore meant to signal a tentative step away from the strident sectarianism and needless infighting of an earlier generation of fundamentalists. Both institutions were envisioned from the start, in other words, as a way of carving out a middle path between the worst excesses of fundamentalism, on the one hand, and the godless unbelief of liberal modernism, on the other. Eventually, Harold Ockenga, Fuller's founding president and one of the chief architects behind the NAE, would popularize the term "new evangelicalism" or "neoevangelicalism" as a descriptor for the kind of third-way approach that organizations like Fuller and the NAE were meant to embody.

But just how far away from fundamentalism the path could go would be another question altogether. At least in the case of Fuller, for instance, everyone involved in the school's founding held tightly to all of the key doctrinal tenets of fundamentalism. As implied by the title of Marsden's indispensable history of the school, *Reforming Fundamentalism*, the point was not to do away with fundamentalist orthodoxy. The point rather was to retain the theological core of fundamentalism minus the worst accretions of its most militant earlier expressions. Although Fuller's founding figures would strive to move beyond the sectarianism and infighting of some fundamentalist leaders, for one crucial example, in the school's early days, the faculty simultaneously attempted to uphold the fundamentalist position on the Bible and its authority: scriptural inerrancy.

For an institution positioning itself as a bastion of an essentially orthodox middle path between fundamentalism and liberal modernism, inerrancy wound up making this kind of third way approach an exceedingly difficult ground to hold. The currents pulling the ship to both the right and the left would consistently prove far too strong. In the years to come, Fuller's eventual internal wrangling over the necessity of inerrancy for its explicitly evangelical identity would furthermore provide in micro a prime example of the self-same battles that would take place in macro among the newly minted, post–World War II, third-force version of evangelicalism for which the school had been tailor-made.

The Evangelical Theological Society

By the time that Fuller was up and running in the late 1940s, neoevangelical luminaries would begin erecting yet another important institutional milestone in the march toward establishing a range of benchmark criteria for evangelicalness in the twentieth-century US American context. In December 1949, a group of sixty or so evangelical scholars from a range of institutions and denominations met in Cincinnati to discuss the need for an academic society that would "foster conservative biblical scholarship."[9] In a plenary address delivered at the meetings, Calvin Theological Seminary theologian Clarence Bouma made the urgency of the situation as clear as possible. Why start yet another theological society when groups like the Society of Biblical Literature (SBL) and the American Theological Society already existed? The answer was simple: such groups were overrun with modernism, no longer truly evangelical, and thus dubiously Christian. Evangelicals needed their own theological society, Bouma explained, because of "the radical divergence between the basis, presuppositions, and consequent methodologies of a sound evangelical theology on the one hand, and that of the prevailing types of theology (which may with a general term be designated as modernist) on the other. . . . This divergence between historic Christian Theology and the currently prevalent modernist Theology—of whatever shape or hue—is so great that the organization of separate scholarly societies for the evangelical theologians is so desirable."[10]

Following the two-day organizational gathering, the group put out a press release announcing the foundation of a new society for evangelical scholars. Despite the denominational diversity among those who had been present, the press release noted, everyone in attendance had been "one in their view of the Scriptures and in the desire to foster true evangelical scholarship." As a result of this consensus, at its 1949 founding, the newly established Evangelical Theological Society (ETS) had thus adopted a statement of faith, which its members would be required to affirm in perpetuity, that was precisely one item long. As stated in article III of the ETS constitution, the sole doctrinal test for membership would be the belief that "the Bible alone, and the Bible in its entirety, is the Word of God written and is therefore inerrant in the autographs."[11]

The 1949 birth of the ETS by no means ended the discussion over what made someone an evangelical. But by the sheer fact of its formation, the organization thereby staked an unequivocal claim on what it meant to do "truly evangelical theology" and provided a more or less official forum for debating its limits. For both the architects and members of the first US American organization explicitly devoted to something called "evangelical theology," the border separating the real kind from everything else furthermore came down to one word: inerrancy. From that point forward, as defined by the ETS, the only truly evangelical theologies would be those that began with the belief that the original copies of the canonical books of the Bible were errorless. By extension, the only truly evangelical theologians would be the inerrantist ones—a group that thenceforth could be most easily found among the members in good standing of the Evangelical Theological Society.

Christianity Today

A little over a year after the founding of the ETS, Fuller Theological Seminary professor Wilbur Smith sent a letter to his close friend Billy Graham describing what Smith believed was yet another serious problem facing the nation's evangelicals. What evangelicals desperately needed, Smith explained, was "a periodical so important that it would be absolutely indispensable for every serious-minded Christian minister in America." Over the course of the next few years, Graham's personal interest in the prospects of just such an important, conservative, Christian periodical was increasingly piqued. By 1954, he and a few close associates had already begun laying the groundwork for the kind of magazine that, in their minds, might serve as an explicitly evangelical version of and clear rival to the mainline, liberal, modernist periodical the *Christian Century*.[12]

In Graham's view, the problems with the *Christian Century* were manifold. The philosophy of the magazine, he would later explain, "was progressive, inclusive, optimistic, and relatively humanistic, within a loose framework of Christian concepts. 'Modernism' was the vaunted label it wore." Worse still was the fact that the periodical had helped contribute to the marginalization of good, conservative, evangelical thought by throwing its weight behind the liberals during the fundamentalist-modernist controversies and by openly embracing higher biblical criticism. For Graham, the magazine's understanding of Scripture in particular was pure anathema. In his telling, according to the *Christian Century*, "the Bible, although it has religious value, was not the inspired Word of God or the objective standard of truth for our faith and practice. Instead, it was a book of human origin, to be approached the same way any other human book was approached—which is to say, critically and even skeptically."[13]

43

Graham believed that the magazine's liberal influence on the nation's Protestant clergy and establishment leaders had been nothing short of disastrous. He also believed that the liberal-mainline churches nonetheless still included "many rank-and-file clergy and lay leaders [who] held more orthodox views and felt discontent with the status quo." The only problem was that this soundly evangelical remnant "had no flag to follow."[14]

Hoping that their new project would give the faithfully evangelical populace a flag that they *could* follow, in 1955 Graham and his team turned their attention to the crucial task of finding an editor for their nascent periodical. After a series of negotiations, the team eventually convinced Carl F. H. Henry, the most influential evangelical theologian of his generation and a recent founding hire at Fuller Theological Seminary, to come aboard. Under Henry's founding editorship, the newly minted, soundly evangelical alternative to the liberal apostate *Christian Century* began circulation in October 1956 under the masthead *Christianity Today (CT)*.[15]

In the inaugural issue, an editorial titled "Why 'Christianity Today'?" straightforwardly traced the magazine's impetus to its founders' belief that "Theological Liberalism has failed to meet the moral and spiritual needs of the people." Evangelical Christianity had been "neglected, slighted, misrepresented," the editorial explained, and therefore needed "a clear voice, to speak with conviction and love, and to state its true position and its relevance to the world crisis." Along with a description of the kinds of topics the new periodical would cover, the opening editorial made the foundational commitments of the leadership team abundantly clear: "Those who direct the editorial policy of *Christianity Today* unreservedly accept the complete reliability and authority of the written Word of God. It is their conviction that the Scriptures teach the doctrine of plenary inspiration."[16]

Christianity Today quickly became precisely the kind of evangelical standard-bearer that Graham had envisioned. During its first year of publication, the magazine rapidly eclipsed the *Christian Century* in terms of readership.[17] It arguably surpassed its liberal-mainline counterpart in terms of influence shortly thereafter. As time marched on, the magazine furthermore became the single most significant publication in all of twentieth-century evangelicalism, increasingly serving as the veritable center ring of the contemporary evangelical world—a place where the evangelical authors featured in its pages would wrestle with the du jour evangelical controversies in full view of the watching evangelical public. It would also offer one of the most influential forums in which evangelical leaders, including most especially its evangelical editors, worked out the unofficial evangelical position on a host of theological, political, and social-ethical issues.

Along with organizations like the NAE, ETS, and schools like Fuller Seminary, *CT* thus became one of the main pillars of a newly institutionalized, post-World War II evangelical establishment that would go on to define and become the mainstream version of US American evangelicalism for the rest of the twentieth century. In every one of the founding examples of this new, capital-E version of Evangelicalism, evangelical identity was clearly and explicitly defined in direct opposition to some combination of the liberal-modernist-mainline troika. Whatever these newly minted official evangelicals were, in other words, they made one thing abundantly clear from the outset: liberals and modernists need not apply. To be counted as safely among *the* evangelicals from that point forward would require proving one's theologically conservative bona fides, usually by recourse to affirming the inerrancy of the Bible.

The Liberal-Modernist Evangelicals and the Possibility of an Evangelical Liberalism

The only problem was that not everyone agreed that defending theological conservatism and inerrancy was what being an evangelical should mean. In the long run, the second-generation fundamentalists behind the midcentury institutionalization of a generally conservative evangelical identity were undeniably successful in their campaign to claim the evangelical field for theological conservatives—which usually meant inerrantists—and for theological conservatives only. But in so doing, the neofundamentalist neoevangelicals who later became just *the* evangelicals first had to successfully wrest the evangelical banner from the hands of a decidedly different group of claimants who were far more reluctant to relinquish their hold for far longer than most histories of twentieth-century evangelicalism acknowledge. Evangelical identity did eventually become strictly synonymous with reactionarily antiliberal theology and rigidly conservative Biblicism. But for a long stretch of the early twentieth century, a number of liberal figures determinedly refused to cede their right to be both explicitly modernist *and* specifically evangelical. Before fundamentalism, inerrancy, and strict opposition to ideas like Darwinian evolution and higher biblical criticism became irrevocably linked to what it meant to be a twentieth-century evangelical, there was a time when an evangelical might also be a modernist or even a liberal.

In the lead-up to, at the height of, and in the wake of the fundamentalist-modernist controversies, such battles were in fact often waged on precisely these terms. Despite what conventional narratives usually suggest, in other words, the modernists didn't necessarily think that they were *fighting* the evangelicals. A number of early twentieth-century liberal Christians believed that they *were* the evangelicals.

Charles Briggs: Modernist Evangelical Biblical Critic

Born and raised in a pious nineteenth-century Christian home, Charles Briggs had his own individual conversion experience during his formative years, thereby fully aligning himself with a traditionally evangelical kind of faith. He went on to study at Union Theological Seminary under Henry Boynton Smith—a "mediating theologian" who believed that scientific knowledge and evangelical faith were perfectly compatible—before finishing his theological education in Germany, where he became an enthusiastic proponent of higher biblical criticism. The discovery of historical criticism was nothing short of a revelation for Briggs, who declared in a letter to his uncle that, through critical study, "the Bible is lit up with a new light." In an attempt to assuage their concerns, Briggs furthermore reassured his family that he had not relinquished "the standards of our church" by adopting the cutting-edge scholarly approach. Far from it. In his mind, critical methodology in fact offered the key to attaining "a more advanced Christian truth."[18]

Briggs believed that higher biblical criticism was by no means a threat to classic Christian orthodoxy and instead offered the most obvious way to retain a soundly evangelical faith in a thoroughly modern world. Critical methods were not merely a *legitimate* tool for faithful Christians, in his view. In reality, the best of contemporary biblical scholarship was *indispensable* for preserving evangelical belief. "True criticism," he later explained, "never disregards the letter, but reverently and tenderly handles every letter and syllable of the Word of God, striving to purify it from all dross, brushing away the dust of tradition and guarding it from the ignorant and profane."[19]

Upon returning to the United States, Briggs joined the faculty of Union Theological Seminary as professor of Hebrew and cognate languages, later moving to fill the school's chair of biblical theology. With its developing reputation as a bastion of liberal evangelicalism, Union was perfectly suited for Briggs and his pious devotion to the best of biblical scholarship. But a large contingent of his fellow Presbyterians were decidedly less enthusiastic about the benefits of higher biblical criticism, and his undeterred commitment to its virtues quickly earned him an equally committed group of denominational critics. Against the backdrop of a broader Presbyterian debate over creedal revision, Briggs's evangelistic belief in the good news of critical biblical scholarship, combined with his support for revising the creed, was increasingly matched by denominational opponents hell-bent on silencing him. The bubbling controversy came to a head in January 1891 when Briggs delivered an address, "The Authority of Holy Scripture," inaugurating his installation as the Edward Robinson Chair of Biblical Theology at Union. In the wake of the address, as news of Briggs's controversial views rapidly spread, his Presbyterian adversaries finally rewarded his passion for biblical criticism by setting into motion the denominational machinery necessary to formally charge him with heresy.[20]

In what became one of the most infamous series of heresy trials in US Christian history, Briggs's opponents would repeatedly suggest that, among other things, he did not believe that the Bible was inerrant. On that point at least, they were exactly right. Although he personally believed and repeatedly affirmed that the Bible was "the only infallible rule of faith and practice," and that any errors it contained were minor "circumstantials," which therefore did not threaten biblical authority, Briggs found the idea of inerrancy absurd. For one thing, he pointed out, the Bible itself never even claimed that it was without error. Inerrancy was in fact a relatively new idea in the history of Christian belief, Briggs argued, representing nothing more than "a ghost of modern evangelicalism to frighten children."[21]

Briggs's protestations were ultimately to no avail. Over the course of three consecutive trials, his Presbyterian adversaries persistently argued that his views were nothing short of heretical. Despite being acquitted of the charges against him in the first two trials, the third time was the charm. In 1893, Briggs was officially convicted of heresy and suspended from ministering in the Presbyterian Church.[22]

In the context of a denomination in turmoil over the rise of modern intellectual trends, Briggs's dogged belief that the Christian faith was not threatened by biblical criticism placed him squarely on the modernist side of the emerging divide between those who believed that such developments undermined the true evangelical faith and those who did not. As one of the earliest casualties in one of the first battles of the looming fundamentalist-modernist wars, when forced to choose, Briggs sided with the modernists every time. He found many of the ideas that became characteristic of fundamentalism—inerrancy and dispensationalism in particular—both repugnant and dangerous, and he never shied away from saying as much.

But even if his acceptance of biblical criticism made him a modernist, in Briggs's mind, that did not mean that he was either a heretical defector from classic evangelical faith or, worse still, a liberal. Although he would eventually describe his work as a kind of "progressive theology," throughout his career, Briggs simultaneously maintained that his approach was in fact the best and most faithful embodiment of "true orthodoxy." When the battle lines were most clearly drawn and the chips were down, given the alternative of the rigid orthodoxism of fundamentalists, he accepted his position among the liberal camp. The fact that higher biblical criticism was fast becoming a litmus test for incipient liberalism furthermore stacked the deck against anyone who might have suggested that he was anything other than a dyed-in-the-wool liberal.[23]

Even so, Briggs refused to go quietly, never accepting the verdict that he was a true, honest-to-goodness liberal. In his view, liberalism was actually a baleful influence on classic evangelical belief, and he wanted nothing to do with it. "It is not a good sign of the times," Briggs judged, "that men boast of having thrown off the restraint of our pious ancestors in praise of a 'liberal Christianity'—one that will allow people to believe whatever they choose."[24] He furthermore stressed that what contemporary Christianity actually needed was not liberalism but "the strong meat, the good, old, strong Calvinistic, Augustinian, and Pauline doctrines" instead.[25] For Briggs, biblical criticism was not a concession to liberalism. By wedding historical critical methodology with a thoroughgoing commitment to the pious study of the Bible, rather, he always hoped to strengthen classic evangelical orthodoxy, not undermine it.

His concern for preserving the good, sound doctrines was not merely an early career fixation either. Despite being forced to side with the modernists when faced with the fundamentalist alternative, Briggs was never totally on board with how far some of his fellow modernists seemed willing to go in liberalizing the faith. Over the years, as his own Union Theological Seminary grew more and more comfortable with its reputation as a liberal institution, Briggs thus grew less and less comfortable with the direction it was heading. Later in his career, for a particularly ironic example, he became so dismayed that his colleague Arthur McGiffert was even willing to question the historical accuracy of the gospels that he—a convicted heretic—confessed to making plans for charging McGiffert with heresy. Although he eventually dropped such plans under advisement, Briggs was never able to shake his impression that some liberals were moving far beyond the legitimate critical interrogation of the Bible's "circumstantials" and were running roughshod over the very essentials of the evangelical faith.[26]

The tendency of conventional narratives to retroactively define him out of the evangelical column notwithstanding, Briggs spent his entire life doggedly insisting that biblical criticism was a tool that enhanced a thoroughly evangelical approach to biblical interpretation. Like his fundamentalist counterparts, he, too, believed that there were some unassailably "fundamental principles of Historical Christianity" upon which to stand in the face of a rising tide of liberalism.[27] Briggs furthermore felt that there was a discernibly evangelical tradition winding its way down through Christian history, and that the evangelical approach to Christian faith was undeniably the best version. He regularly identified various manifestations of this best-of-all kind of faith by pointing to historical and contemporary instances when "the evangelical spirit" was most evident, "true evangelical religion" was lost or recovered, "evangelical truth" was challenged, "evangelical faith" was sustained, and "evangelical life" was most fully lived.[28]

In Briggs's view, there were always a few key characteristics that distinguished evangelical theology and evangelical biblical interpretation from the various other options. For one thing, "evangelical critics" were the interpreters who were most faithful to the principles of the Reformation, which was most easily and accurately tested by alignment with the Westminster Confession. Evangelical interpreters, Briggs suggested, always approached the Bible with a three-step test pioneered by the Reformers: "(1) inquire what the Scriptures teach about themselves, and separate this *divine* authority from all other authority; (2) apply the principles of the *higher criticism* to decide questions not decided by divine authority; (3) use *tradition*, in order to determine as far as possible questions not settled by the previous methods." By following this approach, Briggs argued, evangelical critics thereby avoided the mistakes of both the "rationalistic critics," who applied naturalistic explanations to every biblical text, and the "scholastic critics," who subjected the words of the Bible to "dogmatic a priori systems." Rationalists sacrificed the overall unity of Scripture, seeing only internal variety. Scholastics sacrificed the diversity within the text in favor of homogeny. Only "the true evangelical position," Briggs explained, saw the Bible for what it really was: "a vast organism in which the unity springs from an amazing variety."[29]

The evangelical label meant something definite to Briggs, and he always counted himself as a legitimate claimant to the evangelical tradition. His ongoing need to defend his evangelical credentials derived in no small part from the widening gap between his understanding of what it meant to be an evangelical biblical scholar and the prevailing view among his conservative coreligionists—many of whom increasingly used biblical fidelity as a litmus test and the unquestioned authority of Scripture as a line in the sand. For his part, Briggs remained undeterred. Summarizing the alleged implications of his own position and denying the force of his opponents' challenges all at once, he put the matter succinctly: "Evangelical critics are not forced to deny the inspiration of the Pentateuch because they are convinced that Moses did not write it in its present form."[30] Briggs was not alone in his belief that evangelicals need not adhere to the untenable idea that the words of the Bible had been inerrantly and verbally dictated by God. But in his day and in the years to come, the distinction that he always tried to press—between a legitimately evangelical view of biblical authority that incorporated critical scholarship and the unnecessarily scholastic, dogmatic, and inerrantist position of the fundamentalists—proved an increasingly tough case to make.

Briggs's belief that evangelical biblical critics and theologians must nonetheless avoid becoming *too* liberal was likewise challenged by some modernist thinkers who were far more comfortable with their status *as* liberals. Even Briggs undoubtedly would have felt, for instance, that an admittedly liberal theologian like Shailer Mathews strayed too far afield from the historic evangelical faith.

Shailer Mathews: Modernist Liberal Evangelical Theologian

Born in 1863, Shailer Mathews was also raised in what could be described as a thoroughly evangelical faith. Assuming that he would one day become a minister, Mathews spent his formative years collecting the requisite educational credentials, only to realize somewhere along the way that he was not interested in a life of pastoral work. After seminary, he opted instead for an academic career, taking a position teaching college level "rhetoric and elocution" at his alma mater. Soon enough, he was moved to the History and Political Economy Department but lacked any background in either subject and needed training beyond what his theological studies had provided. Due to an essentially bureaucratic need to change fields, Mathews thus found himself bound for Germany where, like Briggs, he, too, had a career-altering educational experience. Unlike Briggs, Mathews's time in Germany included nothing by way of theological or biblical work. Instead, Mathews's transformative period abroad involved a total immersion in and thorough absorption of a scientific understanding of historiographical methods—an orientation that would shape his work for the rest of his career.[31]

After returning to the United States, Mathews once more found himself in an academic department outside of his disciplinary specialty. Believing that his training made him better suited for a job in the Sociology Department, Mathews nonetheless accepted an offer from the newly established University of Chicago for a position teaching New Testament history at the Divinity School. In light of his earlier seminary education and his "inherited interest in religion," in a sense, his educational journey thereby came full circle.[32]

At Chicago, Mathews became a pioneering figure of a new discipline called "Christian sociology." With the help of the best contemporary social-scientific approaches and modern critical methodologies, Mathews believed that it was at last possible both to clearly understand the actual nature of Jesus's teachings and to rightly interpret their contemporary social implications. His first book, *The Social Teaching of Jesus*, captured the spirit of the newly minted discipline and became a foundational text for the burgeoning social gospel movement. By using his sociohistorical brush to paint a more precise picture of the social-ethical implications of Christianity, Mathews initially concluded that Jesus's goal "was the establishment of an ideal society quite as much as the production of an ideal individual." What's more, he initially suggested, the kingdom of God was and is an attainable possibility involving the societal realization of the underlying principles of Jesus's social teachings. When Jesus talked about the kingdom of God, in Mathews's judgment, what he actually meant was "an ideal (though progressively approximated) social order in which the relation of men of God is that of sons, and (therefore) to each other, that of brothers."[33]

Over time, further scholarly findings and world historical events would force Mathews to revise many of these early conclusions. He later conceded that his previous assumptions about human nature had been overly optimistic, for instance, and the close correlation that he initially found between the social world of the historical Jesus and that of the nineteenth century fared perhaps worst of all. Despite revisiting some of his initial judgments, for the rest of his career, Mathews nonetheless held fast to the legitimacy of a thoroughly social-scientific approach to theology, always maintaining that he had never once "lost faith in a God discoverable in the universe and human history."[34]

In the annals of twentieth-century Protestant history, Mathews often became a paradigmatic example of a liberal-modernism of a bygone era. For some, he was in fact the prototypical example of a modernist who slid ever further down the slippery slope of progressively greater defections from the soundly evangelical faith of his youth. Mathews's role as one of the premiere modernist thinkers of his day made this conventional rendering all the more persuasive. His 1924 book *The Faith of Modernism* became known as one of the three works representing "the defining trilogy" of the fundamentalist-modernist battles, after all. In most standard accounts of evangelical history, that was plenty enough warrant to write Mathews out. In most versions of the story, evangelical faith was on one side of the controversies, liberal-modernist defectors like Mathews were on the other, and never again the twain would meet.[35]

Mathews didn't see it that way though. In his mind, modernists were neither heretical defectors from the evangelical tradition nor even advocates of an entirely new kind of theology. In his view, rather, a modernist was nothing more than a faithful Christian who was willing to employ "the methods of modern science to find, state and use the permanent and central values of inherited orthodoxy in meeting the needs of a modern world."[36] When so defined, Mathews was not merely comfortable with being called a modernist. By all indications, he actually preferred being designated as such. Of all of the various titles that some of his opponents eventually gave him—"rank blasphemer," for instance—modernist was ultimately not so bad.[37]

At the time of *The Faith of Modernism*'s publication, Mathews furthermore felt that modernism and liberalism were actually two distinct phenomena, and, crucially, that modernists were not necessarily liberals. Unlike liberals who were often guilty of "substituting sociology or scholarship or even unbelief for the Gospel," Mathews stressed, modernists began with the "inherited orthodoxy of a continuing community of Christians," remaining steadfast and faithfully anchored in the historic Christian tradition. Unlike liberals, modernists were also convinced that "a religion that psychologizes God into a personification of social values, that belittles sin and the need of salvation through the working of God's spirit, that would merely substitute a liberal theology for a conservative, is impotent to help a bewildered and sinful world toward the Kingdom of God." Mathews also implied that, in light of their willingness to dispense with any real connection to the essentials of the Christian tradition, Unitarians were the real liberals. By way of example, he noted, "a man is not a Modernist because he disbelieves orthodox theology. Modernism is hardly less different from Confessionalism than it is from Unitarianism. Both Confessionalism and Unitarianism are on the same plane of theological rationalism. Modernism is concerned with the historical methods of discovering the permanent values of Christianity, and the religious rather than the theological test of religion."[38] For Mathews, in other words, modernism was merely the best method for preserving and applying the best of the tradition. Modernists, by extension, were faithful to classic Christian beliefs in a way that liberals—Unitarians, for instance—simply were not.

Modernism, in Mathews's estimation, was merely a methodological update for interpreting and applying the essentials of the Christian tradition in contemporary circumstances. Further still, in *The Faith of Modernism*, he argued that it in fact sat thoroughly and comfortably within the *evangelical* tradition. Defining the modernist approach as "the use of scientific, historical, social method in understanding and applying evangelical Christianity to the needs of living persons," Mathews straightforwardly explained that "modernism is the evangelicalism of the scientific mind," and therefore that

"Modernists as a class are evangelical Christians." He went on to clarify exactly what he meant. Modernists were evangelicals, Mathews pointed out, because "they accept Jesus Christ as the revelation of a Savior God." Modernists were not a kind of Christian different from evangelicals, in other words. According to Mathews, they were simply a different kind of evangelical—specifically, "evangelical Christians who use modern methods to meet modern needs."[39]

Long before the neoevangelicals would use the self-same language to describe their decidedly different vision for a rejuvenated kind of Christian witness, in some of his earlier work, Mathews had actually described the socially regenerative version of Christianity that he was envisioning as a "new evangelicalism." In his 1907 book *The Church and the Changing Order*, Mathews framed the task of applying the principles of the Christian faith to the redemption of modern society in precisely those terms. "The new evangelicalism," he argued, "is as passionately devoted to saving men and society as is the old; the older evangelicalism is as passionately devoted to Jesus Christ as is the new. Let them cease to combat each other, and like Peter and Paul preach the same eternal gospel to men of different conditions and acquirements, and thus like the apostles leaven a changing order." For Mathews, the modernist impulse to appropriate the best of contemporary knowledge was simply the most faithful and fruitful way for the church to apply the gospel to the needs of a thoroughly modern world. Why not call it a "new evangelicalism"? After all, modernist theology was no less committed to "evangelical truth" than its fundamentalist opponents. "A theology may be liberal and scientific and not be unevangelical," he explained. Accepting Darwinian evolution, making use of historical criticism, and working toward a renewed social order did not make modernists any less evangelical for the fact. Some theologies certainly failed the test. "Any theology that is unaffected by a conviction of the reality of the risen Christ is not evangelical in the strictly New Testament sense," Mathews judged. But modernists passed that test, regardless of what their fundamentalist opponents might say.[40]

Like Briggs, early on, Mathews refused to accept that modernism was either equivalent to liberalism or unevangelical. Viewing liberalism as a theological approach that willingly abandoned any and all connection to the received traditions of historical Christianity, Mathews initially reserved the label for groups like religious humanists and Unitarians.

Over the course of his career, Mathews nonetheless wound up backing away from many of his early claims. With each new development in his thought, he arguably moved further away from his previous insistence on the binding authority of something essential and intrinsic to the Christian tradition—increasingly embracing and pioneering a particular kind of modernist theology that became known for its "naturalistic, empirical, [and] pragmatic" elements along the way.[41] Unlike Briggs, who could never bring himself to wholly embrace the label, Mathews also eventually accepted that he was something of an "unrepentant liberal."[42]

Regardless of his evolving self-perception, Mathews always remained steadfast in his resolve that theologians should be good historians, that good history was done scientifically, and that Christianity should be thoroughly modern. Unashamedly modernist from the outset—and eventually if belatedly a confessed liberal—he never shied away from provoking the fundamentalists. He also rightfully became known as one of the founding figures of the social gospel. For all of these reasons and more, Mathews's lifelong refusal to relinquish the evangelical label might appear like nothing more than an idiosyncrasy at best. But he didn't see it that way. Despite embracing what was arguably a more thoroughgoingly liberal viewpoint even than Briggs had, Mathews was similarly unable to shake his belief that he was in the end still an evangelical.

He wasn't the only one who thought that unrepentant liberals could be evangelical either.

Harry Emerson Fosdick: Modernist Liberal Evangelical Preacher

Harry Emerson Fosdick was born in Buffalo, New York, in 1878. Like Briggs and Mathews, his journey to becoming the quintessential modernist of his generation began with a thoroughly evangelical religious upbringing. During college, Fosdick's insatiable and lifelong intellectual curiosity brought with it a number of uncomfortable questions about the faith of his childhood. His inquisitive spirit nonetheless meant that the ensuing period of religious turmoil would not last forever. The answer came in the form of his college theology professor, William Newton Clarke, whose willingness "to phrase the Christian faith in the categories of modern thinking" impressed Fosdick tremendously. In his eyes, Clarke's thoroughly modern approach to theology crucially meant that he could retain his faith "without the crucifixion of the intellect." By successfully averting a potential crisis of faith with his professor's help, Fosdick soon realized that he, too, wanted to offer "a contribution to the spiritual life of my generation." Plagued in the ensuing years by a series of personal and familial mental health crises that forced him to navigate an altogether different sort of existential turmoil, Fosdick's student days became fertile soil for the kind of devotional spiritual guidance that later became his trademark.[43]

Although he eventually served as professor of practical theology at Union Theological Seminary, the academy was never Fosdick's primary vocational home. During seminary, he had developed a clear vision of the kind of contribution that he could make, realizing that his task lay outside of the theological ivory tower. "My vocation," he later reflected, "was to be an interpreter in modern, popular, understandable terms, of the best that I could find in the Christian tradition"—which is exactly what he did.[44] During the first few decades of the twentieth century, Fosdick's work as a popular preacher and author brought him a level of national fame and prominence far beyond that of any purely academic theologian. In particular, his three-volume series of devotional reflections—*The Meaning of Prayer*, *The Meaning of Faith*, and *The Meaning of Service*—reached a massive audience and arguably did more to popularize a modernist kind of Christian faith than anything that came before or followed after.[45]

Over the course of his career, Fosdick's thinking and preaching shifted perceptibly on a number of crucial issues. Early on, he was a war booster; later, he became a pacifist. His earliest readings were mostly spiritual and devotional; his later work took an increasingly therapeutic turn. But through it all, his belief that the truths of Christianity were perfectly compatible with the best of modern and scientific thinking never wavered. His commitment to making those truths accessible to the thoroughly modern masses didn't either. Often remembered as the archetypical example of a liberal Protestant churchman, Fosdick was that and more. With his enormously popular writings and widely regarded sermons, in reality he was far and away the most famous preacher and pastor of his time.[46]

He became most *infamous*, however, for his role as the most prominent spokesperson for the modernist cause in the era's most public and explosive battles between fundamentalism and modernism. Although Shailer

Mathews's 1924 book *The Faith of Modernism* offered a more extensive defense of the modernist position, it could not hold a candle to the shockwaves that Fosdick sent through the Protestant world with his 1922 sermon, "Shall the Fundamentalists Win?" In one brief sermon, the popular modernist preacher issued a battle cry that rallied both the modernists and fundamentalists alike to their respective battle stations.

What the fundamentalists were calling modernism, Fosdick explained, was actually nothing more than an honest effort on the part of countless faithful Christians "to think our modern life through in Christian terms and . . . to think our Christian life through in modern terms." What's more, he pointed out, the current crop of modernists wasn't even the first. The attempt to blend "new knowledge and the old faith" had happened numerous times throughout Christian history. The fundamentalist charge that liberals were out to destroy classic Christian orthodoxy was thus both unfair and shortsighted. Fosdick assured listeners that liberal-minded Christians were not all just "reckless radicals," and their acceptance of modern knowledge wasn't motivated by "irreverence or caprice or destructive zeal." Modernist Christians attempted to reconcile the best of contemporary knowledge with their faith, rather, "for the sake of intellectual and spiritual integrity, that they might really love the Lord their God not only with all their heart and soul and strength, but with all their mind."[47]

The sermon also homed in on what Fosdick felt was the most serious fundamentalist offense. Sure, he conceded, the fundamentalists were entitled to their beliefs, no matter how absurd. But their campaign to close "the doors of the Christian fellowship" to their modernist counterparts was unpardonable. Though he obviously disagreed with the fundamentalists' interpretation of what the fundamentals of the Christian faith actually were, Fosdick noted, he would defend their right to such differences of opinion. For Fosdick, the fact that the fundamentalists seemed unwilling to grant him the same courtesy was the heart of the matter. The real question, in other words, was whether anyone had "a right to deny the Christian name to those who differ with him on such points." The implication was clear: if Fosdick could accept that fundamentalists are true Christians, then how dare they suggest that he was anything less.[48]

Fosdick's later suggestion that he had envisioned the sermon's "frank, kindly, irenic plea for tolerance" as a call for unity was naive at best.[49] "Shall the Fundamentalists Win?" was distributed widely and ignited a firestorm everywhere it went. The sermon crescendoed, after all, in a passage highlighting the triviality of the fundamentalists' concerns, with Fosdick bemoaning the "immeasurable folly" of the fact that, "now in the presence of colossal problems, which must be solved in Christ's name and for Christ's sake, the Fundamentalists propose to drive out from the Christian churches all the consecrated souls who do not agree with their theory of inspiration." By emphatically concluding, "Well, they are not going to do it; certainly not in this vicinity," he had furthermore all but challenged the fundamentalists to try as much. Sure enough, like Briggs before him, Fosdick was soon forced to reckon with the prospects of a heresy trial.[50]

As a liberal Baptist pastoring a Presbyterian church, in the early 1920s, Fosdick increasingly drew the ire of conservative Presbyterians hell-bent on forcing him out. In the wake of the increasingly infamous sermon, a group of antimodernist Presbyterians led by William Jennings Bryan launched a campaign to pressure Fosdick either to become a creedal Presbyterian or to resign from his position. Had he converted to Presbyterianism, Fosdick would thereby have made himself vulnerable to a heresy trial at the hands of Bryan and his ilk. In 1925, he resigned from the Presbyterian congregation he had been serving instead. Even though the would-be-fundamentalist Presbyterians succeeded in forcing him out, looking back many years later, Fosdick reflected that the fundamentalist-modernist controversies were "one of the most necessary theological battles ever fought," and judged that the ultimate outcome of the battle was a conclusive win for the liberal-modernist side.[51]

Fundamentalists by no means derailed Fosdick's rise to prominence. He went on to become the most popular preacher and spiritual leader of his generation. For decades, he remained far and away the most famous pastor in the nation—at least until Billy Graham emerged on the scene—and was regularly regarded by secular and religious commentators alike as the most influential US American preacher of the first half of the twentieth century.[52]

The popularity of its most famous publicist notwithstanding, the self-consciously liberal and avowedly Christian perspective that Fosdick made famous received relentless criticism—from both his right and his left—long after the apparent conclusion of the controversies of the 1920s. As the prototypical symbol and veritable embodiment of liberal Protestantism, Fosdick was thus called to the stand in its defense time and time again in the years to come. Over time, he occasionally acknowledged that some of the critics of modernism had made legitimate points. In sermons like "The Church Must Go beyond Modernism," for instance, Fosdick granted that his side had its share of theological problems.[53] But throughout his life, Fosdick never let the increasingly beleaguered state of liberal Protestantism dissuade him from his steadfast belief in the redemptive nature of Christianity, his understanding of the reconcilability of the gospel and modern knowledge, or his commitment to spreading the good news of that message to modern Christians everywhere.[54]

Fosdick's enduring legacy as the paragon of the liberal-modernist side of twentieth-century Protestantism *also* never stopped him from maintaining that he was still an evangelical, come what may. He always readily acknowledged his status as a liberal and upheld the right of any Christian to do the same, but in his view, neither modernism nor liberalism were incommensurable with true evangelical faith. Even in his most infamously controversial sermon, Fosdick defended the modernist position in part by an appeal to the evangelical legitimacy of liberal views. Liberalism, he argued, could be comfortably at home in "evangelical churches." Moreover, he implied that it already *was*. Regardless of what the fundamentalists might think, Fosdick pointed out, liberal views could in fact be found in some of the sincerest hearts of some of the most faithful Christians in the nation's evangelical churches. For that reason, fundamentalist beliefs and liberal beliefs should be understood as nothing more than the real "differences of opinion that exist among evangelical Christians." Evangelical churches had always included diverging theological positions, and evangelical Christians had sincerely disagreed about a host of issues before. By attempting to purge liberalism from the churches, Fosdick argued, the fundamentalists therefore were actually guilty of trying to drive out devoted evangelical Christians who just so happened to be liberals as well.[55]

Fosdick simply believed that evangelicals could be liberals—and, indeed, that liberals could be evangelicals. Perhaps unsurprisingly, his opponents pressed him on precisely that point. In the immediate aftermath of "Shall the Fundamentalists Win?" conservative Presbyterian pastor Clarence E. Macartney issued a rejoinder to Fosdick's sermon with one of his own. In "Shall Unbelief Win?" Macartney acknowledged that Fosdick's "well-deserved popularity" and "splendid emphasis on the social side of Christianity" meant that faithful evangelical Christians might legitimately feel "a sincere desire for the return of Dr. Fosdick to evangelical faith." But he also stressed in no uncertain terms that the liberal preacher's present views were no longer within the bounds of that faith, and indeed were antithetical to it. "If Dr. Fosdick is right, his views ought to prevail," Macartney opined. "But whether he is right, or whether the evangelical position is right, one thing all must now admit: both positions cannot be right; one MUST be wrong."[56] The man himself might renounce his prodigal ways and be reconciled to evangelical truth, in other words, but not as long as he continued defending antievangelical ideas. Macartney was by no means alone in his assessment either. Another conservative Presbyterian pastor lamented the fact that Fosdick "was accepted as evangelical because he called himself evangelical." Judging that it was all a front, yet another highlighted the "widespread impression that [Dr. Fosdick] is a Unitarian under the mask of an evangelical Christian."[57]

Such allegations never stopped Fosdick. Over the years, he continuously argued both for the legitimacy of liberal Christianity and for his right to claim the evangelical label. In a letter to a sympathetic supporter in 1922, he did so unequivocally, plainly stating, "I am an evangelical Christian, believing in the saving grace of God revealed in Jesus Christ, and trusting in him for my redemption." When his congregation was investigated for signs of heresy, he similarly assured the Presbyterian hierarchy in no uncertain terms, "If I did not consider myself an evangelical Christian I surely should not be preaching in an evangelical pulpit."[58] When pressed by a critical interviewer, Fosdick furthermore once proclaimed, "I may be a liberal, but I'm evangelical, too!"[59]

Whither Evangelical Liberalism?

By the latter half of the twentieth century, the words "evangelical" and "liberal" would undeniably become a contradiction in terms in US American discourse. But as the stories of Briggs, Mathews, and Fosdick demonstrate, for the first few decades of the century, the idea that liberal-modernist approaches to theology effectively nullified their essential evangelicalness was not as taken for granted as it eventually became. As Gary Dorrien explains, for many of the era's liberal Protestant figures, "evangelical" was still a "banner word . . . too precious to relinquish," so they didn't. At the time, they didn't have to. For most of the first half of the twentieth century, the idea that there were such people as evangelical liberals—and even liberal evangelicals—was simply neither so unheard of as it might have seemed nor as preposterous as it later became.[60]

In point of fact, the moniker "evangelical liberal" eventually became a popular way for certain kinds of liberal-modernists to distinguish themselves from *other* kinds of liberal theologians who they believed went too far afield from the historic evangelical faith. For a significant stretch of the early to mid-twentieth century, historians and liberal theologians alike regularly identified evangelical liberals as those who believed that there were some irreducible "gospel norms" within the Christian tradition that were permanently binding for all Christian theologians. Ironically enough, liberal thinkers who, on the contrary, refused to be constrained by any previously normative historical essence of the faith increasingly became known instead as the "modernist liberals."[61]

That distinction was arguably too neat, and the reality far messier for a number of reasons. But the crucial point remains: the possibility of describing liberals as evangelical was open for far longer than is often remembered. In an era when "the grammar of contemporary theology" had not yet stabilized, the evangelical label simply did not have the illiberal connotations that it eventually would.[62] What's more, in certain Protestant sectors, the development of a truly, soundly evangelical liberalism—or alternatively, if less frequently of an openly liberal evangelicalism—seemed like a real option and remained the sincere hope of a number of Christian thinkers well into the twentieth century. Fosdick was a case in point. Often remembered as a shining example of liberal Protestantism more broadly, he *also* became known as one of the foremost representatives of the particular kind of liberalism that he always hoped to embody: the *evangelical* kind.

Fosdick wasn't alone in his hopes for an evangelical liberalism either. For decades, Union Theological Seminary—which increasingly became a bastion of liberal Protestantism and thus one of the most putatively unevangelical seminaries in the country—worked toward building an institutional legacy around the necessity of retaining an explicitly and confessedly evangelical basis for liberal theology. In so doing, Union furthermore aimed to distinguish itself from the decidedly less evangelical kind of liberalism that developed in places like the University of Chicago.[63]

In his 1915 address "The Practical Aims of a Liberal Evangelicalism," for example, Union president Henry Sloane Coffin emphasized the importance of keeping liberal theology thoroughly evangelical.[64] Reflecting a generation later on the crucial importance of the title of that address, another Union president, Henry P. Van Dusen, stressed that Coffin always insisted "that the only proper identification of Liberal Theology is 'Liberal Evangelicalism.'" In his 1963 book *The Vindication of Liberal Theology*, Van Dusen went on to explain that Coffin had once put the matter like this: "Liberal evangelicalism! Note which word in our title stands merely in the qualifying position of the adjective and which occupies the position of eminence as the noun. We are first and foremost evangelicals—evangelicals to the core of our spiritual beings. . . . And we are liberals—not liberals in the sense that we cultivate freedom for its own sake, but for the gospel's sake. We are liberals on behalf of our evangelicalism."[65] Coffin's insistence on keeping the evangelical part of the equation securely in the nominative position eventually gave way to the far more frequent rendering "evangelical liberalism." But even so, the idea that the two labels could be combined without contradiction remained part and parcel of Union's institutional legacy for much of the twentieth century.

Van Dusen in particular considered himself an heir of a liberal tradition that unashamedly maintained the legitimacy of its right to claim the evangelical banner. In fact, he spent the better part of four decades arguing that evangelical liberalism was the only kind that remained "fully within the stream of historic Christian development," and thus the only legitimate kind.[66] Further still, in Van Dusen's judgment, evangelical liberalism was actually "the *first* thoroughly and consistently Christocentric theology" in Christian history. The reason? "At the heart of Evangelical Liberalism stands Jesus Christ," he explained.[67]

Despite the best efforts of evangelical, gospel-centered liberals like Van Dusen, the irreconcilability of the two labels eventually became a near universally accepted dictum in twentieth-century Protestantism. No singular development, individual figure, or broader trend deserves absolute or final responsibility for the tough sledding that evangelical liberalism continually faced. But a number of crucial factors had a hand in its diminishing prospects.

First, there were the outside attacks. The idea of a liberal evangelical was clearly anathema to fundamentalists, but they weren't the only ones. Even in the 1920s, evangelical liberals had to contend with the fact that critics to the right *and* left often came to the same conclusion. For example, "An evangelical Christian is not a liberal, in the accepted use of both words," Unitarian magazine editor Alfred Dieffenbach complained in 1924. "They are mutually exclusive terms."[68]

By virtue of their commitment to and experience with defending the middle ground between overbelief and underbelief, evangelical liberals like Fosdick were well prepared to hold their own against outside attacks from either end of the theological spectrum. But evangelical liberalism was far less prepared for the unrelenting *insider* assaults launched by liberal Protestantism's own disaffected descendants.[69]

The already-rough road that lay ahead for all manner of liberal theology—evangelical or otherwise—was made all the more difficult by the successive waves of mutinies mounted by many who were its direct beneficiaries. By the time that the 1930s were in full swing, Reinhold Niebuhr's and H. Richard Niebuhr's withering critiques of liberalism's apparent failures and weaknesses, combined with Karl Barth's putatively wholesale revolt against liberal theology, had already begun heralding what many outsiders and insiders alike took to be the death knell of the entire liberal Protestant theological project. It thus would be hard to overstate the role that an emerging generation of theologians who were disillusioned with their liberal-modernist forebearers—a group that accurately or otherwise became known as the neoorthodox movement—played in cementing the idea that the word "liberal" was an epithet of the worst kind. With the help of neoorthodoxy, in the space of a generation, the idea of calling oneself a liberal or a modernist would lose much of its shine in circles where it might once have been a badge of honor. Against this backdrop, evangelical liberalism had its work cut out for it and then some.[70]

Internal stressors undeniably helped seal evangelical liberalism's fate as an increasingly lost cause. But the institutionalization of the neofundamentalist version of evangelical identity associated with groups like the NAE, schools like Fuller, and publications like *CT* was the nail in the coffin. Defined from the outset in direct opposition to any and all liberal impulses, the midcentury neoevangelical coalition that went on to become the mainstream version of twentieth-century evangelicalism effectively claimed the label as a proprietary trademark. In so doing, the newly self-appointed gatekeepers of evangelicalism overwhelmingly shifted the burden of proof onto the shoulders of any current and future claimants who might disagree with their neofundamentalist and inerrantist definition of what it meant to be a capital-E Evangelical.

Ironically enough, one of the earliest and most enduring test cases for the limits of this understanding of what counted as soundly evangelical theology came in the form of the very same neoorthodox theologians who had similarly positioned *themselves* in opposition to liberal theology. With all of their vaunted rhetoric about the failures of liberalism, it might seem as though Karl Barth, the Niebuhrs, and their subsequent Barthian, Niebuhrian, and neoorthodox offshoots would be able to make some sort of occasional common cause with the explicitly antiliberal neoevangelicals. But a neoorthodox and neoevangelical united front in the battle against liberalism never came about due in large part to one crucial factor. Time and again over the course of the twentieth century, Barthian theology in particular became a line in the sand that evangelical gatekeepers used to signal where evangelical theology ended and godless liberalism began.

The Barthian Revolt . . . or the New Modernism?

In many tellings of the story of twentieth-century Christian theology, Karl Barth's rebellion against the liberal theology of his German Protestant teachers is the opening scene.[71] As Barth himself would later recount, the decisive moment came with the devastating discovery that his theological mentors were among a group of intellectuals who signed a manifesto in support of the German war effort. Shaken to the core by the feeling that he could no longer trust anything he had been taught, according to Barth's own retelling, he increasingly found himself returning to the practical, pastoral problem of learning how to listen with a newfound openness to the Bible.[72] After revising a first edition that he felt was still too reliant on modern liberal presuppositions, Barth channeled his discovery of "the strange new world within the Bible" into a manifesto that would be viewed as the decisive announcement that he was done with his liberal teachers once and for all.[73] With the 1921 publication of the second edition of *The Epistle to the Romans*—the book infamously described as falling "like a bomb on the playground of the theologians"—Barth's dialectical, crisis theology burst onto the worldwide scene, irrevocably shifting the discourse of modern theology forever.[74]

As the 1920s marched on, Barth became the symbolic figurehead of a movement of mostly European theologians who fashioned themselves as an alternative to the impotent and threadbare theological liberalism of the previous generation. By the end of the decade, the movement began extending its influence to US American shores primarily via the work of Emil Brunner. With Reinhold Niebuhr's scathing pronouncements on the failures of liberal Christianity helping to secure the status of liberal as an irredeemable epithet, some American liberal Protestant thinkers of the 1930s were in a similar state of generational revolt. By the 1940s, a range of putatively antiliberal thinkers moving in the orbits of Barthianism and Niebuhrianism were increasingly grouped under the singular heading of neoorthodoxy—a label that Barth, among others, forthrightly rejected.[75]

In the wake of the crashing of the Barthian wave onto American shores, Christian thinkers across the spectrum often struggled with how precisely to categorize both the neoorthodox movement in general and the Swiss theologian's work in particular. Whether neoorthodoxy was the right label, and whether antiliberalism was really the thread uniting the various neoorthodoxies, eventually became a well-established debate among theologians and outside interpreters of twentieth-century Protestant thought alike. Disputes over rightly interpreting Barth and his legacy did as well. Whether the Barthian revolt was as clean a break from liberalism as it seemed, and whether Barth had charted a better path than the liberal theology he purportedly left behind, Barth's titanic and tectonic impact on modern Protestant theology quickly became indisputable. Even when they were unsure what to do with him, in other words, by the middle years of the twentieth century, every Christian theologian was increasingly forced to do *something* with him. One could follow along behind him, attempt to undermine him, work to move beyond him, or try to fight through him, but in Barth's long shadow, there was no way around him.

In the eyes of many of the kinds of thinkers that history eventually consigned to the liberal end of the Protestant spectrum, Barth's theological project seemed hopelessly and disastrously conservative. Throughout the late 1920s and 1930s, Methodist theologian and dean of the Boston University

School of Theology, Albert C. Knudson, consistently said as much, railing against Barth's irrational rejection of reason and experience as legitimate sources for doing theology. If Christian theologians followed Barth backward into the authoritarian enclave of a theology based solely on the self-authenticating divine revelation of an utterly transcendent God, Knudson judged, then Christianity would become utterly incomprehensible to rational modern minds, thereby dooming itself to irrelevance. The zinger came in a 1928 article for the *Christian Century* in which Knudson summarily dismissed Barth's theology as nothing more than "German fundamentalism."[76]

Around the same time, Reinhold Niebuhr had by and large come to the same conclusion. In the face of a rising tide of godless humanism among US American intellectuals, for Niebuhr, Barth's hopelessly otherworldly and fatally subjectivist approach to theology seemed utterly impotent. In his view, Christian theologians needed a better answer to naturalistic relativism than Barth's neosupernaturalist dogmatism.[77] The same year that Knudson described Barthian theology as German fundamentalism, Niebuhr likewise took to the pages of the *Christian Century* with his judgment that Barth's work was either "a new kind of fundamentalism or an old kind of orthodoxy."[78]

Even for many of the first and second generations of theologians who were variously grouped with Barth under the neoorthodox banner, it thus became commonly accepted knowledge that Barth's revolt against liberalism had taken him too far in the other direction. His stubborn insistence on pursuing theology "as church-embedded exegesis of the Word" earned him a reputation, even during the heyday of his influence, as an overly dogmatic defender of the kind of moribund Protestant theology that inevitably became trapped in the safe but sectarian house of orthodoxy.[79] Among the kinds of early to midcentury American Protestant theologians who fully embraced, begrudgingly appreciated, or belatedly admitted their debt to the liberal tradition, in other words, Barth quickly became known as far too conservative to touch.[80]

But by the time that some liberal Protestant thinkers were dismissing Barth as hopelessly conservative, another enormously influential interpreter, Reformed theologian Cornelius Van Til, was reaching exactly the opposite conclusion, deciding that Barth's supposed revolt was a thin veneer atop an obviously liberal core. When it came to twentieth-century *evangelical* thinkers in particular, therein lay the rub. The answer to the question, "what hath Barth to do with American evangelicalism?," would indeed turn on precisely this point: whether Barthian theology was just a repackaged form of liberal modernism. When Barthian ideas first made land on the shores of the American evangelical world, the resulting disputes over whether they were welcome were fought on precisely those terms.

The story of US American evangelicals' relationship to Barth therefore begins with the interpretive paradigm established by Van Til from his post at Westminster Theological Seminary. Formed in the late 1920s under the leadership of the iconic fundamentalist theologian J. Gresham Machen as an alternative to the allegedly liberalizing Princeton Theological Seminary, Westminster was among the most concrete results of the fundamentalist-modernist controversies. In short order, the school became a bastion of fundamentalist orthodoxy for an entire generation of conservative thinkers. As Westminster's founding professor of apologetics—a position he held for more than four decades—Van Til became foremost among its defenders. His take on the merits and implications of Barth's theology thus became one of the earliest and far and away the most important interpretations, setting the tone for every subsequent debate over the compatibility of Barthian ideas with mainstream evangelical thought.[81]

Throughout the 1930s, Van Til published a series of articles warning his fellow Presbyterians of the particularly insidious threat that Barth posed to true Reformed orthodoxy and classic Protestant doctrine. Expressing a measure of gratitude for Barth's alleged attempt "to burn the house of modern theology to the ground," Van Til's appreciation for the theologian's apparent revolt against liberalism quickly devolved into disgust. At first blush, Barth's stated antimodernism might initially have obscured his unorthodoxy, Van Til judged. But in his eyes, Barth's true colors became abundantly clear upon closer inspection. Particularly when it came to Barth's understanding of Scripture, Van Til urgently warned unsuspecting readers that they must not become seduced by a theological system that only sounded orthodox. "Whatever Barth may mean by saying that the Bible is the Word of God," Van Til explained, "it is plain that for him this means something quite different from what it means to the orthodox Christian."[82]

After a decade of consistently reiterating that Barthianism was both unorthodox and dangerous, by the early 1940s, Van Til was ready for a more extensive counterattack. Beginning in 1941, he set to work preparing what would become his first book-length refutation of Barthian theology. Published in 1946 as *The New Modernism*, Van Til's "frankly polemical" book set forth the argument implied in the title.[83] In an effort to expose the obvious liberal-modernist assumptions of Barth's system, Van Til guided readers through several hundred pages tracing the telltale signs—from relativism and subjectivism to an obviously antimetaphysical bias—that had characterized modern philosophy and liberal theology from Kant to Schleiermacher. In the closing chapter, he furthermore invoked his mentor and friend to make the connection between the new modernism and the old modernism as clear as possible. "If the late J. Gresham Machen spoke of the necessity of making a choice between liberalism and Christianity, we should be doing scant justice to his memory if we did less today with respect to the New Modernism and Christianity."[84] Not only were Barth's claims to have rejected liberalism patently false, in Van Til's mind, Barthian neoorthodoxy was fundamentally incompatible with true orthodoxy and therefore altogether sub-Christian.

Much to Van Til's dismay, in the years to come, Barth's ideas eventually received an increasingly receptive hearing—even in some of the more conservative corners of American Protestantism. By way of response, Van Til prepared a second full-length polemic against the Barthian scourge. Published in 1962, *Christianity and Barthianism* similarly pulled no punches. Opening with the matter-of-fact statement, "The present writer is of the opinion that, for all its verbal similarity to historic Protestantism, Barth's theology is, in effect, a denial of it," Van Til railed against Barth's unabashed mimicry of Christian orthodoxy.[85] Worst of all, in his judgment, was Barthianism's deficient view of Scripture as something other than the direct revelation of the words of God.

By once again evoking the spirit of Machen, and by once more making the verdict clear on the title page, Van Til closely followed the pattern established by *The New Modernism*. Only this time, the homage to Machen was even more direct. Just as Machen had argued in *Christianity and Liberalism*—that the two were in fact different religions—from the outset, *Christianity and Barthianism* set out to demonstrate that this was nothing more than new words with the same tune. "Speaking as objectively as we can," Van Til concluded, "we must say that, as in Machen's time 'Liberalism,' while propagated in the church as though it were the gospel, was in reality a man-made religion, so Barthianism, using the language of Reformation theology, is still only a higher humanism."[86]

Van Til's conclusion that Barthian theology in particular and neoorthodoxy more generally were nothing more than liberal-modernism warmed over became the paradigmatic interpretation for mainstream evangelical theologians for the rest of the twentieth century. Although personally ambivalent about the prospects of the kind of broadly evangelical approach to theology that might include non-Calvinists—preferring to focus his energies instead on defending the truth of the Reformed faith—his impact on successive generations of capital-E Evangelicals was outsized nonetheless.[87] Most crucially, Van Til's work was massively influential among the post-World War II generation of neoevangelical leaders responsible for institutionalizing twentieth-century evangelical identity for the first time. In fact, many of the men who helped define mainstream evangelicalism as a kinder gentler fundamentalism no less directly opposed to all forms of liberalism were friends or former students of Van Til. It is perhaps no small wonder then that, according to another, later evangelical theologian, writing during the 1980s, "the new modernism" eventually "became the official evangelical interpretation of neoorthodoxy."[88]

Over the years, when a handful of American evangelical thinkers began initially cautious flirtations with Barthian themes, they would thus be forced to contend with the standard evangelical position on Barth first established and popularized by Van Til. When yet another round of evangelical theologians later attempted to rehabilitate Barth's image among evangelicals—by suggesting, for example, that perhaps he was an honest-to-goodness evangelical after all—the deck remained too stacked against them to make any significant headway. Barth's reputation as a liberal was simply too pervasive, and everyone knew that liberals couldn't be real evangelicals.

But long before the tentative evangelical reconsideration of Barth in later decades, the emergence of an evangelical theologian with Barthian sympathies offered one of the earliest and most direct test cases for the boundaries of the newly official kind of evangelicalism institutionalized by the post-World War II neoevangelicals. During the late 1940s, the surprising appearance of an early defector from the rapidly coalescing evangelical party line on Barth in fact forced a nascent evangelical establishment to issue one of its first official rulings on the limits of mainstream evangelical identity. Appropriately enough, the challenge came from a foreign-born evangelical immigrant not at all accustomed to the workings of the American evangelical world.

Béla Vassady and the First Test Case

Born in Hungary in 1902, Béla Vassady came of age in a country utterly devastated by the ravages of World War I. In addition to the privations associated with growing up in war-torn Hungary, the horrific and untimely death of both of his sisters during his teenage years pushed Vassady even further to the brink of an adolescent existential crisis. He was eventually pulled from the edge of the abyss by what he later described as "a direct and positive [encounter with] the living God," occasioned in part by his reading of a transformational book: a Hungarian translation of *The Manhood of the Master* by Harry Emerson Fosdick.[89] As Vassady later recounted, the book's descriptions of Jesus's personality and the corresponding prayers and Bible verses included with each daily reading had an enormous impact on him. "For the first time in my life," he noted, "I was amazed, thrilled, moved, enriched. 'God speaks to me here,' I wrote in the book's margin. . . . I became an almost regular reader of God's word. Now I began to apprehend that I was not alone. God was with me."[90]

After pursuing theological education in the United States—earning a bachelor of divinity from Central Theological Seminary, a ThM from Princeton Seminary, and becoming ordained as a minister in the Reformed Church—Vassady returned to his native country, embarking on an illustrious career as a professor, seminary dean, chair of dogmatics, and consummate churchman. All of which contributed to his wide renown as one of the Hungarian Reformed Church's most prominent theologians.[91]

But that all came crashing down with the outbreak of World War II. With Hungary increasingly caught in the crossfire of the German and Russian armies, Vassady was forced to witness his beloved homeland being torn apart all over again. After a series of harrowing events—including being forced to house a German officer on the top floor of their home while simultaneously hiding a young Jewish girl in their cellar—the Vassady family realized they would need to escape the country to survive. An invitation from the World

Council of Churches, which Vassady had in fact helped found, to send him on a sixteen-month speaking tour throughout the United States in 1946 and 1947 came just in time. At the end of his tour, a timely offer for a two-year guest professorship at Princeton Seminary provided Vassady and his family a chance to extend their stay in the United States while waiting out the turmoil back home. Fully intending to return to Hungary after his time at Princeton, Vassady was eventually persuaded to reconsider by concerned friends and colleagues—including none other than Karl Barth—who warned that escalating anti-American sentiments in the country might endanger the family's homecoming. Under the advisement of trusted friends, in 1948 Vassady thus began looking for another job in the United States.[92]

That same year, Harold Ockenga, the first president of the newly established Fuller Theological Seminary, heard that Vassady was searching for a teaching position. Attracted by the Hungarian theologian's international renown, Ockenga invited him to join the Fuller faculty as professor of biblical theology. In 1949, Vassady accepted the offer with nothing short of rapturous thanksgiving. For both Vassady and his wife Selena, the fact that Ockenga had emphasized the explicitly evangelical nature of the school was particularly appealing:

> The full name of our native church is the Evangelical Reformed Church in Hungary, meaning a church that is constantly in the process of being re-formed according to the Evangel (Gospel) of Jesus Christ. We praised the Lord for opening before us the same kind of evangelical and evangelistic work in America that we had intended to do in Hungary after our return there. Even the fact that many of our friends called Fuller Seminary a Fundamentalist Institution did not evoke in us any uneasiness or suspicion. In our vocabulary this meant that Fuller was a school training ministers to work on the only valid fundament, the Word of God. That was the very foundation of our vocation, too. What else could we have wanted?[93]

Although the timing could not have been more fortuitous, there were signs of trouble from the start. A number of the school's newly assembled faculty members quickly expressed serious concerns about a couple of items on Vassady's admittedly impressive resume.[94] For one thing, he had recently published an article suggesting that an individual could not totally surrender to God, "without having first given an 'existential response' to God's self-disclosure on the Cross of Christ."[95] In the view of two Fuller professors in particular, Carl Henry and Edward J. Carnell, the mere mention of existentialism sounded suspiciously like what they believed was dangerously neoorthodox language. Deeply influenced by Van Til, and duly attuned to his warnings about "the new modernism," both Henry and Carnell were especially worried by the fact that Vassady would not openly denounce Barthianism and its attendant dangers.[96] For his part, Vassady had unfortunately done plenty to arouse suspicion about his potential Barthian sympathies. He had previously invited Barth to deliver a series of lectures at Hungary's Reformed seminaries, serving as his host and guide during the visit, and had already published two translations of Barth's books. By the time he arrived at Fuller, in other words, Vassady admittedly viewed Barth as an "old friend."[97]

By convincing them that, unlike Barth, Vassady definitely believed that the Bible was the objective revelation and actual word of God, Ockenga successfully allayed the fears of his wary faculty. Fuller thus began the 1949 fall semester with a newly hired, internationally respected, Hungarian Reformed theologian as professor of biblical theology and ecumenics.[98]

Things unraveled pretty quickly from there.

First came the obvious fact of Vassady's association with the international ecumenical movement. A tireless advocate of interdenominational fellowship and church unity efforts, who had indeed helped found the World Council of Churches (WCC), the Hungarian theologian's professorship had the word "ecumenics" directly in the title. The only problem was that a large swath of Fuller's fundamentalist constituency viewed the WCC as an apostate organization that diluted Christian doctrine. Worse still, according to some dispensationalists, the WCC was a likely vehicle for the kind of universal world order that theoretically presaged the end time. When fundamentalist provocateur Charles McIntire caught wind of Vassady's ecumenical sympathies, publishing an article excoriating Fuller for hiring a professor who praised "the modernistic ecumenical movement," Vassady quickly came under fire from none other than Charles Fuller himself.[99] By instructing Vassady to avoid issuing any further uncritical or wholesale approvals of the WCC—and by removing the word "ecumenics" from his title—Ockenga once again defused the controversy. But the peace wouldn't last long. Throughout the semester, Ockenga had already received letters from concerned individuals claiming to have proof in hand that Vassady was a neoorthodox Barthian. Another Fuller faculty member, Wilbur Smith, suspected as much and had also begun his own investigation into the matter.[100]

The entire affair quickly reached what was arguably its logical conclusion when the Fuller faculty decided to prioritize finalizing the school's statement of faith. The most crucial element of the statement, which Carnell had already more or less finished drafting the previous spring, was the wording of the section on the Bible. It read, "The books which form the canon of the Old and New Testaments as originally given are plenarily inspired and free from all error in the whole and in the part. These books constitute the written Word of God, the only infallible rule of faith and practice."[101] Vassady protested the circumstances under which the statement had been hurriedly brought to a vote to no avail. In January 1950, the faculty voted to accept the statement of faith, and that was that. Vassady was unable to sign the newly adopted statement "without mental reservations"—a fact that the Fuller faculty had known full and well from the outset—and thus conceded that he would leave his position by the end of the year.[102]

In Vassady's view, the "literal inerrancy" position adopted by the Fuller faculty was woefully misguided. "I found the statement objectionable," he later explained, "because it is my conviction that we can and should believe in the inspiration and authority of the Scriptures even if we do not have the 'originally given' autographs at our disposal. It is needless to state that they are 'free from all error in the whole and in the part' because the Holy Spirit uses the present text as an authentic source for our salvation."[103]

Worse still was the shamefully unethical inconsistency of the school's initial suggestion that he should highlight his ecumenical work, only to quickly encourage him to hide it instead, and the decidedly unevangelical treatment the faculty subjected him to as a result of the whole fiasco.[104] Although he was profoundly disheartened by the experience, Vassady later noted that at least he had been prepared. "It must have been God's purpose to expose us to totalitarian demands in the name of 'religion' in America after we had encountered the totalitarian claims of both Nazism and Communism in Europe," he reflected. "Evidently this was his way to better equip us to serve him in American Christendom."[105] In Vassady's retrospective judgment, in other words, surviving the Nazis had equipped him for his eventual dealings with the American neofundamentalists, who he had initially but mistakenly believed were evangelicals like himself.

The Verdict

Defined from the outset in direct opposition to any and all liberal tendencies whether real or implied, the version of evangelical identity codified by flagship institutions like Fuller and the NAE effectively ensured that Briggs, Mathews, Fosdick, and those like them were beyond the pale of soundly evangelical thinking once and for all. By midcentury, liberal Protestants, evangelical or otherwise, would never again be welcome inside the safely evangelical walls. Whatever else they were, the capital-E Evangelicals were neither liberal nor modernist from that point forward. Evangelical liberalism became a contradiction in terms consigned to the dustbin of twentieth-century Christian history.

The evangelical status of a theologian like Barth was a tougher question. Barth's stated opposition to liberal theology and his strikingly orthodox language certainly seemed evangelical by many definitions of the word. But if being an evangelical meant subscribing to the inerrancy of the Bible, Barth would never make the cut. The Bible, for Barth, was a witness *to* or record *about* God's revelation. But Jesus was the capital-W Word of God, not the Bible. Under the definition of evangelical theology adopted by groups like the ETS, Barth would thus always be subevangelical at best and heretical at worst. With the help of Van Til, along with his students and friends like Henry and Carnell, Barth was effectively branded a liberal modernist, and his reputation among US American evangelicals would never recover. Try though they might, later generations of evangelical thinkers like Paul Jewett, James Daane, Colin Brown, Geoffrey Bromiley, Donald Bloesch, and Bernard Ramm could never fully rehabilitate evangelicals' impression of Barth as anything other than a dangerous liberal. Even Carnell and Henry's eventual admissions that there might be at least *something* that evangelicals could learn from Barth were not enough. To this day, Barthian theology simply isn't welcome in the flagship institutions of contemporary American evangelicalism. In this particular context, evangelical theology ends wherever it is that liberalism begins, and capital-E Evangelical thinkers can accurately be defined as those who think Barth is too liberal.[106]

At first, Vassady's evangelical credentials were even tougher to parse. Despite his friendship with and appreciation for Barth, Vassady never considered himself a Barthian. But in the end, that didn't matter. His suspected

Barthian sympathies provided sufficient cause for the early Fuller faculty to press him on what they ruled was an insufficiently evangelical and suspiciously liberal understanding of the Bible. Like Barth, Vassady found the idea of a "literally inerrant" Scripture untenable and unnecessary. His arrival on the US American scene at the precise moment that a newly institutionalized version of evangelical identity was inspiring debates over whether evangelicals must be inerrantists made him a prime test case.[107] In the early years of Fuller Seminary, the answer was yes, and Vassady thus found himself surprisingly on the outside of the evangelical city gates.

Arguments over the necessity of inerrancy for true evangelical faith would hardly end with the Vassady episode. Ironically enough, despite continuously rejecting any and all forms of theological liberalism—and neoorthodoxy for that matter—Fuller Seminary would in fact eventually remove inerrancy from the school's statement of faith. Although he was one of the earliest casualties of the midcentury evangelical struggle to elucidate the boundaries of twentieth-century evangelical identity, Vassady would by no means be the last either. Plenty of questions about what it would mean to be a capital-E Evangelical remained, and the answers often came only after strikingly similar processes of excommunication and marginalization.

The midcentury establishment of twentieth-century evangelicalism's bellwether institutions helped define evangelical identity as reactionarily antiliberal, but what made someone liberal? Self-identification as or association with other liberals, obviously. But what else? Neoorthodoxy and Barthianism seemed to qualify, so too did rejecting inerrancy.

But could one be theologically conservative enough to qualify as evangelical without accepting inerrancy?

And even with the litmus test of inerrancy, would that be enough?

two

The Black Evangelicals

When narrating the history of the emergence and trajectory of Black Christianity in the United States, the version of the story that historians usually tell often goes something like this.

By the time that the Atlantic slave trade was finally ended, more than ten million Africans had been kidnapped and sold into slavery in various parts of the world. Nearly four hundred thousand of the many millions of enslaved Africans were taken to North American shores. Although by the start of the American Civil War there would also be nearly five hundred thousand free Black people in the United States, the total population of enslaved Black persons in the United States alone had nonetheless grown to number nearly four million. In the geographical context of what eventually became the United States, the story of Black Christianity thus begins amid the centuries-long brutality, torture, and murder perpetuated under the system of chattel slavery.[1]

In line with their efforts to Christianize the "primitive" and "pagan" peoples of the world, European colonizers frequently justified enslaving Africans on missionary grounds. But in colonial North America, there were initially very few efforts to convert the enslaved to Christianity. Unlike in predominantly Catholic colonial contexts, where slaves were often baptized, slaveholders in the primarily Protestant British colonies were initially unsure whether converting slaves was such a good idea. Believing that slaves were subhuman and therefore either had no soul or were too unintelligent, some slaveholders thought conversion was literally impossible. Others debated the potential implications of Christian slaves: some thought conversion might make better slaves, while others feared it would have the opposite effect. Still others worried that converting their slaves would require releasing them from bondage.[2]

In time, some white Protestant preachers became so driven by the spirit of revival, so motivated to convert the white *and* Black masses, that their willingness to preach to slaves began outweighing reluctance over such questions. During the first and second Great Awakenings in particular, enslaved and free Black Americans began converting to Christianity in large numbers for the first time in US history.[3] For this reason, the origins of Black Christianity in the US context have often been described as decidedly evangelical.[4]

As the practice of preaching to slaves became increasingly popular, Baptist and Methodist churches proved particularly adept at recruiting Black converts.[5] Initially, enslaved Black Baptists and Methodists often attended the same churches as their white enslavers. But enslaved Black Christians were simultaneously developing their own secret, underground, frequently illegal religious life beyond the watchful eyes of white Christians. Try though they might, slaveholders would never wholly curtail the power of what eventually became known as the "invisible institution" of slave religion.

Despite some striking theological similarities between the large numbers of Black and white Christians with evangelical and revivalistic sensibilities, by the advent of the American Civil War, Black and white evangelicalisms had begun heading in irreconcilably different directions. White Christian racism and the ongoing justification of slavery by white Christians had already driven a number of Black Christians to begin founding their own separate congregations and eventually their own denominations, thereby giving rise to what became known as the independent Black church traditions. By the end of the Civil War, despite sharing a number of professed beliefs, white and Black versions of evangelical Christianity were well on their way down the divergent paths necessitated in large part by white evangelical racism.[6]

*

Chapter 1 recovered the stories of some early twentieth-century Christians who believed that embracing modern ideas like higher biblical criticism and evolution by no means disqualified them from being evangelical. But with the advent of the neoevangelical renaissance that began in the 1940s, any idea associated in any way with either liberalism or modernism became effectively off-limits for the newly institutionalized kind of evangelicalism that went on to become the mainstream version of evangelical identity. Barthianism and neoorthodoxy, along with any other theological system that rejected the inerrancy of the Bible, provided an early and perennial test case for the limits of mainstream twentieth-century evangelicalism. Time and again, for most of the rest of the twentieth century, the verdict consistently handed down by the evangelical gatekeepers involved decreeing that theologians like Barth who rejected inerrancy were either obviously liberals—and thus not evangelicals—or dangerously close.

Over time, it nonetheless became increasingly clear that neither theological conservatism more generally nor even inerrancy specifically would be enough to settle a range of difficult questions over the limits of evangelical identity. The array of interpretational discrepancies, denominational particularities, and cultural differences that consistently cropped up even among those who agreed that some version of faithfulness to scriptural authority was indeed an appropriate benchmark for evangelicalness periodically bedeviled evangelical leaders for the rest of the century.

By the turbulent 1960s, a number of theologically conservative and self-professedly evangelical figures brought one such issue fully out into the open by dint of their very existence. The emergence during those years of a group of Black Christian thinkers who unapologetically self-identified as capital-E Evangelicals forced twentieth-century evangelicalism to reckon with a number of questions related, once again, to the nature and limits of what it would mean to be an official evangelical. Largely forgotten both by historians of Black Christianity and scholars of US American evangelicalism alike, the radical Black evangelical movement of the late 1960s and early 1970s was organized as an explicit critique and alternative to a white evangelical culture shot through with racism.[7] By diagnosing the uninterrogated white cultural assumptions of the ascendant version of mainstream evangelicalism, these Black evangelicals prefigured a series of yet ongoing debates over the racial dynamics of evangelical identity by decades.

Because even after clearly establishing that evangelical identity began where liberalism ended, a variety of questions remained unsettled—questions about race in particular. Many of the historically independent Black church traditions were theologically evangelical by just about any definition. Did that mean Black Christians were mostly evangelicals? If so, why did certain Black evangelicals need to clarify as much? Why was it that the only people who seemed to call themselves evangelicals were almost always white?

But before returning to the story of the Black evangelicals who forced such questions, a brief overview of some of the complex historical circumstances that made the very idea of a Black evangelical movement seem so novel will help set the stage.

Evangelicalism in Black and White

The usual story about the historical divergence of white and Black Christians with evangelical beliefs in this country is true enough. Although interpretations of this reality are decidedly mixed, various traditions of Black Christianity in this country can indeed be traced to decidedly "evangelical roots" in the eighteenth and nineteenth centuries.[8] Regardless of their conclusions about the extent and implications of white evangelical influence on early Black Christianity, most historians likewise acknowledge that Black Christians quickly diverged from their white counterparts on a number of pivotal questions for fairly obvious reasons despite holding similar theological beliefs.[9]

The apparently evangelical nature of so much of early Black Christianity, combined with the speed with which it diverged from white evangelicalism, furthermore has led some historians to view much of the independent Black church tradition as its own separate historical stream of Black evangelicalism.[10] According to some such interpretations, when the Black Christians who took their theological cues from white evangelicals were quickly driven out of white evangelical spaces due to white evangelicals' indefatigable racism, they nonetheless retained the major theological tenets of the evangelical tradition. By some accounts, these theologically evangelical Black Christians then began establishing their own congregations and denominations, thereby inaugurating a tradition of Black evangelicalism that would remain almost universally separate from, but no less evangelical than, the majority white tradition usually associated with the descriptor "American evangelicalism." When evangelicalism is defined as a particular set of theological beliefs, it indeed appears not only that the independent Black church traditions have been the conduit for an oft forgotten stream of evangelical faith but also that they have in fact been among the most consistent repositories of evangelical belief in all of US Christian history.[11]

But the idea that Black Christians have therefore almost always been capital-E Evangelicals is not as self-evident as it might seem. The story is more complicated than that. Sweeping suggestions that Black Christians' theological beliefs automatically make them evangelicals are undermined first and foremost by the striking historical reluctance of Black Christians either to view themselves as evangelicals or to identify as such.[12] If the minimum criterion for being counted among the evangelicals is willingness to call oneself an evangelical, in other words, then Black evangelicals have actually been few and far between. This was especially true in the twentieth-century US context, where finding official Black evangelicals became trickier than ever.

To understand why that was the case, one must rewind once again to the fundamentalist-modernist controversies of the early twentieth century. If the story of twentieth-century evangelicalism most always begins with the rise of fundamentalism, then the story of how it is that the capital-E Evangelicals became so white does too.

Fundamentalism and Neoevangelicalism in White

A number of recent efforts to trace the historical trajectories of Black fundamentalism have begun unearthing a long-overlooked aspect of twentieth-century Christian history.[13] As it turns out, Black fundamentalists really did exist. Even so, the fact remains that Black Christians for the most part remained wary of becoming too cozy with the predominantly white fundamentalist movement—and for good reason.[14] All of the most well-known and influential early twentieth-century fundamentalist leaders were white men who, almost without exception, were notoriously, virulently, and unapologetically racist. Despite the fact that a significant number of Black Christians would have shared many of the theological beliefs usually associated with fundamentalism, white fundamentalists like William Bell Riley, John Roach Stratton, John R. Rice, A. C. Dixon, and J. Frank Norris, to name a few, were not the least bit interested in making common cause with Black Christians for any purpose, even fighting modernism.[15]

On its face, the fact that fundamentalism's primary representatives were a group of vocally and openly racist white leaders is perhaps not so remarkable. Many of the most famous fundamentalists of the era indeed were unashamed segregationists who espoused an admixture of biological, anthropological, and theological justifications for their racism. But white fundamentalists were by no means the only Christians with such views.[16] Early to midcentury fundamentalists' opposition to interracial marriage, for one clear example, was an outlier neither among the white citizenry more broadly nor even among more progressive white Christians of the era.[17]

But when it comes specifically to the evolution of mainstream twentieth-century evangelical identity, the fact that white fundamentalism was led by a band of dyed-in-the-wool racists is undeniably significant. Because when the midcentury neoevangelical leaders behind organizations like the National Association of Evangelicals (NAE) cast a vision for a broader kind of evangelical identity, they did so in large part by contrasting mainstream evangelicalism with the worst tendencies of sectarian fundamentalism. In setting the benchmark for what it would mean to be a capital-E Evangelical, in other words, the post–World War II evangelicals consistently portrayed evangelicalism as something kinder, gentler, broader, and better than the fundamentalism of an earlier generation. This version of evangelicalism was supposed to retain the theological core of the fundamentals without the more distasteful parts of the white fundamentalist heritage. Among other things, the neoevangelicals hoped that evangelicalism could remain steadfastly committed to doctrinal distinctives like inerrancy, which fundamentalism had rightly defended, while simultaneously jettisoning the fundamentalist tendency toward infighting and cultural withdrawal.[18]

Their timing could not have been more perfect. No sooner had the midcentury evangelical establishment finally gotten up and running than the newly officialized kinds of evangelicals would be given the perfect chance to make good on their designs. Emerging on the scene during the 1940s and 1950s, just in time for a nationwide hand-wringing over the "race problem," the capital-E Evangelicals were given the perfect chance to demonstrate that they were different from their fundamentalist forebearers, and that one of the key differences was their willingness to bring evangelical faith to bear on contemporary social issues rather than withdrawing to their own sectarian enclaves. The first issue of *Christianity Today*, for one poignant example of a prime opportunity, rolled off the presses in October 1956. A little more than two months later, in December 1956, Martin Luther King Jr. ceremoniously stepped aboard Montgomery, Alabama's first integrated bus.[19] With all of their rhetorical posturing about the need for recapturing the social import of the gospel, in other words, mainstream evangelical leaders of the 1950s were rapidly put to the test by the race problem.[20]

The results?

If the positions that white evangelical leaders took on race and racism during those years served as the measure of the distance from their fundamentalist ancestors, then the distinction between a fundamentalist and an evangelical was a difference of type and not kind. When it came to the race problem, the answers that midcentury evangelicalism offered might have differed from fundamentalism in emphasis and form, but the substance and content were along a remarkably similar range. By the end of the 1950s, a few white evangelical figures had tentatively advocated for integration, others remained among the most ardent of segregationists, and a standard evangelical position somewhere between the two had increasingly become clear.[21]

Articulated by some of the most powerful evangelical leaders, staked out in publications like *Christianity Today*, and effectively supported by organizations like the NAE, the "evangelical moderate" became the default understanding of race for a generation of evangelical thinkers.[22] Although earlier fundamentalists might have been more explicitly and unashamedly open with their racism, the evangelical moderate remained content to denounce only the most overt and blatant kinds of racial prejudice, to equivocate on the inevitability or necessity of segregation, to vehemently oppose "forced integration," and to ignore, critique, or explicitly condemn the burgeoning Civil Rights Movement and its leaders.[23] Occasionally open to symbolic gestures of interracial goodwill, the evangelical moderate had no room for systemic analyses or governmental interventions—which were derided as the kind of thinking preferred by socialists, communists, atheists, and liberals and thus off-limits for good and faithful evangelicals. So too were any tactics that might defy "law and order." Among the mainstream leadership, in other words, the evangelical position that developed in those years was an individualistic, gradualist, conversion-based approach to ending Jim Crow segregation, in which changed hearts and not changed laws were the key.[24]

Despite later hagiographies that played up his relationship to Martin Luther King Jr. and his symbolic decision (eventually) to integrate evangelistic rallies, Billy Graham was the evangelical moderate par excellence.[25] For evangelical moderates like Graham, the race problem was merely an aggregate of the citizenry's individual sins of racial prejudice and the answer therefore was clear. "There is only one possible solution to the race problem and that is a vital personal experience with Jesus Christ on the part of both races."[26] After all, Graham stressed, "any man who has a genuine conversion experience will find his racial attitudes greatly changed."[27]

Despite paying lip service to the need for combating racial injustice, for his part, Carl Henry similarly gave intellectual ballast to the gradualist, conversionary position of the evangelical moderate. Emphasizing the overwhelming importance of avoiding the specter of governmental overreach, *Christianity Today*'s founding editor aimed to strike a balance between both sides—including those on the "segregationist right" and the "integrationist left." In the editorial pages of evangelicalism's newly launched flagship magazine, Henry helped readers see the truly "biblical" view of the problem: forced segregation might be wrong, but forced integration without regeneration was worse. In light of the inevitable disappearance of racial hatred from the heart of the believer, in other words, the personal redemption offered by a regenerative conversion experience was the only viable option to solving the nation's racial crisis—at least, that is, for good, faithful evangelical moderates who could see the "quasi-socialistic political philosophy that shows little sympathy for limited government and States' rights," which was lurking just underneath radical integrationists' calls for a "legislated morality."[28]

Due in no small part to Graham's and Henry's influence, this understanding of "racial reconciliation" and how to achieve it became so intertwined with what it meant to be an official evangelical that it represented the standard white evangelical view for the rest of the century and beyond. In retrospect, it would be no small wonder that Black Christians were so uninterested in becoming official evangelicals.

But even if more Black Christians had been interested in staking a claim for their "right to march in the evangelical parade," for the better part of the century, it would not have mattered much. When the group of midcentury evangelical figureheads at the forefront of efforts to codify what it meant to be a true evangelical sent out the invitations to join the newly officialized evangelical ranks, they neither delivered them to nor intended them for Black Christians. Like their fundamentalist forebearers, the group of architects and leaders behind the midcentury evangelical resurgence were mostly uninterested in any sustained outreach to or cooperation with Black Christian groups. As a result, the mainstream version of evangelical identity that was constructed by a team of universally conservative, mostly fundamentalist, antiliberal white men was *also* tailor-made for the purposes of attracting, uniting, and serving members and constituencies that, perhaps unsurprisingly, without exception were lily white. When the men behind groups like the NAE built what became the flagship gatekeeping institutions of mainstream evangelicalism, in other words, they thus did so without so much as an acknowledgment that Black Christians might be evangelical too.[29]

Among the thousand or so evangelicals who had gathered for the 1942 constitutional convention of the NAE, for example, reports at the time suggested that at least fifty denominations were represented. None of them were of the historically or predominantly Black variety. None of the thirty different denominations that officially joined the NAE by 1947 were Black denominations either.[30] Over the years, the NAE would eventually gain a few individual Black members. But even so, the association's list of official denominational members never included any of the most prominent Black church traditions.[31] The fact that the bellwether organization of the united evangelical movement had furthermore spent the duration of the 1940s tirelessly, albeit unsuccessfully, recruiting staunchly segregationist denominations like the Southern Baptist Convention for membership certainly hadn't helped matters.[32]

For its part, *Christianity Today* would likewise undoubtedly reach an occasional Black reader over the years. But the flagship magazine of twentieth-century evangelicalism simultaneously demonstrated time and again that its evangelical audience was obviously if implicitly white. So too was its staff: the foremost periodical for capital-E Evangelicals would not hire its first Black staff member until 1992, a full thirty-five years after its founding.[33] During the early decades of its history, Fuller Theological Seminary similarly attracted a handful of Black students. But the quintessential evangelical seminary would not hire its first Black faculty member until 1974.[34]

The universally white (and male) leadership of the post–World War II evangelical movement built a coalition that, from the outset, was made up almost exclusively of the kinds of Christians who not only believed like them but who looked like them as well. The movement they built would eventually and necessarily include a somewhat more diverse range of constituents. But even so, by the latter half of the twentieth century, if evangelicalism had been made up solely of those groups and individuals associated in one way or another with one or more of these institutions, then it would have appeared that one of the requirements for being an official, card-carrying evangelical was being white.

In retrospect, the significance of the fact that midcentury white evangelical leaders fashioned a version of evangelical identity calibrated for white Christians, while also adopting an approach to race relations that was effectively an endorsement of the status quo, becomes abundantly clear—especially when it comes to the effects it would have on the racial dynamics of twentieth-century evangelical identity. But long before the major histories of twentieth-century evangelicalism would be written, a group of self-consciously evangelical and explicitly Black Christians who struggled to develop an identity that was equal parts Black *and* evangelical reached essentially the same conclusion: that mainstream evangelical culture was actually *white* evangelical culture, and that it was shot through with uninterrogated racism.

The Black Evangelicals

Despite the fact that the flagship institutions of what became mainstream evangelicalism were not built with them in mind, for one reason or another, a handful of Black Christians slowly and eventually began showing up anyway. By the 1950s, there was a small group of Black Christians who had been trained in white evangelical and fundamentalist institutions—many of whom were among the first Black students admitted to such schools—and who initially believed that most Black churches were insufficiently evangelical.[35] Many of these self-consciously evangelical Black Christians therefore chose to live and work near or within the predominantly white evangelical institutions discussed in chapter 1. Although initially forced to navigate their respective corners of the white evangelical world almost entirely alone, over time they began finding one another and comparing notes.

United by their consistently disappointing experiences with white evangelical racism, by the 1960s a small group of Black evangelicals was increasingly reaching the conclusion that they had received more than just a "biblically sound" education in the white evangelical institutions in which they had been trained.[36] Many came to the realization that what they had been told was merely an evangelical view of the world was in fact a *white* evangelical view of the world, and that a white evangelical view of the world simply would not do.

Developing among a small group of self-consciously evangelical Black Christians as a direct response to their disillusionment with a white evangelical world that could not even see that it was white, the increasingly radical Black evangelical movement of the 1960s and 1970s indicted with its very existence a mainstream evangelical establishment that was unwilling to acknowledge Black evangelical concerns and unable to deal with its own racism. Over time, many of the movement's leaders—a group that included Black evangelical ministers and evangelists like Howard O. Jones, Willian H. Bentley, William Pannell, and Tom Skinner—unsparingly critiqued white evangelical shortcomings and shortsightedness when it came to race. In every case, they reminded white evangelicals that not all evangelicals were white.

Howard O. Jones

Born in Cleveland, Ohio, in 1921, Howard O. Jones grew up in what he would later describe as a middle-class neighborhood in an integrated community. Jones was raised by a devoutly Christian mother. During his early life, Jones's Sunday mornings were spent either going with his mother to her preferred A. M. E. church or staying at home with his reluctantly Baptist father. At his mother's insistence, the family eventually began attending church together. At his father's insistence, Howard and his older brother began music lessons at an early age, both eventually becoming good enough to perform with popular and well-respected jazz and dance bands. Unlike his brother, who went on to a musical career successful enough to get an offer to play trumpet with Count Basie's band, Howard eventually felt called to a decidedly different career path—a journey that first began when he fell in love with Wanda Young.[37]

After eventually convincing her to date him, Jones occasionally joined Wanda for services at Oberlin Alliance Church, an integrated Christian Missionary Alliance congregation that was more than a bit different from his family's all-Black Mount Zion Baptist. Years later, Jones retrospectively wondered whether the discrepancy might have had something to do with the fact that many of Mount Zion's preachers had been trained at the nearby Oberlin Theological Seminary, "which years ago was a good school, but by the 1920s and the 1930s, had become liberal." But at the time, all he noticed was a growing distance between him and Wanda, which first emerged when she decided to give her life to Jesus during a youth revival at her church while Howard was traveling with his dance band one weekend. Soon enough, Wanda stopped accepting his invitations to go to the movies or dancing, eventually giving him an ultimatum. "Unless I gave my heart to Christ, she would stop seeing me." Dreaming of a career as a rich and famous big-band leader, Jones initially decided that he didn't need Jesus or Wanda, but he soon found that his love of music was not quite the salve that he hoped. One Sunday night, in the midst of his teenage spiritual malaise, he thus wandered despairingly into Oberlin Alliance Church, where he heard the message about following Jesus anew. When he later narrated the story of his conversion experience, Jones could not help but acknowledge his belief that God using "the influence of a beautiful young woman to get through to me, in retrospect, was a nice touch."[38]

Although he had already left behind the smoking, drinking, dancing, and other "carnal pleasures" that went along with the life of a "hotshot musician," Jones soon felt that he was being called to quit the band altogether so that he could preach the gospel instead. Toward that end, the newly reunited teenage couple began making plans to jointly attend Nyack College, a Christian Missionary Alliance school known for its strong emphasis on training students for missionary work, leaving Ohio for New York together to enroll at the small Bible college in the fall of 1941.[39]

With a code of conduct prohibiting public displays of affection, requiring assigned seating during meals, and restricting dating to once-a-week outings mandatorily involving at least three couples, Nyack was a challenging place for a young couple in love. The school's racial dynamics made the lives of the handful of Black students all the more difficult. As one of only twelve Black students in a student body of six hundred, Jones later reflected, it was impossible not to feel like he and Wanda were still "test cases." Disappointed to discover that "the same old prejudices and the same distrusting stares" followed them even on a Christian campus, for Jones, the "uneasy questions" that were consistently raised about Black Christians' suitability for missionary service were even worse. As he later explained:

> On Friday nights, we black students would listen as missionaries challenged the student body with the call of the Great Commission—to "go into all the world, and preach the gospel." But when one of us would raise the question about blacks being sent to the mission field, we were given many reasons why it wasn't advisable. For example, some mission boards were concerned that black missionaries would have children who would need to be educated in the same schools as the white missionaries' children. Others said the nationals—or "natives" as they were called then—wouldn't accept the gospel from a black man but would expect him to live "on their level."[40]

With the support of the other precious few Black students on campus, Jones survived the Nyack experience with his motivation to preach the gospel intact. After graduation, the couple returned to Ohio long enough to get married before Jones accepted an offer to become the founding minister of a newly established church plant in Harlem, the Bethany Chapel Christian and Missionary Alliance Church. In New York, Jones launched an ongoing series of Saturday night Soldiers for Christ youth rallies at churches throughout the city, quickly earning a reputation as a rising young ministerial star. After connecting with popular radio evangelist and Youth for Christ founder Jack Wyrtzen, Jones went on to start his own radio ministry, broadcasting live from his Saturday night rallies in a fifteen-minute slot on a local radio station, and eventually upgrading to a live broadcast from his growing Bethany Chapel services in a Sunday evening slot on one of the city's major fifty-thousand-watt stations.[41]

Following his time in New York, Jones accepted an offer to pastor another Christian and Missionary Alliance church in Cleveland, Ohio, where he launched yet another radio ministry. With the help of a Liberian Christian radio station that played recordings of the Cleveland church's choir and its minister, Jones began reaching an international audience as well. His programs eventually became so popular with African audiences that the Sudan Interior Mission invited him to conduct a three-month-long preaching tour and evangelistic crusade throughout various West African countries, which received coverage in *Time* magazine. "The curiosity of a Negro evangelist drawing massive crowds in Africa," Jones later surmised, "proved to be too much for even the mainstream press to ignore."[42]

His impressive resume as a preacher and evangelist soon proved impossible for the broader evangelical world to ignore as well. In May 1957, Jones received a letter from his friend Jack Wyrtzen reporting the details of a conversation that Wyrtzen had recently had with none other than Billy Graham. Lamenting the fact that the crowds at his New York crusade had been overwhelmingly white, the nation's most famous evangelist reportedly asked Wyrtzen whether he knew of any Black evangelists who might be willing to join the Graham team. "Implicit in his question was the idea that this Negro evangelist had to be someone who could transcend racial boundaries," Jones later judged, "someone whose theology was sound and whose approach was non-threatening; someone who understood the subtle intricacies, the manner and vernacular of white evangelical culture. In short, someone who was safe." Wyrtzen knew exactly who to call. For his part, Jones was ecstatic. He enthusiastically accepted the offer in the summer of 1957 and thereby became the first Black pastor to serve as an associate evangelist for a Graham crusade.[43]

Jones's presence on the platform was quickly met with derision both from Graham's white audiences and from a number of his white associates as well. Some nights during the New York Crusade, Jones found himself sitting on one side of the stage with empty seats on either side while some of Graham's white coevangelists conspicuously sat on the opposite side of the stage. His eventual recommendation that, if Graham was serious about increasing Black attendance, they should hold rallies in Harlem and Brooklyn rather than just at Madison Square Garden, combined with Graham's decision to heed Jones's advice, was rewarded with even more criticism from white Christian leaders. Undoubtedly to the chagrin of some such leaders, it worked. By the end of the summer, Black attendance at the rallies had grown significantly.[44]

The following year, Jones joined the Billy Graham Evangelistic Association (BGEA) as the organization's first Black, full-time evangelist. In the years to come, he went on to become instrumental in bringing a handful of other Black associates as well. Throughout his career with the organization, Jones was regularly forced to deal with the racism that was part and parcel of his presence as a lone Black minister in the white evangelical world. In his own later telling, one of the most devastating incidents of all came during a 1966 crusade stop in London where he was dutifully informed that he could not stay in the same hotel where the rest of Graham's team had booked their rooms. Undeterred by the ever-present threat of such indignities, Jones continued working for the BGEA for the next thirty-five years. Even after officially retiring from the organization in 1994, Jones continued preaching for Graham's team via radio for a number of years, with his popular *Hour of Freedom* broadcast coming across the airwaves until 2001.[45]

For his pioneering work as a radio preacher, Jones became the first Black recipient of the National Religious Broadcasters' Hall of Fame award in 1996. Among countless other awards, honors, and positions that he added to his name over the course of his career, he also became one of the early leaders of the self-consciously Black evangelical movement that emerged in the early to mid-1960s—a movement that took its earliest institutional form with the 1963 founding of the National Black Evangelical Association.[46]

William H. Bentley and the National Black Evangelical Association

Although Jones and others provided crucial early leadership, in retrospect, William H. Bentley undeniably became the caretaker and chronicler of the legacy of the radical Black evangelical movement.

Born in Chicago in 1924, Bentley was raised in a Pentecostal tradition that looked askance at higher education. His insatiable intellectual curiosity thus set him at odds with many of his fellow Pentecostals and eventually drove him toward the apologetic and theological writings of neoevangelical luminaries like E. J. Carnell, Wilbur Smith, and Carl Henry. Bentley's commitment to getting as much education as possible carried him through a bachelor's degree from Roosevelt University in 1956, followed by his eventual matriculation at Fuller Theological Seminary, where he went on to become the first Black graduate of the school's bachelor of divinity program in 1959.[47]

During the late 1940s, Bentley had increasingly been attracted to the kind of intellectually serious version of fundamentalism—or neoevangelicalism—that he found outlined in the pages of Henry's book *The Uneasy Conscience of Modern Fundamentalism*. His early exposure and eventual identification with the predominantly white world of fundamentalism quickly taught Bentley some crucial lessons. For one thing, as he later explained, it gave him clear "insight into some of the reasons why Fundamentalists took certain positions on social issues, especially the one concerning Black-white relations. It was the beginning of my struggles to gain understanding of how one could be doctrinally correct and, at the same time, hold backward attitudes toward such an important issue as race in America." His later experience of moving along the neoevangelical path from fundamentalism to a broader kind of evangelical identity furthermore showed him that neither white fundamentalism nor the newly ascendant version of white evangelicalism typified by his alma mater, Fuller Seminary, were particularly hospitable environments for Black Christians. As time went on, he also found that he was not alone in this realization.[48]

At the time, Bentley was Fuller's only Black alumnus. But during the 1940s and 1950s, a handful of other, smaller evangelical Bible colleges and fundamentalist schools—including Jones's alma mater, Nyack College—had likewise begun accepting a few Black students every year. By the 1960s, a number of Black graduates from such institutions had begun discovering that their common experience had given them a very particular kind of worldview. As Bentley later explained, this worldview "included a negative, sketchy, and superficial evaluation of the black church [as] thoroughly corrupt, theologically inept, morally impure, and emotionally out in left field."[49] Rather than working in or with predominantly Black churches, which they viewed as essentially apostate, many Black evangelicals of Bentley's era had chosen instead to pursue their ministries within what they had been taught was the doctrinally pure, predominantly white evangelical world. In Bentley's view, at least two major problems with this arrangement had become abundantly apparent. First there was the unfortunate fact that white evangelicalism was just as infected by racism as any other sector of US American Christianity. Second, much to Bentley's chagrin, it seemed as though white midcentury evangelical leaders were neither capable of addressing nor even interested in considering the evangelistic needs of Black people. If so many Black people—including Black *church* people—were really as spiritually lost as white evangelicals suggested, Bentley wondered, then why were his white evangelical counterparts so reluctant to launch evangelistic efforts in Black communities?[50]

Recognizing an urgent need for connection among the small group of Black Christians moving in the predominantly white evangelical world of the early 1960s—and concluding that white evangelical leaders were not going to support them—Bentley and a handful of others began considering how they might meet their own needs instead. In 1963, a small group of like-minded Black evangelicals met in Los Angeles to do just that. Established with a name that made its purpose as an alternative to the lily-white NAE impossible to miss, that year the organization that would eventually be renamed the National Black Evangelical Association (NBEA) held its first inaugural meeting as the National Negro Evangelical Association.[51]

The NBEA began its life as an organization focused on facilitating Black evangelical outreach to the country's Black communities through three major outlets: missions, evangelism, and youth ministries. This early orientation quickly brought to light some major tensions within the organization that would shape its early identity and determine much of the course of its ensuing history. The first realization had to do with the fact that early NBEA leaders, according to Bentley's later telling, were ill-prepared for meeting the organization's primary goal of reaching Black people. As products of white evangelical institutions, many of the Black evangelicals associated with the new organization had been taught to emulate ministerial and evangelistic practices that were perfectly suited for white communities but not at all relevant for Black realities. NBEA leadership, Bentley later explained, had initially labored under the assumption "that the 'best' and 'proper' methods for reaching our people . . . were those we had learned in the Bible Schools and theological seminaries of white evangelicalism."[52]

The second major ambiguity facing the NBEA, like the first, derived from the early influence of white evangelical frameworks on the organization's thinking. Like the white evangelicals who had trained them, the Black evangelical leaders of the NBEA initially viewed the needs of the Black community as basically spiritual in nature and thus prioritized evangelism above all else. Describing both the prevailing attitude and its implications, Bentley later observed, "It was the soul that needed to be saved, and after that 'all other things would be added'—if necessary!" Combined with a suspicion of anything remotely sounding like "the Social Gospel," which was also inherited from white evangelicalism, the organization's early emphasis on conversion as the key to changing the world initially precluded any real discussion of the social realities of Black life. At best, in other words, social change was viewed as a kind of corollary benefit that would result only from changed hearts.[53]

But according to the history that Bentley would later pen, from the outset, there were always some maverick members of the organization who stressed the importance of a more holistic approach to evangelism, which might also include taking sides on the most pressing social issues facing the Black community. During the NBEA's early years, Bentley himself was foremost among the proponents of a more socially aware Black evangelical perspective, quickly convincing the organization to appoint him as its commissioner of social action. By persistently calling attention to the full range of the gospel's social implications, Bentley and the Commission on Social Action quickly developed a reputation as an abrasive gadfly in the organization, but they nonetheless remained undeterred. "At the heart of the ministry of social action was our strong conviction that whether the wider evangelical community saw it or not, we who were engaged in its promotion, saw it as an indispensable part of the task of proclamation," Bentley retrospectively judged. "We articulated the view that the white evangelical establishment had not shown adequate leadership in this area, and we argued (literally at times) that if Black people in America were to experience social salvation, they would have to, under God, seek their own."[54]

Due in no small part to the commission's explicit critique of the white evangelical establishment, as the 1960s progressed, the NBEA's relationship to the predominantly white world of mainstream evangelicalism increasingly became one of its most controversial internal tensions. Early on, the organization's membership had featured a sizeable contingent of prominent white evangelicals, including, among others, Fuller Seminary professor of English Bible Wilbur Smith and the NAE's Joseph Rian. White evangelicals such as Fuller Seminary professor of theology Paul King Jewett, who was the NBEA's first white board member, also initially served in leadership positions. Although by Bentley's own admission, the organization remained dependent on role models from within the white evangelical establishment for many years to come, the role that white evangelicals should or should not be playing in the NBEA increasingly came to a head during several of the group's annual meetings.[55]

In Bentley's telling, the NBEA had been intentionally structured from the start as a big-tent organization. Through the middle years of the 1960s, it appeared as though the group might indeed be able to successfully hold together both sides of a fault line that was developing between an increasingly radical faction and its more conservative members. Conservatives maintained that personal conversion was the remedy for society's ills and emphasized reconciliation and unity with white evangelicals. Radicals meanwhile increasingly stressed the importance of social activism, critiqued white evangelical paternalism, and became unabashedly committed to promoting Black identity consciousness. For a while, both groups remained together under the organization's umbrella, which initially was big enough to include a handful of white evangelical supporters as well.[56] But that all began to change during the final years of the tumultuous decade when an increasingly radical Black evangelical perspective began coalescing and spreading under the influence of leaders like Bentley, with major help from fiery young evangelists William Pannell and Tom Skinner.

William E. Pannell

Born in 1929 in Sturgis, Michigan—a small town with an even smaller Black community—William E. Pannell grew up wondering why his family had to carpool to a distant city whenever he needed a haircut. During his formative years, Pannell attended a Brethren Assemblies Sunday school, participated in Missionary Church youth group, and officially dedicated his life to Jesus Christ at a revival meeting in 1946. Motivated by the conviction that he was responsible for spreading the gospel, he enrolled at the Fort Wayne Bible Institute the following year.[57]

Though Pannell had already had plenty of exposure to white culture, there were certain aspects of the Bible college experience for which even he was unprepared. Upon arriving at Fort Wayne in the fall of 1947, he naively signed up for the school's missions course with a clear understanding that Africa was the obvious destination and target. "All I knew was that the blacker the person's face, the more desperate his need for salvation," he later explained. Thanks to the "white-oriented education" he received growing up, Pannell had unconsciously absorbed some assumptions about Black people that his faith had done little so far to correct. After all, he later reflected, "When one is taught to think 'white' he isn't changed too much by conversion."[58]

What Pannell had neither anticipated nor fully understood until many years later was the registrar's hesitation when he first enrolled in the missions course. "Did she know," he retrospectively wondered, "that there were few, if any, evangelical mission boards that would have sent me had I finished the course?" The eventual discovery that white evangelicals would train him for work they would never allow him to do might have been shocking. But in hindsight, Pannell judged that it actually might have been for the best that he ended up on a different vocational path: "Had I gone to Africa it would have been disastrous for the same reason it has been for many white Christians. And for another: it is one thing for a white Christian to go to Africa thinking white thoughts about black people; it would be quite something else for a non-white Christian to go there thinking white thoughts about black people." In the end, Pannell's Bible college training unfortunately did nothing to disabuse him of such notions. What it *did* do, however, was to transform him fully into an "anti-modernist, anti-RSV, anti-World or National Council and anti-Roman Catholic" kind of Christian. In other words, he later confessed, "I became a fundamentalist."[59]

Upon graduating from Fort Wayne in 1951, Pannell embarked on a career as an itinerant evangelist. After traveling the country for several years as a preacher and occasional song leader, in 1955 he began working as an assistant youth pastor in the Detroit area, and later served as the area youth director for the Brethren Assemblies churches of the southern Michigan region. But as time marched on, Pannell became increasingly disillusioned with the white Brethren Assemblies congregations in particular and with the broader racial dynamics of the denomination in general. At the same time, at least during his early years in Detroit, Pannell nonetheless believed that the burgeoning Civil Rights Movement had little to do with him as a northerner. According to his later retelling, that all changed in 1963.[60]

Watching the nationally televised images of Bull Connor's police using snarling dogs and water hoses to viciously attack Black men, women, and teenagers in Birmingham, Pannell later recalled, "did more to snatch me awake than any previous event in my lifetime. . . . I felt the spray in Detroit. And I was awake." The dawning realization that he had been underestimating his own sense of racial pride while simultaneously overestimating his white friends' commitments to justice led Pannell to begin rethinking many of his previous assumptions about the Civil Rights Movement. But the clearest turning point in his thinking came later that year when the bombing of Birmingham's Sixteenth Street Baptist Church shattered all of Pannell's remaining religious illusions. After witnessing the removal of the tiny bodies of Carol Denise McNair, Carole Robertson, Addie Mae Collins, and Cynthia Wesley from the wreckage of the church, for Pannell, there was no turning back: "It splintered the walls of my own composure. It yanked me loose from my comfortable moorings in the calm waters of complacency. It blistered my evangelical conscience. . . . I now knew that I could no longer be a standard evangelical Christian, content merely to preach a typical evangelical Gospel. This ghastly event—to be followed by so many like it— happened in the 'Bible belt.' The time had come to re-evaluate the Gospel in terms of its meaning and application for our times. For me, the illusion was over."[61]

The following year, Pannell began working with the evangelical parachurch group Youth for Christ (YFC) as a part-time evangelist. His hopes during the mid-1960s that the organization would begin working harder to reach Black youth were soon dashed, however, and his commitment to helping them try ultimately to little avail. White evangelicals were leaving the cities in droves, groups like YFC were following them into the suburbs, and that was that. As YFC became increasingly suburban, Pannell pressed for the development of an urban ministry division and emphasized the importance and relevance of social action, but the predominantly white ministry possessed neither the will nor the finances to address either issue. The explosion of urban uprisings in 1965 and 1966 sealed the deal. By the time Detroit blew up in 1967, Pannell knew that white evangelicalism was abandoning both the Black inner cities in general and Black evangelicals like him in particular for good. If he wanted to try and reach Black people—and Black youth in particular—he now realized that the all-white flagship evangelical organizations would never do. It was time for a Black-led organization instead. By spring 1968, Pannell had left YFC to join a new evangelistic organization started by Tom Skinner for precisely that reason.[62]

Tom Skinner

Tom Skinner's path to becoming an enormously popular, influential, and eventually controversial evangelist began with a conversion story so powerful that his "testimony" undoubtedly made evangelical preachers throughout the country jealous. Born in Harlem in 1942 to a father who was a Baptist minister, Skinner joined his father's church at the age of seven "because it was the respectable thing to do." But as a precociously and preternaturally intellectual teenager—who could parse the distinctions between existentialism and rationalism by age fourteen—Skinner found the church his father pastored boring and disappointing. In his view, the church seemed like nothing more than meaningless entertainment utterly devoid of spiritual depth and totally disconnected from the realities of the surrounding world. "As a teenager," he later recounted, "I looked around and asked my father where God was in all this? I couldn't for the life of me see how God, if He cared for humanity at all, could allow the conditions that existed in Harlem."[63]

But if his father's Black Baptist church lacked the answers he was looking for, the "hyper-Christian" white ministers he encountered had even less to offer.[64] Worst of all, in Skinner's mind, were the ministers who pointedly and self-consciously called themselves "Bible-believing, fundamental, orthodox, conservative, evangelical" Christians, derided liberals and modernists for biblical infidelity, and quoted Bible verses in response to social problems, but who would never set foot in a place like Harlem. Skinner simply could not relate to an "Anglo-Saxon, middle-class, Protestant Republican" Jesus who wouldn't survive a day on the streets of his neighborhood.[65]

White Jesus might not have fared so well in the Harlem streets, but as a teenager, Skinner became particularly adept at doing just that. An exceptional student, varsity athlete, student-body president, and church youth group leader, Skinner was simultaneously an up-and-coming member of one of the city's most infamous gangs, the Harlem Lords. By excelling in school and dutifully attending his father's church, for several years, he effectively balanced a double life as a respectable preacher's son by day and a rising gang member by night. By the time he was seventeen, Skinner had in fact become the Harlem Lords' undisputed leader. In his own later retelling, that all changed on the eve of what was likely to be one of the gang's biggest battles. That night, as he was mapping out a plan for leading his gang into victory over four rival gangs the following day, Skinner was surprised to hear the regularly scheduled programming on his favorite radio station interrupted by the voice of an unsophisticated radio preacher delivering a familiar message. Only this time, for some reason, he found that his standard philosophical and intellectual objections to the message of salvation began falling away. As a "strong believer in the scientific method," Skinner later explained, that night he realized that perhaps he had actually never truly "put Jesus Christ to the test" and decided to do just that. "I bowed my head and prayed simply, 'God . . . I don't understand all of this. I don't understand how You're going to change my life. I don't even understand why I'm praying to You, but if these things are true . . . if You can transform my life and make me a new person . . . if You can forgive me of every sin that I have ever committed, then I'm asking You to do it."[66]

According to his own retelling, Skinner quit the gang the following day. Shortly thereafter, the newly converted, former gang leader told another gang member his story, invited his friend to pray with him, and by the end of the conversation, "an ex-gang leader, a Christian less than 48 hours, led another gang member to Christ." In the following weeks, Skinner persuaded several more of the Harlem Lords that they, too, should become Christians. Thoroughly convinced by that point that Jesus could and would change people, Skinner took to the streets of Harlem where he began preaching on city blocks, evangelizing from street corners, and spreading his message of redemption wherever he found people willing to listen.[67]

News of Skinner's passion and skill for reaching the city's youth, especially those who were in gangs, spread quickly, and a number of churches throughout the city soon started inviting him to lead youth revivals. His increasingly successful evangelistic efforts brought detractors as well. Throughout his career, Skinner regularly and fiercely criticized Black church clergy—whose ranks, in his mind, included all manner of "phonies, hypocrites, actors, and money-makers." As a young and increasingly popular itinerant evangelist who believed that the pulpits of most Black churches were filled with immoral hucksters, Skinner's lack of support among the city's Black pastors was unsurprising. The fact that he admittedly "de-emphasized church membership" in his preaching certainly would not have helped either.[68]

Over time, Skinner nonetheless developed connections with what he believed were the precious few "earnest, sound evangelical churches" in Harlem. In 1961, he joined with a small circle of like-minded associates to launch the Harlem Evangelistic Association (HEA). The group immediately began laying plans for a large-scale evangelistic crusade at the Apollo Theater the following year. In the summer of 1962, a little over a month after his twentieth birthday, Skinner served as the head evangelist for the week-long campaign, preaching nightly to standing-room-only crowds. Over the course of the following two years, his enormously successful evangelistic efforts expanded to include both international campaigns and a radio ministry. In 1964, the then twenty-two-year-old made the front page of the *New York Times* as the headliner for yet another massive two-week-long crusade in Harlem. That same year, Skinner launched his own organization, Tom Skinner Radio Crusades Inc., which later evolved into Tom Skinner Associates (TSA).[69]

The New Black Evangelicals

As with so many other aspects of twentieth-century US American history, the 1968 murder of Martin Luther King Jr. was a watershed moment for the small but growing Black evangelical movement. That spring, Pannell left the too-white YFC team to join Skinner's Black-led evangelistic organization, where he began helping TSA assemble what became a kind of Black evangelical "dream team" that could finally tackle the kinds of ministries that white evangelicals were either unable or unwilling to even try. If the move to TSA had not made his frustrations with the white evangelical establishment clear enough, the appearance of Pannell's blistering first book that same year removed any lingering doubts.[70]

Published within days of King's death, *My Friend, the Enemy* described Pannell's experience as a Black evangelical navigating a white evangelical world shot through with racism. Tired of dealing with white evangelicals' expectations, weary of the invitations to serve as their window dressing, and disgusted with their hypocritical dismissals of the Civil Rights Movement, Pannell pulled no punches. White evangelicals' mass exodus to suburbia had shown him that they never really cared about Black folks, and if he dared to challenge them on such "worldly" concerns, they just recited verses about the end time and heavenly citizenship. Pannell opened by explaining how hollow white evangelical platitudes rang in the ears of Black people watching their children bleeding in the streets. "But what would my white brother know of this?" he queried. "He taught me to sing 'Take the World But Give Me Jesus.' I took Jesus. He took the world and then voted right wing to insure his property rights."[71] The force of his critique only escalated from there.

Haunted by his own awakening to the importance of the Civil Rights Movement, Pannell's discussion of white evangelicals' views on the matter was perhaps most scathing of all. For years, white evangelicals had invited him to their churches to talk about what his life as a Black person in America was like, asked him to do things like "sing one of your songs," probed and scrutinized his perspective on riots and marches, and regularly explained that his bitterness would only hurt "his cause." Time and again, they had stressed how no responsible person could possibly support "the demonstrators, the liberals, the activists," or the violence that their marches obviously incited. And should he ever become tempted toward a more sympathetic view of King and his ilk, Pannell's white evangelical friends were always wont to remind him that, as an evangelical, he should know "that the issues are basically moral and spiritual" rather than legal, and that changed hearts were the only solution to racism and social problems.[72]

For his part, Pannell could no longer bear to listen to white evangelicals' preaching about individual sin as the source and personal conversion as the solution for *some* social problems when they seemed perfectly willing to press for legal remedies to others. He now realized that such admonitions were a farce, nothing more than the "games conservatives play":

> Because you see, I know that the same conservative brother who refuses to link my social needs with his preaching of the Gospel is the same man who lobbies against the Supreme court, fluoride in the water, and pornographic literature. "Something," he declares, "must be done about creeping socialism. We must speak out against the Communist menace, and by all means we must support the Dirksen Amendment on prayer in the public schools." But mention the inhumanity of a society which with unbelievable indifference imprisons the "souls of black folks," and these crusaders begin mumbling about sin. All right. I'll play the game, my brother. Whose sin shall we talk about?[73]

Later that year, Skinner's electric *Black and Free* first hit bookshelves as well. Skinner and Pannell's books both made it onto the evangelical periodical *Eternity Magazine's* "most significant books of the year" for 1968, and for a while, the invitations to speak to some white evangelical groups continued apace.[74] As Pannell later explained, there was a window during the late 1960s and briefly into the early 1970s when evangelical organizations needed to have one of the two of them—but almost always only one—on the platform at an event to seem "socially relevant." For a period of time, evangelical schools in particular would bring either Pannell or Skinner in to speak to their students, viewing them as relatively safe options. But that window didn't stay open very long. By the late 1960s, their preaching about the kingdom of God, their emphasis on the social implications of the gospel, and their escalating indictments of the majority white evangelical culture were fast earning Skinner and Pannell a reputation as radicals.[75]

Skinner in particular increasingly became known as far too political for white evangelicals' tastes. His unapologetic emphasis on the most pressing issues facing Black communities made his preaching next to impossible for many white evangelical audiences to swallow. Christian radio stations that had once proudly broadcast Skinner's messages, including the Moody Bible Institute's WBMI, quickly began dropping his programs altogether.[76] By the mid-1960s, Skinner's reputation as a dynamic and successful evangelist had earned the young preacher the moniker "the black Billy Graham." Over time, it eventually seemed more appropriate to dub him the "Stokely Carmichael of the evangelical world" instead.[77]

Though many white evangelicals found Skinner and Pannell too radical to touch, their message resonated strongly with a number of Black Christian students on college campuses throughout the country—especially those on distinctly evangelical campuses. When a group of Black students at Wheaton College found that they were studying in a difficult and racially hostile campus environment, for example, they turned to Skinner for advice, successfully lobbying to bring him to campus in 1969. As one of those students, Ronald C. Potter, later recounted, Skinner's example was a boon for Black evangelical students who felt caught between secular Black Power advocates, on the one hand, and white evangelical racism, on the other. "We were experiencing a lot of subtle forms of racism at the time, but we could not describe what it was," Potter explained. "Tom was able to articulate for us what we had been feeling. He helped us differentiate between biblical Christianity and the Christ of the white evangelical culture."[78]

The same year that Skinner was helping Black Wheaton students, the NBEA witnessed the outbreak of a newly "militant emphasis" among its more radical members at the organization's annual meeting in Atlanta. Arguing that the organization should free itself once and for all from any direct dependence on white evangelicalism, the radical wing pressed the group to finally come to terms with its relationship to a white evangelical world that blindly assumed white cultural normativity. After heated debate with some of the more conservative NBEA members—a group that included some who were still affiliated with white evangelical evangelistic organizations—by the end of the convention, the radicals had gained the upper hand. According to Bentley's later account, the results and implications of the debate were clear: "for the first time in the history of the organization, the position was unequivocally expressed that white methods to reach Black people had been historically proven to be inadequate. . . . Uncritical acceptance and imposition of white models, either by Black or white leadership, makes possible a form of sanctified cultural imperialism which must be resisted and set aside as not being relevant to where the bulk of Black Christians are." Pointing to the success of the historically independent Black churches—a sign that some Black evangelicals were ready to reassess *both* their relationship to white evangelicalism *and* their previously critical distance from the traditional Black churches—some of the radicals furthermore stressed that any white leadership within the NBEA must now be moved to the periphery. Even though the emergence of a newly militant emphasis at the convention marked the beginning of a major exodus of both white and Black members from the group, in Bentley's judgment, it was a necessary reckoning.[79]

The following year's annual meeting in New York further signaled the rising tide of a militant Black evangelical movement. At the 1970 convention, the young radicals in particular pressed the NBEA on issues ranging from "the unholy Graham-Nixon alliance" to the need to offer support for Black evangelical activist John Perkins. Columbus Salley, who coauthored a 1970 book titled *Your God Is Too White*, which became something of a militant Black evangelical handbook, delivered the keynote address. That year, the organization furthermore elected Bentley, who was increasingly becoming known as the godfather of Black nationalist evangelical militants, as its president—a development the young radicals viewed as a clear victory.[80]

Even though the NBEA had already begun hemorrhaging its white evangelical members and much of its more conservative Black evangelical membership, with Bentley at the helm, some of the younger Black evangelicals felt that the organization might indeed be repurposed and revitalized by the energy of the young, radical, militant Black evangelicals within its ranks. But if Bentley's election was not enough of a sign that an unapologetically and radically Black evangelical movement had finally arrived, another event that year made it seem all but certain that a new kind of Black evangelical was there to stay.

Urbana 1970

In 1967, InterVarsity Christian Fellowship, one of the most influential institutions on the evangelical scene, hosted its eighth triennial student mission conference in Urbana-Champaign, Illinois. Hoping for a time of fellowship and connection, a group of about sixty Black student members from various InterVarsity chapters had come to Urbana for that year's conference. But as Edward Gilbreath would later report in a 1996 *Christianity Today* article, "What they found instead was a 'white' event, not only in terms of attendance, but also in terms of vision." Carl Ellis, one of the Black evangelical students in attendance that year, had naively expected better: "But it didn't take long for me to realize something wasn't right. I didn't see anybody from my neighborhood there. I didn't see anyone talking about missions to the cities or about the concerns of the black population. And I said to myself, 'I hope these people aren't deliberately doing this.'"[81]

In the wake of the disappointing 1967 meeting, Ellis and some of the other Black evangelical students set out to remedy what they felt was a glaring absence in InterVarsity's near universally white evangelical culture. When they began lobbying to ensure that the next meeting would have a more robust Black presence, Ellis was soon appointed to the national advisory committee tasked with planning the next conference. He knew exactly what to do next. Ellis eventually convinced the organization that the lineup of plenary speakers for Urbana 1970 must include Tom Skinner. News of the decision spread, excitement grew, and it ultimately paid off. "As a result," Gilbreath went on to recount, "in 1970, more than 500 black students and Christian leaders flocked to the Urbana convention. The black evangelical renaissance that the students had prayed about three years earlier actually felt within reach."[82]

The conference began more or less as usual. More than eleven thousand college students spent the first day participating in Bible studies and listening to speakers like John Stott as always. But late in the second day of the five-day conference, that all changed when Soul Liberation, a gospel-funk band that traveled with Skinner's evangelistic campaigns, took the stage to play before the evangelist's keynote address. Sporting "afros, multi-colored attire, and Afro-centric symbols" while playing their song "Power to the People"—a Jesus-centric, Black-Power inflected gospel anthem—in Gilbreath's later retelling, the group had a "sanctified Sly and the Family Stone" aesthetic unlike anything that the predominantly white Urbana crowd had ever experienced. But if the majority of the students gathered that year were caught off guard by Soul Liberation, they undoubtedly were even less prepared for Skinner. With most of the five hundred or so Black students seated together directly in front of the stage, when the band finished playing and Skinner stepped forward, many in attendance later remembered feeling like they were witnessing something historic.[83]

Skinner opened his plenary address, "The U.S. Racial Crisis and World Evangelism," with a whirlwind tour of the long history of American racism, reaching all the way back to 1619 and the arrival of some of the earliest colonial ships. Though the most horrifying part was yet to come, he began, the fact that the colonies had been populated in part by English prisoners in indentured servitude should be enough to disabuse the students of any illusions that they might have that the country "was founded on godly principles." When it was later decided that whites could no longer serve as indentured servants and eventually that Black people could be profitably enslaved, Skinner explained, the practice was upheld not only by the American political and economic systems but crucially by its religious system as well. Pointing to the "group of ad hoc biblical dispensationalists" who had justified slavery by appealing to the "curse of Ham," he then reminded the evangelical college students that such interpretations were by no means a thing of the past, noting, "I can name to you right now at least five Christian colleges and at least a dozen Bible institutions in this country that still teach that in their classrooms today."[84]

For Black people in America, Skinner continued, even emancipation had not ultimately delivered them from oppression. Along with the failure of reconstruction came "a wave of lynchings and murders and drownings and disappearances of black people unequalled in the history of the Western world," for example, and the rest of the twentieth century had been a massive disappointment as well. Enormous numbers of Black people had come to northern cities hoping for liberation only to discover that "integration" was a brief window between their arrival and the departure of the last white families. Forced into segregated ghettoes, the masses of Black people currently living in the slums of places like Harlem were *still* being told that they could simply pull themselves up by the bootstraps. "But, you see," he went on, "this bootstrap theory is one of the most damnable lies being preached in America today. . . . Any of us who are anything at all are there because somebody opened some doors, somebody gave us some breaks, somebody provided some opportunities. In the case of black people, it is difficult to pull yourself up by the bootstraps when somebody keeps cutting the straps."[85]

Skinner saved his severest indictment for an "evangelical, Bible-believing, fundamental, orthodox, conservative church" that had spent the majority of American history supporting slavery, upholding segregation, and underwriting the country's ongoing legacy of racism. Then, if Black people ever dared to rise up in protest, he pointed out, white evangelicals quoted verses like "love your enemy," "do good to them that hurt you," and "obey your masters" to defend the status quo. Even now, scores of white evangelicals were among the voices crying for "law and order," Skinner noted, which the Black community had come to realize actually meant "all the order for us and all the law for them." It was no small wonder then that Black people had turned elsewhere for a message of hope:

> Understand that for those of us who live in the black community, it was not the evangelical who came and taught us our worth and dignity as black men. It was not the Bible-believing fundamentalist who stood up and told us that black was beautiful. It was not the evangelical who preached to us that we should stand on our two feet and be men, be proud that black was beautiful and that God could work his life out through our redeemed blackness. Rather, it took Malcolm X, Stokely Carmichael, Rap Brown and the Brothers to declare to us our dignity. God will not be without a witness.[86]

And how had evangelicals responded to the foremost of the figures who had emerged to declare Black dignity? They had called into question whether he was a real, born-again Christian. "Because you see," Skinner explained, "if we could just prove that Martin Luther King was not a Christian, if we could prove that he was not born again, if we could prove that he did not believe the Word of God, then we think we can dismiss what he said."[87]

The problem with Christians in this country, he went on, was their willingness to accept a dichotomized, either-or interpretation of the gospel. Liberals placed the stress on freeing people from social injustice, while fundamentalists emphasized personal salvation and eternal life. But for Skinner, the message of the gospel included both. If it didn't include *both* the promise of freedom from personal sin *and* deliverance from systemic oppression, he judged, then it was a false gospel that should be rejected. So too was the idea that the gospel had something to do with one's national allegiance or political affiliation. "That is why, just as the Indian Christians had to renounce the British Empire," Skinner confessed, "I as a black Christian have to renounce Americanism. I have to renounce any attempt to wed Jesus Christ to the American system. I disassociate myself from any argument that says a vote for America is a vote for God. I disassociate myself from any argument that says God is on our side. I disassociate myself from any argument which says that God sends troops to Asia, that God is a capitalist, that God is a militarist, that God is the worker behind our system."[88]

The real answer, he preached, could be found only in the one true militant radical, Jesus Christ, who was *both* the personal Savior who cleansed people of their sin *and* the dangerous revolutionary who came to turn all political systems upside down. Driving to the crescendo, Skinner left the students with a charge. "You will never be radical," he concluded, "until you become part of that new order and then go into a world that is enslaved, a world that is filled with hunger and poverty and racism and all those things of the work of the devil. Proclaim liberation to the captives, preach sight to the blind, set at liberty them that are bruised, go into the world and tell men that are bound mentally, spiritually and physically, 'The liberator has come!'"[89]

Many who were there felt that something historic was happening. Pannell, who was sitting on the stage behind Skinner, later described the roaring standing ovation that the evangelist received as "the most powerful moment I've ever experienced at the conclusion of a sermon." Albert G. Miller, who went on to publish some of the precious few historical discussions of the Black evangelical movement, similarly remembered the address as "a pinnacle of visionary and prophetic expression" that "gave both African Americans and whites a vision of what being a black evangelical Christian could be."[90]

Whither the Black Evangelicals?

In the years following Urbana 1970, it seemed for a while that the vision of a radical movement that was equal parts unapologetically Black and self-consciously evangelical was finally coming to fruition. By the mid-1970s, the radical Black evangelicals were being featured in publications ranging from the progressive evangelical magazine *The Other Side,* which devoted an entire 1975 issue to profiling the "New Black Evangelicals," to Gayraud S. Wilmore and James H. Cone's landmark collection *Black Theology: A Documentary History,* which included a chapter by Ronald C. Potter detailing the history of the movement.[91] In the years to come, a number of influential Black Christian figures would furthermore continue working and moving within the confines of the self-confessedly evangelical world. Some would spend decades working to build bridges between Black and white evangelicals. Simply put, there has always been (and there still is) a portion of Black Christians in this country who both consider themselves evangelicals and make their religious home within the self-consciously evangelical world.

But as a separate *movement,* the militant, Black-and-proud, "new Black evangelical" tradition that emerged in the lead-up to and wake of Urbana 1970 arguably reached its peak at the very moment it finally seemed to have gotten off the ground. Hamstrung from the outset by some crucially insurmountable obstacles, the burgeoning group of radical Black evangelicals was persistently forced into an unusual double bind that made developing a full-fledged and sustainable movement next to impossible. As a group, the twentieth-century Black Christians most interested in defending their right to simultaneously claim both their Blackness and their evangelicalness emerged for the most part out of the predominantly white world of mainstream evangelicalism and in response to its racism. But by also drawing a clear line between their fledgling movement and the independent Black church traditions, the early leaders of organizations like the NBEA and TSA had all but guaranteed that their potential constituency would remain niche. On a Venn diagram with one circle representing Black Christians uninterested in, dissatisfied with, or critical of Black churches, and another circle representing Black Christians fed up with the pervasive racism of predominantly white Christian spaces, in other words, the movement's ideal interest group would be found in the overlap. With a Black church tradition that was legitimately suspicious of certain (mostly white) Christians' need to explicitly self-identify as capital-E Evangelicals, on one side, and an evangelical world that often viewed explicitly Black organizations as a form of "reverse racism," on the other, the movement's unenviable position was between the rockiest and hardest of places.[92]

But even still, some persevered. In various chapters that he contributed to larger volumes and in a number of self-published books and pamphlets, Bentley spent the better part of the next two decades codifying, articulating, and caretaking a particular Black nationalist evangelical theological world-view. When a group of progressive, mostly white evangelicals met in 1973 to issue a statement on evangelical social concern, for instance, Bentley (along with Pannell) would not only be found among the few Black signatories but also would in fact go on to offer some of the most trenchant critiques of the document from an unapologetically Black but decisively evangelical perspective. Bentley and a number of the other new Black evangelicals aggressively pushed the gathering of progressive, socially concerned, white evangelicals who issued what became known as "the Chicago Declaration" to include "a strong statement on the complicity of white evangelicalism in the individual manifestations and group mechanisms that originated and perpetuate racial oppression in America" in the document. But in a written response included with the published version of the declaration, Bentley pulled no punches when it came to his ambivalence about the ultimate results. Although it was probably the strongest social statement contemporary white evangelicals had yet produced, he judged, "the declaration would not be adequate for a purely black constituency."[93] White evangelicals, even the progressive kind, simply could not forthrightly reckon with the overwhelming legacy of the country's racism and their tradition's ongoing participation in its perpetuation.

Despite Bentley's tireless individual advocacy, his beloved NBEA's early militant turn and the subsequent exodus of so many of the organization's conservative members began a long and gradual decline from which the group would never fully recover. Even though Bentley himself regularly went on to admit that the Black evangelical movement had unnecessarily distanced itself from the independent Black churches—frequently explaining that he now believed that most Black Christians in those churches were soundly evangelical whether they identified as such or not—the NBEA continually struggled to make any lasting inroads with the historically Black denominations. In recognition of the fact that the politically conservative connotations of the word had likely been one of the organization's major sources of friction with Black churches, the group periodically considered dropping the word "evangelical" from its name altogether. Still later, as Bentley and some Black evangelicals became increasingly interested in engaging with the work of Black liberation theologians like James Cone, yet another rift emerged in the organization—one that eventually led to the departure of some members who felt that "Black theology" compromised the biblical emphasis of "Black *evangelical* theology" and thus should be rejected out of hand.[94]

Unlike Bentley, who spent many more years trying to keep the dream of an explicitly Black nationalist and self-consciously evangelical movement alive, Skinner's electrifying Urbana 1970 address arguably marked the high point of his direct leadership in the upstart movement. Already a pariah in much of the predominantly white world of mainstream evangelicalism, during the early 1970s, Skinner's marital troubles and eventual divorce gave many white evangelicals the excuse they were waiting for to write him off for good. His meteoric rise to personal fame, which eventually included a stint as an NFL chaplain, and subsequent self-distancing from Pannell and the rest of his associates furthermore led to the departure of most of the Black evangelical dream team from TSA's roster. By 1975, Tom Skinner Associates was mostly defunct as a result.[95]

By focusing more on high-profile Christian leadership development than on mass evangelism, Skinner's career nonetheless entered a new phase with an altogether different sphere of influence during the 1980s. In 1981, Skinner married Barbara Williams, an attorney who served as the secretary for the Congressional Black Caucus, and with her help began making connections with some of the traditional Black political and ecclesial elite for the first time. When Skinner died tragically from leukemia in 1994 at the age of only fifty-two, the range of mourners in attendance at his funeral was duly reflective of his unusual career. Along with numerous colleagues from his early evangelistic days, a number of widely influential Black leaders like Maya Angelou, Jesse Jackson, Betty Shabazz, and Louis Farrakhan were there as well—a guest list that would be utterly unfathomable for any evangelical *but* Tom Skinner.[96]

Unlike Skinner, who eventually moved somewhat afield of the evangelical mainstream, in the last two decades of the twentieth century, some Black evangelicals dove back into its most difficult territory. Throughout the 1980s and 1990s, a number of Black evangelical leaders took on the all-too-thankless work of what often became known as the "racial reconciliation" movement—a protracted, sporadic, and often haphazard series of efforts to unify (mostly) Black and white evangelicals. For perhaps the most famous example, with his lifelong pursuit of racial reconciliation, tireless advocacy for holistic community development, and noteworthy contributions to ongoing struggles for civil rights, the minister and activist John M. Perkins became one of the most influential Black evangelicals of the twentieth century.[97]

Although some wound up leaving the evangelical world behind altogether, some of the Black evangelical leaders who were associated in one way or another with the movement would spend the duration of their careers struggling desperately to carve out some space for Black evangelicals in the majority white culture of mainstream evangelicalism. Some such figures went on to become like lighthouses for future generations, often serving as the only beacon in sight for young Black Christians needing help navigating the inevitably stormy waters of a lastingly and overwhelmingly white evangelical world. After leaving TSA in 1974 to join Fuller Theological Seminary as its first Black faculty member, Pannell shouldered precisely that burden and carried it throughout a forty-year-long career at the flagship evangelical school—where he eventually spearheaded the development of the Theological Studies Program for Black Ministers, which the school eventually renamed the William E. Pannell Center for African American Church Studies in his honor. For many Black evangelical students who came through Fuller's halls over the years, Dr. Pannell served as *the* signal proof that being unashamedly Black and self-consciously evangelical was even possible.[98]

By the dawn of the twenty-first century, more than three decades after Urbana 1970, the mainstream version of US American evangelicalism remained as mired in race problems as it was when *Christianity Today* was platforming segregationists in the 1950s. Perhaps unsurprisingly, for the rest of the twentieth century and well beyond, Black Christians who would willingly and unflinchingly self-identify as evangelicals continually remained something of an anomaly on the religious landscape. Sizeable percentages of Black Christians may indeed have held theological beliefs that were evangelical by most standard definitions, but by and large they simultaneously remained decidedly uninterested in a predominantly white evangelical world with a seemingly intractable racism problem.

Black evangelicals, of course, have always existed, and their existence has regularly challenged widespread popular and scholarly preoccupation with white evangelicals. But just how rare Black evangelicals actually were (or are) turns almost exclusively on precisely what the label means. On the one hand, evangelical sentiments have perhaps been more historically pervasive among Black Christians than any other group. But then, on the other hand, the label eventually became so closely associated with a kind of Christianity that was culturally white without knowing it that joining the roster of official evangelicals has often seemed to require "thinking white thoughts"—precisely as Pannell suggested more than a half century ago. Ongoing reluctance to identity as capital-E Evangelicals, even among Black Christians who might otherwise fit the theological criteria, in other words, is far less surprising when one recognizes that mainstream evangelical identity has been constructed, controlled, and policed almost exclusively by and for white Christians. As Edward Gilbreath so incisively pointed out, when it comes to the evangelical label, Black Christians grasp that "there's just something about that name."[99]

Joining *Christianity Today* in 1992 as the flagship evangelical periodical's first full-time Black staff member, Gilbreath would know better than most just what was so peculiar about that name too. He spelled it all out in his 2006 book *Reconciliation Blues: A Black Evangelical's View of White Christianity*. In Gilbreath's telling, the reluctance to embrace the label had become so widespread that even Black Christians like himself—those who had chosen to live and work in the mainstream evangelical world and its institutions—were often profoundly uncomfortable with describing themselves as evangelicals.

Regardless of whether they self-identified as evangelicals, Gilbreath furthermore explained, so many of the Black Christians that he encountered who had at one time or another been involved in predominantly white evangelical spaces during the 1990s and early 2000s had eventually confessed to him how lonely, tired, and disappointed they were. They were lonely from having to work as one of if not the only Black persons in their respective organizations, tired of the very idea of "racial reconciliation," and disappointed at white evangelicals' provincialism and naivete when it came to the realities of structural and institutional racism. The Black evangelicals that he knew continuously felt "disconnected, patronized, marginalized, misunderstood," and Gilbreath knew exactly how they felt: "And that, in essence, is what this book is about—the loneliness of being 'the only black,' the frustration of being expected to represent your race but being stifled when you try, the hidden pain of being invited to the table but shut out from meaningful decisions about the table's future. These 'reconciliation blues' are about the despair of knowing that it's still business as usual, even in the friendly context of Christian fellowship and ministry."[100]

Though published nearly four decades after *My Friend, the Enemy* first hit the shelves, *Reconciliation Blues*'s subsequent chapters painted a picture in which "business as usual" for Black evangelicals during the late twentieth century and early twenty-first century meant having to constantly reckon with the same struggles Pannell identified in 1968. The patterns appeared to be repeating themselves time and again with each new generation. Black evangelicals were still prodded with questions like "why do all the Black students sit together?" With their very presence, they were still periodically integrating evangelical institutions for the first time. Once inside those institutions, they were still being subjected to uninterrogated cultural assumptions that were unmistakably white, and like so many Black evangelicals before them, they were often eventually becoming so fed up and exhausted that they were forced to leave evangelical spaces for their own well-being.[101]

As Gilbreath went on to explain, Black evangelicals were also continually facing an especially intense level of scrutiny from their white evangelical friends and colleagues when it came to the question of partisan politics. In the chapter "Is Jesse Jackson an Evangelical?" he recounted a particular manifestation of the phenomenon in his own career. Admittedly a fan of Jackson, Gilbreath nonetheless knew that most of his white evangelical colleagues detested the man. But even that awareness did not prepare him for the reaction when he pitched a profile of the provocative preacher and civil rights leader for *Christianity Today* in the early 2000s:

Call me naïve, but I underestimated the repulsion my bosses would have toward Jackson. Several working lunches later, I was given the okay to do the article. But that was only the beginning. . . . Once the article was written, I received a number of unannounced visits from at least two high-ranking members of *Christianity Today*'s editorial management team. Both men shared their concerns about publishing the article, that it could be a potential powder keg with our readers. Though they both agreed that I had written a balanced profile, it became apparent that, in this case, balance wasn't enough. I gathered that they wanted to make certain the story was not too kind to Jackson and it clearly distanced *Christianity Today* from any hint of sympathy for the man.[102]

The article eventually ran with minor adjustments, but the ultimate lesson for Gilbreath was clear. White evangelicals were still profoundly uncomfortable with any discussion of the "loud and impolite aspects of the race issue," especially if it meant that they would have to do something about it.[103]

As he would later conclude, they were also leery of Democrats and anyone who might have reason to view Democratic policy positions with sympathy. Recognizing that Black people were often overwhelmingly in one or the other of those groups, white evangelicals were automatically predisposed to view Black Christians with suspicion—so much so in Gilbreath's experience that they even tended to question the legitimacy of Black evangelicals' faith. "Sometimes I get the feeling," he confessed, "that some white evangelicals won't consider an African American believer a real Christian unless he or she subscribes to their conservative political views."[104]

In the concluding chapter, Gilbreath highlighted the recent publication of a landmark book, *Divided by Faith: Evangelical Religion and the Problem of Race in America*, that offered clear sociological evidence of a sobering reality that he and countless other Black evangelicals had already lived and experienced. Coauthored by sociologists and self-identified evangelicals Michael O. Emerson and Christian Smith and published in 2000, *Divided by Faith* detailed the findings of an extensive study designed to learn more about how "ordinary evangelicals" explained racial inequality, how they viewed the country's "race problems," as well as what kinds of solutions they would offer to address them. The book was a bombshell. By *both* garnering high praise from the secular academic community *and* earning wide circulation, discussion, and debate among popular religious audiences, it pulled off a rare feat indeed.[105]

In Gilbreath's telling, the buzz was duly warranted. Driven in part by the meteoric 1990s rise of the Promise Keepers—a widely popular evangelical movement that encouraged Black and white Christian men to come together in a shared commitment to taking charge of their families—the evangelical world had recently become rife with "reconciliation excitement" and was overdue for a reality check.[106] *Divided by Faith* delivered in spades. "Despite devoting considerable time and energy to solving the problem of racial division," Emerson and Smith ultimately concluded, "white evangelicalism likely does more to perpetuate the racialized society than to reduce it."[107] Not only were white evangelical "racial reconciliation" initiatives ineffective, in other words, they were actually part and parcel of a mainstream evangelical culture that made the nation's racial problems even worse.

In Emerson and Smith's judgment, the problem could be traced to a few key sources. US American evangelicalism's particular history, including "its thorough acceptance of and reliance on free market principles," was partially to blame. So too was the contemporary evangelical tendency toward demographically homogenous congregations. White evangelicals furthermore had developed a particular "subcultural tool kit" for interpreting both the world around them and their place in it, and the "theologically rooted" tools in the white evangelical cultural tool kit, the authors explained, "tend to (1) minimize and individualize the race problem, (2) assign blame to blacks themselves for racial inequality, (3) obscure inequality as part of racial division, and (4) suggest unidimensional solutions to racial division."[108]

Groundbreaking though the thesis might have seemed, for Gilbreath and many of the other Black evangelicals he knew, the signs had been there all along. Black evangelicals moving in the predominantly white mainstream evangelical world didn't need *Divided by Faith* to tell them "that the preaching and theology of white evangelicalism [was] infected by a crippling case of individualism," or that "evangelical theology" was afflicted by but blinded to its own whiteness.[109] They already knew that. Despite decades of periodic calls for "racial reconciliation," and several lifetimes' worth of work on the part of some Black Christians like Pannell and Perkins who tried to help white evangelicals get past their racial naivete, being Black and self-consciously evangelical in the early years of the twenty-first century *still* meant fighting for space in a white evangelical culture that subtly and not so subtly sent the message that they did not belong. To be a capital-E Evangelical still meant trying to fit somewhere inside a religious identity originally meant only for white people. For Black evangelicals, the distance between Urbana 1970 and the early aughts was effectively nil.

Some, like Gilbreath, refused to give up anyway. But doing so always came with a cost. Black Christians who could not shake the conviction that the mainstream evangelical world was somehow their home would *still* be forced to wrestle with their place in a faith tradition that *still* could

not shake its insistence on "thinking white thoughts about Black people."
As Gilbreath ultimately concluded in *Reconciliation Blues*, being Black and
evangelical in the early twenty-first century inevitably required "grappling
with what it means to live with this strange DuBoisian dichotomy—a 'double-
consciousness' that often requires them to see their faith through a white
cultural lens."[110] The cost of admission for contemporary Black evangelicals
remained just as high, in other words, as the price demanded from the radical Black evangelicals nearly a half century before. Joining the ranks of the
card-carrying evangelicals still required coming to terms with a mainstream
evangelical culture closely associated with whiteness. With a ticket price
that high, is it any wonder that so few were interested in admission?

three

The Progressives

When historians recount the twentieth-century history of evangelical politics, which they do more often than any other aspect of US American evangelical history by far, the way they usually tell the story goes more or less like this.

The antievolution crusades of the early twentieth century culminated in the embarrassing spectacle of a fundamentalist defeat at the Scopes trial. With the old-time religion in apparent retreat, evangelicals of all varieties seemingly disappeared from US American public life for the next several decades. But that all changed with the post-World War II appearance of the neoevangelical movement, when it appeared that the uneasy conscience of evangelicalism had at last been reawakened and that a new period of evangelical social reengagement might finally have dawned.

In the wake of the neoevangelical emergence, neoevangelicals and neofundamentalists spent the middle decades of the century furiously building a subcultural network of parachurch organizations and institutional connections. Over time, it nonetheless became clear that midcentury evangelicalism's social conscience was slower to emerge than promised. During the 1940s, 1950s, and into the 1960s, even the closest observers of the so-called evangelical resurgence would never have considered the idea that evangelicalism was a potentially potent social force or that the evangelical masses were an enormous voting bloc awaiting activation. When it came to US American politics, in those years, it wasn't even that evangelicals were dismissed as irrelevant so much as it was that they weren't really considered at all. Evangelicalism, in other words, spent the middle decades of the twentieth century as a nonfactor on the national political scene. But that all changed in the 1970s when evangelical politics went from bust to boom like never before.

Conventional narratives of the rise of the Religious Right generally paint a picture of the formation of a grassroots coalition of long-dormant conservative evangelical citizens, concerned with the ethical decline of the nation, mobilized primarily by opposition to abortion, and driven by a desire to put an end to the rampant immorality and moral relativism that they believed were by-products of the country's headlong dive into godlessness. The countercultural turbulence of the 1960s stirred the sleeping evangelical giant, the story often goes, and *Roe v. Wade* finally woke evangelicals up to the direness of the situation.

In 1979, the founding of the Moral Majority marked the institutionalization of a newly reunified political interest group, the evangelicals, who were committed to bringing America and its government back to a state of halcyon godliness by realigning the country with biblical values. With the full weight of the rising evangelical tide behind him, Ronald Reagan was elected the following year.

By the time the 1980s were in full swing, the Religious Right's political platform—for traditional family and against feminism, pro-life and against abortion, for prayer in schools and against secularism—was fast becoming the calling card of evangelicalism. It also became the scorecard for politicians hoping to secure the votes of the newly reactivated evangelical masses. By promising to fulfill each item on the Religious Right's wish list, the Republican Party eventually did just that. The evangelicals, in turn, did their part. By the close of the twentieth century, they had become the most reliably partisan constituency in all of American politics.

*

As discussed in chapter 1, the 1940s emergence of the neoevangelical movement marked the beginning of the end of any lingering hopes that evangelical identity could make space for Christians who unabashedly championed modern ideas like higher biblical criticism and evolution. From that point forward, to be an official evangelical meant wholeheartedly embracing theological conservatism—usually by affirming the inerrancy of the Bible. As indicated by the stories recovered in chapter 2, theological conservatism would never be enough unless you were also white, however. But even then, the question of whether all theologically conservative white Christians would make the cut still remained.

This chapter moves into a period when another item was emphatically added to the list of unofficial qualifications, exploring a question that became the most determinative feature of late twentieth-century debates over the limits of evangelical identity—namely, could card-carrying, theologically conservative (white) evangelicals ever embrace progressive politics?

By the close of the twentieth century, the answer was clear. Mainstream evangelicalism had become known above all else for its conservatism in general and its conservative, specifically Republican, politics in particular. But this outcome was by no means inevitable.

The midcentury evangelical leaders who codified what it meant to be an official evangelical were neither theologically liberal nor politically progressive by any stretch of the imagination, and many such figures either implicitly or explicitly defined evangelicalism in opposition to *all* forms of liberalism. But before the Religious Right helped irrevocably link evangelical identity with contemporary Republican politics like never before, for a while it seemed like there might be at least some space for political difference among the ranks of the capital-E Evangelicals. In fact, for much of the latter half of the twentieth century, a small but committed group of self-consciously evangelical figures persistently argued that evangelicalism's increasingly partisan political alignment was selling out the historic evangelical faith. Evangelical theology, in their view, need not yield Republican politics. At times, Christian principles indeed would demand voting against Republicans, and faithful evangelicals should be allowed and prepared to do so. Eventually known as the "evangelical left," many of these progressive evangelical leaders spent decades fighting tooth and nail against the increasingly close association between theological and political conservatism. They also desperately tried to prevent their fellow Christians from making US American nationalism the sine qua non of the evangelical faith.

The various individual figures and organizations associated with the evangelical left eventually coalesced into a modest but promising progressive evangelical movement—the emergence of which actually predated the official establishment of the Religious Right by several years. But the fight to keep a left-wing evangelical option alive was an uphill battle from the start, and when the evangelical forces of the Christian Right came on the scene, they came on strong. The combination of a broader evangelical subculture in which political conservatism had long been the assumed de facto position with the ascendance of an increasingly influential movement that successfully cemented an explicit link between evangelical belief and Republican politics in the minds of insiders and outsiders alike meant that the leaders of the evangelical left had their work cut out for them. No matter what they did, they would always be forced to make their appeals from the margins of the mainstream evangelical world.

Despite the length of the odds, a small but devoted group of evangelical progressives nonetheless spent the last few decades of the twentieth century tirelessly fighting for a version of evangelical political engagement that could serve as an alternative to the reigning option on offer from the right. Even as evangelical identity was becoming increasingly coupled with a narrow set of right-wing political priorities and the possibility of a robust evangelical left-wing was drifting into history as a long-forgotten dream, the scrappy cadre of figures eventually known as the evangelical left kept on protesting that being an evangelical did not and should not mean being a Republican.

An Emerging Vanguard

The Alexanders, Freedom Now, *and* The Other Side

One of the earliest institutional forums for what became the evangelical left was born in one of the seemingly unlikeliest places. Formed in 1933 when a group of fundamentalist members of the Northern Baptist Convention realized that the liberal-modernists could not be driven out of their denomination and that the only option for maintaining doctrinal purity was to form a new one instead, the General Association of Regular Baptists (GARB) represented the most sectarian kind of white fundamentalism, refusing even to cooperate with conservative evangelical organizations like the Billy Graham Crusades or the National Association of Evangelicals (NAE).[1] As a white fundamentalist minister ordained in such a strictly separatist denomination, Fred A. Alexander's conservative theological bona fides were as sound as they come. But in the context of the white fundamentalist and evangelical worlds of the 1960s, his eventual willingness to question the prevailingly segregationist orthodoxy on the "race problem" put him in a lonely position indeed.

After inviting a gospel quartet made up of students from Faith Bible Center, a Black fundamentalist college in nearby Cleveland, Ohio, to sing at his church, Alexander developed a connection to the school that eventually led to him teaching classes there. When Fred's son John graduated in 1964 from Trinity College—the undergraduate counterpart to Trinity Evangelical Divinity School—the younger Alexander moved to Cleveland, joined his father as an instructor at Faith Bible Center, and soon became actively involved with the NAACP.[2]

During his undergraduate days at Trinity, John had been forced to radically rethink his own faith. Initially joining the only campus organization that affirmed inerrancy, InterVarsity Christian Fellowship, which was still too liberal for his own fundamentalist tastes, Alexander had eventually become profoundly disillusioned with the group and its beliefs for a decidedly different reason. His first major faith crisis had in fact occurred during an InterVarsity gathering when the group explicitly refused to collect an offering for the poor and hungry, suggesting that "Christians are concerned about souls not bodies." Hearing it put so bluntly drove Alexander to the brink of giving up on Christianity altogether. "If the Christian god was like that," he later recounted, "I was not a Christian." In a process that would become nothing short of transformative, Alexander nonetheless decided to give the Bible one last read through. By the end of his journey reading from Genesis to Revelation, he had come to the staggering realization that "every section of Scripture is jammed with teaching about the poor," ultimately discovering that somewhere along the way, he had both "utterly rejected the god of my Inter-Varsity group" and simultaneously fallen "in love with the God of the Bible."[3]

John Alexander wasn't the only one rethinking aspects of his faith either. Convicted by the voices of the rising Civil Rights Movement and transformed by their experience teaching and living in inner-city Cleveland, during the early to mid-1960s, John and Fred Alexander were both radically reconsidering the prevailing fundamentalist position on race.[4] Rejecting fundamentalism's segregationist logic was only the first step, however. While teaching at Faith Bible Center, John Alexander discovered that many of the Black preachers who were his students "had a better understanding of the Bible's social ethic than I did," and that his efforts to teach them "how to speak standard English" were merely reinforcing his own "false image of white superiority and black incompetence." He was eventually forced to rethink his own position in the struggle for racial justice as well. Ultimately concluding that the white-savior role they were playing at the school was actually perpetuating racial oppression, by 1965 both John and his father left their positions at Faith Bible Center.[5]

The Alexanders nonetheless felt that there was *something* they should and could do with their newfound convictions about racial justice. With the help of Anne Alexander, Fred's wife and John's mother, as well as a few family friends, in 1965 the father-son team thus began printing a twelve-page newsletter, specifically "written from a Bible-believers' viewpoint," "especially directed to the white fundamentalist," and explicitly intended "to encourage interracial understanding and communication." Under Fred's editorship, with John serving as associate editor, the first issue of the monthly periodical *Freedom Now* rolled off of the Alexanders' personal (and antiquated) printing press that August.[6]

With its message that "segregation is sin" and that the country's churches ought to be at the forefront of saying so, *Freedom Now* initially faced considerable obstacles in trying to reach its intended fundamentalist audience.[7] Though the magazine unsurprisingly received its share of angry letters, its signal didn't carry far enough into segregationist fundamentalist territory to receive all that much attention at first. Eventually realizing that their potential audience would not be found primarily among the kind of sectarian fundamentalism associated with small separatist denominations like the General Baptists, the editors (John in particular) soon began considering a different sort of Bible-believing readership. The recent rise of the broader, paradenominational, though mostly still fundamentalist, evangelical network associated with institutions like Fuller, the NAE, InterVarsity, and Wheaton College provided the magazine with both a ready-made opportunity and a fighting chance. Around the same time that he moved to Chicago to pursue graduate work in philosophy at Northwestern, John Alexander thus began reaching out to the more neoevangelical, less sectarian kinds of readers who *did* seem interested in the sort of Bible-believing integrationism that the magazine was articulating.[8]

While at Northwestern in 1966, John also began teaching at nearby Wheaton College, where his passion for racial justice soon placed him at the center of a rising tide of political progressivism among the student body. As one Wheaton student who went on to work for Alexander at the magazine later recounted, in those years, the fact that Alexander was "the most eloquent and convincing voice on campus speaking out against the war in Vietnam and against racial injustice" meant that he quickly became known as a troublemaker on the staid, conservative campus—so much so in fact that *Freedom Now* was eventually banned from the Wheaton bookstore.[9]

By the time that the magazine was getting blacklisted at Wheaton, John Alexander had become coeditor, taking on most of the responsibility for selecting content and setting the overall editorial tone. Under John's influence, during the final years of the 1960s, the magazine slowly but perceptibly began expanding its coverage beyond its original emphasis on race to include discussions of social issues like national and global poverty as well. Eventually deciding that the periodical needed a new name to reflect its new directions, the editors issued an announcement in the September 1969 issue explaining how the magazine's new title, *The Other Side*, had been chosen. "The America of TV serials, glossy magazines, and first grade primers is full of people who are prosperous, healthy, young, and of Northern European extraction," the editorial noted, but that was only one side of the country. On the *other* side were the "hungry, defeated, and miserable," including those who "live in old folks homes, migrant workers camps, Indian reservations, inner-city ghettos, and declining mining towns. These are the forgotten Americans, the representatives of the other side."[10]

The announcement was undeniably ambitious. Hoping that the magazine would be able to raise readers' awareness so that they would then be motivated to combat social injustices "by applying the whole gospel of Jesus Christ," the editors expansively defined "the other side" to include suffering communities the world over.[11] In the editors' views, American evangelicals needed to start caring about those living on the other side of society both at home *and* abroad.

But along with this global emphasis came the unavoidable question of what the magazine would be willing or able to say about one of the era's most defining political issues. Despite a developing reputation for falling at the leftmost end of the evangelical political spectrum, internal debates over what the truly biblical position on war and violence ought to be meant that even the pluckily progressive periodical spent the final years of the 1960s assiduously avoiding any discussion of the Vietnam War. The heart of the matter came down to a divergence between father and son: although John Alexander was increasingly wrestling with the call to nonviolence, Fred Alexander was not. Over time, with the waning of the elder Alexander's editorial input, the magazine began including a range of views on war and violence that increasingly skewed toward pacifism—though it would not be until many years later that John Alexander realized that he was indeed a pacifist himself. But when it came to the question of war in general and Vietnam in particular, internal disagreements were by no means the only potential pitfall. As John Alexander later explained, for instance, the magazine's eventual decision to openly editorialize against the Vietnam War earned them "a lot of negative reaction from people who had been supporting us on other issues." For some of *The Other Side*'s evangelical readership, reconsidering race and poverty was one thing. Calling into question the righteousness of their country and its military was quite another.[12]

In the US American evangelical world of the late 1960s, *The Other Side*'s willingness to challenge prevailing views on race, poverty, and, slowly but surely, violence and war often put the periodical and its staff in a lonely position. But even then, they weren't entirely alone. By the time that *Freedom Now* was announcing its new name, another evangelical thinker, Ronald J. Sider, who was similarly influenced by the Civil Rights Movement, was already teaching evangelical college students about the radical implications of the biblical message regarding the poor and oppressed. But unlike with the Alexanders, for Sider nonviolence and the path of pacifism were nearly second nature.

Ron Sider

Born in rural Ontario in 1939, Ron Sider grew up on a small farm owned and tended by his deeply religious family. In addition to farming, Sider's father served as a Church of the Brethren pastor, and both of his parents modeled an Anabaptist and perfectionistic piety that he regularly credited as the single most formative aspect of his upbringing. Although his mother would never be able to convince him that she was anything less than fully sanctified, Sider later explained, he was enormously relieved the first time he ever heard his father curse because it meant that at least one of his parents had not yet attained perfection. The combination of perfectionist holiness and Anabaptist streams in his parents' faith also resulted in a thoroughgoing "concern for peace and justice and for the poor," which was anything but theoretical.[13] As Sider eventually recounted, for instance, when his parents had once encountered a child in need of a home, they adopted her, and that was that. The four Sider children got a new sister. When Ron Sider "knelt at the altar and accepted Jesus Christ" during a revival meeting when he was eight years old, he was thus converted to a kind of evangelical faith in which it was simply "assumed that devout Christians shared the gospel . . . and also cared for the poor."[14] The Canadian, Anabaptist, holiness kind of evangelical religion of his youth was also largely immune to "the kind of God and Country stuff" so prevalent among his evangelical neighbors to the south.[15]

Matriculating at Waterloo Lutheran University in the late 1950s as a first-generation college student, Sider's first taste of political activism came during his undergraduate days when he joined an agnostic history professor at a demonstration protesting the 1960 Sharpeville massacre. His first exposure to the "modern skepticism" of the secular university also caused his first real crisis of faith. Sider's eventual rescue from the sea of doubt came in the form of a serendipitous lifeboat from a surprising source. During his junior year, the school replaced the "secular agnostic" chair of the History Department with evangelical historian and zealous Christian apologist John Warwick Montgomery, who subsequently became a mentor and friend for Sider. Montgomery's influence was decisive. Deciding that he, too, could mount a vigorous defense of Christian belief from within the walls of the secular university, after graduation, Sider gratefully accepted a fellowship to pursue a PhD in history with an emphasis on the Reformation at Yale University.[16]

After two years of doctoral studies, Sider took a three-year leave of absence from his work in the History Department to pursue a bachelor of divinity degree at Yale Divinity School—a decision that, by his own account, was ironically motivated by a desire "to understand fully the strongest arguments against historic Christian orthodoxy" in preparation for his anticipated career in secular academia. Envisioning himself as a historian of the Renaissance-Reformation era, he initially planned to serve the Christian students at whatever secular university he found himself in by working simultaneously as an advisor for InterVarsity Christian Fellowship. Sider's plans nonetheless began to partially unravel during his time at Yale in the late 1960s due in no small part to his deepening concern for social justice in general and racism in particular.[17]

In addition to his Yale training, living in the predominantly Black part of New Haven provided the Sider family an entirely different sort of education. Becoming friends with their Black landlords and witnessing the anger and frustration of his Black friends' youngest son in particular were profoundly moving experiences for Sider, who soon decided that he "could not just go on reading Latin and German for my dissertation."[18] In 1967, he joined the NAACP. By the end of that same year, he was organizing a voter registration drive. When Martin Luther King Jr. was murdered the following year, the experience of sitting with his Black friends as they mourned King's death only deepened Sider's developing commitment to the work of social justice. "Most of what I know about oppression," he later reflected, "I've learned from black Americans."[19]

Increasingly convinced that contemporary evangelicalism desperately needed a renewal of biblically based social concern to complement its near-exclusive emphasis on evangelism, Sider felt called to help make it happen, eventually deciding "to do everything in my power to make sure that as evangelicals became more concerned with social issues, they would not lose either their passion for evangelism or their grounding in historic Christian orthodoxy."[20] In 1968, his prior plans to teach Renaissance-Reformation history at a secular university officially came to an end when Messiah College, a small Christian Brethren school in Pennsylvania, sent a letter inquiring whether he might be interested in helping launch a new satellite program in Philadelphia. The opportunity to live and work in the inner city while teaching courses such as Christianity and Contemporary Problems was an offer Sider could not refuse. Later that year, the family moved to Philadelphia, where their education in racial solidarity recommenced when they began attending a Black Presbyterian church—where Sider developed and led seminars on racism and poverty for suburban and rural white audiences—and sending their sons to the nearest all-Black public school.[21]

In addition to his advocacy for the poor and oppressed, in the years to come, Sider's long-standing commitment to pacifism became one of the many issues on which he persistently served as a gadfly on the social conscience of late twentieth-century evangelicalism. With his Canadian Anabaptist roots, he furthermore always came by his antiwar and anti-nationalistic convictions naturally. As opposed to many of the progressive evangelicals whom he would increasingly help lead, Sider had little need to personally overcome the close link between Christian faith and patriotism that became so prevalent among his US American-born counterparts. Having grown up outside of midcentury American evangelical culture, he simply never needed to seriously reckon with the implications of an evangelicalism thoroughly drenched in nationalism. For Jim Wallis, another young evangelical driven into progressive politics during the 1960s largely due to his disappointment with white evangelical racism, dealing with the "God and Country stuff" would take up far more energy.

Jim Wallis and the Post-American

Born into a comfortable, suburban, middle-class home outside Detroit, Jim Wallis spent his 1950s childhood attending a conservative Plymouth Brethren church where he was immersed in a resoundingly evangelical faith—a fact that he later explained by noting, "I was 'saved' at six and baptized at eight in the little evangelical church my dad and mom helped to establish." As a "white kid from everything that was 'middle' about America," Wallis's coming-of-age in the 1960s quickly upended both his respectably middle-class upbringing and the version of American evangelicalism that he felt went along with it. In his later telling, the earliest cracks in his boyhood worldview came from the realization that there were Black people living in nearby Detroit whose lives were nothing like his. Finding out that some parents didn't have jobs, that many children did not get to attend good schools, and that, unlike in his family, not everyone "believed that we lived in the best city in the best state in the best country in the world," Wallis began asking the kinds of questions—like why his Black friends' parents warned them to *avoid* the police if they were ever lost in a strange neighborhood, when his own parents taught him to *look for* the police in the same scenario—that eventually led to a shattering disillusionment with his childhood faith.[22]

As a teenager in the 1960s, Wallis developed friendships with Black coworkers while working in downtown Detroit, struggling to come to terms with the discrepancies between their experiences of America and his own. He first learned that there was something called the Civil Rights Movement during high school and eventually began reading books like *The Autobiography of Malcolm X* and the Kerner Report to try to better understand why his Black friends were so angry. Increasingly indignant over his newfound realization about the horrors of racism and the unjust treatment of Black Americans, Wallis brought his concerns to his parents' congregation, hoping the church would share his anger. He was bitterly disappointed at their dismissive response. "The more I learned from my black friends and co-workers in inner-city Detroit," he later recounted, "the more I felt disillusioned, hurt, angry, betrayed, and rejected by the church. I became separated from the church and, in the process, I felt I had lost my faith." In Wallis's telling, his evangelical upbringing thus included two different kinds of conversion experiences. The first was personal, private, abstract, and largely disconnected from "any concrete historical realities." The second, "deeper" conversion experience involved a crisis of faith and the ultimate rejection of the all-white, comfortably middle-class kind of evangelicalism associated with the first.[23] "Detroit was my early baptism by fire," he later reflected, "teaching me how racism had betrayed the ideals I had been taught as a child."[24]

By the time he enrolled as a freshman at Michigan State University in the fall of 1967, Wallis's initial estrangement from the church had become a near-total divorce. But the deeper conversion that began in downtown Detroit kept haunting him, and his search for answers soon brought him into the fold of a decidedly different kind of community. Unable to reconcile himself to a faith tradition that viewed the pursuit of social justice as a political matter unrelated to spiritual issues, Wallis eventually found common cause instead with the kinds of political radicals that he had grown up fearing. Realizing that there were plenty of other college students who shared his passionate opposition to "racism, poverty, and war," in his own later telling, "My community, and in many ways my family, became those who were struggling for civil rights and an end to the war in Vietnam."[25]

With a college career that coincided almost perfectly with the rise of widespread dissent over the country's involvement in Vietnam, Wallis poured himself into student antiwar activism. His position in student government, his membership in Students for a Democratic Society, and his work organizing large-scale student protests eventually earned him a reputation that stretched beyond just the Michigan State campus. But by his senior year in 1970, the realization that the now massive student antiwar movement, which he had helped build, was in danger of collapsing under the weight of both external forces and its own internal inconsistencies forced Wallis to reconsider the nature of his calling. If the chaos and disillusionment that he witnessed in the final years of the student antiwar movement were partially responsible for its eventual undoing, he wondered, where might one turn to find a framework for social change with deeper "spiritual roots"?[26]

According to his later accounts, it was about that time that Wallis began reading the New Testament again for the first time in years. What he found in its pages stunned him. "Throughout my student years I could never quite shed myself of Jesus," he later explained. "Now I encountered him as never before. I read the Sermon on the Mount and realized that Jesus was talking about a whole new order. He called me back, or maybe he called me for the first time."[27] Initially dissatisfied with evangelicalism's dichotomization of personal morality and social justice, Wallis had left the church of his youth, experienced a deeper kind of conversion through his involvement in political movement-building, eventually become "disillusioned with political liberalism," and, finally, by the end of college, returned to his roots.[28] In his own retelling, "I had come full circle . . . applying my tradition in a new way to new realities."[29] After graduation, Wallis closed the circle of his circuitous journey back into the evangelical fold by enrolling as a seminary student at Trinity Evangelical Divinity School, which he admittedly chose out of a desire "to go to a place where the Bible was believed and its message taken seriously."[30]

Wallis's evangelical homecoming might have changed the tenor and nature of his activism, but it by no means quelled his passion for decrying injustices wherever he found them—especially when he found them among his evangelical coreligionists. During seminary, his devotion to social justice combined with his rediscovery of the radical teaching of Jesus gave him both a new mission, calling evangelicals to repentance for their racism, militarism, and indifference to poverty, and a new kind of community in the form of a group of like-minded seminarians who increasingly rallied around him. Staid and conservative Trinity was ill-prepared for the kinds of protest that its small cadre of student activists soon ignited. By pamphleting the campus with a manifesto decrying the hypocrisy of the American church, by drafting other seminary students for antiwar demonstrations, and by generally occasioning fiery debates wherever they went, Wallis and his band of co-conspirators quickly became controversially renowned as Trinity's resident radicals. Wallis's personal reputation was especially dismaying both to the seminary's conservative administration, who once set up a series of "special interviews" to determine whether he would be allowed to remain at the school, and to its board of trustees, who once requested that he appear before them in order to provide his "personal testimony of faith in Jesus Christ." In Wallis's mind, the subtext was perfectly clear: "I think the trustees needed to be convinced that I was really a Christian."[31]

Trinity's resident radicals and its foremost offender were not content with critiquing evangelical devotion to the political status quo solely from within the seminary's walls and soon took their message to a much larger audience. In the summer of 1972, Wallis and several others traveled to Dallas, Texas, for Campus Crusade for Christ's Explo '72 conference toting signs that read "Stop the war in Jesus' name" and "Choose this day—make disciples or make bombs, love your enemies or kill your enemies." Despite initial interventions by event officials who explained that the group's literature was "not in harmony with the purposes of Explo," Wallis and his fellow dissenters were able to successfully distribute their "Christian peacemaking" materials. They also managed to convey their message via a public demonstration at one of the conference's most prominent events. During the Explo Flag Day celebration, held one evening at the Cotton Bowl, Wallis and his friends gathered in a far corner at the top of the stadium where they unrolled banners reading "Cross or Flag" and "Christ or Country." When the event's speaker requested "a moment of silence to remember our boys in Vietnam," the small group began chanting "Stop the War! Stop the War!" The reaction, in Wallis's telling, was swift: "soon a hundred thousand faces turned and looked up at our banners. The largest billow of 'boos' I have ever heard came rushing back at us. The noise was frightening, and I was scared that we might be attacked. Fifty police rushed up and surrounded us. One of them asked, 'Who's in charge here?' Peter Ediger, a Mennonite pastor, answered, 'The Holy Spirit.'"[32]

The protest made the front page of the next day's edition of the *Dallas Morning News*. "War vs. Peace at Explo '72" explained that "the Christian militants of the Prince of Peace and the might of the military were both in evidence last night in the Cotton Bowl," which might have indeed been the case.[33] But between militants for peace and military boosters, only one side was represented en masse. The young evangelicals in attendance at Explo that year were enthusiastically supportive of the event's most patriotic elements, they gave the South Vietnam banner a standing ovation during a parade of international flags, and they were overwhelmingly conservative in their political preferences. The crowd reportedly favored Nixon, for instance, by a margin of more than five to one.[34] As "evangelical Christians who believe that faithfulness to Christ calls us to abandon all carnal warfare," with the message that "the evangelical church's silent complicity with the immoral American involvement in Indochina is a tragic example of misplaced allegiance," in retrospect, Wallis's "militants of the Prince of Peace" had their work more than cut out for them.[35]

But Wallis and the small group of evangelical radicals—who eventually began describing themselves as the People's Christian Coalition—were undeterred. In fact, in addition to protesting at Explo, the disaffected seminarians had already gone public with their message in an even more concrete way. In the spring of 1971, they had moved in together and started laying the groundwork for a magazine that could get their ideas out into the broader evangelical world. That summer, the group put together the inaugural issue of a "sixteen-page tabloid" with a title, *Post-American*, chosen to reflect their efforts "to put forward a Christian faith that broke free of the prevailing American civil religion."[36] With a few hundred dollars of their personal money, a typesetter rented from a local underground newspaper, the help of a nearby printing shop that specialized in countercultural fare like the *Black Panther*, and without so much as a mailing list of potential subscribers, the People's Christian Coalition printed thirty thousand copies of the first edition of the *Post-American*. With a picture of Jesus draped in the American flag above a caption reading "and they crucified Him" on the cover, volume 1, issue 1 pulled no punches. "The message," Wallis later reflected, "was clear. Jesus was being crucified again by American Christianity."[37]

The first issue went on to describe the team behind the magazine as a "chief-less movement from two tribes." First there were the student radicals who rejected the institutional church in favor of identification instead with Jesus of Nazareth as "an ally, a liberator, a Lord."[38] The second group included Christians who had discovered that the New Testament demanded a lifestyle of radical discipleship at odds with the values of the American church. As a grassroots coalition of "radical Christians," Wallis explained, "we seek to recover the earliest doctrines of Christianity, its historical basis, its radical ethical spirit, and its revolutionary consciousness," noting that "we dedicate ourselves to no ideology, government, or system, but to active obedience to our Lord and His Kingdom, and to sacrificial service to the people for whom he died."[39]

Suspecting that somewhere out among the conservative evangelical heartland there was an audience hungry for precisely this kind of religiously pious and politically radical message, the *Post-American*'s editors took their newly printed first issue on the road. Wallis and the team distributed their provocative tabloid throughout the Chicago area, canvassing the region's seminaries and evangelical colleges in the hopes of finding an audience in disaffected students like themselves. Selling copies for twenty-five cents or sometimes simply giving them away, in the ensuing months, the *Post-American* secured its first two hundred or so paid subscriptions at the introductory rate of "two dollars or whatever you can afford" for the first year. Within two years, the periodical had no less than twelve hundred subscribers.[40]

A Burgeoning Alternative Movement

Under the influence of a small group of self-confessedly evangelical but politically progressive leaders like Wallis and Sider, and with the help of a modest but growing level of interest in progressive evangelical periodicals like *The Other Side* and the *Post-American*, by the early 1970s a burgeoning left-wing evangelical movement was beginning to take shape. From the outset, movement leaders necessarily framed their position as an alternative to the evangelical political status quo. Although the official organizational debut of the Religious Right was still several years away, much of the evangelical world had been reflexively politically conservative for decades—a fact with which progressive evangelicals were well acquainted—and some of the era's most influential evangelical figures were developing increasingly close associations with Republican politicians at the upper echelons of American political power.

By the advent of the 1970s, in fact, the single most famous evangelical figure of the twentieth century, Billy Graham, was already wielding his unsurpassed influence to drum up as much evangelical support for his close friend Richard Nixon as possible. Despite later insistences that his ministry was apolitical, Graham was all too willing to work closely with the Nixon administration. Among other duties, Graham had already been involved with helping plan the era's unprecedented White House worship services, and in the lead-up to Nixon's reelection campaign, he was more than happy to play a crucial and ongoing role as connector and facilitator of meetings between the president and other influential evangelical figures. In 1971, for instance, he coordinated a meeting between Nixon and a group of evangelical leaders including W. A. Criswell and Harold Lindsell, who at the time was the editor of *Christianity Today*. Graham also later organized a meeting between Henry Kissinger and a few dozen of Graham's friends and associates—including men like Oral Roberts, whom Graham personally encouraged Nixon to develop further contact with.[41]

The following year, as the electioneering of 1972 intensified, Graham began meeting regularly with White House aide H. R. Haldeman to discuss strategies for locking up the evangelical vote. He encouraged Nixon's team to build a connection with Campus Crusade for Christ director Bill Bright, for one example, in the hopes that the president might make an appearance at the organization's Explo '72 event—the same event that Jim Wallis and friends protested.[42] Though Bright's team ultimately declined to invite Nixon to the conference, the organizers nonetheless played a telegram that the president sent to the more than eighty thousand evangelical young people gathered in Dallas that June. During the very same week as the Watergate break-in, the Explo attendees thus heard the president remind them of the need for a "deep and abiding commitment to spiritual values," as well as the fact that "the way to change the world for the better is to change ourselves for the better," which closely echoed one of Graham's favorite refrains.[43]

For his part, Graham spent the rest of the election season offering Nixon as much help and encouragement as he could—from providing the president's team the names of influential evangelical youth leaders and coordinating further discussions with evangelical figures, to sending Nixon news clippings emphasizing the importance of the "emerging evangelical strength in the country" and letters assuring him of "constant prayers on your behalf." In September 1972, Graham took his support for the president a step further by publicly endorsing a candidate for the first time.[44] That October, *Christianity Today* quoted Graham as suggesting that Nixon "will probably go down in history as one of the country's greatest presidents."[45] In the final few weeks before the election, he nonetheless made sure Nixon knew that he was willing to help with "anything you can think of you want me to do."[46] But by providing the president with his enormously important imprimatur, Graham had already done more than his fair share. Due at least in part to his success with wooing the kinds of voters for whom Graham's endorsement meant a great deal, Nixon won the November election in a landslide.[47]

Evangelicals for McGovern

But progressive evangelicals had not given up without a fight. While Graham was busy helping Nixon's team strategize, Ron Sider and a handful of emerging politically progressive evangelical figures had organized and launched Evangelicals for McGovern (EFM) in the hopes of building upon what they believed was a "rising tide of theologically orthodox Christians who are not chained to conservative politics."[48] Suggesting that George McGovern's platform was more closely in line with biblical values than Nixon's, in 1972 EFM made its appeal in a letter that was eventually sent to more than eight thousand evangelical leaders throughout the country. By supporting EFM and its campaign to offer an alternative voice, the organization noted, evangelicals might finally be able to "end the out-dated stereotype that evangelical theology automatically means a politics unconcerned about the poor, minorities, and unnecessary military expenditures."[49]

Despite the organization's uphill battle among the broader evangelical world—the group wound up raising only around six thousand dollars, for instance, and *Christianity Today* would later describe the operation as a "shoestring political organization" with a "man-bites-dog name"—EFM's preferred candidate had a message that nonetheless found strong resonance within certain evangelical spheres.[50] The son of a Methodist preacher, George McGovern had previously considered becoming a minister himself, going so far as enrolling for a year at Garrett Theological Seminary, before eventually deciding to transfer to Northwestern University to pursue a graduate degree in history instead. He nonetheless carried an affinity for "the social application of Christianity"—which he first picked up when he became enthralled with the writings of Walter Rauschenbusch during his undergraduate days at Dakota Wesleyan—throughout his graduate work and beyond.[51]

With regular references to the social teachings of the Bible throughout his 1972 campaign, McGovern offered some evangelicals a clear alternative to the default support for Nixon that they saw all around them. Fuller Seminary ethicist Lewis Smedes, Eastern College sociologist Tony Campolo, and Wheaton College theologian Robert Webber all lent a measure of evangelical credence to EFM's mission by joining the organization's board.[52] *The Other Side* boosted the signal, running articles and editorials ranging from impassioned critiques of evangelicals' uncritical support for the president to point-by-point explanations of why evangelicals could and should vote for McGovern. But one of the clearest evangelical votes of confidence in favor of a different kind of religiously motivated politics came when the South Dakota senator made a visit to "the evangelical Harvard," Wheaton College, shortly before the election.[53]

The fact that progressive evangelicals had been successful in lobbying to bring McGovern to Wheaton to address its student body at an October 11, 1972, chapel service was no small wonder in and of itself. In an article for the *Christian Century* that December, future Fuller president and then professor at Calvin College Richard J. Mouw provided readers some context and insight into the "conservative-evangelical" college climate, explaining how one of the professors during his own undergraduate days had been forced by the administration to remove a Kennedy sign from his home. Given the widespread assumption among contemporary evangelicalism "that any evangelical who did not like the sort of attitude and policy Richard Nixon stood for kept quiet about it," Mouw furthermore intimated that both McGovern's invitation to Wheaton and the fanfare surrounding it—including a breakfast meeting before the event during which the candidate met with some fifty evangelical leaders from organizations like Youth for Christ and InterVarsity—were all the more striking.[54] In an article for his school's student newspaper, Gordon-Conwell professor Stephen Charles Mott echoed Mouw's sentiment, admitting that the McGovern event had prompted him to reflect on his own time at Wheaton, "when Jack Kennedy was not allowed even to rent the college gymnasium for a rally."[55] If measured solely by the reception that McGovern received at Wheaton in 1972, something certainly seemed to have changed since Mott and Mouw's days as evangelical college students. After a speech full of direct and indirect references to the biblical charge to seek justice for the "least of these," the

Wheaton crowd gave McGovern a standing ovation—some pro-Nixon signs and some student booing notwithstanding.[56]

Though McGovern's showing at the polls that year were ultimately abysmal, neither EFM's efforts to rally evangelical support to his cause nor the associated stirrings of a politically progressive evangelical awakening had gone unnoticed. Writing for the *Reformed Journal*, Wheaton philosophy professor Arthur F. Holmes admitted both appreciation for and hesitation about the surprising turn of events. "Evangelicals supporting George McGovern for the presidency have been greeted by other evangelicals with the emphatic invective, 'Evangelicals are *not* for McGovern,'" he began, "as if the Republican party line follows logically from evangelical theology." The South Dakota senator's appeals to the biblical precedents behind his political principles were obviously sincere, Holmes went on to explain, and his willingness and ability to connect political issues to fundamental ethical questions were both refreshing. But even if evangelical support for McGovern was a perfectly reasonable idea, according to Holmes, it had nothing to do with the fundamental evangelicalness of his Wheaton speech. In fact, he continued, "Far from it. One of his dominant themes, the brotherhood of all men under the fatherhood of God, stirs ghosts of the theological past; and his conception of personal redemption remains vague."[57] Sure, the Democratic candidate's appeal might have been an appropriate indictment of the abysmal state of political discourse in general, in other words, but his theology sounded like the social gospel, which should give all good evangelicals pause.

In the same issue of *Reformed Journal*, another influential evangelical philosopher, Nicholas Wolterstorff, rendered a similar judgment about the implications of McGovern's favorability for both evangelical political thought and the broader American scene. For Wolterstorff, both the senator's willingness to openly discuss the concrete ways his personal Christian faith informed his political views and his divergence from the standard practice of politicians who merely referenced God at the conclusion of speeches to underwrite whatever they just said were a welcome breath of fresh air. There were only two major problems. For one thing, though *some* evangelicals were breaking ranks by signaling their support for McGovern's platform, Wolterstorff predicted that *most* evangelicals would vote the other way. "Confronted with the chance to vote for someone who has heard the radical social message of the prophets, they will have voted for cynical, power-hungry, sanctimonious manipulators who promise to do nothing to disturb American values," he noted. The second major problem came down to McGovern's underlying theology. Although he had been raised in a fundamentalist evangelical tradition, Wolterstorff explained, the senator had apparently parted ways with the theology of his youth "because it neglected social structures and concentrated all its attention on the salvation of individual souls." But in so doing, McGovern had thereby embraced the "heretical liberalism of the social gospel" due in part to a reaction against the "heretical escapism of fundamentalism"—a fact that, in Wolterstorff's telling, should give evangelicals serious pause.[58]

In the end, Wolterstorff's predictions about how evangelicals would vote were essentially on target. For his part, Sider later admitted to feeling that EFM had thus largely been a failure.[59] But with its message that, when it came to politics, "Billy Graham does not speak for all of the nation's evangelicals," the organization had at least offered an alternative to the evangelical status quo, signaling that a small but rising tide of progressive political sentiment was beginning to take shape in certain corners of evangelicalism.[60] Sider could see it, and he remained determined to help corral it into something more sustainable and organized. By early 1973, he had already begun circulating letters to other sympathetically progressive evangelical leaders, highlighting the pressing need to develop some sort of national organization that could offer structure and direction for what was clearly a nascent movement of evangelicals concerned with social justice. That spring, Sider began meeting with a small band of coconspirators to lay the groundwork for the kind of organization he had been envisioning.[61] Deciding that the first step toward addressing "the need for strengthening evangelical social concern" required convening as many sympathetic evangelical leaders as possible, the group soon sent out a call inviting participants to a Workshop on Evangelicals and Social Concern, slated for Thanksgiving weekend of 1973.[62]

The Chicago Declaration and Evangelicals for Social Action

When considering whom to include on their list of potentially sympathetic invitees, the Thanksgiving Workshop's planning committee decided to cast a narrow net as broadly as possible. As Sider later explained, the planners specifically chose to include only "those who were 'evangelical'" on the guest list. With the acknowledgment that "definitions are always slippery," in a retrospective essay, Sider referenced a definition previously offered by neo-evangelical pioneer Harold Ockenga in the pages of *Christianity Today* as a particularly useful guiding framework for whom the planning committee had had in mind. "An evangelical is one who believes, on the basis of the Bible, which is the inspired, authoritative Word of God and hence the norm for faith and practice, the basic doctrines of historic Christianity—the deity of Christ, the sinfulness of man, justification by faith alone through Christ's death on the Cross, and regeneration." With this theological rubric in hand, the committee nonetheless aimed for as much intraevangelical diversity as they could muster, inviting younger and older evangelicals, evangelicals from the North and the South, evangelicals from denominations like the Southern Baptist Convention that were not associated with the NAE, as well as evangelical members of mainline churches. They furthermore held out hope that they could "avoid just a token representation" of evangelical women and Black evangelicals.[63]

The planning committee's recruitment efforts proved successful—at least up to a point. When the fifty or so evangelical leaders who accepted the invitation arrived at a YMCA in downtown Chicago on November 23, certain kinds of diversity were better represented than others. With participants ranging from conservative "evangelical elder statesmen" like Carl Henry to a number of more progressive younger evangelicals, generational diversity was certainly on display.[64] But the vast majority of participants were still white and male, and the range of attendees falling at the most conservative end of the evangelical spectrum was drastically limited by some glaring absences. Neither proudly fundamentalist figures like Bob Jones Jr.—who reportedly later explained that "no Fundamentalist would be caught dead in this kind of meeting"—nor evangelicalism's most famous spokesperson, Billy Graham, were in the room.[65] Early on in the weekend's activities, the diversity that *was* represented nonetheless quickly gave the attendees plenty enough disagreement to work through during their short time together.

From the outset, the group had planned to issue a public statement representing a soundly evangelical vision of "biblical social concern," the initial draft of which had already been drawn up in advance.[66] The first version of the document went over like a lead balloon. John Alexander thought it sounded like "leftist propaganda." *Christianity Today* editor Frank Gabelein reportedly thought the first draft was nothing short of heretical.[67] The contingent of evangelical women in attendance were incensed that it said next to nothing about sexism, and the handful of Black evangelicals in the room, a group that included Bentley and Pannell, rejected the first draft outright due to its insufficient treatment of evangelical racism. Mennonite theologian and pacifist John Howard Yoder furthermore bemoaned the fact that "blacks have a paragraph they can redo; women have a word they can redo; but there is nothing at all about war."[68] After a full day of lengthy and heated debates over what the document did and did not say, the group agreed to form a new drafting committee to rework and rewrite the statement in the hopes of reaching some kind of consensus by the end of the weekend. After further debate, and despite a number of ongoing differences on certain issues, the Thanksgiving Workshop ultimately and unanimously approved a significantly revised version of what became known as the Chicago Declaration.[69]

With an opening that signaled the signers' evangelical soundness as clearly as possible—describing themselves as "evangelical Christians committed to the Lord Jesus Christ and the full authority of the Word of God"—the Chicago Declaration took immediate aim at the many ways in which the nation's evangelicals had failed to demonstrate "the love of God to those suffering social abuses," to proclaim "his justice to an unjust American society," and to "defend the social and economic rights of the poor and the oppressed." Taking care to avoid endorsing any specific political party or program, the document attacked economic inequality and US American materialism. "Before God and a billion hungry neighbors," the declaration charged, "we must rethink our values regarding our present standard of living and promote more just acquisition and distribution of the world's resources." Going on to explain that "we proclaim no new gospel, but the gospel of our Lord Jesus Christ, who, through the power of the Holy Spirit, frees people from sin so that they might praise God through works of righteousness," the signers once again anticipated the critiques of those who might impugn their evangelicalness by reiterating the fundamentally orthodox nature of their theological views.[70]

In anticipation of the very real possibility of significant pushback from their conservative evangelical peers, throughout the conference, the planners consistently stressed that no one should feel pressured into signing. In Sider's later telling, one particular story offered a perfect illustration of how much was truly at stake for some of the participants: "One older evangelical leader, who had experienced increasing alienation and isolation in recent years because of his forthright demand for more social concern among evangelicals, felt uncertain. He first affixed and then removed his signature. But after a few minutes of inner anguish, he concluded that he must support the call for greater evangelical social concern, whatever the cost."[71]

In the weeks and months following the declaration's release, commentators and observers from across the religious and secular spectrum took notice. The *Chicago Sun-Times* described the event as a historic U-turn for evangelicals.[72] In his widely syndicated Religion Today column, the Associated Press's George Cornell similarly emphasized the significance of the declaration's origins from among "a broad cross-section of doctrinally conservative evangelicals"—especially given the fact that "the 'evangelicals' traditionally have been averse to applying gospel principles to society's political and economic problems, concentrating instead on personal conversion and individual salvation."[73] Cornell also contrasted the event with the seemingly waning emphasis on social action among liberal Protestants, and he was by no means alone in situating the gathering of evangelicals in opposition to the mainline. In a special correspondence for the *Christian Century*, *Washington Post* writer Marjorie Hyer stressed that the declaration itself would merit little more than a footnote in standard social gospel literature, but its implications were mind-boggling in light of its evangelical authors. "If 40 million evangelicals in this country should start taking seriously all those problems that every religious convention 'resolutionizes' about," Hyer judged, then it "could well change the face of both religion and politics in America."[74]

Judging by the widespread, largely hopeful, and mostly positive reactions that the declaration received from both outside and inside the evangelical world, at least some of the astounding possibilities that Hyer envisioned seemed possible, at least for a while. In addition to favorable coverage in evangelical periodicals including *Christianity Today*, *Eternity*, and the *Reformed Journal*, as well as in a number of denominational magazines, the statement gained an impressive list of institutional endorsements and additional individual signers. Groups ranging from the Social Action Department of the Baptist General Convention of Texas—a state-level denominational body representing nearly two million of the state's Southern Baptists—to the mainline National Council of Churches (NCC) ultimately lent varying kinds of official and unofficial support.[75] The NCC's Division of Church and Society eventually went so far as to issue its own, largely adulatory statement directly responding to the document. Admitting appreciation for "the degree to which [the] statement lessens the distance that is often assumed to separate 'evangelical Christians' from 'ecumenical Christian,'" and a distaste for "the use of such labels as though they were mutually exclusive," the NCC's response expressed a measure of hope that "a new understanding, a new dialogue, and possibly a new reconciliation" between mainliners and evangelicals might soon be possible.[76]

Along with major institutional endorsements, a number of influential evangelical professors, editors, denominational officials, and leaders of parachurch organizations eventually added their names to the original list of around fifty signers. But some high-profile evangelical leaders simply could not get on board. In a September 1974 editorial for Bob Jones University's in-house magazine, *Faith for the Family*, Bob Jones inveighed against the Chicago Declaration, bemoaning its embrace of "the socialist-communist line," lambasting its rejection of "old-fashioned American patriotism," and pillorying its complete disregard for "what the Bible has to say about . . . a woman's true place in society." The individuals responsible for the statement, he suggested, were obviously of a piece with all manner of liberals, fellow travelers, and socialists. Ascribing such views to the so-called New Evangelicalism, Jones stressed that the ideas espoused by the leaders of this group were not a new position at all and in fact were nothing more than "a half-way house between Biblical orthodoxy and apostasy."[77] He wasn't alone in his criticisms either. A number of more moderate evangelical figures similarly found certain aspects of the declaration unacceptable.[78] Although he would later suggest that he could support much of the document's content, Billy Graham, for the most notable instance, ultimately would not join the list of the declaration's cosigners due apparently to its concession that evangelicals had "encouraged men to prideful domination and women to irresponsible passivity," and its subsequent call for both women and men to live instead in "mutual submission" to one another.[79] For Graham, there were certain lines that simply could never be crossed, and any compromise on the idea of God-ordained gender roles apparently was one of them.

Even without Graham's all-too-important official endorsement, the inaugural Thanksgiving Workshop and the resulting Chicago Declaration helped show the outside world that conservative politics were not an inevitable result of evangelical theology. The battle to convince the broader evangelical world to reconsider the equation of the two was always going to be uphill, but in the declaration's wake, the message that evangelicals could and should care about traditionally progressive political questions seemed to be gaining resonance. In the hopes of keeping the momentum alive, and using the declaration as the founding charter, Sider subsequently helped launch a new organization called Evangelicals for Social Action (ESA) primarily as a way to continue planning and hosting annual follow-ups to the original Thanksgiving Workshop. If the following year was any indication, momentum was indeed building: the second meeting of what had then become ESA's annual conference successfully attracted more than twice as many participants as the inaugural workshop.[80]

But like the first meeting, subsequent conferences were wracked by a series of theological and political debates over the nature, rationale, and desired ends of the group's progressive activism. Due in part to such internal disagreements, by the time that ESA was finally institutionalized with a full-time staff and a national headquarters in Philadelphia, the organization had already undergone a perceptible shift in focus and purpose. Rather than serving as a channel for direct evangelical political activism, at the time of its official establishment in 1978, ESA would primarily function instead as a national membership organization and educational think tank.[81]

Growth and Controversy

By the mid-1970s, it was becoming increasingly clear that there really was a subset of evangelicals out there who were hungry for something other than the de facto political conservatism of mainstream evangelical culture. Rallying them behind any given cause or uniting them under any single banner would never be easy, of course. But when it came to the prospects of a sustainable and united alternative evangelical political movement, internal controversies among politically progressive evangelicals would ultimately prove the least of their worries. External obstacles were arguably a far more serious threat, and the outside attacks were unrelenting. Although swift and severe backlash almost always followed closely on the heels of each bit of success and growth, a beleaguered but unbowed evangelical left spent the rest of the decade fighting for space in an evangelical world that regularly told them that they did not belong.

The constant criticism that accompanied the modest growth of *The Other Side* offered a case in point. Though the market for a magazine combining an explicitly evangelical theological orientation with an increasingly liberal political outlook would never rival the demand for the consistently conservative *Christianity Today*, through the middle years of the decade, the pluckily progressive periodical had slowly but surely expanded its reach. Under John Alexander's editorship, *The Other Side* earned a reputation as one of the most politically open forums for evangelicals interested in viewpoints outside the range of acceptably mainstream evangelical options. With articles and entire issues devoted to subjects ranging from evangelical debates over the authority of the Bible to "the homosexuality question," the editors' willingness to push the envelope was regularly rewarded with both high praise from loyal supporters and vehement denunciations from detractors.[82] Angry letters and canceled subscriptions were a given. Some critics charged the magazine with "reverse racism," deriding the "crass hypocrisy" of the "reprehensible racists" who wrote for it. Others accused it of offering liberal humanism disguised behind Christian language. Still others encouraged the editors to move to Russia.[83]

Many of the messages came from the evangelical rank and file, but denunciatory letters with high-profile evangelical names in the signature line occasionally rolled in as well. A 1972 letter from Butler University theologian and neoevangelical kingmaker Gordon H. Clark suggested that the magazine was quite clearly beyond the pale of soundly Christian principles.[84] When the magazine had later dared to even discuss some of the potential problems with the idea of biblical inerrancy, a flurry of criticism from evangelical professors and theologians soon poured in. Along with messages decrying the "unscriptural, compromising, illogical material" and "pseudo-intellectual tripe" espoused by the "young evangelicals" in the pages of *The Other Side* came dire warnings from influential evangelical thinkers about the dangers of abandoning inerrancy.[85] Writing all the way from Switzerland in a 1976 letter, and putting the matter as apocalyptically as he was wont to do, the massively influential evangelical thinker Francis Schaeffer warned that any deviation from the idea of a perfectly errorless Bible would drive the current generation of evangelicals straight to Barthian neoorthodoxy, universalism, and eventually death-of-God theology.[86]

The Other Side and its provocative editor nonetheless remained undeterred by such criticism. Alexander in particular spent the better part of the 1970s fending off attacks from fundamentalists and evangelicals who dared to question the magazine's soundly evangelical credentials. By reiterating time and again that the magazine and its staff were unwaveringly committed to biblical authority, and by successfully riding the small but rising wave of disaffection with the narrowly conservative political limits of the era's evangelical mainstream, the progressive periodical was furthermore able to attract, retain, and slowly grow its religiously conservative readership. Bypassing the three-thousand-subscriber mark in 1975 and the seven-thousand-subscriber milestone by 1978, as the decade wore on, *The Other Side* became one of the foremost forums for anyone interested in ideas that challenged the evangelical status quo on issues ranging from race and sexuality to poverty and war.[87]

Even though Alexander and the allegedly "socialist sheet" that he helped publish caused plenty of stir, they were neither the only nor the most controversial group in the world of 1970s evangelicalism.[88] That title unquestionably belonged to Jim Wallis and the post-Americans.

Sojourners

In addition to publishing the *Post-American*, in the early 1970s, the community of disaffected seminarians behind the magazine had also simultaneously been busy trying to sustain an experiment in communal living. In the fall of 1972, the small but growing group had ultimately decided to move from the house they shared in the suburbs into two adjacent apartments in a low-income neighborhood on Chicago's North Side. The community's exploration of "new ways of being the church" eventually included a period of fragmentation and division, with a number of original members calling it quits.[89] But a small core group of the radical post-Americans had stayed together, and some new community-seekers had joined along the way. All the while, the group kept churning out issues of their increasingly popular progressive periodical, which soon gained a sizeable team of important supporters and allies both among the evangelical establishment and on the national political stage.[90]

During his student days at Trinity, for instance, Wallis had already gained the support of one of the generation's most important evangelical theologians, Clark Pinnock, and in the early years of the magazine, a number of in-fluential evangelical thinkers—including David Moberg, Richard Mouw, and Robert Webber—had come aboard as contributing editors.[91] The first issue of the *Post-American* furthermore had made an instant impression on Oregon senator Mark Hatfield, a liberal antiwar Republican and self-identified evan-gelical. After reading the magazine and coming to the startling realization that he was *not* in fact the only evangelical against the war, Hatfield had im-mediately started making phone calls, desperately trying to reach someone connected to the publication to offer his encouragement and support.[92]

In 1975, Wallis and his small but dedicated group of post-Americans de-cided to leave the rapidly gentrifying North Side of Chicago for a new start in Washington, DC. That fall, the troupe of "eighteen adults, two babies, a puppy, and a cat" moved into a side-by-side pair of dilapidated houses in DC's Columbia Heights neighborhood. Soon after arriving in their new city, the post-Americans chose a new name, "sojourners," to reflect their commitment to living "as aliens who are citizens of another kingdom, fully present in the world but committed to a different order."[93] The following year, the formerly post-American evangelical radicals now known as so-journers changed the name of their signature periodical, officially adopting the *Sojourners* title that thenceforth became its calling card. Within a few short years of moving to the nation's capital, the sojourners community quickly captured the attention of both the secular press and the evangelical world with their progressive advocacy and activism. By 1977, the group had already been involved in more than forty nonviolent protests in and around the DC area, including demonstrations against everything from gentrifica-tion and real-estate developers to nuclear weapons.[94] *Sojourners'* popularity and reach grew apace: the progressive evangelical periodical jumped from around five thousand subscribers in 1976 to almost twenty-five thousand by the end of 1977.[95]

Over the course of the 1970s, the post-Americans-turned-sojourners be-came far and away the most well known of the various groups and organiza-tions associated with the era's small but growing tide of evangelical political dissent. By simultaneously developing a reputation for consistently falling at the leftmost end of the progressive evangelical spectrum, they also be-came the most controversial.[96] Though the broader sojourners community received a fair deal of attention, the lion's share of the considerable backlash that consistently came their way was reserved for the group's radical magazine and its dynamic editor. Beginning with their earliest appearance on the scene, Wallis and his closest coconspirators had rapidly inspired a coterie of consistent critics who proved ready and willing to charge them with everything but murder and to label them anything but evangelical. Their early antiwar activism had earned the group plenty of scorn to be sure. But as the decade wore on, the fiercest and most recurrent accusations made against both Wallis and *Sojourners* magazine came as a result of the *economic* views articulated in the pages of the periodical and in its editor's books. If their antiwar views had called their evangelical credentials into question—and it had absolutely done that—the group's trenchant criticisms of capitalism had removed any and all doubts.

As was so often the case, there were certain lines that faithful evangelicals simply could not cross. Considerations of alternative economic arrangements were one such line. In the minds of many of the era's evangelical leaders, socialism and communism and Marxism were not just unevangelical and anti-Christian, they were interchangeably evil species of godlessness and atheism. The fact that anticapitalism was also anti-American was perhaps worst of all. Emerging against the backdrop of a neoevangelical resurgence in which anticommunism had long gone hand in glove with the movement's goals of returning the country to its halcyon state as the pinnacle of Western civilization, the economic analyses of progressive evangelical thinkers sounded positively satanic to many of the most influential and conservative evangelical figureheads.

For his part, Wallis consistently tried to fend off such accusations. As early as 1974, he had taken to the pages of *Christianity Today* to respond to charges levied by one of twentieth-century evangelicalism's most respected elder statesmen, Carl Henry, that radical young evangelicals like Wallis were developing Marxist sympathies.[97] Such accusations, Wallis countered, completely overlooked the fact that many young, politically radical evangelical thinkers were actually offering sophisticated critiques of Marxism—especially its problematic eschatology and anthropology—from a soundly Christian point of view. In his telling, Henry had apparently missed the radical insistence on the part of groups like sojourners "that a Christian's basic allegiance be to the kingdom of God and that all ideologies, systems, and governments stand under the judgment of Jesus Christ and his kingdom."[98]

Despite Wallis's protestations to the contrary, as the decade wore on, accusations that *Sojourners* was promoting Marxism (or socialism or communism) only increased. Along with the usual critics, some previously sympathetic observers eventually began joining the fray as well.[99] Although his 1974 book *The Young Evangelicals* had treated the emergence of a new generation of politically progressive but theologically orthodox evangelicals as a salutary development, within a few short years, Richard Quebedeaux became far less convinced that young evangelical radicals like Wallis were heading in a good direction.[100] He said as much in a 1978 book, *The Worldly Evangelicals*, which represented an about-face from his previous assessment. Along with a handful of other radical evangelical communities—like the one associated with *The Other Side*—Quebedeaux could now see that Wallis and the sojourners community were "gradually moving toward an espousal of some form of Christian socialism, tinged with Marxism." More so than any other progressive evangelical outfit, in his judgment, *Sojourners* had quite clearly become far and away the most comfortable with "using New Left and Marxist categories (including arguments raised by liberation theology) as part of its critique" of the dominant forms of US American Christianity. Though he had previously judged that radical evangelicals like Wallis could simultaneously embrace progressive politics while remaining "genuinely faithful to the Gospel," with *The Worldly Evangelicals*, Quebedeaux made it clear that he was no longer sure.[101]

Quebedeaux was by no means alone in his impression that *Sojourners'* dangerous leftward march outflanked the rest of the progressive evangelical spectrum. On the whole, Wallis's group ultimately caught more flak from conservative evangelical leaders than anyone else. But when it came to igniting fiery debates in the evangelical world of the late 1970s, Ron Sider wound up giving even the radical post-Americans a run for their money.

Rich Christians in an Age of Hunger

Sider's shot across the bow began with an early 1970s article for InterVarsity Christian Fellowship's *His* magazine in which he wrestled with what precisely Christians ought to do about world poverty. At the time, Sider had proposed a "graduated tithe": the richer the Christian, the schema went, the greater the percentage of income that should be voluntarily donated. When

InterVarsity Press later approached him about the possibility of publishing a more in-depth exploration of the article's themes, Sider set to work on a manuscript that he initially thought would receive little attention. Despite its titular indictment of many readers, when the resulting book was finally published in 1977 as *Rich Christians in an Age of Hunger*, its impact rapidly surpassed the modest expectations of its author.[102]

Sider's argument was straightforward. In light of the abject suffering of the nearly one billion people around the world living in or near absolute poverty, wealthy US American Christians living in "comfortable clubs of conformity" with a society that worshiped its standard of living above all else were thereby sinning against their needy neighbors and thus desperately needed to repent. In three stepwise sections, Sider advanced his controversial thesis that the utter discrepancy between the complacently affluent lives of American Christians and the sickness, starvation, and death confronting so many of the world's poorest people was a profound violation of the will of God. Part 1 emphasized the increasingly unequal distribution of the world's resources. Part 3 offered readers examples of various individual and structural changes—from adopting simpler lifestyles to advocating for the kind of public policy measures that "enable everyone to earn a just living"—that could begin addressing the problem.[103]

But the axis on which the entire argument turned came with the second section's articulation of "a biblical perspective on the poor and possessions." In light of the fact that there were millions of relatively affluent Christians out there who would let nothing stop them from fulfilling what they believed were the clear commands of God, Sider explicitly emphasized the biblical basis of his thesis as the most important piece of the puzzle. The Bible, Sider explained, neither romanticized poverty nor suggested that prosperity was inherently evil. But Scripture was nonetheless abundantly clear both that God was on the side of the poor and that the rich were in constant danger of all manner of sins. Fortunately, he continued, the Bible included a helpful metric for determining how God would judge the wealthy. "The crucial test," he noted, "is whether the prosperous are obeying God's command to bring justice to the oppressed. If they are not, they are living in damnable disobedience to God." For Sider, the implication of the biblical perspective on poverty and possessions was irrefutably clear: "The righteous person distributes his riches freely to the poor."[104]

Directly targeting the argument at evangelicals, Sider found his mark. Early reactions and initial responses were resoundingly positive. Reviewers praised the book as both courageous and disquieting while simultaneously cheering its author's deep and obvious commitment to the evangelical cause. One particularly ringing endorsement from a British supporter favorably compared *Rich Christians* to Martin Luther's ninety-five theses. Much to Sider's own surprise, the book did almost unbelievably well to boot. Over the course of its eventual five editions and translations into eight languages, *Rich Christians* ultimately went on to sell as many as four hundred thousand copies, quickly turning its Canadian Anabaptist author into one of the most talked about figures in the US evangelical world. [105]

Book sales and glowing reviews notwithstanding, many evangelical thinkers found Sider's ideas mistaken at best and heretical at worst. A 1977 *Christianity Today* article gave *Rich Christians* a measured but direct dressing down and chided its author for his economic naivete, for one early example, but that was just the beginning. [106] Within a few short years, the critiques of the book would escalate into a full-fledged backlash with a number of conservative evangelical figures waging an all-out and enduring crusade to undermine and refute Sider's views at every turn. Whether in spite or because of the growing controversy around it, *Rich Christians* became only more influential as time went on, however. Regular charges that its author was a socialist or a Marxist or a "stateist"—and thus obviously un-Christian— were unable to prevent the book from becoming a perennially popular and lastingly influential text within certain corners of the late twentieth-century evangelical world. Many years later, even *Christianity Today* would ultimately wind up featuring Sider's manifesto on multiple retrospective best-of lists—including a spot on *Christianity Today*'s top one hundred religious books of the twentieth century, as well as the seventh-place slot on the magazine's ranking of the fifty most influential books that shaped post-World War II US American evangelicals. [107]

The Peak

With a stable of increasingly popular leaders, organizations, and publications, by the dawn of the 1980s, the still small but nonetheless significant cadre of progressive evangelicals eventually known as the evangelical left had gained a solid foothold in the US American evangelical world. Although much of evangelicalism retained the default political conservatism that figures like Sider, Wallis, and Alexander had hoped to change, at the time, evangelical identity had not yet become as inextricably linked with contemporary Republicanism as it eventually would. They were by no means in the majority, but a sustainable alternative movement of theologically conservative evangelicals with progressive political views looked like a real possibility for much longer than many outsiders and evangelical insiders often remember.

In retrospect, the dream lasted through at least the middle years of the 1980s. Ever the underdog in a generally conservative twentieth-century evangelical culture, by the early part of the decade, progressive evangelicals were increasingly being forced to play the role of David to the Goliath of an ascendant Religious Right. In an era representing both the heyday and twilight of the evangelical left as a movement, they rose to the challenge. Directly combating the evangelical forces of the new Christian Right and explicitly countering their unwavering support for Ronald Reagan and his policies, for a while, organizations like Sojourners—which undeniably became the movement's most influential torchbearer—successfully inspired serious and ongoing debate over evangelical political engagement. Due in no small part to the influence of figures like Wallis and Sider, whether evangelicals could or should critique American imperialism and the inequalities and injustices of global capitalism without thereby becoming godless communists, for instance, remained an open question for several years. But by forcing such debates, progressive evangelicals ultimately won more enemies than friends. The more influence they gained, the more vicious and vocal their persistent critics became. Along with the movement's peak came a massive backlash that had been accelerating all along.

The clearest example of the ongoing persistence of a viable evangelical left came in the form of an astoundingly successful movement to disrupt, interrupt, and stop Reagan's interventionist military tactics in Central America. With the mid-1980s campaign resisting Reagan's foreign policy, the evangelical left arguably also reached its apex as a movement.[108] From that point forward, whatever influence progressive evangelicals once had was increasingly decimated by a totalizing turn in US evangelicalism toward hard-right politics.

The Witness for Peace and Pledge of Resistance

After decades of direct and indirect US American interventions aimed at controlling the region, the 1970s had witnessed a tide of insurgent revolutions that challenged the United States' long-standing domination of Central America. On the heels of a decade of waning confidence in America's global hegemony, during the early 1980s, President Reagan began insisting that the revolutionary instability of the region posed an imminent threat to the United States. Believing that the only thing standing in the way of ending the spread of global communism was US American reluctance to act decisively in the third world, the president furthermore concluded that swift military intervention was the only viable option. In Nicaragua specifically, over the course of the decade, the Reagan administration would go on to funnel more than one billion dollars' worth of aid—in the form of funds, weapons, and various kinds of logistical and technological equipment and support—to the Contras' counterrevolutionary forces in their struggle against the leftist Sandinista government.[109]

On the home front, evangelical leaders associated with the Religious Right stood behind Reagan and his interventionist campaigns. But progressive evangelicals were unconvinced. Consistently critical of the injustices and human rights violations perpetrated in the name of US American interventionism, a number of the evangelical left's prominent leaders got involved like never before after visiting Nicaragua with the Evangelical Committee for Aid and Development (CEPAD), the country's largest nongovernmental relief agency.[110]

During the early 1980s, CEPAD president Gustavo Parajón led representatives of evangelical groups ranging from ESA and Sojourners to InterVarsity and the NAE on tours of the country. Taking the groups to regions that had been decimated by the Contras and sections that had been revitalized by the Sandinistas, Parajón explained to his US American evangelical visitors that Nicaraguan evangelicals were far better off under the Sandinista government and that they were in fact experiencing an era of unbridled religious freedom. Upon returning to the United States, evangelical outlets including *Sojourners* and *Christianity Today* transmitted the news that Reagan's policies were having disastrous effects and that evangelicalism was thriving under the Sandinistas to their evangelical audiences.[111]

In response to their experiences in Nicaragua, for their part, progressive evangelical leaders soon launched a direct-action campaign to do something about their discovery. Spearheaded by Jim Wallis and Joyce Hollyday, and in cooperation with CEPAD and a number of Nicaraguan religious and political leaders, by 1983, Sojourners had taken the lead in developing a plan to forestall Contra attacks on Nicaraguan towns by strategically situating US evangelical volunteers in communities under assault. With an advisory committee that included Ron Sider, the Sojourners-helmed Witness for Peace campaign quickly captured national attention in December 1983 when NBC's *Today* show provided live coverage of one of the earliest interventions. News of Witness for Peace and its "shield of love" spread like wildfire. As historian David Swartz recounts:

> The direct action quickly expanded to dozens of towns, often at the request of Nicaraguan evangelicals disturbed by the patrols of Contra forces on the northern mountains near the Honduran border. Volunteers, who attended a one-week training program on nonviolent reactions to mortar attacks, kidnappings, and rapes from Contra insurgents, flooded Sojourners' Washington office with offers to pay their own travel expenses to the Nicaragua-Honduran border. By the early months of 1984, Witness for Peace was maintaining a constant presence in Nicaragua with four rotating teams. In the first six months of 1984, 260 Americans traveled to Nicaragua in 13 delegations.[112]

In addition to the Witness for Peace campaign, CEPAD's connections with the evangelical left led to yet another major operation aimed at deterring Reagan's interventionist dealings in the region. Following the US American invasion of Grenada in late 1983, Sojourners responded to Parajón's pleas for help by launching the Pledge of Resistance. Drafted by Jim Wallis and Jim Rice, the pledge threatened a direct-action campaign that would send countless North American Christians to form a nonviolent barrier blocking the path of any US forces attempting to invade the country. With more than forty thousand signatures affixed, as Swartz goes on to explain, Sojourners delivered the pledge "to every member of Congress, the Departments of State and Defense, the CIA, and the White House." Soon enough the nation witnessed the true extent of the progressive evangelical organizers' willingness to follow through. In the wake of the Reagan administration's decision to enact a full trade embargo on the country and Congress's decision to extend millions more aid dollars to the Contras, Swartz points out, "Pledge signers demonstrated in 200 cities across 42 states. Police arrested more than 1,200 activists for civil disobedience. As Congress debated eight more Contra aid bills in 1986, tens of thousands of Pledge activists occupied congressional offices for days, blocked gates at military bases, staged funeral processions and 'die-ins,' disrupted traffic in major cities, and rented airplanes that carried 'U.S. Out of Nicaragua Now!' banners over sporting events. By mid-1986 organizers had gathered 80,000 signatures."[113]

Many of the organizers behind the Pledge of Resistance had initially expected that the campaign would focus mainly on the most pressing short-term goal of preventing a Nicaraguan invasion, imagining that it would thus last no more than a few months. But the movement ultimately wound up lasting through the end of the decade, encompassing dozens of individual campaigns, and involving more than one hundred thousand protesters—more than ten thousand of whom were arrested for acts of civil disobedience. As one part of a broader Central America Peace Movement, in other words, the Witness for Peace and Pledge of Resistance proved almost impossibly successful in mobilizing widespread opposition to the Reagan administration's interventionist campaign.[114] Over time, the movement increasingly attracted a primary constituency from beyond the evangelical world. "Within a few years," Swartz notes, for example, "most of the ground troops were being supplied by mainline participants, Catholics, peace denominations, and nonreligious sources."[115] But the fact nonetheless remains: without the crucial support and leadership provided by an oft-forgotten group of progressive evangelical activists, the movement might never have even gotten off the ground.

Whither the Evangelical Left?

In light of the movement's surprising successes during the 1970s and 1980s, the question becomes this: whatever happened to the evangelical left? The most straightforward explanation for why left-leaning evangelical politics became increasingly inconceivable can be found in the countless sociological, political, and theological accounts of the historical rise of the evangelical forces of the Christian Right.

What happened to the evangelical left?

In short, the Religious Right happened.

Just as the message that traditionally conservative evangelical theology need not yield contemporary Republican politics seemed to be gaining some traction, a group of enterprising evangelical figures began organizing their own political movement based on precisely the opposite conclusion. Whether it was their genius political maneuvering, successful fundraising, media savvy, or simply an intuitive grasp for the kinds of issues that could rally millions of generally conservative Christians to their cause that ultimately did the trick, the architects of the Christian Right were effectively able to summon a unified voting bloc from among the nation's disparately evangelical citizens. In so doing, they also became late twentieth-century evangelicalism's unofficial spokespeople and consistently conveyed the message that to be an evangelical was to be a theologically and politically conservative (white) Christian.

Along the way, conservative evangelical leaders successfully catechized countless millions of rank-and-file evangelicals into a Manichean worldview that pitted a "moral majority" of conservative Christian citizens concerned with preserving the God-fearing, freedom-loving, capitalism-supporting, traditional "family values" of the US American city on a hill against the ever-present onslaught of atheistic communists, socialists, third-world dictators, and their leftist domestic supporters, thereby recruiting massive swaths of the nation's Christians into what they believed was an all-out war between good and evil. At home, the enemy was often known as secular humanism, which influential evangelical thinkers like Francis Schaeffer increasingly blamed for untold societal ills, from abortion-on-demand, moral relativism, and sexual permissiveness, to anti-Christian bias. Abroad, the enemy was a combination of anti-American, communist, Marxist, socialist, atheistic totalitarianisms. Though some mainstream evangelical leaders of the 1980s carefully distanced themselves from some of the most extreme forms of right-wing activism, even the more moderate evangelical figures of the era by and large accepted the underlying assumption that Christian America, including its economic and foreign policies, was an unrivaled force for good and that all manner of liberals, socialists, and countercultural agitators were aiding and abetting a rising tide of anti-American, anticapitalist, anti-Christian forces of evil.[116]

Thanks in large part to the Religious Right's predominance in the popular imagination, a large portion of the countless books about twentieth-century US American evangelicalism that have been published during the past several decades have been narrowly focused on this story. Studies of evangelicalism centered on evangelical politics have furthermore tended toward one or two major interpretive approaches. On the one hand are accounts that view late twentieth-century evangelical partisanship as inevitable and determinative. On the other hand are studies that portray such developments as contingent—for example, by contextualizing the Religious Right within a much broader, longer, and more variegated evangelical tradition.[117] Whether the picture they paint is one of inevitability or contingency, the vast majority of accounts nonetheless share one striking commonality: the evangelical left is included as a mere footnote if at all.

In the past several years a handful of important studies have begun filling this glaring gap in twentieth-century evangelical history, however. In the 2011 book *Countercultural Conservatives*, for instance, Axel R. Schäfer challenges the idea of a politically monolithic evangelicalism, arguing that twentieth-century evangelicals' eventual partisan alignment was neither a foregone conclusion nor as rapid a process as it might have seemed to outside observers. Before the Religious Right successfully helped ensure that evangelicals would remain the most consistently Republican voting bloc in US American politics, Schäfer argues, twentieth-century evangelicalism underwent a long period of fierce debate between various internal constituencies with a fairly diverse range of political views. The left wing of evangelicalism was never huge in his telling, but it posed a legitimate challenge to an increasingly predominant right-wing for far longer than many insiders and outsiders alike remember. Though an ascendant cadre of fiercely politically conservative leaders hellbent on pushing the evangelical establishment firmly to the right ultimately succeeded, Schäfer concludes, they had first to effectively marginalize their "intramovement adversaries" from the evangelical left.[118]

Focusing primarily on Evangelicals for Social Action, Sojourners, and *The Other Side* as the key institutional representatives, Brantley Gasaway's 2014 book *Progressive Evangelicals and the Pursuit of Social Justice* argues that progressive evangelicals successfully built a "coherent yet complex" political movement by effectively positioning themselves as an explicit alternative to both the Religious Right and the secular left. Though massively overshadowed during the 1980s and 1990s by the size and influence of the Religious Right, in Gasaway's telling, the progressive evangelical network inaugurated with the 1973 Chicago Declaration became a strong and sustainable alternative minority movement lasting well into the twenty-first century.[119] David Swartz's 2012 book *Moral Minority: The Evangelical Left in an Age of Conservatism* similarly argues that the evangelical left not only represented a dynamic movement with real momentum, it also *predated* and paved the way for the later emergence of the organized Religious Right. Highlighting the sheer contingency of the eventual alignment between late twentieth-century evangelicalism and contemporary Republicanism, Swartz furthermore concludes that the evangelical left was ultimately defeated by its political homelessness, but that the most crucial source of the movement's failure was internal fragmentation "along gender, racial, and ideological lines." According to Swartz, in other words, "identity politics" hamstrung the movement from the outset.[120]

Schäfer, Gasaway, and Swartz all dutifully acknowledge that one of the challenges the evangelical left always faced came from conservative evangelical leaders who consistently vilified and cast aspersions on the theological credentials of progressive evangelicals like Alexander, Sider, and Wallis. But the countless denunciations aimed at the evangelical left also regularly shared one common feature that even their groundbreaking work tends to mention only in passing: when politically conservative evangelicals impugned and marginalized their politically liberal adversaries, they frequently did so by either implicitly questioning or explicitly challenging the evangelical left's very evangelicalness.[121]

Despite the fact that the more explicit convergence between evangelical political identity and the GOP party line took more time to develop than conventional narratives often suggest, and though the post–World War II neoevangelical movement represented a tenuously configured coalition with a broader range of political views than is usually remembered, from the beginnings of the midcentury evangelical resurgence onward, none of the most powerful and well-known evangelical leaders ever fell much further to the political left than what might generously be described as a right-leaning moderate position. Both in terms of sheer numbers and in access to mainstream evangelicalism's positions of power, in other words, the evangelical left were underdogs from the outset. As the struggle to solidify evangelical political identity progressed, the fact that the evangelical left was so consistently marginalized should come as little surprise. By the time a progressive interevangelical movement was finally getting off the ground in the mid-1970s, the politically conservative leaders of the evangelical establishment were already engaged in the unremitting vilification of left-leaning evangelicals, and part of the reason why is that they had the power to do so.

One of the most effective and simultaneously least discussed ways in which politically conservative evangelicals were able to corner the market on evangelical identity came not so much from the frequency of their denunciations of evangelical liberals—though it surely helped—as it did from the content of their gibes. In the ongoing contest over the political soul of twentieth-century evangelicalism, conservative evangelical leaders' consistent willingness to portray their liberal evangelical opponents as subevangelical or unevangelical demonstrated that there was even more at stake in debates over whether an evangelical could be a Democrat than met the eye. By fighting the war for the direction of evangelical politics on the basis of the very essence of what it meant to be a true evangelical, conservative evangelical leaders were playing a zero-sum game. In the eyes of many establishment evangelical figureheads, progressive evangelicals were not just wrong, they weren't even true evangelicals. Worse still, in the minds of many conservative evangelical leaders, progressive evangelicals weren't even really Christian. Although angry letters and canceled subscriptions had been a constant reality for progressive evangelical institutions like Sojourners and The Other Side from the very beginning, by the 1980s, the steady stream of such attacks became an all-out war.

In some instances, publishing polemical takedowns of liberal evangelicals developed into a cottage industry. Sider's widely influential Rich Christians was a case in point. In light of their Christian reconstructionist framework—a movement inaugurated by R. J. Rushdoony advocating government based directly on Old Testament law—a small group of authors behind the Institute for Christian Economics (ICE) made destroying Sider's arguments their personal mission.[122] Believing that Rich Christians was rife with the most dangerous and damnable kind of heresies imaginable, ICE president and Rushdoony's son-in-law Gary North and ICE economist David Chilton became Sider's most prolific and virulent critics.[123]

In North's view, the fact that no one was stepping up to challenge Sider's views furthermore indicated "just how intellectually bankrupt the supposed defenders of Christian orthodoxy really are." So, when Gordon-Conwell invited him to engage in a public debate with Sider in 1980, he unsurprisingly jumped at the chance to prove once and for all that US American Christians who accepted Sider's disturbing thesis were thereby aiding and abetting "the forces of domestic and international socialism that are threatening the survival of the West." Refusing to view the Gordon-Conwell event as a friendly "sharing of ideas between Christians," North steadfastly maintained that his debate with Sider should be understood as "all-out intellectual and theological warfare." In anticipation of the battle, he furthermore urged Chilton to quickly complete a book-length refutation of Sider that he was already developing. On the night of the debate, North set up a table offering the audience the chance to purchase the first publicly available copies of Chilton's not so subtly titled book *Productive Christians in an Age of Guilt-Manipulators: A Biblical Response to Ronald J. Sider*.[124] In short, the book argued that Sider's "philosophy of Christian socialism" amounted to "legalized theft," that "statism" and socialism were in contradiction to the truly biblical system of free-market capitalism, and that any opposition to the divinely sanctioned system of "biblical free enterprise" would bring God's judgment upon a nation.[125]

In North's judgment, his debate with Sider, Chilton's book, and ICE's raison d'être were all one and the same: to warn evangelicals of the dangerous heresies lurking in popular books like Sider's and to thereby save them from apostasy before it was too late. The matter could not be any simpler, the task any more urgent, or the goal any clearer. For North, the struggle between capitalism and socialism was in fact a struggle "between the kingdom of God and the society of Satan," and the "only way to turn the tide in this nation is to capture the minds of the evangelical community" with a rigorous defense of "the biblical nature of the free market system."[126] Chilton's book, North furthermore suggested, provided just the sort of intellectual firepower necessary for exposing the "threat to orthodox Christianity and the free market" posed by Sider's theology. Lest orthodox Christians despair that Sider's popularity with the "literally thousands of supposedly evangelical pastors who have been compromised by the liberalism of the universities and seminaries they attended" meant the battle was too far gone, North stressed that the struggle by satanic-socialist-Marxist forces to overcome Christianity and capitalism would not prevail. "Satan is going to lose," he told readers, "despite Soviet missiles, Cuban surrogate troops, liberation theology, Ronald Sider, and Inter-Varsity Press. Then we will have that most godly of economic arrangements: *rich Christians in an age of hungry socialists*."[127]

Fringe though ICE's reconstructionist views might have seemed, the idea that progressive evangelicals like Sider were lining up on the wrong side of the divide between good and evil were rife among mainstream evangelical leaders as well. After retiring in 1978 from his longtime role as editor in chief of *Christianity Today*, for instance, Harold Lindsell turned his attention to the more sustained kinds of apologetic arguments that needed book-length treatments. Warning Christians of the creeping influence of socialism in the churches was one such cause that was near and dear to Lindsell's heart. Weeding out false evangelicals was another. In his 1982 book *Free Enterprise: A Judeo-Christian Defense*, he put it plainly. On one side stood the only economic arrangement consonant with the Judeo-Christian tradition: the good, rational, ethical, and democratic free enterprise system. On the other side stood the irrational, statist, totalitarian system known as socialism, which was associated with a host of evils from atheism and moral relativism to slavery. Worse still, Lindsell warned, was the fact that socialism was infiltrating the church. It had already spread through the Roman Catholic Church "under the guise of liberation theology," and it was increasingly seducing Black theologians like Union Theological Seminary's James H. Cone. The fact that socialism was even gaining a hearing among some Christians who considered themselves evangelicals was most disturbing of all, and there were some obvious culprits. "*Sojourners* is a so-called evangelical religious magazine edited by Jim Wallis, who introduced a sort of communal community into the Washington headquarters of the operation," Lindsell reported, and "undermining America's belief in the free enterprise system is precisely what *Sojourners* is all about." The group might have sounded Christian, but unsuspecting evangelicals should not be fooled. Sojourners was a socialist group with a Marxist view of the world and "a thin veneer of Christian faith covering over it," he explained.[128]

The former editor in chief of evangelicalism's flagship magazine was not the only one concerned about the dangerously socialist group either. In addition to books like Lindsell's, the early 1980s witnessed a variety of conservative outlets publishing reports on the true and insidious nature of Sojourners. Commissioned by the right-wing group Accuracy in Media and authored by Joan Harris, *The Sojourners File* purportedly offered clear proof that Wallis's group followed "the Soviet Party line . . . on fifty-three topics ranging from revolution, liberation theology, and the PLO, to Senator Hatfield, the Super Bowl, and the disabled."[129] In a 1983 article about the report, *Conservative Digest* recommended the "massively documented" study to its readers, highlighting "the covert and overt support given these radicals by Senator Mark Hatfield" as particularly egregious and disturbing.[130] The National Christian Action Coalition agreed. Later that same year, during Hatfield's reelection campaign, they issued a press release announcing that "Senator Mark Hatfield Promotes Radical Magazine, according to New Book: Exposé on Sojourners Documents Leftist Ties of Christian Publication," which was distributed along with *The Sojourners File*.[131]

Though Sider continually received his fair share of attacks, by the mid-1980s, it had become increasingly clear that Wallis and his group were public enemy number one for conservative evangelical thinkers. With articles like "First Church of Christ Socialist" in a 1983 issue of *National Review*, and the 1985 book *The Generation That Knew Not Josef: A Critique of Marxism and the Religious Left*, author and regular *Christianity Today* columnist Lloyd Billingsley sounded the alarm that nefarious communist, socialist, Marxist, and Stalinist ideologies—which had long been prevalent in havens ranging from secular enclaves like Hollywood to liberal religious groups like the National Council of Churches—were increasingly detectable in once-safe evangelical spaces. "Increasingly, the evangelical community takes the Sojourners mentality seriously, to the point that it is widely thought that the majority of professors of social ethics in seminaries adhere to a leftist line," he warned.[132]

Though his critiques were a bit more measured than Billingsley's diatribes, over the course of the decade, evangelical philosopher and Reformed Theological Seminary professor Ronald H. Nash devoted even more time and energy to combating the influence of the evangelical left. Beginning with the 1983 volume *Social Justice and the Christian Church*, Nash consistently stressed that free-market capitalism was the most rational and the only morally defensible economic system available, that liberal evangelicals' criticism of capitalism was based on bad economics *and* bad theology, and that Wallis's unrestrained "enthusiasm for Marxism" made him the worst offender of all.[133]

Couched as the work of a disinterested observer describing evangelicals for an audience of nonspecialist outsiders, Nash's 1987 *Evangelicals in America: Who They Are, What They Believe* once again singled out *Sojourners* and its editor as the worst of the worst. In spite of the fundamental wrongness of their political views, Nash granted, there were *some* left-leaning evangelicals whose essential evangelicalness was sound. But there were others like Wallis who were far more questionable. Over the years, as "some careful readers of *Sojourners* found it increasingly difficult to find any evangelical content in the magazine," he explained, most reasonable evangelicals had begun realizing that Wallis's group was obviously beyond the pale.[134]

Nearly ten years later, in a 1996 exposé titled *Why the Left Is Not Right: The Religious Left; Who They Are and What They Believe*, Nash went on to put it as bluntly as possible. There were three major figures who were largely responsible for the persistence of leftist ideas in evangelical circles: Ron Sider, evangelical sociologist Tony Campolo, and the "super-radical of the Evangelical Triumvirate," Jim Wallis. Sider and Campolo had admirably reconsidered some of their previously leftist views on certain issues over the years, and both men seemed willing to affirm the essential tenets of soundly evangelical theology. Wallis was another case altogether. Despite the fact that he had sometimes cast himself as a centrist, Nash warned readers, Wallis had consistently demonstrated that he was nothing more than a "quasi-Marxist" whose "compulsive anti-Americanism" and indefatigable commitment to "far left ideology" had apparently proven far more important to him than his supposedly evangelical theology.[135]

For decades, progressive evangelicals in general and Wallis and Sojourners in particular were subjected to an unrelenting torrent of publications calling them everything but evangelical. But in terms of their influence on the broader public, few such publications could match the sheer effectiveness of a well-timed quote by the Reverend Jerry Falwell.

In 1985, Sojourners sponsored "Peace Pentecost," a multiday event in Washington, DC, organized to promote a "consistent prolife ethic." That May, around thirteen hundred Christians traveled to the nation's capital to join Wallis and his group in declaring "that all life is sacred from the beginning of the life cycle to the end," emphasizing that the lives of "unborn fetuses, death-row inmates, young people in South Africa and Nicaragua, families in Afghanistan suffering from the Soviet invasion, and families in America suffering from poverty" were all worth defending. The event concluded with a day of protests and civil disobedience that resulted in the arrest of more than two hundred of the gathered attendees.[136] That same day, Falwell held a press conference to offer his own take on the matter. The protestors, he explained, were merely "pseudo evangelicals."[137] As a reporter for the *Wall Street Journal* recounted, "For his part, Mr. Falwell questions whether the radicals are evangelical. 'I think these men are theological liberals,' he says, calling themselves evangelicals as a 'cloak of respectability' to appeal to an evangelical audience. 'They're entitled to their point of view,' he says, 'but they shouldn't pretend it's an evangelical point of view.'"[138]

For *his* part, Wallis stressed that Falwell was not his enemy. As *Christianity Today* later reported, Wallis suggested instead that "we are asking Reverend Falwell to join us in promoting a consistent ethic of life for all people which crosses political lines and boundaries." But the Moral Majority leader could not have been less interested in joining forces with someone he obviously viewed as an enemy. "Jim Wallis is to evangelicalism," Falwell told reporters, "what Adolph [*sic*] Hitler was to the Roman Catholic Church."[139]

Nearly twenty years later, when NPR host Tavis Smiley refereed a debate between the two men during a segment on religion and the 2004 presidential election, Falwell employed a different simile to convey essentially the same message. After asking Wallis to admit that he had not voted for George W. Bush, George H. W. Bush, or Ronald Reagan—he indeed had not—Falwell rested his case: Jim Wallis was clearly "about as evangelical as an oak tree," he told the audience.[140]

*

From the founding of bellwether institutions like the NAE and *Christianity Today* forward, the evangelical-moderate position was about as far to the left as the evangelical establishment was willing to allow respectable evangelicals to go. Some tried to push the boundaries anyway, but their work was cut out for them from the start. Despite the best efforts of a persistent progressive minority to open up some space for a liberal evangelical option, by the dawn of the twenty-first century, evangelicalism's most prominent and politically conservative leaders effectively forged a kind of evangelical identity politics. "Evangelical," in other words, ultimately became the name of an aggrieved white political interest group with a self-image as an oppressed conservative minority belied only by its countless millions of members.

When it came to the ability to define evangelical political identity, by the end of the twentieth century, the Religious Right had decisively seized the reins of power. By effectively convincing millions of evangelicals that they were indeed a part of a "moral majority," and by simultaneously positioning themselves as the spokespersons for the conservative Christian masses, politically conservative evangelical leaders became *the* evangelicals. Conservative evangelical figures' willingness to question the evangelical authenticity of their political opponents was a devastatingly effective tool for marginalizing intraevangelical opposition. When voting for a Democrat was enough of a transgression to disqualify someone from claiming the evangelical name, sustaining a progressive alternative movement became next to impossible.

four

The Feminists

Throughout US American history, the majority of the Christians sitting in the pews of the nation's churches have been women, and evangelical churches have been no exception.[1] The majority of the history books about those churches full of women nonetheless have been both full of and written by men. Before turning to the story of the late twentieth-century evangelical feminist movement, then, an overview of how the history of the complex relationship between evangelicalism and women—and evangelicalism and feminism—is most often told will help set the stage.

Even though official ministerial credentialing was often off the table, over the course of the nineteenth century, women who came from traditionally evangelical faith traditions served as leaders of some of the country's most dynamic religious and social movements. From Harriet Beecher Stowe, Phoebe Palmer, Anna Howard Shaw, Sarah and Angelina Grimké, Antoinette Brown, Lottie Moon, Frances Willard, Elizabeth Cady Stanton, and Susan B. Anthony, to Ida B. Wells-Barnett, Mary McLeod Bethune, Mary Church Terrell, and Nannie Helen Burroughs, a host of pathbreaking white and Black Christian women were the primary drivers and leaders of an enormous variety of missionary, benevolence, education, social reform, and politically activist organizations. In ways both direct and indirect, the birth of the modern US American feminist movement can indeed be traced to some of the work done by these Christian women.[2]

Along with shifting traditional gender norms and waning Victorian notions about marriage and family afoot in the broader American culture, however, the turn of the century brought a religious backlash. Women never stopped wielding enormous influence in evangelical circles. But during the first few decades of the twentieth century, what had once been a *predominantly* male group of fundamentalist and evangelical leaders became increasingly *exclusively* male by explicit design. Rejecting earlier generations' idealization of women as the morally superior sex, many of the most prominent fundamentalist and evangelical leaders began stressing that what the churches really needed instead was a strong, masculine defense of the faith against an increasingly feminized (and liberal) culture. Men were intrinsically equipped for such a task. Religious leadership by extension was obviously men's work. As the inherently weaker sex, women were seen as "theologically and morally untrustworthy." Increasingly told that their appropriate place was in the home, Christian women were encouraged to use their inherent gifts for that "valuable form of 'ministry'" for which they were designed: marriage.[3]

Believing that "bobbed hair, bossy wives, and women preachers" were among the surest signs that American society was headed in the wrong direction, in the years leading up to World War II many fundamentalists and evangelicals began linking the idea that God made women to serve in domestic roles with the notion that male headship and female submission were obviously an intrinsic aspect of the God-ordained created order. By the time the post–World War II neoevangelical movement began taking shape, the view that a gendered hierarchy had been built into the very fabric of creation was fast becoming one of the most staunchly defended aspects of true evangelical belief.[4]

When some of the mainline Protestant denominations began ordaining women in the late 1950s, the rising neoevangelical movement's reflexive antifeminism meant that most groups most closely associated with the evangelical name did not follow suit. For most of the rest of the twentieth century, the mainstream evangelical movement unsurprisingly resisted women's leadership at every turn.[5]

*

Chapter 1 showed how the institutionalization of the midcentury neoevangelical movement signaled the end of the possibility that evangelicals could be anything other than theologically conservative. Thenceforth inerrancy was in, and higher biblical criticism and evolution were by and large out. Evangelicals who could agree to those terms were usually safe—unless of course they were Black, which was the story of chapter 2. Chapter 3 returned to a period before voting Republican became an additional qualification required for official evangelicals. This chapter moves to an era when evangelicals began fiercely debating yet another potential credential for admission to the capital-E Evangelical parade: could either self-proclaimed feminists or at least those who believed in the egalitarianism of the sexes in all aspects of church life and leadership still be truly and faithfully evangelical?

The clearest source of the most controversial version of this debate began in the late 1960s with the emergence of a movement of evangelical women who began arguing not merely that evangelicals could be feminists but that evangelicals in fact *should* be feminists. Some of the women associated with the late twentieth-century evangelical feminist movement never explicitly identified as feminists per se. But by arguing that women were fully equal to men and that they should be viewed as such in marriage, the church, and the world, even the nonfeminist-identifying women who were involved in some way with the movement inspired enormous controversy in evangelical circles.

In the end, the question of whether feminists, egalitarians, and so-called complementarians could all be counted as among the real evangelicals was effectively answered with a resounding no. The evangelical feminist movement inspired a massive backlash in the form of a rising "biblical manhood and womanhood" movement that spread throughout late twentieth-century evangelicalism like wildfire. Feminists in particular were increasingly demonized, and egalitarianism in general was often driven to the margins of the evangelical world. By the time the twenty-first century was fully underway, evangelical identity had become closely wedded to a particular worldview that sees a hierarchical gender binary and an accompanying sexual complementarity as fundamental and essential aspects of the entire created order.

But long before complementarianism became the du jour orthodoxy for US American evangelicals, a determined and devoted group of feminist and egalitarian evangelicals spent decades fighting for their right to claim the evangelical name. In their view, interpreting a few biblical passages differently by no means undermined their fundamental theological soundness despite what their opponents often claimed.

Background: Women in Fundamentalism and Neoevangelicalism

As previously discussed, the decision makers and power brokers behind the official establishment of flagship evangelical institutions like the National Association of Evangelicals (NAE) were almost universally white and conservative. They were also all men. At face value, that fact might not be all that surprising. Men had been running Christian institutions for centuries after all. But there were a number of particularities in this case that made it abundantly clear that the building of a twentieth-century, pandenominational kind of evangelical identity was a project that began and ended with evangelical men in mind.

Twentieth-century evangelicalism's flagship magazine was a case in point. Launched with the goal of becoming required reading "for every serious-minded Christian minister in America," and founded under the auspices of a group of men who all would have believed that only men could be ordained ministers, *Christianity Today*'s initial target audience presumably would have been almost universally male.[6] As an organization similarly designed for a constituency comprised of the nation's evangelical leaders and pastors, the NAE also began as an all-male affair. Though there were precisely zero female delegates at any of the NAE's early meetings, at least one woman, Elizabeth Evans, was in the room at the organization's 1942 founding. Despite the fact that she had previously had extensive training for missionary work and years of experience as an itinerant preacher, evangelist, and Christian educator, Evans's role at the inaugural gathering was exclusively clerical. "You see," she later recounted, "NAE was for the men . . . and some of us single girls were there to help out." After all, someone had to take notes. In light of her background and experience, the NAE eventually appointed Evans to its Commission on Education where she also served as secretary. With the 1946 formation of the "women's auxiliary," which "provided fellowship for wives of its membership and the opportunity to work for 'enterprises of the parent organization in which women may effectively engage,'" the NAE called on Evans once more. Once again, she served primarily as the auxiliary's secretary.[7]

As Evans's story highlights, in the early years of the midcentury neoevangelical movement, there was at least one nonmatrimonial role in which women could occasionally participate. By the time that organizations like the NAE were up and running, there was an established legacy of fundamentalist and evangelical schools with programs specifically designed to prepare women for certain teaching and evangelistic roles in a field frequently known as "religious education." In the early decades of the twentieth century, one of evangelicalism's least well-known yet massively influential figures, Henrietta Mears, in fact became a groundbreaking pioneer in the field.[8]

Mears began her educational career teaching an enormously popular girl's Bible study class, which quickly grew from five to five hundred students, at fundamentalist icon William Bell Riley's church in Minnesota. From there, she was hired as director of Christian education at Hollywood Presbyterian Church in southern California, where she oversaw a Sunday school program that similarly grew from a few hundred to several thousand students in a few short years. In the same time frame, she also cofounded Gospel Light Publications, which went on to become an enormously influential source of educational materials in fundamentalist and evangelical circles. At the height of her prolific career, Mears furthermore served as a close personal mentor for some of the nation's most famous and influential evangelical figureheads, including both Campus Crusade for Christ founder Bill Bright and the most famous evangelical of all time, Billy Graham, who called her "one of the greatest Christians I have ever known." As historian Margaret Bendroth notes, Mears's emphasis on mentoring male students like Bright and Graham was intentional. She resolutely believed that the "building of spiritual empires" was a task for men and that women should be helpers who followed their lead.[9]

The evangelical men building a spiritual empire at Fuller Seminary in Mears's own southern California agreed. From the outset, the founding faculty had assumed that any involvement that women might have in the life of the seminary would be as the wives of the male students. During the inaugural semester in the fall of 1947, the faculty furthermore decided to disallow women from taking classes and to discourage auditors. The following year, the school established two organizations that women could join instead: the Fuller Seminary Auxiliary, a fundraising and scholarship organization, and the Philothean Fellowship, a group specifically for the wives of students and faculty. In addition to holding weekly fellowship meetings and high teas, during its first year in existence, the Philothean Fellowship petitioned the seminary to consider letting academically qualified wives begin taking classes for credit. With the caveat that the credit could not be applied toward the bachelor of divinity (BD) degree, the faculty eventually relented.[10]

The following year, the school softened another of its initial restrictions by allowing unmarried women to take classes as "occasional special students."[11] But when one such "special student," Helen Clark, asked for the chance to enroll as a BD student, the faculty faced a conundrum. Though her request was unprecedented, Clark's excellent academic credentials—including an undergraduate degree from Wellesley—made it hard to simply ignore. For a number of the faculty members, the idea was out of the question for one simple reason: granting a BD to a woman would amount to supporting her ordination. With that problem in mind, later that year, the school came up with a seemingly perfect solution. Rather than admitting women to a program that could led to ordination, they would simply design a whole new degree specifically for women. Recognizing the school's "responsibility in the training of exceptionally qualified candidates who are seeking to labor in the broader field of Christian teaching," but "without endorsing the training of women for the Gospel ministry," in the fall of 1950, the Fuller faculty thus voted to establish the bachelor of sacred theology (BTS) degree as an alternative to the BD.[12]

In place of the traditional preaching and pastoral counseling electives, which would be reserved for male BD students, the faculty furthermore decided that female students in the BTS program would take electives in Christian education. That meant that they also needed a new, full-time professor in the field. Acknowledging the fact that the faculty undoubtedly wanted "nothing but men teaching on its staff," Fuller president Harold Ockenga nonetheless noted that it would be "a stroke of genius" on the seminary's part to offer the job to "the greatest Christian education leader in America today," Henrietta Mears. Given that the students in the program would be mostly women, the rest of the faculty by and large were willing "by way of exception" to consider hiring a woman for the position. But Mears's dynamic personality gave some of the men pause. Feeling that Mears might "be difficult to keep within bounds," some of the faculty thus suggested that the school should instead consider hiring Dr. Rebecca Price, an in-demand professor of Christian education at Wheaton College. Though Price's academic credentials were exceptional and extensive, it was her "quiet and submissive" personality that apparently sealed the deal. After a bit of back-

and-forth—before ultimately accepting the offer, Price initially turned them down, at which point they offered the job to Mears, who also turned them down—in the fall of 1952, Rebecca Price joined the Fuller Seminary faculty as the inaugural head of its Department of Christian Education and the school's first female professor.[13]

An Emerging Vanguard

For women interested in some sort of leadership role in the world of mainstream midcentury evangelicalism, this kind of arrangement became the main option. Christian education, in other words, often functioned as a safe way for evangelical organizations to reconcile a long-standing tension in fundamentalist and evangelical circles. According to most midcentury evangelical leaders, women should neither be ordained nor serve in positions of leadership over men. But without women leading classes and Bible studies in churches, Sunday schools, independent Bible colleges, and pretty much anywhere that twentieth-century evangelicals gathered, there would not have been very many classes. By the 1950s, the unofficial evangelical position on the matter was more or less decided by default: women could not preach, but in certain circumstances, they could *teach*. But by the 1960s, some evangelical women (and a few evangelical men) were beginning to wonder whether evangelicalism was needlessly stifling the gifts of the women in its midst.

Letha Dawson Scanzoni

Born in Pittsburgh, Pennsylvania, in 1935, Letha Dawson Scanzoni grew up believing that girls could do anything that boys could. A prodigiously talented trombonist by the time she was in middle school, in 1951 the sixteen-year-old Scanzoni earned admission to the prestigious Eastman School of Music. During her first year at the Rochester, New York, school, she learned more than just music, however. While at Eastman, Scanzoni also started attending local Youth for Christ meetings, began learning what it meant to live a separated life, and soon discovered that there was a place called Moody Bible Institute, which had a sacred music program. Having grown up in a Lutheran church, in her own later telling, this period in her life represented Scanzoni's first involvement with real fundamentalism.[14]

Scanzoni had already begun wrestling with deep questions about how her faith should impact her life prior to her move to Rochester. As a teenager, she had been struck by one of the main characters in Charles M. Sheldon's novel *In His Steps: What Would Jesus Do*, a woman who sang in rescue missions as a way of using her musical talents to serve God. Unable to shake the conviction that she should do the same, during her first year and a half at Eastman, Scanzoni played trombone for numerous religious rallies and church gatherings. Somewhere along the way, she also began developing a different set of skills. In some of the churches where she played, Scanzoni occasionally led adult Sunday school classes as well. In some of those classes in certain churches, some of the members occasionally suggested that she should consider becoming a minister. Other times and in other venues, Scanzoni received a decidedly different message. When she played trombone for a local Billy Graham rally, for instance, she was told that women should not teach classes with men in them. When a local minister later invited her to give her testimony before a trombone performance for an all-male group of prison inmates, Scanzoni dutifully pointed out that this would seem to violate prohibitions against women teaching men. Assuring her that in certain cases it was perfectly all right, the minister clarified. Women could not *teach* or *preach* to men, he told her, but giving a testimony was fine.[15]

After three semesters at Eastman, in 1954 Scanzoni matriculated at Moody Bible Institute's Sacred Music Department. As she later recounted, however, "like so many women following the societal expectations and prescriptions of the 1950s," Scanzoni married young, eventually cutting her degree short to focus on being a wife and mother. But even that didn't slow her down.[16] During the late 1950s, she worked for a time with a rural missionary organization, and in the early 1960s, she continued teaching Sunday school classes, leading Bible studies for college students, and eventually began a career as a prolific freelance writer. All the while, Scanzoni was simultaneously studying, researching, and rethinking what had become the unofficial orthodoxy among evangelicals on the question of biblical teaching about "women's and men's roles in home, church, and society." In Christian organizations that kept telling her things like, "If you have a new idea, let the man think it's his idea," and in evangelical circles where she was constantly reminded that "a woman's role and goal was to get married, have children, and make a lovely home for her family," Scanzoni later explained, she simply could not help but wonder, "Is that all there is in terms of God's will for our lives? What about our gifts, our talents?"[17]

The tipping point came in the form of the November 1963 edition of her favorite evangelical periodical, *Eternity*, which featured a pair of point-counterpoint articles discussing "women in the church." In the first article, Canadian minister H. H. Kent argued that the Bible was rife with precedents of women exercising their considerable gifts for leadership. In the second article, Dallas Theological Seminary professor Charles C. Ryrie stressed that "a woman may not do a man's job in the church any more than a man can do a woman's job in the home." Scanzoni was thrilled by Kent's emphasis on some of the biblical passages that she had long treasured and appalled at Ryrie's bombastic misogyny. After reading the reactions to both articles in the following month's Letters to the Editor section, she immediately sat down to compose one of her own, detailing what she believed were the many biases and inconsistencies in Ryrie's argument. When the letter became far too long, she decided to shelve the draft for the time being, however, filing it in a folder labeled "The Woman Issue" as potential material for a longer-form article later on. By the time Scanzoni was finally ready to revisit the draft, she had already published her first book and finished a second. But neither of those books would cause nearly as much controversy as the finalized version of the article she had been waiting years to write. In mid-1965, Scanzoni submitted a finished draft of her article, "Women's Place, Silence or Service?" to the editors of *Eternity*. With a bit of editorial revision, it first appeared in the magazine's February 1966 issue.[18]

Citing historical examples ranging from Tertullian to Augustine of Christian men demonizing women, highlighting the various textual debates over what the apostle Paul really meant in 1 Corinthians and 1 Timothy, and pointing to the many practical implications that would result if women were truly silenced in churches, Scanzoni's article challenged the magazine's evangelical readership to openly reckon with some of the troubling inconsistencies associated with the idea that women were spiritually inferior to men. Recognizing that many male pastors believed the question was already settled, Scanzoni nonetheless pressed the matter. "If it's permissible to teach children," she queried, "how does one determine at what point a teen-age boy ceases to be a child? May a woman lead youth groups? Serve as Christian education director? . . . And what about writing? Is it all right for a woman to write Bible study materials, yet not permissible to teach them in the local church? . . . In all of this, aren't we overlooking the sovereign distribution of gifts by the Holy Spirit?"[19]

Even though the editors had actually excised some of her potentially most controversial statements, reactions to the article were swift and fierce. "Mrs. Scanzoni's article," one letter to the editor judged, "is a perfect example of why a woman is admonished to be silent in the church."[20]

Whether in spite or because of the controversy the first article inspired, *Eternity* invited Scanzoni to submit another article on "some aspect of 'the woman problem'" the following year. Having already outlined her next book, which was slated to consider the role of women in the home, the church, and the world, Scanzoni was happy to oblige. In mid-1967, she submitted an article titled "Christian Marriage: Patriarchy or Partnership?" to the magazine's editors. That October, she received a response from the editors thanking her for the draft, paying her the fifty dollars they owed her, and asking her to add a section on "male headship" so that the article might "communicate more clearly" with *Eternity*'s readers.[21]

Scanzoni was torn. On the one hand, such an addition might dilute the article's argument that "egalitarian marriage could be biblical," and its suggestion that Christian marriages need not succumb to the inevitable master-slave dynamic associated with the idea of "wifely submission." On the other hand, if she could at least show evangelicals that when the Bible spoke of "the husband's leadership," it was not thereby mandating a "'caste system' with vested privileges for the male sex," then it might be worth including a caveat about instances of "marginal disagreement" in which the husband might serve as "the final court of appeals." Ultimately deciding that the caveat was not too large a price, Scanzoni revised the article accordingly. In May 1968, she finally received word on the status of her revisions when a letter from *Eternity*'s newly hired assistant editor, Nancy Hardesty, arrived in her mailbox. Assuring Scanzoni that her article would run in the July issue, Hardesty explained that "some members of the staff" nonetheless had one additional request: could she send them "a picture of you and your husband" to run along with the article? "I guess to show that he approves of your writing such 'radical' stuff," Hardesty added parenthetically, before closing the letter with a personal admission. "I've just finished editing your article and I'm really impressed by it—and I don't think it's radical or provocative at all. It's just right and true and like it should be," she noted. "But then I'm only a woman!"[22]

Scanzoni obliged. Along with the requested picture, she included a note to *Eternity*'s mysterious new female assistant editor. "It sounds as though your views on this subject of woman's roles, etc. are quite similar to mine. Would love to discuss it with you sometime," she concluded. With the new title "Elevate Marriage to Partnership," the article finally ran in July 1968. But the fact that she "had apparently found a sister Christian feminist," which meant that "the road ahead looked a bit less lonely," was far more important to Scanzoni than the article itself.[23]

Nancy A. Hardesty

Scanzoni's new sister Christian feminist, Nancy A. Hardesty, was born in Lima, Ohio, in 1941. She was raised in the Christian and Missionary Alliance denomination, actively participated in Youth for Christ growing up, and went on to the crown jewel of US American evangelical higher education, Wheaton College. While at Wheaton, Hardesty developed an interest in journalism, eventually serving as editor for the school's newspaper, the *Wheaton Record*. Graduating with a BA in communications in 1963, followed by a master's degree in newspaper journalism from Northwestern, she began working as an editorial associate for the *Christian Century* in 1964. After a little over a year at the mainline magazine, Hardesty was hired as an associate editor for the evangelical *Eternity* in 1966.[24]

By the time she arrived at the evangelical magazine, Hardesty had already experienced an initial awakening of her own feminist consciousness—a development she later attributed to her time working under a demanding female editor at the *Christian Century*—and her next few years at *Eternity* only deepened her growing interest in feminism. Witnessing the evangelical magazine's decision to pay a less qualified male candidate more than his more qualified female counterpart, and hearing the justification that it was "good stewardship" to do so because men had to support families, was particularly bracing for Hardesty's emerging feminist sensibilities. Her contact with Letha Scanzoni was too.[25]

In October 1969, Scanzoni wrote Hardesty once again. Only this time, the correspondence was not as an author to her editor. Scanzoni had been considering a new project, a book about women and their "'place' in the home, society, and church," and had begun wondering whether Hardesty might be interested in working on it together as coauthors. After all, Scanzoni explained, they were both obviously interested in the subject, and working together might ameliorate the inevitable loneliness of the project. What's more, Hardesty was single, Scanzoni was married, and their unique backgrounds, perspectives, and expertise might just be the perfect complement for an evangelical "women's liberation" book.[26]

Hardesty was receptive. Homesick for the Midwest and disappointed with the current direction of her life, she had recently left the East Coast to accept an offer for a job teaching English and writing at the evangelical Trinity College in Deerfield, Illinois. But having previously vowed that she would never teach and that she would also never again work for a Christian organization, Hardesty found her new job situation less than ideal.[27] Frustrated and overwhelmed by work and the ongoing difficulties of being a single, professional, Christian woman, in her reply to Scanzoni she admitted that, for her, the stakes of "the woman question" were not merely theoretical. Excited by the possibility of having at least one project that she cared deeply about, after much hedging, Hardesty closed her reply letter with precisely the answer Scanzoni had been hoping for. "So if you still would like to work together," she wrote, "I would like to try it."[28]

Thus began a prolific, sometimes near-daily correspondence between the two women as they planned, researched, and wrote a manuscript prospectively titled *The Christian Women's Liberation* over the next couple of years. In the process, they quickly developed what became a close and lifelong friendship, which Hardesty once described as a deep "spiritual communion," providing constant encouragement for each other's ongoing vocational and educational endeavors.[29] It soon became clear that their mutual support for one another was going to be invaluable. The book was essentially finished in 1970, but its journey to publication was only just beginning. By the end of that year, Scanzoni and Hardesty began what became an excruciatingly difficult and ultimately yearslong process of searching for a publisher willing to take on what the two women realized was a controversial manuscript.[30]

As it turned out, Scanzoni and Hardesty were not the only evangelicals keeping tabs on feminism. They were by no means alone in feeling the need to develop an appropriately evangelical, soundly biblical response to women's liberation either. The only problem was that the standard evangelical alternative to secular feminism was not nearly as liberating as budding feminists like Scanzoni and Hardesty would have hoped.

While the two women were struggling to get their book published during the early 1970s, for example, *Christianity Today* was regularly printing articles by evangelical authors who stressed that the divinely ordained male-female hierarchy was the only secure basis for a stable marriage and that the leadership of husbands was the only workable solution for lasting marital fulfillment. In a 1970 article, the editors painted a particularly bleak picture of the potentially disastrous effects of feminism and women's liberation. "In the beginning," the editors explained, "Eve bit into forbidden fruit and fell into subjection to Adam." Though their temptation toward "equality with man instead of with God" was not quite as great, the editorial continued, it had become abundantly clear that Eve's contemporary descendants were just as eager to taste their own "forbidden fruit."[31] That same year, Billy Graham offered a similar take on the dangers of women's liberation in an article, "Jesus and the Liberated Woman," for the *Ladies' Home Journal*. Feminist demands for liberation, Graham explained, were merely an indication of what was an underlying spiritual problem. Driven by boredom with the God-ordained purpose and "appointed destiny of real womanhood," contemporary women fighting for equality with men and for the opportunity to venture into the workforce were searching for fulfillment in the wrong place. Women were biologically designed for their role as "wife, mother, homemaker," Graham noted, and they would only ultimately "be happiest, most creative—and freest—when they assume and accept that role."[32] Male evangelical leaders were not the only ones pushing back against the secular women's liberation movement either. Writing for *Christianity Today* in May 1971, Mary Bouma echoed Graham's sentiments. "The truly liberating option for modern mothers lies in a broadened sense of homemaking," she observed.[33]

In the context of early 1970s evangelicalism, Scanzoni and Hardesty thus had their work cut out for them. Fortunately, they were not entirely alone. In addition to the standard antifeminist fare, signs of dissent had begun cropping up in evangelical circles as well. A 1971 *Christianity Today* article by Ruth A. Schmidt called evangelicals to task for treating women like second-class citizens of God's kingdom and indicted churches for their failure to support women's equality.[34] That same month, Hardesty posed similar questions in an *Eternity* article titled, "Women: Second Class Citizens?"[35] The following year, the *Christian Herald* ran a piece, "Women's Liberation and the Bible," offering biblical support for female equality. Its author, Virginia Ramey Mollenkott, first joined forces with Scanzoni shortly thereafter.[36]

Virginia Ramey Mollenkott

Virginia Ramey Mollenkott was born in Philadelphia in 1932 to a deeply religious working-class family who attended services at their storefront Plymouth Brethren church every time the doors were open. Raised by a physically and sexually abusive mother in a family that always prioritized their only son's schooling, Mollenkott was a precociously intellectual child who dreamed of getting the best education she could despite the circumstances. From an early age, she chafed at the idea of a divinely ordained gender hierarchy. Recognizing that women could sometimes take on leadership roles in foreign mission fields, Mollenkott decided that becoming a missionary offered her the best chance at the education she hoped for.[37]

But when her mother later discovered that Mollenkott had become romantically involved with an older woman, shipped her off to a Southern Presbyterian boarding school in Florida as a result, and effectively outed her to the school's administrators in the process, it was by no means the kind of education she wanted. As she later explained, at boarding school, she first learned "that whenever a woman dared to 'do theology,' the result was always heresy." Though they also taught her that her "condition was unchangeable and incurable," the school's administration remained intensely interested in Mollenkott's sexuality and regularly found new ways to shame and punish her for it. After a particularly long period of forcible isolation and false accusations, Mollenkott unsuccessfully attempted suicide. Nightmarish though the entire experience was, she ultimately survived the boarding school thanks in large part to the support of some of the other students.[38]

For college, Mollenkott went to Bob Jones University—because Wheaton was too expensive—and survived *that* experience only because the administrators had no idea about her sexuality. She escaped the pressure of the school's fundamentalist theology and infamously strict rules by diving headfirst into a lifelong love affair with British and American literature. But by her senior year, there were some cultural expectations that Mollenkott had yet to shake. Having once admitted her attraction to women to a professor who told her "that if only [she] would pretend to be heterosexual long enough, eventually heterosexual feelings would emerge," Mollenkott married a man in the desperate hope that it might just work. In addition to a passion for studying literature, she thus also left Bob Jones with a husband—one who believed that it was her divinely decreed obligation to wait on him hand and foot.[39]

Mollenkott went on to complete an MA in English from Temple University in 1955 and a PhD in English from New York University in 1964. Along the way, with the help of her extensive literary training, she simultaneously began reconsidering some of the strictly fundamentalist beliefs that she had been taught. In her own later telling, it all began with the shocking discovery that the book of Genesis included two different creation stories. Realizing that she had devoted far more time and scrutiny to close readings of classic literature than to the word of God, sometime in the early 1960s, Mollenkott began using her considerable interpretive skills to approach the Bible anew. When she did, she was stunned by what she found.[40]

During her doctoral studies at NYU, Mollenkott developed a fascination with the work of John Milton. With the help of the "great Puritan poet and theologian," she began discovering a fresh new world of possibilities for reading the Bible. By immersing herself in Milton's hermeneutics, Mollenkott later recounted, she learned how to "notice linguistic anomalies" in the text, how "to pay attention to the central impact of literary images" as well as "the historical circumstances surrounding the text," how to "interpret analogies only within the context where they originally were presented," and, perhaps most importantly, "how to read the Bible through liberationist lenses." With the help of John Milton, she thus gained a set of tools that she could not have gotten from feminist biblical scholars at the time. "The fact that feminist scholars could offer no *biblical* way for a woman to find freedom," she later explained, "the fact that they *agreed* with the patriarchal interpretations I had learned in my youth—would have drained me of hope. It would not have helped to know that feminist scholars disapproved of the heteropatriarchal meanings they found in the Bible. I was not free to turn away from the text; what it 'really said' was what mattered to me."[41] Upon closer inspection, her discovery that the Bible did not really say that women must obey whatever orders their husbands might give—that such interpretations were merely that: *interpretations*—was nothing short of life-changing.[42]

During the late 1960s, while working as an English professor at William Patterson College, Mollenkott also began giving herself permission to explore the literature coming out of the rising feminist movement. At the time, in her later telling, she found the radical feminist theology of someone like Mary Daly terrifying. But when articles by women like Letha Scanzoni and Nancy Hardesty began appearing in publications like *Christianity Today* and *Eternity*, Mollenkott took notice. In 1972, she was finally ready to make her first public statement in defense of a Christian view of women's equality with an article on "Women's Liberation and the Bible" for the *Christian Herald* magazine. The following year, Mollenkott was invited to lecture on the question "What do women want?" at the conference Evangelical Perspectives on Women's Role and Status. With a presentation titled "Women's Role in Christian Ministry," Letha Scanzoni presented at the same conference, where she and Mollenkott met for the very first time.[43]

*

During the early 1970s women like Scanzoni, Hardesty, and Mollenkott thus began sprinkling a bit of feminist leaven in the overwhelmingly male-dominated evangelical world. Though egalitarian and feminist evangelicals—and even just evangelical women interested in taking on leadership roles—were always going to have their work cut out for them, as the decade wore on, their already-uphill battle became steeper than ever as antifeminist sentiments became an increasingly integral part of late twentieth-century evangelical culture. By the time that egalitarians were becoming regular contributors to a variety of evangelical forums, a decidedly different vision of evangelical womanhood began spreading like wildfire. For many evangelicals in the early to mid-1970s, the ideal woman was not the liberated woman. The *total* woman was.

"A total woman," evangelical author Marabel Morgan explained in her 1973 manifesto, "is not just a good housekeeper; she is a warm, loving homemaker. She is not merely a submissive sex partner; she is a sizzling lover. She is not just a nanny to her children; she is a woman who inspires them to reach out and up." In Morgan's telling, the first essential step to becoming a total woman, with a "husband more in love with you than ever before," was to make sure that one was applying biblical principles to the ordering of one's marriage. "The biblical remedy for marital conflict is stated, 'You wives must submit to your husbands' leadership in the same way you submit to the Lord,'" she explained. For any marriage to work, in other words, it first and foremost needed to begin with the realization that "God planned for woman to be under her husband's rule."[44] The book became a runaway best seller. It sold somewhere near a half million copies in 1974 alone, making it the best-selling nonfiction book in the country, and many more millions in the years to come.[45]

Morgan was by no means alone in her belief that a divinely ordained and biblically mandated sexual hierarchy was a far better alternative to the freedom and equality touted by feminists. She wasn't the only evangelical woman writing about the subject either. As the decade progressed, Elisabeth Elliot, widow of the famous missionary Jim Elliot, became a leading voice of evangelical opposition to all things feminist. With articles like "Why I Oppose the Ordination of Women" in outlets like *Christianity Today*, and with books like *Let Me Be a Woman*, Elliot made it something of a personal mission to remind evangelical women that there were intrinsic differences between masculinity and femininity, that such differences required men "to exercise authority in Church and Home," and that the idea of "mutual submission" was a subversion of God's will. The only way for women to find true fulfillment, Elliot reiterated time and again, was by joyfully accepting that they had been created by God with submission in their very nature. With her vocal endorsement of the divinely mandated and ultimately rewarding nature of sexual hierarchy, throughout the 1970s and beyond, Elliot often became the go-to female voice proffered by male evangelical leaders as proof positive of the manifold blessings of womanly submission.[46]

The Formation of a Movement

In an evangelical culture long dominated by male leaders who believed that only men could be leaders, women like Morgan and Elliot were widely celebrated by men and women alike. But while many evangelicals were increasingly singing the praises of the total women, other evangelical women were growing weary of being treated like second-class citizens. And even though they were *mostly* alone, budding evangelical feminists like Scanzoni, Hardesty, and Mollenkott had begun discovering that they were not *entirely* alone in their discontent with the evangelical status quo. Along with a small group of like-minded colaborers, they had furthermore begun doing something about it.

All We're Meant to Be

The shot across the bow came in 1974. After a long string of unsuccessful bids and failed negotiations with numerous evangelical publishing companies, by 1973 Scanzoni and Hardesty had nearly given up hope that anyone would be willing to publish their "Christian Woman's Liberation" manuscript. Their luck finally changed that year with the welcome news that Word Books was willing to take on the project. At long last, Scanzoni and Hardesty's yearslong efforts to get their book into the hands of the evangelical public was realized in August 1974 when *All We're Meant to Be: A Biblical Approach to Women's Liberation* first hit the shelves. In relatively short order, it became both indispensable reading for egalitarian evangelicals and the founding manifesto of an incipient evangelical feminist movement.[47]

The book's argument was as deceptively simple as it was powerful. Regardless of what the so-called biblical literalists might claim, *All We're Meant to Be* argued, the Bible always required interpretation. When it came specifically to the passages supposedly prohibiting women from having authority over men, apparently mandating wifely submission, and purportedly prescribing sexual hierarchy, Scanzoni and Hardesty pointed out that such views were merely one possible interpretation and, crucially, that there were actually better ways of reading the text. Rather than reading it as *prescribing* female subservience, for example, Genesis should be understood instead as a *descriptive* account of the creation of all humankind in God's own image. When the apostle Paul demanded that women remain silent and keep their heads covered in church, the book argued, such injunctions must be understood in the context of "practical local cultural problems," and not as universally binding mandates. There are "theological and doctrinal" passages in the Bible, Scanzoni and Hardesty stressed, and there are "culturally conditioned" passages. Some passages are descriptive, and others are prescriptive. Careful study of the textual references, the book proposed, made it abundantly clear that, rightly interpreted, the Bible's message to women was nothing short of an affirmation of their full equality.[48]

With its clarion call for evangelicals to reconsider whether the Bible really mandated women's submission, *All We're Meant to Be* made more than a little splash. Emerging in an evangelical culture in the earliest throes of an ongoing backlash against secular feminism, its popularity would never rival that of Morgan's "total woman" manifesto. But if the early reviews were any indication, it nonetheless seemed that the kind of evangelically feminist approach that Scanzoni and Hardesty were articulating was beginning to earn a hearing in some of mainstream evangelicalism's most influential spaces. Though there were some initial detractors, the book was largely well received, earning appreciative reviews in outlets ranging from *Christianity Today* and InterVarsity Christian Fellowship's in-house magazine to the *Journal of the Evangelical Theological Society*. In 1974, it made *Christianity Today*'s year-end list of significant books, it was chosen as *Eternity* magazine's book of the year in 1975, and it soon became unavoidable. For weal or woe, as time marched on, *All We're Meant to Be* was increasingly interpreted as *the* authoritative statement of what an emerging group of evangelical feminists believed.[49]

The Evangelical Women's Caucus (EWC)

The year 1974 was a watershed year for evangelical feminism—and not just because of *All We're Meant to Be*. Nancy Hardesty in particular spent the year providing crucial leadership to a small but growing group of budding feminist evangelicals. Along with several other women in the Chicago area, she had recently begun holding a feminist Bible study group that started publishing a newsletter, *Daughters of Sarah*, in the fall of 1974 as a way of connecting evangelicals who might be interested in feminism. Over the course of the year, Hardesty had also been busy working behind the scenes to ensure that the second annual Thanksgiving Workshop included a robust feminist presence. Her efforts eventually paid off in spades.[50]

For Hardesty, the inaugural 1973 meeting of progressive evangelicals had been disappointing. One of the precious few women in attendance at the first Thanksgiving Workshop, she had had to fight hard for the group to give sexism and women's rights any real consideration as major issues for evangelical social concern. Much to her dismay, some participants of the first year had been almost completely oblivious to the many issues facing women both in society and in "so-called 'Christian' organizations," and the initial version of the "Declaration of Evangelical Social Concern" was a perfect indication.[51] After discovering that the first draft included only one passing word about sexism, Hardesty had been compelled to speak on behalf of "the other half" of evangelicalism by lobbying for the statement to include a more substantial section on women's rights. Though she had not been included on the (all-male) redrafting committee, she had nonetheless written a new statement about men, women, and their relationship that had ultimately made it into the final version of the declaration. Thanks in large part to Hardesty's advocacy, when the Chicago Declaration was finally published, it had included a section reading, "We acknowledge that we have encouraged men to prideful domination and women to irresponsible passivity. So we call both men and women to mutual submission and active discipleship"—which none other than Billy Graham had apparently pointed to as the source of his refusal to sign it.[52]

In the wake of the disappointing 1973 meeting, Hardesty had taken several steps to help avoid a repeat in 1974. When the group that began describing itself as Evangelicals for Social Action (ESA) had subsequently formed a variety of specialized task forces, she had taken on the role of chair for the women's task force. By allowing her to invite as many evangelical women who were interested in challenging the evangelical status quo on questions of sex and gender as possible, her decision to also serve as secretary on the planning committee for the following year's meeting had arguably been even more significant, however.[53] As she later recounted, when the delegates finally arrived for the second annual Thanksgiving Workshop in 1974, and when Hardesty convened the group tasked with addressing sexism, she discovered that "all but one or two of the women I invited became part of it."[54]

Over the course of the second annual conference, the women's task force offered no less than twelve proposals outlining various ways to support women and combat sexism within the evangelical world. One proposal called for a study of sexism in evangelical Sunday school literature, while another called for investigating Christian bookstores for sexist material. One proposal lobbied for equal opportunities for women in evangelical schools, another called for the ESA to educate its own members about the use of sexist language, and still another urged the ESA to endorse the recently reintroduced Equal Rights Amendment (ERA). Another group of proposals called for launching regional conferences that would help build a grassroots movement, developing a directory of evangelical feminists, and using the recently launched *Daughters of Sarah* newsletter to circulate feminist materials, all of which were aimed at sustaining the emerging connections between feminist evangelicals and extending the reach of feminist sentiments into the broader evangelical culture. By the end of the meeting, all of the proposals offered by the women's task force passed successfully.[55]

It had nonetheless become clear to many of the women in attendance that the group's work was only just beginning. With the approval of the gathered delegates, the women's task force thus decided to officially call themselves the Evangelical Women's Caucus (EWC) and to use the *Daughters of Sarah* to coordinate their future endeavors. When a number of women from the Washington, DC, area volunteered to host a separate conference dedicated entirely to issues facing evangelical women, the newly formed EWC furthermore began laying the groundwork for its own separate meeting as an independent body.[56]

The following Thanksgiving, nearly four hundred women (and a handful of men) gathered at a YWCA camp in DC for "Women in Transition: A Biblical Approach to Feminism," the first annual conference hosted by the EWC. In a presentation outlining "a basic biblical feminist exegesis," Virginia Ramey Mollenkott opened the 1975 event with the straightforward claim, "the Bible supports the central tenets of feminism."[57] Along with hearing plenary speeches from the vanguard of evangelical feminist leaders, conference attendees participated in a wide array of workshops exploring issues ranging from biblical interpretation to self-esteem, marriage, and singleness.[58] They also voted in favor of a resolution affirming the ERA, and another expressing solidarity with Roman Catholic women who were meeting that very same weekend to discuss women's ordination and roles in the church. Letha Scanzoni made a speech highlighting the "whole new world" that was becoming available to women, and Nancy Hardesty delivered an address that gestured toward the distinctive contribution that evangelical feminists might make in that world.[59] Evangelical, biblical feminism, Hardesty explained, should be understood as "the commitment of those Christians who believe it is essential to have a personal relationship to God through Jesus Christ, who accept the Bible as God's inspired word, who have a deep concern for love and justice between the sexes, and who desire to find the whole counsel of God on this issue."[60]

If Hardesty's speech helped define what a specifically evangelical kind of feminism ought to look like, a press release on 2 December 1975 helped clarify one of the most pressing tasks at hand for the newly institutionalized evangelical feminist movement. In the wake of its inaugural meeting as an independent body, the group issued a statement making it abundantly clear that "providing organized opposition to Total Woman, Inc., is an immediate goal of the EWC."[61]

Due in part to a lack of funding, the EWC was initially forced to scale back its national presence significantly in the wake of the 1975 meeting. The steering committee was discontinued, and the only full-time staff position was reduced to a part-time secretarial role. Even though the prospects of holding annual national conferences proved similarly unsustainable, for several years thereafter, the organization and the movement it represented were kept alive in part by a number of strong local and regional chapters. When the EWC eventually reunited for its second national conference a few years later, the group of evangelical egalitarians and feminists that showed up would ultimately be bigger than ever.[62] In the meantime, feminist evangelical thinkers kept up the fight, continuously pressing their case for a biblically based view of women's equality in evangelical circles rife with hostility to their cause and welcoming whatever support they could get along the way.

Allies in the Struggle

With the help of a small but growing evangelical feminist movement, by the mid-1970s, the idea that evangelicals could *both* affirm the authority of the Bible *and* interpret it as supporting the full equality of women in the home, church, and world had begun creating a stir in the wider evangelical world. Thanks in part to the increasingly unavoidable *All We're Meant to Be*, it furthermore seemed that a biblically based feminist perspective might just register as a legitimately evangelical option. But evangelical debates over what the Bible really said about women and their place were far from over.

The same year that the EWC hosted its first independent meeting, Fuller Seminary professor of systematic theology Paul King Jewett published a major book, *Man as Male and Female*, that inspired even more controversy than Scanzoni and Hardesty's. Like *All We're Meant to Be* before it, Jewett's 1975 book came as a boon to the small but growing evangelical feminist movement. Given his background and training, Jewett's emergence during the mid-1970s as one of the only prominent, mainstream, male, evangelical theologians to argue that the Bible affirmed the full equality of the sexes came as something of a surprise to many of his peers. To others, it came as a profound disappointment. [63]

Along with midcentury evangelical luminaries like Carl Henry and E. J. Carnell, during his undergraduate days at Wheaton, Jewett had been one of the prize students of Calvinist philosopher and strict inerrantist Gordon H. Clark. After graduating from Wheaton in 1941, he had gone on to study at Westminster Seminary before ultimately pursuing a doctorate in theology at Harvard, where he wrote a dissertation flatly rejecting the idea that the Bible was merely a human witness to God's revelation rather than the actual words of God. When Fuller Seminary hired him in 1955, Jewett had joined his fellow Clark-trained inerrancy-defenders on the faculty with a reputation for the potential to become the Charles Hodge of his generation. [64]

But with the 1975 publication of *Man as Male and Female*, Jewett clearly signaled that he no longer subscribed to the strictly inerrantist position of his former teacher and many friends. In what quickly became a massively controversial book, he argued that the New Testament passages mandating the subordination of women were actually the result of what was essentially a theological mistake. When read as a whole, Jewett explained, the writings of the apostle Paul clearly reflected a man struggling to overcome some of the previous views that he had inherited from Judaism in light of the new insights of the Christian gospel. Upon closer inspection, for instance, the Pauline passages that seemingly advocated female subordination were obviously based on a particular rabbinical interpretation of the second creation story in the book of Genesis. More importantly, Jewett noted, this rabbinical interpretation was clearly at odds not only with the first creation story and with the example set by Jesus but indeed with Paul's own teaching in Galatians "that in Christ there is no male and female." In Jewett's telling, the real difficulty had less to do with the apostle's inconsistent application of the gospel's message that men and women were radically equal in Christ and more to do with a rigidly inerrantist view of biblical inspiration. The only solution, he therefore stressed, was to recognize and acknowledge that the Bible was a divinely inspired book with some human qualities. "As divine," he explained, "it emits the light of revelation; as human this revelation shines in and through the 'dark glass' of the 'earthen vessels' who were the authors of its content at the human level." [65]

When it came to the question of the thrust of broader biblical teaching about marriage and gender roles, Jewett ultimately concluded that Christians should embrace a model based on partnership rather than hierarchy. Despite what some evangelical thinkers tried to suggest, he furthermore argued, the idea of subordination without hierarchy—that the mandated submission of women did not necessitate female inferiority and male superiority—was not merely disingenuous but actually impossible.[66]

With his extensive evangelical bona fides, Jewett's willingness to go on record with such arguments made him a crucial ally for the burgeoning evangelical feminist movement. "If *All We're Meant to Be* was the genesis of evangelical feminist theory," Virginia Mollenkott later judged, "Paul King Jewett's *Man as Male and Female* is its watershed."[67] For Mollenkott in particular, Jewett was something of a godsend. At a time when she had still felt the burden of needing male imprimatur to be able to reconsider the default evangelical orthodoxy on gender, Jewett provided it. Suggesting that her background in literary studies was actually the perfect preparation for the task of theology, he also invited Mollenkott to write the foreword for *Man as Male and Female* and encouraged her to pursue her own theological work, which she did. In 1977, Mollenkott published a book-length articulation of her own evangelical feminist position in *Women, Men, and the Bible*.[68]

Arguing that the majority of the biblical evidence stood in favor of egalitarianism, Mollenkott stressed that neither the "Marabel Morgans of modern evangelicalism" nor some of the most "militant feminists" had it quite right. The most truly Christian and consistently biblical way for people to relate to one another came instead via "the voluntary and loving submission of each individual to all the others." When it came to the question of Paul's teachings about women, Mollenkott furthermore noted, the best interpretive approach involved recognizing that the apostle's letters occasionally bore witness to the workings of a finite human mind. What's more, she judged, acknowledging that the Bible sometimes reflected Paul's internal "thought-processes" by no means undermined the authority of Scripture. The mere inclusion of the apostle's "inner conflicts," which must have been "recorded for our instruction in righteousness by the inspiration of God," was not a mistake. "But *we* are in error," Mollenkott concluded, "to absolutize anything that denies the thrust of the entire Bible toward individual wholeness and harmonious community, toward oneness in Christ."[69]

Reactions to the "Jewett-Mollenkott view of Scripture" were predictably swift, especially fierce, and they had already begun by the time Mollenkott published her book.[70] The previous year, *Christianity Today* editor and aggrieved former Fuller professor Harold Lindsell had already taken aim at Jewett in particular and egalitarians in general for their alleged rejection of the authority of Scripture. In his 1976 manifesto *The Battle for the Bible*, Lindsell singled out Jewett's book as a prime example of an allegedly widespread problem in the evangelical world: a mass defection from the inerrancy of Scripture.[71]

According to Lindsell, countless institutions that had once been safely and soundly within the bounds of classic evangelical belief were abandoning what he believed was the most irreducibly essential evangelical belief. By revising its original statement of faith from an affirmation of biblical inerrancy to the claim that the Bible was "the only infallible rule of faith and practice," he charged, even the once-great Fuller Seminary had recently taken the first step down a slippery slope and thereby opened the floodgates for professors like Jewett to take it a step further. "Down the road," Lindsell predicted, "whether it takes five or fifty years, any institution that departs from belief in an inerrant Scripture will likewise depart from other fundamentals of the faith and at last cease to be evangelical in the historical meaning of that term." The school's rejection of inerrancy indicated that it was already dubiously evangelical at best. Jewett's suggestion that the apostle Paul was wrong about female subordination, which was tantamount in Lindsell's view to rejecting the infallibility of scriptural authority altogether, meant he was already gone.[72]

But Jewett probably wasn't the only one. That same year, in the March 26 issue of *Christianity Today*, Lindsell impugned the theological trustworthiness and questioned the evangelical soundness of all manner of egalitarian arguments—not just Jewett's. In his editorial "Egalitarianism and Scriptural Infallibility," Lindsell put it plainly. "At stake here," he warned, "is not the matter of women's liberation. What is the issue for the evangelical is the fact that some of the most ardent advocates of egalitarianism in marriage over against hierarchy reach their conclusion by directly and deliberately denying that the Bible is the infallible rule of faith and practice. Once they do this, they have ceased to be evangelical: Scripture no longer is normative."[73]

In the evangelical world of the mid to late 1970s, Lindsell by no means was alone in such views. Though he was always among the loudest and most influential accusers, the implication that evangelical feminists' interpretations of the Bible fell beyond the bounds of evangelical orthodoxy went far beyond Lindsell and his ilk. As a result, egalitarian evangelicals were forced into a near-constant state of defense against the charge that they had become feminists only by abandoning a soundly evangelical view of Scripture—an accusation that they routinely and forthrightly denied. As another evangelical feminist, Patricia Gundry, once explained, "You are denying the inspiration of the Bible," eventually became "an all-purpose silencer" wielded by opponents of evangelical feminism from all sides.[74] But like so many of her feminist evangelical counterparts, Gundry refused to remain silent.

In her 1977 book *Woman Be Free*, Gundry published the results of her own in-depth exploration into what the Bible really had to say to women. When it came to the so-called problem passages, she explained, the only real problem was for Bible-believing evangelicals who rightly emphasized "that the very words are inspired." For those who rejected the notion of divine inspiration, the answer was simple: disregard such verses "as the work of misogynists or writers with a patriarchal bias." But for evangelicals like herself, things were not so easy.[75]

In Gundry's telling, the crux of the issue came down to an all-important distinction. The same evangelical thinkers who were quick to affirm biblical *inspiration* were slow to acknowledge the importance of *interpretation*. Those who commendably stood firm on the divinely inspired nature of the text, she noted, often simultaneously failed to admit that the Bible always requires interpretation and that, crucially, "interpretation leaves room for human error." By relegating women to "second-class citizenship" in the church, the traditional evangelical interpretations of the problem passages were rife with human error—the first and foremost of which was relying exclusively on a set of universally male evangelical interpreters. "If the experiences of half of Christendom are not applicable to the careful study and translation of the Scriptures," she pointed out, "then we are bound to miss a great deal and perhaps make mistakes a wider experience would prevent." Overlooking the historical and cultural context behind the apostle Paul's teaching about wifely submission or appropriate female worship attire was one such mistake.[76]

Paul's writings communicated God's instructions for Christians in a specific time and place, Gundry explained, and contemporary Christians were obligated to abide by the *principles* underlying those instructions. But the *application* of some of those principles was bound to change in different cultures and contexts. What's more, she judged, traditional evangelical interpretations that insisted on "a rigid, literal, transcultural application" of certain Pauline passages often undermined the very principles behind them. To suggest that all of Paul's instructions to women were binding mandates for all Christians in every era amounted to applying *social* teachings in a way that directly contracted Scripture's *doctrinal* teachings. The Bible made it clear that God provided all manner of gifts, including the gift of leadership, to both men *and* women. Ironically enough then, when contemporary evangelicals made elaborate arguments against women's leadership based on single words "like *submit* or *head*" that were taken out of context, they tacitly subverted their own deeply held belief in divine inspiration by "making the word mean something God did not intend."[77]

Inspired by his wife's relentless pursuit of a deeper understanding of the Bible, Patricia Gundry's husband Stan eventually began his own reconsideration of traditional evangelical interpretations of the problem passages. Upon discovering that he agreed with her analysis, he, too, began identifying as a "biblical feminist," which Patricia Gundry later defined as "one who is committed to the authority of the Scriptures and whose feminism follows from that conviction." The only problem was that, in addition to being the wife of a feminist author, Stan Gundry also happened to teach at Moody Bible Institute. Though the Gundrys got away with the publication of Patricia's 1977 book—largely due to the fact that Moody's constituency mostly ignored it—it was only a matter of time. When she later delivered a lecture on women's rights in a nearby town, and when the school was subsequently flooded with letters objecting "to the fact that the wife of a Moody professor had given a pro-women's-rights speech," the Moody administration asked Patricia Gundry to kindly use her talents for other causes. When she nonetheless refused to cancel an upcoming interview about her biblical feminist views, the school banned her from its media platforms. Although the school had never before articulated an institutional position on feminism, and Patricia's views thus did not violate any official doctrinal statement, in August 1979 Moody asked Stan Gundry to resign based on charges that "he and his wife had become an 'embarrassment' to the school." Within a few short weeks, in October 1979, Moody made its first public stand explicitly denouncing feminism.[78]

Rise and Fall

The odds of building a sustainable alternative movement that could subvert and counteract the growing antifeminist animus among twentieth-century evangelicals were always long. As the decade progressed, the sledding only got tougher. In addition to the enduring popularity of figures like Morgan and Elliot, the 1970s also witnessed the meteoric rise of a network of widely influential authors, speakers, and teachers who captured the attention of the evangelical world with a tide of books and conferences and media defending "traditional"—usually meaning hierarchical and patriarchal—understandings of gender, marriage, and family. With the emergence of Larry Christenson's popular *The Christian Family*, the ascent of James Dobson's marriage-and-parenting-help empire, and the relentless advance of Beverly and Tim LaHaye's virulently antifeminist writings and activism, by the late 1970s, evangelicalism had become absolutely inundated with materials touting the benefits of a divinely ordained sexual hierarchy.[79]

Growth and Peak

Still, evangelical feminists, biblically based egalitarians, and their allies and supporters alike remained undeterred. With the help of a small vanguard of key leaders and the tireless work of various grassroots outposts, the evangelical feminist movement made it through the middle years of the 1970s mostly intact. Whether in spite or because of their context, evangelical feminists had actually begun witnessing some significant enough signs of growth that the waning years of the decade in fact looked more promising than ever.

After scaling back in the wake of its inaugural 1975 national meeting, for instance, the movement's most crucial institutional home, the EWC, was finally ready for another nationwide event in 1978. That year, with the help and cosponsorship of Fuller Theological Seminary, the organization's leaders and regional chapters began laying plans for a second national meeting slated for mid-June in Pasadena with the title, "Women and the Ministries of Christ." When the day finally arrived, the conference drew crowds far surpassing those at the first meeting. This time around, nearly a thousand women and fifty or so men descended upon southern California for the eleven plenary sessions and more than ninety different workshops—including a number led by Fuller faculty members and one by Fuller president David Hubbard—held during what was ultimately EWC's largest conference ever.[80]

From start to finish, "Women and the Ministries of Christ" was rife with exhortation, encouragement, and the occasional bit of levity from evangelical feminists who offered their perspectives on the past, present, and future of the movement. Noting that the word "daughters" should be interpreted generically to include men as well, Fuller psychology professor Phyllis Hart opened the conference by addressing the gathered participants as the "daughters of Abigail, Priscilla and Sarah."[81] During the closing worship service, Virginia Mollenkott delivered a sermon acknowledging the inevitable difficulty of trying to change the church's long-held views, emphasizing the power of the Holy Spirit, and challenging the audience with biblical proclamations. In a keynote address on the final day of the conference, Letha Scanzoni offered both a retrospective account of how far evangelical feminism had already come and a prospective vision for what it might become.[82]

"The Evangelical Women's Caucus," Scanzoni stressed, "is much more than a warmed-over, imitative, Christianized version of secular feminism." Despite what some critics were suggesting, she explained, evangelical feminists were not trying to retroactively square Christianity with a preexisting feminist ideology. In reality, they were Christians long before they were feminists and actually only became feminists as a result of their faith. Evangelical feminists, she explained, had thus formed a movement based on their conviction that the church was contradicting "God's will for women" and desperately needed correction. In Scanzoni's telling, evangelical feminism had finally moved past the initial awakening phase, and evangelical feminists were now facing the kinds of crucial identity questions that were necessary to build and sustain the movement. A clear next step for the biblically based, specifically evangelical feminists of the EWC, she concluded, involved filling the gulf between secular feminists, on the one hand, and "those Christians who are fearful, misinformed, and afraid to take a new look at woman's role because they believe to do so is to go against Scripture," on the other.[83]

Following Scanzoni's keynote, the EWC held a business meeting to discuss the details necessary for incorporating the group as a nonprofit organization. On the final day of the 1978 conference, before parting ways, the gathered members voted unanimously in favor of both an official set of bylaws and an institutional statement of faith. Carefully crafted to clearly convey that their organization was a soundly and evangelically orthodox group that nonetheless supported women's equality rather than just a religious knockoff of secular feminism, the EWC's statement of faith read:

> We believe that God, the Creator and Ruler of all, has been self-revealed as the Trinity. We believe that God created humankind, female and male, in the divine image, for fellowship with God and one another. We further believe that because of human sinful disobedience, the right relationship with God was shattered, with a consequent disruption of all other relationships. We believe that God in love has made possible a new beginning through the Incarnation, in the life, death and resurrection of Jesus Christ, who was, and is, truly divine and truly human. We affirm a personal relationship with Jesus Christ as Savior and Lord. We believe that under Christ's headship and through the work of the Holy Spirit we are freed to exercise our gifts responsibly in our churches, homes, and society. We believe that the Bible which bears witness of Christ is the Word of God, inspired by the Holy Spirit, and is the infallible guide and final authority for Christian faith and life. We believe the church is the community of women and men who have been divinely called to fellowship with God and one another to seek and do God's will, looking forward to God's coming glorious kingdom.[84]

With the success of the 1978 conference in Pasadena, it seemed like the evangelical feminist movement was finally gaining momentum. In the judgment of one of the conference's organizers, Fuller Seminary professor Roberta Hestenes—who was then the chair of the school's Ministry Division and later became the first tenured woman in Fuller's School of Theology—the gathering indeed represented a clear indication "that biblical feminism has come of age."[85] At long last, it appeared that the EWC was evolving from a smattering of loosely connected local groups into a financially sustainable national organization with a stable and growing base of members. In the first few years after the 1978 gathering, the organization added at least ten new regional chapters and nearly doubled its membership rolls. The addition of at least one Canadian chapter eventually also called for an updated name: in 1980, the EWC officially became the Evangelical Women's Caucus International instead. Although the crowds never surpassed the peak of the cosponsored Pasadena gathering, attendance at several subsequent national meetings furthermore remained relatively high through the early 1980s. The organization and the movement it represented thus entered a new decade with a seemingly promising future of expanding influence.[86]

Controversy and Fracture

In addition to the overwhelming external obstacles the movement always faced, internal controversies nonetheless began bubbling to the surface right as evangelical feminism seemed to be gaining a foothold on an evangelical world that was increasingly hostile to their cause. By the time the EWC was reveling in the success of its 1978 meeting, some of the first signs of trouble had already begun cropping up.

Earlier that same year, Letha Scanzoni and Virginia Mollenkott had finally published a coauthored book that they had been working on for several years. What began as a project covering a wide range of social-ethical issues had eventually evolved into a book-length treatment of one especially controversial issue. Due in part to Scanzoni and Mollenkott's ultimate conclusion that this particular question needed far more than a chapter for sufficient treatment—as well as Mollenkott's decision to come out as lesbian to her friend and collaborator—the two had ultimately decided to devote the entire project to an in-depth exploration of the complex relationship between Christianity and homosexuality.[87] Published in 1978 as *Is the Homosexual My Neighbor?* their resulting manuscript was one of the earliest book-length discussions of homosexuality in any tradition of US American Christianity—evangelical or otherwise. Opening with the straightforward claim, "The question that makes up the title of this book shouldn't be necessary," Scanzoni and Mollenkott's landmark book proposed a measured reinterpretation of the traditional views of homosexuality espoused by so many Christians, ultimately arguing that evangelicals ought to reconsider the ethical legitimacy of gay and lesbian relationships in light of the fact that the precious few scriptural passages apparently condemning homosexuality actually had next to nothing to do with modern understandings of sexual orientation.[88]

Broader evangelical reactions to Scanzoni and Mollenkott's argument were mixed and equally so among their evangelical feminist counterparts.[89] Some thought it was anathema, others found it right on target, and the EWC had its share of feminist evangelicals in both groups. Mollenkott felt the divide acutely. In the wake of the book's 1978 publication, some EWC members began asking pointed questions about her sexuality even though she had not yet come out publicly. Others simply shunned her entirely.[90] At the same time, it was also becoming clear that Mollenkott was not entirely alone. The EWC membership included a small lesbian minority that began meeting together as a group at national conferences during the early 1980s for the very first time.[91]

In the hopes of maintaining a united front on their already controversial message that women were fully equal to men in every way, for a while the EWC successfully navigated simmering internal tensions over potentially fraught issues like homosexuality or abortion by declining to take official positions on anything other than women's equality. But when it came to the "homosexuality issue," by the time the 1980s were fully underway, two diverging factions were emerging within the organization. On the one hand, there were those who believed that the EWC should both support "homosexual persons" and explicitly say so. On the other hand, whether for moral or strategic reasons, there were those who felt that there were no circumstances under which the evangelical feminist movement should ever even hint at approving homosexuality.[92] The delicate balance between the two groups could last only so long.

The true extent of the divide became clear at the EWC's sixth national conference in 1984. From its first meeting forward, the organization had consistently voiced official support for the Equal Rights Amendment. But this time around, during the business meeting, the delegates brought forth a number of additional resolutions addressing everything from pornography to racism. Unsurprisingly, the most controversial of all was a resolution proposing that the EWC take "a firm stand to support with love homosexual persons in an attitude of justice which is against the oppression involved in sexism, racism, classism, heterosexism, or homophobia." After lengthy debates and emotionally charged discussions, the delegates ultimately settled the matter by agreeing to table the resolutions until the next national gathering. In the meantime, the EWC would conduct a follow-up study including surveys to better understand the views of its members. In 1985, the study results showed just how evenly split the membership actually was: 50 percent of EWC members wanted the organization to take explicit stands on a broader range of political justice issues, and 50 percent wanted the organization to pass no resolutions beyond supporting the ERA. The following year, the institutional home of the evangelical feminist movement met for the final time as a tenuously united front.[93]

When the EWC gathered in Fresno, California, in July 1986, attendance was down, money was tight, and controversy was looming. The business meeting once again featured a number of proposed resolutions, open disagreements over whether the group should even be considering additional resolutions, and lengthy debates over one resolution in particular. After voting in favor of resolutions addressing racism and violence against women, the delegates moved on to consider a third resolution that read, "Whereas homosexual people are children of God, and because of the biblical mandate of Jesus Christ that we are all created equal in God's sight, and in recognition of the presence of the lesbian minority in the Evangelical Women's Caucus International, EWCI takes a firm stand in favor of civil rights protection for homosexual persons." With eighty yeas, sixteen nays, and about twenty abstentions, the resolution ultimately passed. An exodus of angry and disappointed members began almost immediately.[94]

In the wake of the 1986 conference, a wave of resignations by both individuals and entire local chapters cost the organization nearly half of its members. One regional outfit, the Minnesota chapter, withdrew both its membership and its offer to host the 1988 national conference in one fell swoop. Motivated by their belief that evangelicals could not condone homosexuality, as well as a feeling that their erstwhile organization had effectively ruined its chance of impacting the broader evangelical world by doing so, a small group of the newly ex-members of the EWC furthermore spent the rest of 1986 making plans to start a new organization. A *Christianity Today* article reporting on the controversial gathering and its aftermath gave notice that Catherine Kroeger, a member of the Minnesota chapter, was currently helping to lead the nascent group, which would strictly emphasize biblical feminism.[95]

The following spring, a handful of the newly christened "biblical" evangelical feminists began publishing *Priscilla Papers* to spread the message that supporting the full equality of the sexes need not and should not mean affirming homosexuality. By August 1987, the biblical feminists were ready to launch their new organization, Men, Women and God: Christians for

Biblical Equality, with a mission statement emphasizing their goal "to make known the biblical basis for freedom in Christ to those in evangelical and conservative churches," and a nine-point statement of faith that concluded with an affirmation of their belief "in the family, celibate singleness, and heterosexual marriage as the patterns God designed for us." Officially established in January 1988 as Christians for Biblical Equality International (CBE), the new group named Catherine Kroeger as the first president and official spokeswoman. In July 1989, more than two hundred biblical feminists made their way to Saint Paul, Minnesota, for CBE's first inaugural conference. That same year, the group joined the unofficial ranks of mainstream evangelicalism by becoming an organizational member of the National Association of Evangelicals.[96]

The logic beyond CBE's emergence and subsequent framing was clear. In the eyes of many CBE members, when the EWC decided to support homosexuality, it thereby rejected the authority of the Bible. Since it was no longer biblical, the EWC was no longer evangelical enough to warrant the name. By explicitly refusing to affirm the moral legitimacy of homosexuality, CBE successfully signaled that it was a soundly biblical and therefore faithfully evangelical alternative to an EWC that had moved beyond the pale. For some evangelical groups like the NAE, that was enough.

But for a number of influential evangelical thinkers and leaders, even the explicitly antigay version of sexual egalitarianism that became CBE's trademark was theologically suspect. In their view, supporting the full equality of women in the home, church, and world was tantamount to rejecting the clear teachings of the Bible, which made CBE nearly as dubiously evangelical as their EWC counterparts. Both evangelical feminism and biblical egalitarianism, in other words, were contradictions in terms. And not only that. They were an insidious threat that needed to be stopped at any cost.

Backlash

Due in no small part to the enormous influence of some of the late twentieth century's most politically conservative and publicly recognizable evangelical leaders, by the end of the 1980s, feminism had been so thoroughly stigmatized in the minds of huge swaths of the American public that it was effectively untouchable—including among evangelicals and nonevangelicals alike. In evangelical circles in particular, "feminist" became an epithet at least as bad and probably worse than "liberal." Feminists were godless secularists hell-bent on destroying the traditional way of life that good, God-fearing evangelicals held so dear, and that was that. As busy as they were with stopping the spread of the "secular feminist agenda," many of the era's most passionately antifeminist evangelical political crusaders would have paid precious little attention to the idea that there might be something called an evangelical feminist, much less an entire movement. But by the mid-1980s, some evangelical theologians and pastors had started taking notice. Feminism and egalitarianism were infiltrating their once-safe evangelical organizations, and a small team of evangelical thinkers decided to take a stand against it. In so doing, they thereby set off what arguably became the most concerted, explicit, and largely successful intramovement backlash in the history of twentieth-century evangelicalism.

One of the main architects behind the efforts to stop evangelical feminism, evangelical theologian Wayne Grudem, first began feeling that "the church was being led astray by misleading and false information . . . put forth by evangelical feminists" during his years as a PhD student at Cambridge in the mid-1970s.[97] While later working as a professor at Bethel College in Minnesota, he came across a 1979 *Christianity Today* article arguing that the biblical idea of "headship" did not mean that husbands had "authority over" their wives. Though he found the article disturbing, he initially lacked the time and resources to write a rebuttal.[98] But a few years later, he was finally ready to launch an all-out war to turn the tides.

Grudem's crusade against feminists and egalitarians began in earnest at the 1986 meeting of the Evangelical Theological Society. That year, six plenary speakers offered presentations under the title, "Manhood and Womanhood in Biblical and Theological Perspectives." Five of the presenters, one of whom was Catherine Kroeger, were egalitarians.[99] As the sixth and only nonegalitarian speaker, Grudem came to the meeting with a chip on his shoulder from the start. After discovering that he wasn't the only one who believed that the "five-to-one situation" by no means accurately reflected the percentage of egalitarians among the organization's rank-and-file membership, he gathered a small group of coconspirators for a secret meeting to discuss what might be done about the fact that "egalitarians were taking over . . . in a way contrary to the convictions of the vast majority of the members of ETS." At the end of the meeting, Grudem took the stage to announce the development of a new organization toward those ends, inviting anyone interested to join their cause.[100]

The following month, he invited a small group of evangelical leaders to meet in Dallas, Texas, to develop a more concrete plan for stopping "the spread of unbiblical teaching" about sex and gender in evangelical circles.[101] With the help of evangelical pastor and theologian John Piper, by the end of their time together, the group had sketched out a rough draft of "a statement on principles for manhood and womanhood." Later that year, in the days leading up to the December 1987 ETS meeting, they came together once again in a hotel in Danvers, Massachusetts, to finalize their manifesto. During the course of their clandestine gathering, the group put the finishing touches on what became the "Danvers Statement on Biblical Manhood and Womanhood," discussed the importance of being present at future ETS business meetings to ensure like-minded candidates were elected for leadership, and voted the Council on Biblical Manhood and Womanhood (CBMW) into existence.[102]

With a package that included everything from promotional materials to a neologism, the organization's public rollout came the following year during the 1988 ETS meeting. That December, Grudem later recounted, "We announced the formation of the Council on Biblical Manhood and Womanhood (CBMW) and handed out brochures. We even had a press conference (*Christianity Today* showed up, but nobody else). We coined the term 'complementarian' as a one-word representation of our viewpoint. So we were now known to the ETS, but not yet in the general evangelical world."[103] That all changed the following month when the group first took its message to the evangelical masses with a full two-page ad in the 13 January 1989 issue of *Christianity Today*. Along with an announcement of the organization's formation, the first page included a detailed list of council and board members, a series of questions and answers about the group, and a form that readers could submit to join the CBMW mailing list. The second page printed the ten-point rationale, fivefold purpose, and ten key affirmations of the Danvers Statement in full.[104]

The rationale was simple. From "the increasing promotion given to feminist egalitarianism" to "the increasing prevalence and acceptance of hermeneutical oddities devised to reinterpret apparently plain meanings of biblical texts," there were a number of deeply disturbing "contemporary developments" afoot in the evangelical world. The CBMW was formed to combat such disastrous trends by studying, articulating, and promoting the only adequate remedy: "the noble Biblical vision of sexual complementarity." As clearly demonstrated in Genesis, the statement continued, God's original intent for humanity involved male headship and female submission. But the divinely ordained structure for male-female relationships had become distorted in the wake of Adam and Eve's fall into sin. For anyone interested in "removing the distortions introduced by the curse," the good news was that redemption and return to the rightful order of the family and church was possible. "In the family," the statement explained, "husbands should forsake harsh or selfish leadership and grow in love and care for their wives; wives should forsake resistance to their husbands' authority and grow in willing, joyful submission to their husbands' leadership. In the church, redemption in Christ gives men and women an equal share in the blessing of salvation; nevertheless, some governing and teaching roles within the church are restricted to men." In Grudem's telling, the ad prompted an enormous and overwhelmingly positive response—a sure sign of God's blessing on their work. [105]

The following year, Grudem joined forces with fellow CBMW executive council member John Piper in coediting a massive, nearly five-hundred-page-long volume of twenty-six essays from various authors detailing different aspects of the complementarian position. Published in 1991 with a title that made both its purpose and impetus clear on the cover, *Recovering Biblical Manhood and Womanhood: A Response to Evangelical Feminism* was the first book-length project sponsored and endorsed by the CBMW. Piper and Grudem opened the tome with a preface sounding the alarm about the disastrous trend wreaking havoc on the country's evangelical churches. The torrent of abominable feminist ideology that had long eroded the morality of the broader society now had a counterpart within the previously secure walls of evangelicalism. Even though "the vast majority of evangelicals have not endorsed the evangelical feminist position" because "it does not really reflect the pattern of Biblical truth," they noted thankfully, the number who had was too high already and it was time to name names. Along with a handful of others, Letha Scanzoni, Nancy Hardesty, Paul Jewett, Patricia Gundry, and Catherine Kroeger were sowing doubt and confusion about the Bible's clear teachings. By introducing new interpretations of key passages, evangelical feminists were undermining the divinely ordained distinctions between the sexes and thereby threatening the stability of evangelical families and churches everywhere.[106]

Twenty-five essays later, Piper and Grudem concluded the book with a chapter painstakingly detailing the crucial differences between the CBMW and another evangelical organization, Christians for Biblical Equality, that had recently emerged within the evangelical world. "Its members are the primary persons we debate in this book," they suggested. The reason was simple. Although the evangelical feminists of the CBE were playing the kinds of dangerous games that opened the door to wholesale liberalism, at least for the time being the group seemingly still affirmed the authority of the Bible, and therefore, "it would be fair, we believe, to describe this group as theologically conservative, evangelical feminists." Lest there was any confusion, Piper and Grudem noted, their debate with the feminists who were still evangelical but on shaky grounds was far more than "a minor intramural squabble," and the stakes were immeasurably high. "Yet we sense a kinship far closer with the founders of CBE," they confessed, "than with those who seem to put their feminist commitments above Scripture." Leaving nothing to the imagination, the editors pointed to one particular feminist as a prime example of the kind beyond the evangelical pale: Virginia Mollenkott.[107]

For the rest of the twentieth century, the book, its authors, and the organization they represented became massively influential in the US American evangelical world. From its late 1980s invention forward, complementarianism spread like wildfire. Numerous groups, dozens of major evangelical organizations, and countless evangelical leaders began emphasizing its antifeminist, nonegalitarian interpretation of a divinely mandated sexual hierarchy as the default evangelical view on sex and gender. As the driving force behind the popularization and spread of complementarianism, Grudem, Piper, and the CBMW could justifiably claim a lion's share of the responsibility for making that happen. Grudem in particular made combating evangelical feminism at every turn *the* centralmost focus of his long and ongoing career as an evangelical theologian.[108]

Whither Evangelical Feminism?

To suggest that evangelicalism entered the twenty-first century with a well-earned reputation as resoundingly antifeminist would be an understatement. Since there really was a time when a rising evangelical feminist movement seemed to be gaining ground though, it is certainly worth pausing for a moment to consider the question: *What then happened to the evangelical feminists?*

The answer, at least in part, is *nothing*. Both of the major evangelical feminist organizations remained (and remain) in existence. Both groups furthermore continue working in their respective way to carve out some space in an evangelical culture that never stopped being hostile to their message. In the past few years, they've also been joined by a fresh tide of evangelical women working to convince as many of their fellow evangelicals as possible that revisiting the question of whether the Bible *really* says that women are inherently made for submission is both worthwhile and crucial.

But once again, feminists and egalitarians who also happen to be evangelical have their work cut out for them. What began as an uphill battle in the late 1960s and early 1970s only became steeper as time went on. The virulently antifeminist messaging of the Religious Right during the 1980s made any kind of feminist message infinitely harder to hear, and the CBMW's concerted and explicit backlash against evangelical feminism in particular was wildly successful. Over the course of the 1990s, the overwhelming resurgence of explicitly masculinist, muscular styles of Christianity within evangelical circles by no means helped things. From the softer patriarchy of the Promise Keepers movement, to the flood of literature featuring a warlike Christ as the ideal model for wild-hearted, godly, and masculine pastors, fathers, and husbands, to the unabashedly chauvinistic teachings of evangelical men like Mars Hill Church pastor Mark Driscoll, defending a particular set of contemporary white US American middle-class conservative ideals about marriage, sex, and family arguably became late twentieth-century evangelical culture's most determinative feature.[109] In this context, it is no small wonder that "feminist" became a four-letter word.

Having to compete with gender-essentialist, manly man, womanly woman views in the marketplace of popular evangelical ideas undeniably proved one of the most lastingly insurmountable obstacles preventing evangelical feminism from truly catching on among twentieth-century evangelicals. Feminist and egalitarian evangelicals were simply never able to gain the level of widespread support from evangelical masses that the Marable Morgans and Elisabeth Elliots, the Grudems and Pipers and Driscolls, or the Dobsons and LaHayes most certainly did. Between the two alternatives of feminism or complementarianism, the egalitarian option wound up losing almost every time.

But something else happened, too, and that something had to do with perennial struggles over the nature and limits of evangelical identity. In their ongoing efforts to define and enforce the inherently porous boundaries of evangelicalism, twentieth-century evangelical leaders consistently made a variety of ad hoc decisions about who was in and, more importantly, who was out of the evangelical tent. Whenever someone (or a group of someones) challenged the prevailing interpretations of the evangelical establishment, somehow, someway, the dissenter's right to march in the evangelical parade would be called into question. Put another way, although outcompeting an opponent by winning converts to one's team was always an obvious path to victory, getting the referees to rule the opposition out of bounds—or better still, proclaiming oneself the referee—was just as effective and far more efficient.

Evangelical feminism may very well have lost the competition for converts. But its enduring marginal status among twentieth-century evangelicals was most effectively ensured by successive generations of mostly, if never exclusively, male evangelical figureheads who consistently derided feminists as godless, dangerous, and inherently *unevangelical*. By suggesting that evangelical feminists were not merely wrong but were actually dubiously evangelical and questionably Christian, antifeminist evangelical leaders successfully defined certain interpretive conclusions as intrinsically off-limits for true evangelicals. Declaring that evangelical feminists could not have become feminists if they had followed the evangelical rules of interpretation allowed twentieth-century evangelical power brokers to effectively erect a new boundary between evangelical identity, on the one hand, and feminist identity, on the other. This understanding of what it means to be evangelical arguably became so pervasive, in fact, that even some outsider historians have told the story of the late twentieth-century evangelical feminist movement through this lens.

If one accepts the idea that there were certain conclusions about biblical teachings on maleness and femaleness that no real evangelical could ever reach, for instance, the divergent paths of the EWC and the CBE seem clear-cut and self-evident. The only major published history of the movement indeed tells the story in essentially this way. In so doing, it thereby becomes a history of two kinds of evangelical feminism: a soundly evangelical kind and a dubiously evangelical kind. One story, the CBE's, is about a group of "traditionalist biblical feminists" who held firm to biblical authority, maintained evangelically sound scriptural interpretation methods, and thereby remained safely and "solidly evangelical." Their story begins with the decision to leave the EWC over its apparent rejection of the authority of the Bible. The second story, the EWC's, is about an organization that began within the established boundaries of evangelicalism only to become less and less evangelical as time went on. Over the years, the "progressive evangelical feminists" of the EWC consistently demonstrated that their feminist identity was more important than their evangelical identity by increasingly capitulating to the broader surrounding culture. In light of the fact that the EWC clearly succumbed to the influences of pluralism and the secular feminist movement, in this version of the story, their marginalization within evangelicalism makes perfect sense. Despite continuing to call themselves evangelicals, EWC-style feminists openly and willingly flouted established and accepted evangelical rules, which is why the soundly evangelical feminists of the CBE had to leave. The EWC abandoned evangelical norms, and the CBE was founded to retain them.[110]

According to this version of events, one particular "liberal evangelical feminist," Virginia Mollenkott, represented both the prototypical example and the major influence behind the EWC's ultimate turn away from evangelicalism. Mainstream evangelical theologians like Piper and Grudem, by this account, eventually stopped engaging feminists like Mollenkott and the EWC because they were no longer true evangelicals.[111]

That's one way of telling the story.

But it's neither the only way nor the way that Mollenkott told it. Over the course of her career, throughout all of her work in biblical interpretation and theology, Mollenkott consistently and persistently stressed that she was an evangelical Christian whose loyalty to the Bible never faltered. Even though she had been regularly attacked both by those who wanted to toss out feminism *and* by those who wanted to toss out the Bible, Mollenkott refused to concede that the two were inherently contradictory. Despite the charges that were relentlessly leveled against her, she once explained, "I continue to regard the Bible as given by God for my doctrine, reproof, correction, and instruction for my righteousness." Although many of her evangelical counterparts found it hard to believe, she furthermore noted, "never have I consciously taken a position in defiance of or unconcern about biblical teachings."[112]

In the 1992 book *Sensuous Spirituality*, Mollenkott reiterated her commitment to scriptural authority, pointing out that rigorous biblical study was in fact the basis for her ongoing motivation as an "evangelical lesbian feminist" to demonstrate "that one cannot be a good Christian without struggling against heteropatriarchy, just as Jesus and (up to their respective lights) Paul and the other apostles did."[113] Then in a 1994 article for the *Daughters of Sarah* magazine, she went on to explain the two main sources behind her identification as an "evangelical liberationist." The first was a belief that "the gospel should not be reduced exclusively to a political theology." The second was "because I hold a strong view of biblical authority and have in fact been radicalized by the Bible."[114]

And as to the charges that she nonetheless had eventually rejected the accepted evangelical rules of biblical interpretation? Mollenkott would hear none of it. In her telling, historical accounts suggesting that her early work began within the boundaries of soundly evangelical interpretation and that she later moved beyond them were patently false. In light of the fact that she had maintained "*the very same hermeneutical principles*" from her 1975 keynote at the first meeting of the EWC throughout all of her subsequent work, Mollenkott later stressed, "then I must be evangelical, whether or not the traditional evangelical community likes the conclusions I have reached."[115]

What about the accusation that she had eventually begun deferring to the authority of outside influences such as reason and experience in developing her interpretations of the Bible? Nonsense. Such judgments were disingenuous at best and self-deceptive at worst. Regardless of whether they could admit as much, all interpreters approached the text from within the context of their own experience and presumably used their reasoning capabilities when they did so—her acceptably mainstream evangelical critics included. In Mollenkott's estimation, the origins of such naivete were clear. "If we spend our entire life in a community that interprets Scripture as we ourselves do, and if we are able to fit our behaviors comfortably within that community," she pointed out, "we tend to develop the illusion that our view of Scripture is THE view of Scripture, the only set of interpretations worth bothering with. The illusion is possible because everybody in our interpretive community joins us in ignoring the Bible passages that might make us uncomfortable by casting doubt upon our community's tacitly accepted point of view."[116]

Although some people could afford to live with this illusion, Mollenkott continued, there were a number of reasons why she simply could not:

> I was called and gifted to study theology in a community that denied women any voice in theology. I was born lesbian in a community that saw homosexuals as deliberately defiant toward God. I was born with many "masculine" leadership traits in a community that required women to be subservient to men and to obey the gender roles and rules of "total femininity." I could have walked away from Christianity, but instead I used the abilities I had been given to work and study my way into what seems to me to be an open, clear, responsible way of life as a follower of Jesus the Christ, whom I dearly love.[117]

*

Another way of telling the story of the rise and fall of the evangelical feminist movement might thus emphasize the complex internal power dynamics involved in the perennial struggle to safeguard the often porous boundaries of twentieth-century evangelical identity. As the progressive evangelical feminists continued studying and interpreting the Bible for themselves, in *this* version of the story, their resulting conclusions about its meaning and application look less inherently unevangelical. Instead, they begin to look more like alternative interpretations that were merely at odds with those of the majority male gatekeepers with the power to police the borders of evangelicalism.

If being an evangelical always meant only what the most influential twentieth-century leaders thought it meant, then evangelical feminism was indeed outside the bounds of evangelicalness. Put differently, if faithfulness to the authority of the Bible also meant staying within a range of interpretive conclusions set by evangelical power brokers, evangelical feminists were out of luck.

But accepting the idea that certain kinds of evangelical feminists who interpreted and applied certain passages in a certain way were thereby obviously and necessarily beyond the pale is simultaneously to accept that the finer details of what it meant to be an official evangelical were clearly established, already settled, and that they were what many of the most powerful, mainstream, male evangelical figures said they were.

five

The Gay Evangelicals

Conventional narratives about the history of Christianity and homosexuality usually go something like this.[1]

For the better part of the past few centuries, in most traditions of Christianity, the official teaching about sex held that the only morally legitimate kind happened within the confines of a legally recognized, church-sanctioned, lifelong, monogamous marriage between a man and a woman, usually for the express purpose of procreation. For most modern Christians, in other words, the only ethically recognized options were procreative married sex or celibacy.

Although the idea of a morally acceptable sexual relationship between two men or two women would almost never have been considered, Christian thinkers throughout history nonetheless were relatively silent about homosexuality. They weren't the only ones either. As some scholars eventually began pointing out, the very idea of a fundamental orientation known as homosexuality—or heterosexuality for that matter—was a relatively recent development in the history of human thought. Discussions of homosexuality therefore have been a decidedly modern affair.

When it comes to the history of US American Christianity more specifically, the story thus unsurprisingly begins in relative silence. Whether because of the relative novelty of the idea of sexual orientation, the common assumption that same-sex sexual relationships were unspeakably wrong and obviously contrary to the will of God, or a mixture of both, for much of the twentieth century, most varieties of Christians had precious little to say about homosexuality.

The earliest signs of even subtle change to the blanket assumption in Christian circles that "homosexuality" was self-evidently sinful and verboten first emerged during the latter half of the century. On the heels of the radical social changes of the 1960s in general and in the wake of the first clear emergence of the post-Stonewall version of the mainstream gay rights movement in particular, a small minority of US American Christians began cautiously reconsidering whether unequivocal condemnation was the only legitimate response to the increasingly open secret that there were gay and lesbian people in the pews of the nation's churches. By the early 1970s, a handful of Protestant denominations subsequently embarked on a decades-long series of discussions, debates, studies, task forces, and ecclesial negotiations increasingly known as the "homosexuality debates."[2]

The debates continued almost uninterruptedly for the rest of the twentieth century. As time went on, they spread to an ever-growing list of denominations with varying results. In some churches, the explicitly prohibitive view gave way to either accommodation or cautious approval. In others, the traditionally denunciatory position was upheld. For some denominations, the debates lasted well into the twenty-first century. But regardless of the outcome, the kinds of Christians engaged in the late twentieth century's homosexuality debates were almost universally united by one important characteristic: they were all associated with the liberal-mainline Protestant tradition. While some self-identified evangelicals within certain mainline denominations fought to maintain the traditional position, most of the broader evangelical world simply refused to have the discussion. To be an evangelical in the twentieth-century US context, in other words, was to be steadfastly against the mere consideration of legitimizing gay and lesbian anything.

*

With the end of chapter 1 came the end of the possibility that evangelical identity might include enough room for Christians who accepted modern intellectual developments like evolution and higher biblical criticism. From that point forward, being evangelical meant being as theologically conservative as possible, and the quickest and easiest way to draw that line was between those who affirmed the inerrancy of the Bible and those who did not.

By the end of chapter 2, it nonetheless became clear that theological conservatism and fidelity to biblical authority were not enough if one also happened to be Black—in which case one also needed to be able to think "white thoughts about Black people."

Over the course of chapter 3, evangelicalism became inextricably tied to political partisanship, progressive politics of any sort became sufficient cause for excommunication, and voting Republican ultimately became a sine qua non of contemporary evangelical identity.

As chapter 4 ended, feminists, egalitarians, and anyone who disagreed with the idea that female submission was God-ordained had discovered the hard limits of acceptably evangelical views of the Bible's message for women. Evangelical feminists' reward for daring to challenge prevailing interpretations of certain passages was constant vilification, targeted marginalization, and the clear message that believing in the full equality of women was beyond the pale for true evangelicals.

But as the story of the split between the EWC and CBE showed, the fault lines created by competing understandings of what counted as a sufficiently evangelical interpretation could emerge even within an otherwise unified group. This chapter turns to the question that was at the heart of the evangelical feminist divide: could evangelicals who affirm the authority of Scripture disagree over what the Bible had to say about gay and lesbian people?

At first blush, the answer was an obvious and emphatic no. Contemporary evangelicalism developed a well-earned reputation as overwhelmingly antigay, and conventional histories of the homosexuality debates rightly emphasize their primarily mainline context.

During the past half century or so, nearly every one of the approximately seven denominations usually associated with mainline Protestantism did indeed hash and rehash debates over their official positions on homosexuality with near-clockwork consistency. Countless mainline congregations, denominational bodies, and parachurch organizations spent decades considering and reconsidering whether to enshrine an official institutional position on homosexuality, what that position should be, what it should or should not endorse, and what it might or might not mean for everyone involved. The fault lines in such debates most frequently formed around disagreements over whether gay and lesbian people should be openly welcomed and affirmed as church members, whether those who were members should be eligible for ordination, whether the church should offer institutional recognition of gay and lesbian partnerships, and whether denominationally sanctioned ministers could perform same-sex marriages. In certain instances, the nay side of the debate was represented by an in-house evangelical faction. In many cases, ongoing debates were driven by the emergence of a denominationally specific gay and lesbian support group or caucus, which themselves were sometimes founded in direct response to the official adoption of prohibitive policies. Regardless of the individual particularities, over time, almost all of the mainline denominations wound up following a strikingly similar path in their deliberations. As Chris Glaser highlights, for instance, the standard pattern went something like this: "An assigned task force or committee would study and report favorably on homosexuality, only to have a national governing body reject recommendations for changing church position, while at the same time supporting gay civil rights."[3] Many of the mainline denominations that began this sequence during the 1970s and 1980s in fact repeated the very same pattern every few years for the rest of the twentieth century.

While mainline Protestants were debating the status of gay and lesbian Christians in their midst, mainstream evangelical thinkers were mostly either dismissing such discussions as one more sign of liberal accommodation or simply doubling down on the traditional position that homosexuality was patently sinful and expressly forbidden by Scripture. As they nonetheless were eventually forced to reckon with the fact that there also happened to be gay and lesbian Christians in *their* midst, evangelical leaders increasingly turned to what became the standard late twentieth-century evangelical response to LGBTQ people: "love the sinner, hate the sin." Over time, this general posture furthermore contributed to the development of a characteristically evangelical solution to the problem in the rise of a network of denominational and parachurch ministries dedicated to helping anyone interested in escaping the homosexual lifestyle. By the end of the twentieth century, the default evangelical position on the matter thereby became clear: the most loving thing that Christians could do for gay people was to help them change.

From the 1970s through the end of the century, the vast majority of mainstream evangelical figures undeniably fell somewhere in the narrow window between the most vitriolic antigay rhetoric imaginable and the kind of quieter, subtler, homophobia that lovingly stressed the possibility of liberation from a lifestyle that was obviously worth changing. But before the so-called ex-gay movement became the official evangelical answer, there was *some* internal debate over what exactly evangelicals should think, say, and do about homosexuality. During the early years of the mostly mainline versions of the debates, in fact, a handful of evangelical thinkers had similarly begun rethinking the traditional position, advocating a different interpretation of the biblical passages that presumably prohibited homosexuality, and all while reaffirming their distinctively evangelical commitment to the authority of Scripture.

Though few and far between, in other words, there really were progay evangelicals, and they were around much earlier than many insiders and outsiders alike might assume.[4] Some emerged from within the innermost circles of the 1970s evangelical world, and one in particular made it his personal mission to challenge the developing consensus that gay and evangelical were necessarily a contradiction in terms.

Ralph Blair and Evangelicals Concerned

Ralph Blair became a Christian during junior high school and realized he was gay sometime during high school. Unlike many young evangelicals who just so happen to be gay, Blair was not all that troubled by the apparent irreconcilability of his faith and his sexuality, however. As a teenager, he later explained, "I came to a growing understanding of who I was as both gay and Christian and what these two facts meant for my lifestyle. I had committed myself to Christ and it flowed then, that I'd committed myself to either be celibate or to be in a faithful relationship with another guy someday."[5] Comfortable with the fact that he was both gay and an evangelical Christian, after graduating from high school Blair went on to enroll at the only Christian college he had ever heard of, Bob Jones University, where he first ran afoul of the evangelical authorities as a freshman in 1956.[6]

His transgression was the most stereotypically evangelical offense possible: sticking up for Billy Graham. After a chapel speaker had viciously criticized Graham's decision to include nonfundamentalists in his upcoming crusade at Madison Square Garden, Blair complained about it. Unfortunately, someone overheard him, turned him into the administration, and he was immediately summoned to the dean's office for a thorough dressing down. As Blair later recounted, among the group of administrators gathered to address his insubordinate "griping" about the guest speaker was none other than Bob Jones Sr., who apparently chastised Blair for thinking that he knew more about the appropriate methods of mass evangelism than "Dr. Bob." Duly aware that the campus was always on high alert for signs of heresy, Blair bided his time at BJU until 1958 when he transferred to Bowling Green State University. After college, he returned to the card-carrying evangelical world, studying both at Dallas Theological Seminary and Westminster Theological Seminary before ultimately pursuing graduate studies in religion at the University of Southern California.[7]

While studying at USC during the early 1960s, Blair continued his journey throughout the mainstream evangelical world by joining InterVarsity Christian Fellowship. He also began expressing his belief that gay Christians should be encouraged to form and supported in sustaining committed relationships. For a while, he got away with it too. In Blair's later telling, his particular Inter-Varsity chapter apparently seemed none too offended by the idea, but it was only a matter of time. His days with evangelicalism's flagship college ministry were already numbered. After graduating from USC in 1964, Blair accepted a job as an InterVarsity staff member at the University of Pennsylvania. The position lasted exactly one year. He made a presentation at a Christian students' meeting at Yale University, InterVarsity caught wind of his progay views, and the organization declined to reappoint him for the following year.[8]

In 1965, Blair went on to work instead as an interim chaplain at Penn State, where he subsequently began doctoral studies exploring "the etiology and treatment of homosexuality." His findings? The cause of homosexuality remained unclear, the relevant psychological studies were woefully inadequate and ultimately contradictory, and none of the various interventions designed to treat homosexuality by "reorienting a homosexual to heterosexuality" had ever proven particularly successful. With a dissertation debunking both the idea that homosexuality's cause had been definitely determined and the notion that it could somehow be cured via therapeutic intervention in hand, in 1969 the newly minted Dr. Blair moved to New York City to begin working as the director of counseling at a City University of New York community college. In 1971, he went on to found the Homosexual Community Counseling Center, began editing its quarterly publication, *The Homosexual*

Counseling Journal, in 1974, and established his own private psychotherapy practice in the meantime. By the mid-1970s, Blair had also begun offering seminars to help other health-care professionals better understand how to care for their gay and lesbian clients.[9]

At the same time, he had simultaneously become increasingly aware of another, more specific problem that he was uniquely qualified to address. In Blair's later telling, when a nationally known evangelical leader reached out to him for guidance about his own sexuality, and when Blair also began receiving a number of responses to an ad about gay evangelicals that he had placed in the gay newspaper *The Advocate*, he finally realized it was time to act.[10] The evangelical world desperately needed a "ministry of reconciliation" that could both reach gay and lesbian evangelicals struggling with their sexuality in isolation and help the broader evangelical community better support its gay and lesbian members.[11] So, in 1975, Blair founded Evangelicals Concerned (EC) as a first-of-its-kind organization aimed at doing just that.[12]

The official public announcement came the following year at a time and place strategically chosen for maximum exposure. As a member of the National Association of Evangelicals (NAE), in February 1976, Blair traveled to Washington, DC, for the organization's annual meeting. After distributing pamphlets advertising the new ministry to his fellow NAE members, Blair convened a separate meeting across the street from the NAE's gathering for the handful of evangelicals who were either interested in or sympathetic to the group's mission.[13] Lest anyone be misled, the early promotional materials made it abundantly clear that, even though the two groups shared some members, the new organization had "absolutely *no* official connection" to the NAE.[14] By simultaneously pointing out that EC's statement of faith would follow the NAE's, and that its membership included both card-carrying NAE members and members of "various evangelical churches," Blair nonetheless was equally as emphatic about the soundness of his new organization's evangelical credentials.[15]

Later that year, a team of members from the fledgling group brought one of Blair's longtime dreams to fruition. While working for InterVarsity Christian Fellowship more than a decade earlier, Blair later explained, he had once imagined "a time when we could present God's love to gays just as we present it to others." In December 1976, EC representatives thus traveled to the Mecca of evangelical college ministry gatherings, InterVarsity's annual Urbana missions convention, to do just that. In their efforts "to declare His Glory both to gays and non-gays who will be ministering among the nations to and with gays, maybe without even realizing it," on the night that Billy Graham was slated to speak to that year's meeting, a few EC members joined one another for a time of prayer before gathering outside the assembly hall.[16] As the approximately sixteen thousand delegates filed out of the hall following Graham's address, EC representatives handed out pamphlets giving notice that there was a mission field "white unto harvest" that remained virtually untouched by evangelicals who refused to see gay people as anything other than unrepentant sinners. "But guess what!" the pamphlet continued. "Our Lord's love is greater than the short-sightedness, ignorance, and homophobia of some people. We're here in Urbana to bear witness to the fact that we, too, are washed in the blood of the Lamb and are trying to live responsible lives as the homosexual Believers we know ourselves to be. . . . We and you come from the same backgrounds and we share the same Christian faith and fellowship, but maybe you have not noticed. And some of you are us. That's why we're here this week."[17]

With evangelical language, an evangelical audience, and an evangelical mission, from EC's 1976 emergence on the evangelical scene forward, the group thus consistently made it clear that the specifically evangelical emphasis was the entire point. The organization's fundamental evangelicalness indeed was its very raison d'être and Blair always stressed that EC should be understood primarily as "a group of evangelical Christians who happen to be gay and lesbian" rather than the other way around.[18] Explicitly formed as "a national ministry of evangelical Christians concerned about the misunderstanding of homosexuality among evangelicals and the misunderstanding of the Gospel among homosexuals," from the outset, the two main pillars of Blair's vision for the organization involved educating the former and supporting the latter.[19] The wider evangelical world needed to understand that homosexual orientation was neither unnatural, chosen, or inherently sinful. Gay and lesbian evangelicals needed help and encouragement with learning "to live their homosexuality responsibly as unto their Lord" by forming committed partnerships. Both were undeniably ambitious goals that quickly became all the more difficult.[20]

As it turned out, just as EC was getting up and off the ground, so too were a range of evangelical organizations based on an increasingly popular idea that was in diametric opposition to everything Blair's organization stood for. As the evangelical world increasingly turned toward a new kind of gay ministry as the standard approach, EC's vision of a future in which gay and lesbian evangelicals were affirmed and supported was rapidly eclipsed by one in which they were encouraged instead to seek answers from a cadre of organizations touting the ability to help them change.

The Birth of the Ex-gay Movement

After a characteristically evangelical conversion experience in 1973, Frank Worthen became convinced that he had been living in sin for many years, renounced "his homosexual lifestyle," and started attending a charismatic Christian church in the Bay Area of his native California.[21] At the urging of Kent Philpott, a minister from another local church, Worthen soon began offering counseling to a handful of gay and lesbian people during weekly meetings at Philpott's church. Shortly thereafter, the group adopted the name Love in Action (LIA) and thereby established one of the earliest known examples of a new breed of ministry that eventually became known as the ex-gay movement.[22] With the publication of a 1975 book arguing that homosexuality was obviously a choice—explaining, for instance, "that there is no such thing as a bisexual or a homosexual according to God's established order"—Kent Philpott furthermore helped invent what was effectively a new genre of publication: the ex-gay testimonial.[23] Based on a series of interviews with LIA participants, Philpott's book *The Third Sex?* chronicled the personal struggles of six people who, like Worthen, had decided to leave "the gay lifestyle" behind for good. In so doing, Philpott also helped establish a narrative blueprint for the countless stories of deliverance from homosexuality that soon proliferated in a burgeoning ex-gay movement as proof positive that change was indeed possible.[24]

Initially convinced that LIA was the only organization of its kind, Worthen soon discovered that the group was by no means alone in its mission to help gay people change. In 1975, Worthen connected with the Ex-gay Intervention Team (EXIT), an Anaheim, California–based group led by Michael Bussee and Jim Kaspar. The following year, Worthen, Bussee, Kaspar, and Barbara Johnson, a woman who had reached out to Worthen after finding out that her son was gay, joined forces for the first time. On the weekend of 10–12 September 1976, the group held a conference in Anaheim at the Melodyland Christian Center organized around their shared interest in "helping homosexuals find freedom."[25] By the end of the weekend, in true evangelical fashion, the sixty or so attendees decided to establish a new umbrella ministry called Exodus International that would function as a "Christian referral and resource network" for groups and individuals dedicated to helping people gain "freedom from homosexuality through faith in Jesus Christ."[26] Beginning with its 1976 founding and continuing through the end of the twentieth century, the organization explained its mission with a statement that read, "EXODUS is an international Christian effort to reach homosexuals and lesbians. EXODUS upholds God's standard of righteousness and holiness, which declares that homosexuality is sin and affirms HIS love and redemptive power to recreate the individual. It is the goal of EXODUS International to communicate this message to the Church, to the gay community, and to society."[27]

Early on, Exodus faced a number of internal and external obstacles that made institutional growth difficult. Internally, there were disagreements over both what "overcoming homosexuality" actually entailed and the most appropriate methods for bringing about the desired change. Some organizational leaders believed that transforming homosexuals into heterosexuals was the ultimate goal. Others were less sanguine about whether that kind of total change was possible. Although many members advocated therapeutic interventions, some were more interested in pursuing deliverance from demonic possession as the surest cure for anyone hoping to escape the "homosexual lifestyle." Some of the fledgling organization's constituent ministries were also divided over whether instantaneous change or long-term remedial efforts were most feasible. By the second annual convention, external stressors began cropping up as well when gay advocacy groups began protesting outside the organization's meetings.[28]

They weren't the only ones protesting the ex-gay concept either. By the time that groups like Exodus began proliferating in the mid-1970s, Blair had already spent years arguing that evangelicals should support committed same-sex partnerships instead of wasting so much time condemning those who happened to be gay. As ministries advertising their ability to repair or convert gay and lesbian people through some combination of questionable therapeutic and spiritual methods began spreading among his fellow evangelicals, he unsurprisingly responded by taking every possible opportunity to denounce the dangerous implications of the emerging ex-gay enterprise.[29]

As a professional psychotherapist, Blair saw the promises of homosexual to heterosexual conversion for what they were: dubious and often patently false claims based on junk psychology and limited anecdotal evidence. He knew for instance that the broader psychological community had recently begun to reverse course on the idea that homosexuality was a pathological disorder in need of a cure. Emerging on the heels of the American Psychological Association's (APA) decision to remove homosexuality from its Diagnostic and Statistical Manual (DSM) in 1973, the ex-gay movement's admixture of spiritual-pastoral and pseudopsychotherapeutic approaches to fixing homosexuality increasingly placed it on the fringes of mainstream psychology and Blair knew as much.[30] He also knew that, behind the growing tide of testimonials about deliverance and healing from homosexuality, the ex-gay movement had an open secret that would only stay secret for so long.

Ex-ex-gay

In Blair's later telling, while he had been holding the renegade meeting for the newly established EC across the street from the February 1976 gathering of the NAE, another gay ministry, Liberation in Jesus Christ, was advertising its services from a booth situated comfortably inside the exhibit hall.[31] Founded by Guy Charles—who famously claimed to have been converted to heterosexuality after accepting Jesus—Liberation in Jesus Christ was billed "as a Christian ministry within the Episcopal Church in the United States to help individuals with sexual problems, especially homosexuality and lesbianism."[32] Due in part to a chapter that he contributed to a 1976 book edited by evangelical psychologist Gary R. Collins, Charles's claims soon began receiving a wide hearing, with evangelical media outlets quickly latching on to his story as evidence that "homosexual healing" was possible.[33] Blair would have none of it. During a public debate with Charles, hosted by radio personality Barry Farber on a May 1976 edition of his nationally broadcast radio show, he said as much, openly contesting the very idea that one could experience total deliverance from homosexuality.[34]

Soon enough, Charles himself offered tragic proof that Blair was right. Following an investigation by charismatic Christian newspaper *The National*

Courier, which alleged that he had been sexually involved with some of the young men he was counselling, Charles resigned from Liberation in Jesus Christ in 1977.[35] For his part, Blair took no pleasure in Charles's struggle. As he later recounted, "Charles has suffered at the hands of homophobic zealots who encouraged him to deny his sexuality and who exploited his 'testimony' to suit their ignorance and bigotry. Now he, too, is a victim of that stupidity that masqueraded as miracle and that he himself was sucked into promoting."[36]

Although the end of Liberation in Jesus Christ was little cause for celebration, in Blair's mind, its demise at least offered an early example of the fundamental fraud at the heart of the entire ex-gay enterprise. He begged evangelical leaders who were beginning to repeat the "miraculous healing" stories of "those who have been changed from homosexual orientation to heterosexual through Christian conversion, prayer, exorcism, Spirit-baptism, or divine healing" not to be fooled. All previous psychotherapeutic efforts to reverse sexual orientation had proven woefully unsuccessful, and the psychological community had finally begun realizing that homosexuality was not a mental illness and should not be treated as such. With the theo-therapeutic "hocus-pocus" they were peddling, ex-gay ministries were attempting the impossible. Neither the psychological literature nor the recent pseudopsychospiritual approaches of the ex-gay movement had ever produced any "validated evidence" of true transformation from heterosexuality to homosexuality in Blair's telling, and he thus tried to warn evangelicals of the potential embarrassment awaiting those who continued touting "wished-to-be-true" ex-gay conversion narratives like Charles's.[37]

By that point, the evidence of the misleading, at best, and fraudulent, at worst, nature of ex-gay advocates' claims had in fact already begun piling up, Blair had the receipts, and he laid them all out in a booklet published in 1977. Referencing numerous examples from the rising tide of testimonies distributed by groups like EXIT, LIA, and Ex-Active-Gay-Liberated-Eternally (EAGLE) in which ex-gay advocates were simultaneously claiming deliverance from homosexuality while nonetheless admitting "that they still are 'on fire' with very strong temptations to commit homosexual acts, but have, through self-control, refrained from 'falling,'" he highlighted a fundamental problem with the movement's very premise: so many of the individuals who were supposedly converted from homosexuality nonetheless remained "sexually attracted to members of the same sex." Upon closer investigation of several instances of the recent phenomenon, Blair furthermore reported that he had personally spoken with a number of ex-gay leaders who admitted that most ex-gay men were still attracted to men, including one who confessed that "of course he did not know *any ex-gay* who was not still tempted by attractive men."[38]

By the late 1970s, precisely as Blair warned, the high relapse rate among ex-gay organizations had indeed become an open secret with the potential to undermine the entire movement. Even *Christianity Today* eventually took notice. When evangelicalism's flagship magazine later began reporting on the ex-gay movement, for instance, one article noted that four of the six people profiled in Kent Philpott's influential ex-gay book *The Third Sex?* had ultimately "reverted to their homosexual lifestyles" and lobbied unsuccessfully for the publisher to pull the book.[39]

Neither Guy Charles, nor Blair's examples, nor Philpott's subjects were the only ones either. Before the decade was over, Exodus founding member Michael Bussee and Exodus volunteer Gary Cooper gave the ex-gay movement its most infamous embarrassment of all. As Bussee later told the story, he and Cooper fell in love during their years working together at Exodus and finally realized as much in 1979 while on their way to give a presentation at a church in Virginia. Instead of giving their usual ex-gay testimonies, Bussee and Cooper delivered a rewritten speech to the unsuspecting congregation, confessing that they now believed that the church should accept gay people. The two men subsequently left Exodus and the ex-gay movement behind for good, later got married at a Metropolitan Community Church, and ultimately went on to become two of the most prominent and vocal opponents of the organization that Bussee had helped found. By the late 1970s, a number of similar defections had already given rise to a new trend that eventually became known as the "ex-ex-gay phenomenon."[40]

An Emerging Evangelical Debate

Throughout the 1960s and for most of the 1970s, evangelical leaders had largely taken for granted that the mere willingness to reconsider the moral legitimacy of homosexuality represented one more sign that the country's sexual permissiveness was sending it to hell in a handbasket. In their eyes, the fact that some liberal mainline Protestants were beginning a series of theological debates over homosexuality might have been disappointing but was by no means surprising. As evangelical theologian Robert K. Johnston explained, for instance, a diverse range of positions was always in play in "wider ecumenical circles where pluralistic approaches to theological authority are taken." But in evangelical circles where the Bible was the ultimate authority, there had been next to no controversy over homosexuality so far, "for evangelicals have traditionally held the Bible to be clear on this point." By the late 1970s, the near-unanimous evangelical consensus on homosexuality had seemingly developed some cracks, however, and Johnston thought he knew why. With the 1979 book *Evangelicals at an Impasse*, he ventured an explanation.[41]

The problem, Johnston explained, ultimately came down to the crucial distinction between biblical authority, on the one hand, and its interpretation and application, on the other. Since the rise of the post–World War II neoevangelical coalition, allegiance to the authority of the Bible was the most commonly used glue that held official evangelicals together. But by the time a second generation of card-carrying evangelicals emerged, it was becoming increasingly clear that a variety of theological, social-ethical, and political debates were threatening the tenuous unity that the first-generation neoevangelical leaders had forged. Evangelicals, he argued, indeed were different from other Christians in their express commitment to the authority of Scripture. They were also continually at odds over how exactly to translate an authoritative Bible into practice. Tying evangelical identity to a firm belief in scriptural authority was all well and good, in other words, until it came time for the interpretation and *application* of the authoritative Bible, at which point all bets were clearly off. The question of homosexuality was a perfect recent example of this perennial problem.[42]

Much to the surprise of many evangelical leaders, Johnston noted, a range of theological approaches to homosexuality had apparently gained a hearing among the nation's evangelicals. Although both the evangelical laity and most evangelical theologians still overwhelmingly believed that homosexuality was obviously sinful and forbidden by Scripture, a small but growing number of evangelical thinkers had recently begun arguing that Christians could and should reconsider the standard position, sparking instantaneous debate in the process. When *Christianity Today* surveyed evangelical leaders in its first 1978 issue, for example, many had pointed to the controversies surrounding homosexuality as the most significant religious development facing the nation's churches. The debate, in other words, had finally reached the evangelical world. In Johnston's judgment, by that point, it had furthermore become clear that the spectrum of theological positions on homosexuality was nearly as wide among evangelicals as it was among liberal Protestants.[43]

At one end, he observed, there was the "rejecting-punitive" approach, which had mostly disappeared among mainline thinkers but was increasingly prevalent among evangelicals due in part to the rising influence of evangelical political leaders. With rhetoric singling out gay people as deserving of the worst kinds of punishment, popular figures like Jerry Falwell, Anita Bryant, and Jack Wyrtzen were turning pervasive antigay prejudice among evangelicals into a hysterical backlash. Their rejecting-punitive approach was merely inflaming "prevalent Christian bigotry" against homosexual people and in Johnston's mind was therefore indefensible.[44] The next option, he continued, was a "rejecting-nonpunitive" approach that stressed the sinfulness of homosexual behavior, argued against the ordination of "practicing homosexuals," encouraged gay people to try becoming heterosexual, but stopped short of vilifying those who were inclined toward an "active homosexual life-style." For examples, Johnston pointed to two evangelical thinkers who had recently been involved in the United Presbyterian Task Force on Homosexuality and who had recently written books on the subject, Richard Lovelace and Don Williams.[45]

From there, Johnston moved to the "qualified acceptance" of homosexuality as found in the work of both German theologian Helmut Thielicke, who had recently become increasingly popular among American evangelicals, and Fuller Seminary ethicist and theologian Lewis B. Smedes. Both Thielicke's 1964 *The Ethics of Sex* and Smedes's 1976 *Sex for Christians*, Johnston explained, crucially diverged from Williams and Lovelace on an important methodological assumption that clearly affected their respective conclusions. Whereas Williams and Lovelace stressed the irrelevance of contemporary findings—whether via "personal testimony or empirical evidence"—for determining the appropriate Christian position on homosexuality, Smedes and Thielicke emphasized the *pastoral* importance of taking "contemporary opinion concerning homosexuality" into account when dealing directly with the problems of "real people with real suffering." Both thinkers, he argued, acknowledged the biblical witness's clear portrayal of male-female sexual pairing as the divinely ordered pattern of creation and homosexuality as a disordered and abnormal result of a fallen world. But in light of the fact that it appeared unlikely that anyone had ever consciously chosen this disordered orientation, both theologians *also* stressed that homosexual persons should not be condemned for what seemingly was beyond their control. According to Smedes and Thielicke, Johnston noted, homosexual people should "be encouraged to seek healing and/or to practice abstinence." But in a fallen world in which curing a disordered but unchosen orientation was not always possible, as a pastoral concession, the two theologians nonetheless cautiously advocated the occasional "qualified acceptance" of stable, loving, monogamous homosexual partnerships as a less than ideal but best possible arrangement in some instances.[46]

By crucially continuing to acknowledge that heterosexuality was quite obviously "the wider Biblical norm," in Johnston's judgment, both Smedes and Thielicke had offered careful reconsiderations of certain aspects of the church's position without venturing too far afield "from traditional theological judgment." But the evangelical thinkers like Letha Scanzoni, Virginia Mollenkott, and Ralph Blair who had recently begun arguing for the "full acceptance" of homosexuality were quite another story. Their suggestion that the apparent scriptural injunctions against homosexuality were addressed primarily to certain contextual practices such as idolatry or gang rape, and that such prohibitions had not been made with either the reality of a permanent and fixed sexual orientation or the idea of a lifelong, committed, homosexual relationship in mind, carried the full-acceptance advocates far beyond the traditional view.[47]

In Johnston's assessment, the varied reactions of the evangelical establishment to Scanzoni and Mollenkott's argument in their recent book *Is the Homosexual My Neighbor?* were a clear demonstration of just how deep the controversy went. Few evangelical reviewers agreed with the book's conclusions, he judged, but some had at least acknowledged the need to carefully consider its arguments. The same could not be said about the other major advocate for the full acceptance of homosexuality. With his unequivocal judgment that the Bible by no means condemned committed, monogamous, homosexual relationships, his consistent reminder that Christian views on homosexuality desperately needed to consider social-scientific findings about its cause and treatment, and his constant pleading for evangelicals to acknowledge that homosexuality was neither chosen nor reversible, Ralph Blair, Johnston argued, was "less careful in both his Biblical and theological analyses and more doctrinaire than Scanzoni and Mollenkott concerning scientific evidence." Unlike Scanzoni and Mollenkott's hotly debated book, he concluded, "Ralph Blair's writings have been largely ignored by the wider evangelical establishment."[48]

After reviewing all of the available arguments, Johnston ended with a proposal for an "evangelical agenda" on homosexuality. First, he argued, evangelicals needed to consider social-scientific findings and personal experiences while simultaneously subjecting them to the correction offered by an "objective encounter with the Spirit in Scripture." Contemporary observations need not be cast aside—as Lovelace proposed—but should be used only as a secondary supplement in the process of considering what the Bible had to say about God's will for homosexuality and never as an ultimate norm. Despite Mollenkott's, Scanzoni's, and Blair's attempts, Johnston continued, there still was no convincing biblical argument for the moral legitimacy of homosexual relationships, and evangelicals therefore needed to remain firm in their assertion that "homosexual activity" is always sinful. At the same time, evangelicals also needed to address their widespread homophobia and antigay prejudice. It seemed likely, he judged, that evangelicals would rightly continue affirming the sinfulness of homosexuality. But they also desperately needed to stop treating it as a particularly detestable sin that was somehow related to a conscious embrace of perversion. Evangelicals, in other words, were plenty good at hating the sin, but the "loving the sinner" part needed a lot of work.[49]

*

By the end of the 1970s, as Johnston pointed out, evangelicals indeed had begun debating their default position on homosexuality. Before the decade was over, a variety of evangelical periodicals had already included major features on homosexuality, with some devoting entire issues to the question. Though precious few evangelical editors, reviewers, and interpreters were willing to grant the legitimacy of their conclusions, evangelical dissenters like Scanzoni and Mollenkott had at least been able to force the debate into the evangelical mainstream.

Over time, the resulting controversy slowly but surely gave rise to an emerging consensus among evangelical leaders. When it did, the evangelical answer to homosexuality was strikingly similar to the analysis, conclusions, and agenda Johnston offered in 1979. Scanzoni and Mollenkott's work was treated as impressive but ultimately unpersuasive. Evangelical thinkers doubled down on their affirmation that the biblical norm prohibited homosexual behavior. A variety of evangelical figures echoed Johnston's admonition that evangelicals needed to avoid the harsh and prejudicial rhetoric of figures like Falwell. And his suggestion that Blair was largely being dismissed or ignored by mainstream evangelical leaders continued apace.

Johnston's judgment that a fundamental dividing line between Blair and much of the evangelical establishment came down to a disagreement over whether a cure for homosexuality was either possible or appropriate furthermore remained true and became truer as time went on. In Blair's view, curing homosexuality was both impossible *and* inappropriate. With the dawn of a new decade, it became abundantly clear that evangelical leaders increasingly disagreed with him on both accounts. Evangelicals Concerned and its views on homosexuality, in Blair's later telling, were already considered "*too* divergent, *too* deviant" to be considered a legitimate evangelical option by the close of the 1970s. With the exception of the progressive evangelical periodical *The Other Side*, he explained, mainstream evangelical publications were already refusing to let Blair's organization place ads in their pages. While simultaneously suggesting that there were a variety of specific interpretive issues on which evangelicals might disagree, in other words, the evangelical establishment had quickly ruled EC out of bounds.[50]

But worst of all in Blair's mind was the fact that his most dire warnings were falling on deaf ears. In developing the standard evangelical approach to homosexuality, much to his dismay, mainstream evangelical leaders increasingly agreed that change indeed was preferable, possible, and most readily on offer in ex-gay ministries.

A Developing Evangelical Consensus

Over the course of the 1980s, mainstream evangelical leaders' standard response to debates over homosexuality would consistently involve doubling down on the idea that the Bible expressly condemns homosexual behavior as sinful, reiterating the subevangelical nature of progay biblical interpretations, and standing firm in their defense of "traditional family values" against an increasingly godless and permissive secular culture. Christians, evangelical leaders regularly stressed, must never concede that "Gay is Good" despite what a rising tide of gay rights activists might say.

True to the post–World War II neoevangelical vision of a mainstream evangelical identity that was less angry than its most bellicose fundamentalist representatives, many evangelical leaders also increasingly urged the evangelical laity to avoid the most inflammatory kinds of rhetoric when talking about gay and lesbian people, occasionally encouraging them to put hurtful myths about homosexuality to rest as well. They needed to do so in no small part to distance themselves from evangelical political figures like Falwell and Bryant, who were capturing the public's attention with their controversial speeches. Although they definitely agreed with Falwell that homosexuality was sinful, a number of evangelical thinkers thus began emphasizing the need for compassion. Some called for their fellow evangelicals to put an end to the kinds of demeaning labels often used by the Religious Right. As the 1980s progressed, in other words, mainstream moderate evangelical leaders regularly agreed that Christians needed to continue "hating the sin" and "loving the sinner," but they needed to do so with far more compassion.

But if Christians were going to do more than simply rail against homosexuality, evangelical leaders began recognizing, then they needed a better alternative. Evangelicals needed to minister to gay and lesbian people instead of just condemning them. The eventual realization that groups like Exodus International were already doing just that ultimately gave mainstream evangelical leaders a tailor-made solution to their problem: change, it seemed, really was possible. Loving gay sinners, evangelicals decided, meant helping them change.

From the Fringes of Psychology to the Evangelical Mainstream

For a while, the ex-gay movement remained relatively small. The slow but ongoing depathologization of homosexuality that began in the 1970s had increasingly pushed reorientation efforts to the outskirts of the professional psychological community, and widespread evangelical homophobia had initially ensured that gay ministries like Exodus remained mostly confined to the shadows of the evangelical world. But with the help of one sensational, widely referenced, and enormously controversial study, which bridged the gap between mainstream psychology and evangelicalism, at the dawn of the 1980s, the ex-gay movement received a shot in the arm, a new measure of respectability, and a nudge away from the shadows and into the light of day all at once.

The study in question was conducted by E. Mansell Pattison, a professional psychiatrist, licensed minister, and eventual editorial board member of the journal *Pastoral Psychology*, whose credentials perfectly positioned him to address the strange juncture between the clinical mental health and evangelical worlds. Throughout the 1960s and 1970s, Pattison had published dozens of studies and articles on topics ranging from the treatment of alcoholism to faith healing in secular psychology and psychiatry journals. With articles in outlets like *Christianity Today* and the evangelical *Journal of the American Scientific Affiliation*, he had also periodically lent his psychological expertise to the evangelical community. When it came specifically to the question of homosexuality, in Pattison's view, there had clearly been a great deal of contradictory ideas and competing claims circulating in both the evangelical and professional psychological communities. By the mid-1970s, he thus began doing what he could to try to correct some of the prevailing confusion in both worlds.[51]

Homosexuality, Pattison argued, could be traced to early disturbances in the normal process of sexual identity development, which resulted in an orientation driven by the effort "to compensate for missing elements in the acquisition of identity."[52] Although homosexuals were justified in protesting their ongoing social persecution, "the polar extreme of Gay Lib militancy" was taking things too far. Replacing "Gay is Bad" with "Gay is Good," Pattison explained, was not the answer.[53] Homosexuality was "a developmental aberration" that would not be fixed by eliminating broader societal discrimination.[54] The good news, he pointed out, was that the aberration might not be permanent. What homosexual people needed most was neither scorn nor approval. What they really needed, Pattison suggested, was help changing.

By the late 1970s, in Pattison's telling, both the gay-liberation movement and much of the mainstream psychological community had ultimately concluded that changing sexual orientation was effectively impossible. In light of the existing data on the subject, which consistently demonstrated that the process was indeed intensive, difficult, and frequently unsuccessful, Pattison furthermore confessed that he, too, had once been pessimistic about the prospects of reorientation efforts. But that all changed, he went on to explain, with a discovery that forced him to reconsider his previously negative judgments. In a 1977 article in the *Journal of the American Scientific Affiliation*, Pattison enthusiastically reported some initial observations about his discovery. "I am happy to report," he noted, "that some exciting and intriguing events have occurred over the past five years. Across the country in various places, Christian men and women have achieved successful changes in their homosexual orientations, their lifestyles, and achieved major emotional and spiritual growth. Although I plan to publish later a series of scientific studies on this process, I should like to share some preliminary observations." It appeared, Pattison continued, that the prevailing assumptions about the impossibility of reversing sexual orientation were mistaken. Christian groups were helping people do just that. The implication of this discovery was nothing short of amazing, he concluded, "for it suggests that homosexual orientations are indeed amenable to profound change and it highlights the importance of the Christian community for such a process."[55]

The real bombshell came when Pattison finally published the results of his subsequent study in the December 1980 issue of the secular *American Journal of Psychiatry*. Although the conventional wisdom among secular mental health professionals held that change in orientation was impossible, Pattison began, he had recently been given the opportunity to study the question in a thoroughly scientific way. A "religious hot-line crisis program" that offered "lay crisis services to homosexuals" was claiming that a number of its clients had successfully changed from an exclusively homosexual orientation to heterosexuality. Recognizing that the organization's claims offered the perfect circumstances for an in-depth psychological study, Pattison had jumped at the chance. The results, he reported, were nothing short of groundbreaking. Based on a thorough review of the program and personal interviews with a number of its clients, Pattison concluded that all eleven of the subjects that he studied "demonstrated a strikingly profound shift in sexual orientation," which represented the first major documented evidence that homosexuals could become heterosexual "without long-term psychotherapy." What's more, he continued, it seemed that the religious program at the center of his study was not the only group of its kind. It appeared that a network of similar, religiously based, informal self-help peer groups, akin to Alcoholics Anonymous, was beginning to emerge, and the implications were revolutionary. This "lively social movement," Pattison suggested, might just be offering the effective method for changing sexual orientation that had eluded the mainstream psychological community. Change really was possible, and this was the proof.[56]

The organization in Pattison's study was the group started by Melodyland Christian Center that eventually became known as EXIT. What Pattison had discovered, in other words, was the ex-gay movement. With the 1980 article reporting on his findings, "'Ex-gays': Religiously Mediated Change in Homosexuals," he thereby introduced the label into the scientific literature for the very first time.[57]

In the wake of the article's publication, evangelical authors wasted little time delivering the news from the annals of secular psychology into the hands of the evangelical public. When mainstream evangelical thinkers began converging in the early 1980s on a consensus view of what they were supposed to say about homosexuality, Pattison's research became grist for those who believed that helping gay people change struck the appropriate balance between compassion and denunciation.[58]

By offering evangelical readers some "Biblical guidance through a moral morass," an early 1980 *Christianity Today* editorial helped set the tone for the decade. While simultaneously reaffirming the biblical truth that any and all homosexual behavior was sinful, for their part, evangelicals needed to stop promoting unhelpful stereotypes about gay people. Evangelicals, the editors noted, were missing a crucial opportunity to "show compassion" to gay people by offering them "teaching, preaching, and counseling that strengthens and supports those who see their need of help and who want to change." Homosexuality, the editors explained, was neither normal nor incurable. Although change was difficult, they noted, it was certainly possible, and homosexual "Christians, of course, should have the highest motivation to change."[59]

In early 1981, evangelicalism's flagship magazine did its readers one better, moving a step beyond "biblical guidance" with an in-depth feature offering clear evidence of how a number of ministries were courageously helping "Christians with homosexual problems" change. In an article, not so subtly titled "Homosexuals Can Change," Tom Minnery pointed out that evangelical negativity and fear was driving homosexual people to look elsewhere for help. The astounding recent growth of the gay-positive Metropolitan Community Church was a prime example. Based on the testimonies of "some two dozen homosexuals" that *Christianity Today* had interviewed, the article continued, it was clear that evangelical churches were failing to minister to gay people. If more evangelicals would only listen to the courageous stories of people like Frank Worthen, whose organization Love in Action was out there doing the difficult work of homosexual ministry, perhaps then they would realize "that change from the homosexual lifestyle is more likely if straight Christians don't scare them off."[60]

After profiling a number of ex-gay leaders, Minnery went on to highlight the true significance of ministries like LIA. In spite of the hateful condemnation of so many Christians, the lack of financial support from the nation's churches, and the opposition of progay propagandists, ex-gay organizations were experiencing real success in their efforts to deliver people from homosexuality. "The evidence is too great to deny it," he noted. Evangelicals looking for solid proof needed only to consider the results of a recent study by Mansell Pattison, which Minnery quoted at length. Pattison's study, the article explained, included examples of eleven formerly homosexual men who had successfully developed attraction to women, eight of whom "no longer have homosexual dreams, fantasies, or physical arousal. In other words, these eight were cured—something gay activists often claim is impossible." Further still, Minnery noted, "Pattison's findings are significant, because Evangelicals Concerned, an organization of self-styled Christian homosexuals, is adamant about the failure of true homosexuals to be able to change their sexual orientation . . . the homosexuals in Evangelicals Concerned do all they can to discredit Love in Action and all 'ex-gay' ministries."[61]

The following month, in the March 1981 edition of the *Reformed Journal*, Robert K. Johnston similarly stressed the importance of Pattison's study for recent evangelical debates about homosexuality. The driving force behind the debate, Johnston argued, was the twofold claim that reversing homosexual orientation was both *inappropriate* and *impossible*. In light of their argument that the traditional position was based on an incorrect interpretation of a handful of biblical passages, evangelicals like Scanzoni and Mollenkott had suggested that attempts to cure homosexuality were *inappropriate*. Given his suggestion that there was no validated evidence of successful change from homosexuality to heterosexuality, Ralph Blair was the most representative example of the argument that such attempts were also impossible. If either argument—that a cure was neither appropriate nor possible—was successfully proven, Johnston confessed, then evangelicals would indeed need to revise the traditional position. For this reason, he explained, Pattison's findings were unavoidably significant. The study offered the first clear and documented scientific proof of successful reorientation, which ultimately meant that "we can no longer speak of the impossibility of change in one's sexual orientation, and thus of the 'naturalness' of homosexuality among one group of people." Like alcoholism or drug addiction, homosexuality really was curable.[62]

Blair's response to both articles was as quick as it was trenchant. In letters to the editors of both magazines, he castigated Minnery's shoddy reporting and Johnston's oversight in failing to give the Pattison study a much-needed closer look. In subsequent booklets, conference papers, and articles, he tried his best to warn anyone who would listen that its problems were too numerous to count. The results, he explained, were neither as airtight as the two articles had made them seem nor even as substantial as Pattison's original report had claimed.[63]

Blair consistently argued that the entire study was invalidated by a number of crucial flaws—not the least of which was the tricky double standard that Pattison used when talking about homosexuality and heterosexuality. "So eager are they to see change," he noted, "that they speak of a person's being 'heterosexual' even though there are continued homosexual dreams, fantasies, and impulses and no heterosexual acts, but they speak of a person's 'homosexuality' in terms, fundamentally, of overt homosexual acts." Sure, some of the men had apparently been able to avoid "homosexual acts." But in reality, there were only two men in the entire study who reported experiencing absolutely "no homosexual dreams, fantasies, or impulses," and the sample set was far from random anyway. From among the three hundred who had attempted the program, the leaders of EXIT had handpicked the records of thirty men who had been successfully cured, only eleven of whom had agreed to be interviewed. Based on a set of onetime retrospective interviews with a handpicked group who were willing to tell their stories, in Blair's telling, the report might have seemed like a legitimately scientific psychological study, but it wasn't. The willingness on Pattison's part to accept two out of three hundred as a measure of success represented the kind of willful ignorance brought on by wishful thinking, Blair judged, and the predominantly evangelical ranks of those who were excitedly referencing the results were merely seeing what they wanted to see.[64]

In retrospect, the reality behind the Pattison study was actually worse than Blair had initially imagined. Although he knew that Michael Bussee and Gary Cooper had still been involved with EXIT at the time and that they had also been involved in selecting the files that Pattison considered, Blair was likely unaware that their role in the research was even deeper still. In a 2011 interview, Bussee later confessed that he and Cooper had in fact been "Subject Number 2" and "Subject Number 1" in Pattison's study. At the time, both of the men who later became some of the most prominent critics of the ex-gay movement had reportedly gone from an exclusively homosexual Kinsey 6 to an exclusively heterosexual Kinsey 0. The only problem, as Bussee later explained, was the study's assumption that a group of men who were desperately hoping that they had in fact changed would be willing or able to answer the questions with complete honesty. "We professed that we had been healed—past tense," Bussee recounted, "because it was part of the theology to claim your healing in order to bring it about."[65]

Change Is Possible

Despite Blair's persistent protests, as the 1980s progressed, evangelical thinkers repeatedly doubled down on the possibility of change. For many moderate mainstream evangelical leaders, the consensus view became a twofold refrain: evangelicals needed to be nicer to gay people than Jerry Falwell was, and the clearest way to do so involved paying attention to groups like Exodus that were already doing the work. Ex-gay ministries, in other words, offered mainstream evangelicals a middle-ground solution that they could point to as a way of showing more compassion to gay people than the Religious Right was often willing to consider.

Christianity Today's ongoing coverage was a case in point. Editor Kenneth S. Kantzer's 1983 article "Homosexuals in the Church" called for both "godly attitudes toward homosexuals" and "godly faithfulness by the homosexual." Godly attitudes toward homosexuals, Kantzer explained, required "loving the sinner while condemning his sin." Godly faithfulness by homosexuals involved trying to change. Although it was admittedly a difficult process, Kantzer noted, "Change can occur by the power of God working through the gospel and the spiritual resources of the Christian community."[66] The following year, Beth Spring struck a similar note in an article profiling the ex-gay leaders who were hard at work marshaling the spiritual resources necessary for helping gay people "escape from homosexual lifestyles." In light of the dubious claims of the gay rights movement and other kinds of "church organizations for gays" that homosexuality was no different from being left-handed, the article explained that evangelical ex-gay organizations were offering a desperately needed service "by demonstrating a scriptural way out of homosexuality." In the absence of more evangelical churches willing "to offer a third alternative" between the increasing societal acceptance of homosexuality as an unobjectionably natural variation and the outright condemnation of all homosexual people, Spring concluded, groups like Exodus, "staffed by people who have endured the pain of passage out of homosexual behavior," were committed to filling the gap with "authentic models of change for men and women still struggling with a misplaced sexual identity."[67]

An article in the 9 August 1985 issue continued the theme. Randy Frame's "The Homosexual Lifestyle: Is There a Way Out?" once again gave favorable coverage to the rising tide of "former gays." The article likewise portrayed the ex-gay movement as a kind of via media between the most extreme antigay rhetoric of some Christians—pointing by way of example to R. J. Rushdoony's infamous defense of capital punishment for homosexual practice—and the most extreme arguments of the "prohomosexual camp" that the church's traditional reading of scriptural prohibitions needed revising. It also highlighted the recent gathering of nearly two hundred mostly ex-gay Christians, who were "living testimonies that practicing homosexuals can become heterosexuals," at the tenth annual meeting of Exodus International.[68]

In addition to its coverage of ex-gay organizations as crucial alternatives to progay perspectives, Frame's 1985 article went on to explain that there was an important theoretical development taking place in the ex-gay movement. Recently, he noted, many of the leaders of Exodus had begun rethinking their previous understandings of homosexuality, its cause, and how best to treat it. In Frame's telling, the shift had come in large part due to the influence of British psychologist Elizabeth Moberly, whose recent book *Homosexuality: A New Christian Ethic* developed a fresh interpretation of the origins and remedies of homosexual orientation.[69]

According to Moberly, homosexuality was not an intrinsic abnormality but instead resulted from normal developmental needs that had gone unmet. Homosexual desires, she theorized, were traceable to early ruptures in a person's relationship with members of the same sex, most especially between the child and their same-sex parent. These fractured relationships resulted in resentment toward members of one's own sex, which then yielded a "defensive detachment." Same-sex sexual attraction was thus a product of what Moberly termed the "reparative drive"—a natural urge to compensate for a broken relationship with one's parent by seeking an inappropriate substitute. "Sexual sin," she explained, "is contrary to God's intention, but homosexuality, although often an occasion for sexual sin, is essentially a state of incomplete development." Homosexually oriented people hoping to reach developmental maturity in their relationships with members of their own sex, in Moberly's view, needed something that the church had crucially failed to provide: a nonjudgmental context in which they could develop appropriate, nonsexual, same-sex friendships and relationships.[70] During the early 1980s, Frame's article pointed out, this solution was becoming increasingly popular among ex-gay leaders.

Though mainstream psychology had long since rejected the underlying assumptions of Moberly's framework—specifically, the idea that homosexuality was pathological and that its origins were a sign of developmental immaturity—by that point, her reparative approach was indeed becoming all the rage among the ex-gay movement. By drawing on a variety of older psychoanalytic theories about the origins of homosexual orientation, which the contemporary psychological community viewed as discredited and out of date, and linking them with a theological belief that homosexual activity was "contrary to the will and purposes of God for mankind," with her 1983 book, Moberly furthermore introduced the world to what became known as "reparative therapy" for the very first time.[71]

For Blair, the ongoing publicity that *Christianity Today* was giving to ex-gay organizations was unconscionable. He responded to Frame's article with yet another letter to the editor, which ran in September 1985. "Why can't *CT* at least be honest about homosexuality?" he queried. "Disagree, but tell the truth." Ex-gay people, Blair pointed out, regularly admitted that their same-sex desire continued. But ex-gay ministries kept claiming that their clients had been transformed into heterosexuals, and *Christianity Today* kept buying it and promoting it.[72]

Two months later, the magazine addressed Blair's specific argument in favor of affirming monogamous same-sex relationships head-on by inviting a "biblical analysis" from influential evangelical theologian John R. W. Stott. In a preface to the essay, the editors explained their rationale. "An increasingly more vocal Christian gay community (characterized by such groups as Evangelicals Concerned and the Metropolitan Community Churches) is actively challenging the church's traditional understanding of homosexual behavior and its sinfulness," they noted. Given this challenge, the editors had reached out to Stott for a rebuttal to the gay Christian community's arguments, and he had not disappointed. The resulting essay presented an extensive case for "why same-sex partnerships are not a Christian option." With a title that made the conclusions clear from the outset, *Christianity Today* in turn gave Stott's article "Homosexual 'Marriage'" top-line billing as the issue's cover story. As readers might have come to expect, the widely respected evangelical theologian made all the key evangelical points. The Bible was clear: homosexual orientation was obviously a disordered result of the fall, and all homosexual behavior was clearly sinful. Although change was difficult, Stott furthermore stressed, Christians were people of hope, and they must therefore refuse to acquiesce to the "despairing opinions of the secular mind" that healing for the homosexual was impossible.[73]

Special Rights and an Immorality Disease

In addition to their belief in the possibility of change, during the mid-1980s, mainstream evangelical leaders added two more items to the list of semi-official evangelical consensus positions on homosexuality. The first was a response to gay rights activism. The second was a response to AIDS.

While moderate evangelical thinkers were championing ex-gay ministries as a more productive and compassionate response to homosexuality than the tirades of the Religious Right, they were simultaneously becoming increasingly alarmed by the rising tide of the mainstream gay rights movement. By the middle of the decade, for instance, *Christianity Today* was regularly reporting on the developing culture war between Christians and gay rights advocates.[74] Around the same time, the most official organization in the unofficial evangelical establishment, the NAE, furthermore made it abundantly clear that mainstream evangelicals opposed "special rights" for gay people with a 1985 "Statement on Homosexuality" that checked all of the consensus boxes.[75]

Opening with a clear condemnation of homosexual activity as a degrading and unnatural abomination that brought "grave consequences" both in this world and beyond, the statement nonetheless noted that homosexual people who repented and accepted the gospel could be forgiven. Through prayer and with God's help, it continued, they could also have hope for healing and deliverance. For their part, pastors, theologians, and medical specialists therefore needed "to expand research on the factors which give rise to homosexuality and to develop therapy, pastoral care and congregational support leading to complete restoration." The NAE saved its most extended exhortation, however, for the nation's politicians and legislators. Stressing the organization's belief that homosexuality was by no means in the same morally neutral category as race, gender, or nationality, the statement declared:

> While homosexuals as individuals are entitled to civil rights, including equal protection of the law, the NAE opposes legislation which would extend special consideration to such individuals based upon their "sexual orientation." Such legislation inevitably is perceived as legitimatizing the practice of homosexuality and elevates that practice to the level of an accepted moral standard. While maintaining our opposition to proposed so-called "Gay Rights" legislation, where such legislation has been enacted into law, NAE strongly urges that churches and religious organizations be exempted from compliance by amendment to the law. The position and practice of such organizations regarding homosexuality are determined by their religious convictions. This we hold to be a grave matter of religious freedom.[76]

With its 1985 statement, the NAE thus accurately captured, reflected, and helped codify the consensus of the evangelical world: homosexuality was forbidden by Scripture, and homosexuals could hope for deliverance through conversion. It also demonstrated the convergence between evangelicalism's more moderate mainstream and its most conservative right-wing flank on the particular question of how evangelicals should respond to public debates over gay rights. Already by the mid-1980s, in other words, whatever the *pastoral* response to homosexuality might be, it was already clear that the evangelical *political* position on gay rights involved a twofold platform with both offensive and defensive components. On offense, evangelicals would oppose special rights for homosexuals at all costs. On defense, they would defend the religious freedom of Christians to claim exemption from any such laws.

The same year that the NAE issued its first official statement on homosexuality, most of the broader American public simultaneously became aware of the AIDS epidemic for the first time when the 1985 coverage of Rock Hudson's death from AIDS-related complications propelled the crisis into the national consciousness. By the time that religious periodicals like the *Christian Century* and *Christianity Today* began covering the epidemic in 1985, the Religious Right had already set the tone for the public's perception of Christian reactions to the crisis. Reverend Jerry Falwell in particular would infamously be quoted as suggesting that AIDS was "a gay plague," that it was "the wrath of God upon homosexuals," that it represented "a definite form of the judgment of God upon a society," and indeed that it was the "lethal judgment of God on America" for tolerating and endorsing homosexuality.[77] As a result of the outsized influence of figures like Falwell in the public imagination, for the rest of the decade, both the moderate evangelical mainstream and the mainline Protestant churches would be forced to define their respective answers to AIDS in the shadow of the "wrath of God" rhetoric that had been so effectively deployed by the rising Religious Right.[78]

Although there were always some exceptions, in the years to come, the standard evangelical response to AIDS might have differed from Falwell in tone but not so much in substance. Across the board, it became incumbent upon evangelical thinkers of all varieties—from conservative to progressive—to emphasize that sinful behavior had real-world consequences. Many were less willing than Falwell to attribute the virus directly to a particular divine intervention signaling God's displeasure for a nation that condoned homosexuality. But the vast majority nonetheless affirmed the sentiment that there was an intrinsic link between AIDS and immorality.

In the wake of Rock Hudson's death, a *Christianity Today* article by Calvin Seminary professor Cornelius Plantinga Jr. set the tone. For evangelicals struggling to make sense of their newfound awareness about the epidemic, Plantinga emphasized that "serious Christians are reminded by the AIDS phenomenon that God is not mocked. When someone sins, someone pays."[79] The following year, in a 1986 sermon, Billy Graham similarly wondered aloud whether AIDS "might be a judgment of God upon us" or perhaps "just a warning from God."[80] That same year, Southern Baptist Convention (SBC) president Charles Stanley forthrightly argued that "AIDS is God indicating his displeasure" with gay people.[81] In 1987, the SBC made its official position on AIDS clear with a resolution that stopped short of declaring that the virus represented the judgment of God, but that nonetheless denounced safe sex campaigns as a concession to "perversion" and explicitly condemned "any mass and indiscriminate distribution of condoms or other sexual devices which seem to encourage an acceptance of immorality or deviant behavior."[82] In a book published that same year, *Power in the Blood: A Christian Response to AIDS*, Christian reconstructionist David Chilton captured the prevailing sentiment among evangelicals. Even though it might not be a universally "homosexual disease," Chilton argued, it was quite clearly an "'immorality disease,' and most of those 'really nice' but immoral people contracting and spreading it are homosexuals."[83]

Although many of Chilton's reconstructionist ideas were undoubtedly on the fringes of 1980s-era evangelicalism, his understanding of AIDS as an "immorality disease" was not. Time and again, fundamentalists like Falwell had reiterated such claims, mainstream leaders like Billy Graham had suggested as much, the SBC had implied the same thing, and *Christianity Today* had agreed. The NAE came to the same conclusion shortly thereafter. In its 1988 "Statement on AIDS," the bellwether organization of the evangelical mainstream pulled no punches in identifying the source of the problem and the only acceptable solution. Sure, the statement admitted, there were "innocent sufferers." But the disease obviously had moral dimensions that government and private organizations alike were ignoring. "The nexus between immoral behavior and the spread of the AIDS virus is self-evident," the NAE judged, and the only real answer to the AIDS crisis would thus be found in the promotion of "biblical sexual morality."[84]

Even progressive evangelical thinkers agreed. Writing for the *Christian Century* in January 1988, Ron Sider offered an "evangelical perspective" on AIDS in which he, too, emphasized "the importance of the connection between homosexual promiscuity and the transmission of AIDS." The idea that God had recently created the disease to uniquely punish a specific sin was unbiblical and empirically false, he noted, and evangelicals certainly needed to do much better caring for people with AIDS. But violating the divine mandates that were clearly built into the created order came with consequences, and evangelicals were right to condemn homosexual practices as one such violation. "To the extent that there is a link between AIDS and homosexuality," Sider therefore declared, "the major point that must be made is that it is homosexual promiscuity that stands condemned, not evangelical belief that homosexual practice is wrong."[85]

Solidifying the Evangelical Position

By the late 1980s, mainstream evangelical leaders had thus spent the better part of the decade forging an unofficial consensus view that homosexual activity was obviously sinful, that such immoral behavior was inextricably tied to the AIDS crisis, that gay people should not be granted any special rights, and that evangelicals needed to do better at loving gay sinners. Although some were beginning to realize that the cure on offer by ex-gay ministries was neither as instantaneous nor as guaranteed as some had hoped, many evangelical thinkers continued stressing that groups like Exodus were at least trying to help people change. The mainstream evangelical position by that point furthermore held that such efforts were unquestionably sincere, admirable, and worth supporting. Homosexuality, most evangelical leaders agreed, was neither natural nor inborn, and change was possible. To suggest otherwise was to risk one's evangelical credentials.

Progressive evangelical sociologist Tony Campolo recognized as much. When he deviated ever so slightly from the consensus view, he was fully aware that doing so would likely "incur the wrath of many of my evangelical friends," which it did. The infraction came in a 1988 book, *20 Hot Potatoes Christians Are Afraid to Touch*, in which Campolo provocatively asked, "does Christianity have any good news for homosexuals?" From the outset, Campolo made it abundantly clear that he would in no way be suggesting that evangelicals change their view on the sinfulness of homosexual *behavior*. The problem, in his telling, was that the standard evangelical reaction to anyone with a homosexual *orientation* was revulsion and disgust. Pointing out that he personally knew and admired many "brave saints" with a homosexual orientation who nonetheless remained celibate in light of their belief that the Bible clearly prohibited homosexual activity, Campolo stressed that the typical evangelical solution—demanding "that to be saved, homosexuals must also be free from their homosexual orientation"—was often making things worse.[86]

By continuously promoting the healing and transformation of homosexuals into heterosexuals, Campolo argued, evangelicals were simultaneously making both a theological and a scientific error. Theologically, this viewpoint confused "what God *can* do and *what* He will do" to potentially tragic ends—including, for example, a young man he knew of who prayed long and hard for deliverance from homosexuality but never experienced it and ultimately committed suicide as a result. Scientifically, the ongoing promotion of this overly simple understanding of deliverance reflected evangelical ignorance of the most up-to-date findings and research. Sociologists and physiologists increasingly agreed, for instance, that homosexual orientation was neither chosen nor caused by parental failures and likely arose through some combination of biological and hormonal factors. The theological implications of the scientific data, in his telling, were profound. "If many of those who have a homosexual orientation are the way they are through no fault of their own, but rather as a result of inborn conditions or hormonal changes," Campolo concluded, "then it becomes dubious that much can be accomplished simply by asking such persons to repent and choose to be heterosexuals." If evangelicals wanted to truly serve their homosexual brothers and sisters, he explained, they needed to move beyond simplistic and unhelpful admonitions to change and instead find ways to love and support them in Christian community.[87]

In July 1989, Living in Freedom Eternally (LIFE), a New York–based ex-gay ministry, published a newsletter denouncing Campolo's views of homosexuality as "unbiblical and harmful," arguing that his book had "given 'aid and comfort to the enemy' by distorting and avoiding the truth." Later that year, *Christianity Today* covered the controversy in an article explaining that the debate ultimately came down to the fact that Campolo had a fundamentally different understanding of the origins of sexual orientation: groups like LIFE and Exodus believed *nurture* was responsible, whereas Campolo seemed to emphasize that *nature* was the source. For his part, the article furthermore explained, Campolo had issued a brief statement responding to the organization's accusations in which he granted that perhaps some people might have the possibility of miraculous delivery from homosexuality, while nonetheless reaffirming that demanding deliverance from all homosexual people was unwise and unfair.[88]

That same year, *Christianity Today* finally put the debate over whether the ex-gay movement was "delivering on deliverance" and how successfully, if so, front and center with an issue featuring three separate articles addressing the question emblazoned on the front cover, "Ex-gay: Can Homosexuals really change?" In the straightforwardly titled "Homosexuality according to Science," Wheaton College Department of Psychology chair Stanton L. Jones challenged the increasingly widespread but, in his mind, patently false notion that change was utterly impossible. Change in orientation was difficult but possible, Jones explained, and nothing in the scientific literature should convince evangelicals to abandon the view that homosexual behavior was obviously sinful.[89]

Readers hoping for evidence could simply turn the pages to the article "I Found Freedom," in which Colin Cook recounted his "labyrinthine" path from homosexuality to heterosexuality. After losing his first ministry in 1974 due to the initial exposure of his homosexuality, followed by the 1986 collapse of Quest Learning Center—a "homosexual healing ministry" that he had spent years building but ultimately lost because his "recovery . . . was not yet complete"—Cook assured readers that he had finally overcome homosexuality with God's help. Despite the obvious embarrassment of having his failures recounted once again in print, Cook explained, he simply had to tell his story as confirmation that change was possible lest "thousands of Christians . . . yield to the despairing persuasion that homosexuality is an irreversible fate."[90]

Senior staff writer Tim Stafford's article profiling the then ten-year-old ex-gay movement echoed Cook's conclusion: leaving the homosexual life-style was difficult but possible. The ex-gay movement clearly had plenty of critics and a record of high-profile failures, he explained, but its successes could not be denied. After in-depth research and interviews with Exodus leaders like Frank Worthen, it was clear that ex-gay organizations were doing important work, and Stafford was duly impressed. Far less impressive, the article continued, was the "absolute and unyielding" perspective of "the arch critic of the ex-gay movement, Ralph Blair." Although his investigation had primarily involved interviews with insiders, Stafford had done his journalistic due diligence by traveling to Manhattan for an interview with

Blair. "The founder of Evangelicals Concerned (EC), a group that promotes monogamous relationships between Christian homosexuals," Stafford explained, "Blair publishes a newsletter with his caustic reviews of evangelical books that discuss homosexuality, and a sarcastic diatribe against the ex-gay movement." The contrast between Blair's views and the ex-gay movement, he continued, were stark in more ways than one.[91]

At first, Stafford reported, Blair seemed mild, composed, and generally charitable. But that all changed when the topic of the ex-gay movement came up. Angrily denouncing ex-gay organizations as nothing but PR, in Stafford's telling, Blair inflexibly refused to consider that changing orientation might be possible. Unable to square the image of a fraudulent ex-gay movement with his own experience interviewing its leaders, Stafford felt that Blair's anger was unjustifiable and misplaced. In his judgment, the problems with Blair's perspective only became more obvious as the interview progressed. In particular, the suggestion that demanding celibacy from all homosexual people was cruel and unnecessary, Stafford explained, clearly reflected a belief that "makes some sense in our modern therapeutic society, but none at all in biblical thinking." His experience with ex-gay leaders, on the other hand, had left a far more positive impression. "I went doubtful; I came away with a cautious optimism," Stafford confessed. The ex-gay leaders he had interviewed seemed "open, sincere, and vulnerable." They were self-aware and comfortable with the reality of the gradual process of change. In his view, in other words, the ex-gay movement was offering realistic hope, and it was long past time for evangelicals to stop holding organizations like Exodus at arm's length.[92]

In Blair's view, the 1989 *Christianity Today* issue on homosexuality was a mixed bag. On the whole, the magazine's overwhelmingly positive spin on the ex-gay phenomenon was more of the same disappointing coverage. But at least he had been able to explain himself. Articulating his perspective in the pages of the most influential evangelical publication meant that the broader evangelical world might at least get to hear a counterargument to the consistent "change is possible" refrain.[93]

Much to Blair's dismay, that refrain only got louder as time went on. With the advent of a new decade, the magazine's ongoing willingness to publish news items, editorials, articles, and book reviews authored by, covering, featuring, and promoting ex-gay leaders and their work only helped solidify the evangelical consensus that reorientation efforts were legitimate and worth supporting. From the early through the mid-1990s, *Christianity Today's* regular coverage of the ex-gay movement reflected a growing awareness among mainstream evangelicals that they could not simply ignore homosexuality as an "outside issue." Evangelicals needed to know about "the homosexual crisis," and they needed to be able to offer a soundly evangelical response. Based on their widening recognition that conservative Christians were neither immune to homosexuality nor doing enough about it, evangelical leaders thus reiterated what was already the standard refrain. To be able to take a firm stand against the incorrect view of homosexuality advanced both by the secular progay agenda and by allegedly evangelical organizations like Blair's, evangelicals needed to know that change was possible. Mainstream, moderate evangelicals needed to be the "loving opposition" to the loudest voices of the gay rights movement by hating the sin and loving the sinner. The most loving thing to do for those who had learned a homosexual orientation was to let them know that ex-gay organizations offered hope. As the decade marched on, mainstream evangelical thinkers increasingly enshrined this view as the best, truest, and only legitimate evangelical position.[94]

The Rise and Fall of the Ex-gay Movement

From its earliest emergence in the early 1970s through the mid-1990s, the ex-gay movement had been forced to labor mostly on the fringes of both the mainstream psychological community and the wider evangelical world. Despite the publicity and coverage offered by mainstream evangelical leaders, ex-gay leaders' regular appeals for support from major evangelical organizations went mostly unanswered, and the movement perpetually struggled to remain sustainable. In Frank Worthen's later telling, in reality, ex-gay organizations spent nearly twenty-five years feeling "ignored by the church and the culture." Although organizations like Exodus had effectively convinced many moderate evangelical thinkers that their work was worthwhile, in other words, when it came time to put their money where their leaders' mouths were, evangelicals had mostly looked the other way.[95]

The fact that the ex-gay movement's emergence had coincided with the rise of the Religious Right certainly didn't help matters. Even though many in evangelicalism's moderate mainstream had increasingly come around to the idea that the ex-gay movement represented a valuable and important pastoral response to the homosexuality crisis, their constant reiteration of the message that change was possible was often drowned out by evangelical political activists' cries against special rights for homosexuals, the Religious Right's harsher denunciations of homosexuality as a perverse lifestyle, and constant calls to arms for evangelicals to stop the rapidly advancing gay agenda before it was too late. A handful of evangelical thinkers occasionally conceded that homosexuals deserved human rights, but even the most progressive evangelical figures had consistently balked at the prospect of comprehensive gay rights protections. For evangelicals across the board, the fact that homosexuality was gaining acceptance in the broader culture always took precedent. The conversation began and ended, in other words, with a clear declaration that evangelicals must necessarily reject all homosexual behavior as inarguably immoral and oppose any and all societal efforts to suggest otherwise to boot.

Though the evangelical consensus on that point would by no means change, a number of crucial developments during the 1990s nonetheless helped move the idea that change was possible from a motto that many mainstream evangelical leaders accepted to a rallying cry that was widely embraced across the evangelical world.

In the in-depth study of ex-gay organizations *Straight to Jesus*, for example, Tanya Erzen recounts how powerful evangelical organizations like Concerned Women for America, Focus on the Family, and the Family Research Council spent the 1970s and 1980s all but refusing to acknowledge that the ex-gay movement even existed. Ex-gay leaders like Worthen, Erzen explains, spent years trying to gain a hearing from the leaders behind such organizations to no avail. One of the first major signs that the ex-gay movement was beginning to move from the evangelical periphery to the main stage, she furthermore argues, came when James Dobson's Focus on the Family began subtly shifting its antigay rhetoric in the late 1980s.[96]

Although his organization continued deploying the kind of "promotion of perversion" and "no special rights" rhetoric it had long used in fighting the societal normalization of homosexuality, by the early 1990s, Dobson had also started publishing articles with titles like "There Is Hope for the Homosexual." Then, when Focus on the Family hired ex-gay leader John Paulk in

1994, Erzen points out, the polemical tone of the organization's publications began rapidly giving way to the kind of "hope for change" language that the ex-gay movement had been using for years. In many ways, the support of such an influential group was the boon that the ex-gay movement had long been waiting for.[97] As *Christianity Today* later judged, for example, no other development deserved as much responsibility for bringing the ex-gay movement "into the mainstream of evangelicalism" as the endorsement of Dobson and his organization.[98] In 1998, Focus on the Family furthermore began sponsoring Love Won Out, its own ex-gay conferences overseen by Paulk and aimed at spreading the word that change was possible throughout the evangelical world. Over time, Erzen explains, Dobson also began referring his untold millions of readers and listeners to organizations like Exodus and eventually started recommending ex-gay therapy to parents with children who were showing signs of homosexuality.[99] In the later judgment of another ex-gay leader, Alan Mendinger, the "tremendous support" of Focus on the Family "made a huge difference" in the ex-gay movement.[100]

The ex-gay movement's biggest promotional break of all came when the Center for Reclaiming America solicited the help of fourteen other Christian organizations to launch a massive national advertising campaign called "truth in love" as a counter to the ongoing "hostility and intolerance" toward those "who dared to call homosexuality a sin." During the summer of 1998, the group ran a series of advertisements in a host of major newspapers—including full-page ads in the *New York Times*, the *Washington Post*, and *USA Today*—featuring testimonies from numerous ex-gay figures. Some versions of the ads featured John Paulk's wife Anne, with captions like "wife, mother, former lesbian," and taglines like, "I'm living proof that Truth can set you free." Others included pictures of the nearly "850 former homosexuals" at a recent Exodus gathering with a headline proclaiming, "We're standing for the truth that homosexuals can change."[101] Shortly after the ads appeared, *Newsweek* featured John and Anne Paulk on its 17 August 1998 cover in a story, "Can Gays Convert?" that cemented their status as two of the most prominent representatives of the ex-gay movement.[102]

The convergence of groups like Focus on the Family with the long marginal ex-gay movement catapulted groups like Exodus into the national spotlight like never before. By the late 1990s, ex-gay organizations had finally become the poster child for evangelicals hoping for a better alternative to the "gay agenda"—so much so that even Jerry Falwell seemed to have come around. Addressing the audience of the National Coming Out of Homosexuality Day in October 1999, Falwell made what Erzen rightly describes as "an unusually conciliatory" gesture by suggesting that "homosexuality is not more sinful than heterosexual promiscuity."[103] That December, *Christianity Today* made note of Falwell's "tamed rhetoric" in a news feature describing how the fiery preacher had recently "made a surprising about-face in his war of words with homosexuals."[104] Within a few short years, the man who had long vilified homosexuals as depraved sodomites would in fact go on to serve as the headline speaker at one of Exodus's annual conferences. By the dawn of the twentieth century, in other words, the ex-gay movement had even brought Jerry Falwell on board.

With major evangelical groups like Focus on the Family and once-hostile figures like Falwell finally endorsing it, the ex-gay movement had finally earned a hearing from a crucial sector of the evangelical world that had long ignored it. The newfound publicity and support paid dividends. By 2002, Exodus leaders were estimating that the 150 affiliated ministries in seventeen different countries were reaching nearly 250,000 people with their message of change. At its peak in years to come, the organization would ultimately grow to include twenty-five employees, an annual budget of more than one million dollars, and more than 400 affiliated ministries operating under its umbrella network. By the mid-2000s, Exodus had furthermore become increasingly involved in broader political debates over gay rights, eventually testifying before congress and attending press conferences with President George W. Bush in support of the "Marriage Protection Amendment." Its late 1990s–early 2000s convergence with existing evangelical political forces and emergence as its own increasingly powerful public presence brought the ex-gay movement more than just growth and influence, however. Along with a newly earned place in the national spotlight, the ex-gay movement's turn-of-the-century resurgence and progressive politicization also brought to light a number of the more complicated fissures and uncomfortable complexities that ultimately led to its undoing.[105]

The fall of the ex-gay movement was precipitated by a number of internal and external factors that began converging in the wake of its precipitous turn-of-the-century rise. *Externally*, the movement's claim to fame that change was possible began attracting more intense criticism from a variety of sectors than ever before. Having consistently concluded that change was neither possible nor necessary, the mainstream scientific and psychological communities had increasingly begun suggesting that reorientation efforts were potentially harmful and likely unethical to boot. By the mid-2000s, the movement was also being forced to reckon with the challenge posed by an increasingly vocal and mobilized countermovement of "anti-reorientation activists," which included a growing number of "ex-ex-gay" and "ex-gay survivors" groups that undermined the entire ex-gay project.[106] The decision during the same era to begin targeting minors—a shift that retiring Exodus president Bob Davies described in a 2002 *Christianity Today* interview as "moving into more intervention with youth"—would eventually earn the ex-gay movement its most concentrated scrutiny and vehement protests to date.[107] By the late 2000s, groups like the American Psychological Association were issuing reports explicitly and unequivocally condemning any sexual orientation change efforts (SOCE), and within a few short years, a number of states subsequently began passing laws banning the use of SOCE with minors.[108]

Although the counterwitness of ex-ex-gay testimonies, the outcry of gay activist groups, and the mainstream psychological community's rejection of its premises all played undeniable roles, the ultimate collapse of the ex-gay movement was most directly precipitated by the perennially open *internal* secret that change was rarely as straightforward as advertised. Over the course of the 2000s, the highly public failures of some of its most prominent leaders arguably became the tipping point that forced the ex-gay movement to confess its secret to the public: ongoing same-sex attraction was part and parcel of the ex-gay experience.[109]

Despite the fact that many evangelicals continued enthusiastically endorsing ex-gay ministries, by the early 2010s, even then-president of Exodus Alan Chambers had begun publicly admitting that "99.9 percent" of the people he had met over the years through the ex-gay movement had not experienced a reversal in their sexual orientation. When Chambers *also* began suggesting that "there are people who are living a gay Christian life. An active gay Christian life. God is the one who called them and has their heart. They are in relationship with God," evangelical leaders both in and outside of the ex-gay movement were apoplectic. Many cried heresy. In the wake of Chambers's honest admissions, Exodus began hemorrhaging affiliate ministries. When he announced at the annual 2012 conference that the organization "would no longer support or recommend reparative therapy," several staff and board members resigned in protest.[110] For many ex-gay leaders, orientation change was the very purpose of their work, and questioning its efficacy was anathema. That September, several former Exodus-affiliated ministries and ex-gay leaders thus went on to found a new organization called Restored Hope Network to continue the work that Chambers was no longer willing to do. The following year, in June 2013, the members of the Exodus Board of Directors announced that "the oldest and largest Christian ministry dealing with faith and homosexuality" would be closing its doors and disbanding for good.[111]

Whither Gay Evangelicals?

By the second decade of the twenty-first century, the shifting tides of the evangelical world had once again reversed the course of the ex-gay movement. Although some evangelical leaders continued touting the possibility of reorientation, over time, even many conservative evangelical leaders began denouncing reparative therapy and the ex-gay enterprise as a "severely counterproductive" endeavor based on "an inadequate view" of sexual orientation, which had unfortunately become widespread among evangelicals.[112]

The broader turn against the ex-gay movement left a vacuum in the evangelical world and doubly so for gay evangelicals. "For years," as religion reporter Sarah Pulliam Bailey later recounted, "gay evangelicals had three options: leave the faith, ignore their sexuality or try to change."[113] But with the eventual shift away from exhortations to change as the de facto evangelical position, many gay evangelicals uninterested in leaving the faith and unable to simply ignore their sexuality unsurprisingly began looking for other options. In the lead-up to and wake of the demise of Exodus, an emerging group of gay evangelical advocates took the lead in developing their own answer. Some began suggesting that embracing an identity as "celibate gay Christians" offered a better way of reconciling their faith and their sexuality than the old ex-gay model. Others began advocating monogamous, committed, same-sex partnerships or marriages as perfectly legitimate and morally defensible options for gay and lesbian Christians.[114] Regardless of their differences, almost all of the new gay evangelicals began pointing out that evangelicals might just so happen to be gay and that neither identity need preclude the other. When they did, the predictable backlash from many evangelical leaders was often swift and brutal.

After spending his teenage years wrestling with the discrepancy between the promises and realities of the ex-gay movement, Justin Lee ultimately realized that being gay was not something he could change. He also knew that he was a Christian and an evangelical one at that. Feeling caught between the gay community and the evangelical community, in 2001 Lee founded the Gay Christian Network to help provide connection, fellowship, and support for gay Christians like himself. In 2012, he published a memoir, *Torn: Rescuing the Gospel from the Gays-vs.-Christians Debate,* in hopes that his story might help those who similarly felt too Christian in gay circles and too gay in Christian circles. The organization grew in the meantime, and so did the controversy around it.[115] In a 2006 article highlighting his work, the *New York Times* explained that "Justin Lee believes that the Virgin birth was real, that there is a heaven and a hell, that salvation comes through Christ alone and that he, the 29-year-old son of Southern Baptists, is an evangelical Christian." According to Pittsburgh Theological Seminary New Testament professor Robert Gagnon there was no such thing. When invited to comment, Gagnon's reply was unequivocal. "If by gay evangelical is meant someone who claims both to abide by the authority of Scripture and to engage in a self-affirming manner in homosexual unions, then the concept gay evangelical is a contradiction," he explained.[116]

A few years later, in 2010, gay evangelical Harvard student Matthew Vines took a leave of absence from college to conduct an in-depth study of homosexuality and the Bible. In March 2012, he presented the results of his findings to a church in his hometown of Wichita, Kansas. The speech was recorded, uploaded to YouTube, and soon went viral. As the *New York Times* later reported, Vines's presentation tackling the "traditional interpretations of all six Bible passages that refer to homosexual acts, arguing that they don't actually condemn, or even address, the modern understanding of homosexuality," had quickly inspired both admiration and vicious backlash. The article went on to explain, for example, that one minister recorded five hours' worth of podcasts attacking Vines and his arguments, another "self-described reformed homosexual" Christian blogger "published a blistering 1,700-word rebuttal," and a number of commentators "compared Mr. Vines to Satan."[117]

Undeterred, in 2014 Vines published a more extensive version of his argument in *God and the Gay Christian: The Biblical Case in Support of Same-Sex Relationships*. Aimed at convincing evangelicals that celibacy was not the only evangelically legitimate option for gay Christians, the book straightforwardly argued that the Bible never directly addresses same-sex orientation and that the traditional interpretations of the passages that seemed to mention homosexuality had nothing to do with the idea of gay Christians in committed relationships.[118] Moody Bible Institute professor Christopher Yuan was unconvinced. Reviewing the book for *Christianity Today*, Yuan admitted that the historic evangelical answer to gay and lesbian people—promoting reorientation efforts and reparative therapy—had been an abject failure. "If our goal is making people straight, then we are practicing a false gospel," he warned. But Vines was wrong too. For same-sex-attracted Christians who wanted to remain faithful to Scripture, Yuan judged, the only option was celibacy. Despite a professed commitment to "a 'high view' of the Bible," he therefore suggested, Vines's arguments were by no means consistent with "uncomfortable biblical truths."[119]

If a scathing *Christianity Today* review offered a reliable indication that someone had run afoul of the contemporary evangelical establishment, a book-length refutation provided the surest sign that evangelical leaders saw that particular someone's views as not only wrong but also dangerous. Within months of his book's appearance, that is precisely what Vines received when a group of Southern Baptist Convention leaders published *God and the Gay Christian? A Response to Matthew Vines*. Edited by Southern Seminary president R. Albert Mohler Jr.—and made available free of charge for good measure—the book contained five essays aimed at systematically refuting every one of Vines's arguments.

In Mohler's view, the book-length refutation was born out of absolute necessity. The stakes could not be any higher. "Given the excruciating pressures now exerted on evangelical Christianity," he suggested, "many people—including some high-profile leaders—are desperately seeking an argument they can claim as both persuasive and biblical. The seams in the evangelical fabric are beginning to break, and Vines now comes along with a book that he claims will make the argument so many are seeking." The only problem with Vines's argument, according to Mohler, was everything.[120]

Throughout their responses, Mohler and the team of Southern Baptist professors assembled therein consistently stressed that the audacious young author was neither faithful to Scripture nor a real evangelical—no matter what he might claim. The scholars whom Vines cited, in Mohler's telling, were either "far left" biblical scholars "or on the fringes of the evangelical world," and his overall argument echoed the kinds of claims made by liberals.[121] For his part, Boyce College professor of theology and church history Owen Strachan derided Vines as one among a group of "professing evangelicals currently queuing up to endorse same-sex marriage and curry favor from the cultural elite when the moment is right."[122] Boyce College professor of biblical studies Denny Burk took the charges a step further. Not only was Vines a false evangelical, Burk argued, he was deliberately faking it. "Vines has rejected the straightforward commands of Scripture," he warned. "He just does not want to admit that this is indeed what he has done. He wants to give an appearance that he is still in the evangelical fold. But make no mistake. He is not. As he gives lip-service to biblical authority and to the need for salvation, his sheep costume looks really convincing. But do not miss that there really is a wolf concealed within—one that would like to devour as many sheep as possible with a Bible-denying, judgment-inducing error. The stakes really are that high."[123]

*

Gay evangelical advocates like Lee and Vines thus received the clear message that they were beyond the pale. Mainstream evangelical leaders might finally have moved away from defending the ex-gay movement as the evangelical answer, in other words, but many simultaneously spent the early twenty-first century refusing to entertain the alternatives proposed by a rising tide of new gay evangelicals. By the post-Exodus era, antigay animus had become so essential to contemporary evangelical identity that any deviation from the mainstream consensus was treated as tantamount to heresy. Even if the ex-gay movement had been a failure, all true evangelicals still seemingly needed to remember that the Bible obviously condemned homosexuality as unspeakably evil—and only liberals suggested otherwise—that Christians must oppose the societal normalization of homosexuality at any cost, and that the words "gay" and "evangelical" must necessarily be a contradiction in terms. Due in part to the nature of many of the most high-profile debates, openly gay and lesbian evangelicals defending the moral legitimacy of their partnerships often bore a lion's share of their fellow Christians' vitriol on this front. But there was plenty to go around for celibate gay evangelicals, for any and all LGBTQ evangelicals, as well as for anyone who deviated even slightly from the unofficial evangelical consensus.

After admitting in a 2008 interview that he was rethinking his opposition to gay marriage and becoming open to the idea of same-sex civil unions, NAE vice-president for Governmental Affairs Richard Cizik was quickly reminded of the boundaries of acceptably evangelical views. Cizik apologized for the statement shortly thereafter, but the damage was done. A little over a week later, he resigned from his position at the NAE in a decision that president Leith Anderson described as "reluctantly mutual."[124]

The following year, one of the nation's most influential evangelical pastors, Rick Warren, heard the message about what faithful evangelicals must believe loud and clear. After initially encouraging his California megachurch to support the Proposition 8 amendment, which sought to ban same-sex marriages in the state, Warren seemingly distanced himself from the amendment during a 2009 interview with Larry King. In response, evangelical leaders castigated Warren for what they believed was a sign of backpedaling. Shortly thereafter, a spokesperson for Warren issued a statement clarifying that the pastor "remained committed to the biblical definition of marriages as between one man and one woman."[125]

In 2014, World Vision learned the hard way that charities were not immune to the demands of the unofficial evangelical consensus. That year, when the massive evangelical organization announced that they would no longer prohibit the hiring of "gay Christians in same-sex marriages," the backlash was instantaneous and overwhelming.[126] Within forty-eight hours of the initial announcement, *Christianity Today* reported that the organization had already recanted. World Vision president Richard Stearns went on to make a statement apologizing profusely, lamenting "the confusion we caused for many friends who saw this policy change as a strong reversal of World Vision's commitment to biblical authority, which it was not intended to be," and begging the organization's evangelical supporters for forgiveness.[127]

That same year, evangelical ethicist David P. Gushee published a series of articles explaining how he had personally reconsidered the consensus evangelical view, which he had previously defended, that same-sex relationships were never a morally legitimate option. The publication of a 2014 book based on the articles, *Changing Our Mind*, made it official: he was now calling for the full "inclusion of LGBTQ Christians in the church on the same terms as everyone else."[128] True to form, evangelical leaders reacted swiftly and decisively. As evangelical schools where he had once spoken began withdrawing their invitations for him to come back, and as evangelical publishers that he had often worked with began politely explaining that they could no longer publish his material, Gushee quickly realized that he had thereby traded his status as "every liberal's favorite evangelical" for a new position as "every (conservative) evangelical's least-favorite liberal ex-evangelical."[129]

Tony Campolo announced his change of mind the following year. In 2015, Campolo explained that he was finally ready to join his wife Peggy, who had long since decided as much, in calling "for the full acceptance of Christian gay couples into the Church."[130] Shortly thereafter, retired editor in chief of *Christianity Today* David Neff confessed that he, too, had changed his mind and now believed that "the ethically responsible thing for gay and lesbian Christians to do is to form lasting, covenanted partnerships." A June 2015 editorial from Neff's former employer lamented his defection. Although Campolo's shift was not all that surprising, in editor Mark Galli's telling, Neff's agreement with Campolo was incredibly disappointing. Despite the fact that a number of their fellow evangelicals were beginning to change their minds "to accord with the current secular thinking on this matter," he explained, *Christianity Today* had long defended the Bible's clear teachings about marriage and would continue to do so come what may.[131]

For his part, Ralph Blair could not help but note the oversight at the heart of Galli's lament. In addition to the news about some evangelicals' recent change of heart, 2015 also marked the fortieth anniversary of Evangelicals Concerned. By that point, Blair pointed out, some evangelicals had thus been supporting same-sex couples for decades. To imply that doing so somehow made someone less evangelical, in his estimation, was a clear demonstration that Galli was either unaware or unwilling to acknowledge the fact that there were many different kinds of evangelicals. Despite the fact that the word "evangelical" had come to mean nothing but bad news for so many outsiders and insiders alike, Blair explained, evangelicals were supposedly a denominationally diverse group of Christians united by their belief in the good news of the gospel. Anyone paying attention could furthermore see that evangelicals with a range of diverging theological interpretations on a host of issues often formed their own internal subgroups. Some evangelical groups agreed about some questions and disagreed about others, and a variety of evangelicals fell in a variety of camps on a variety of controversial topics—including this one. "There are," Blair observed, "Evangelicals for Social Action, Evangelicals for Life, Evangelicals for Peace, Evangelicals for Middle East Understanding, Evangelicals for Biblical Immigration. There's the Evangelical and Ecumenical Women's Caucus, the National Association of Evangelicals, The Evangelical Theological Society. And there are those in each of these and other evangelical organizations who agree with Evangelicals Concerned and there are those who don't. So it's at least silly, if not unchristian, for some evangelicals to set themselves up as *the* spokespersons for *all* evangelicals or to say that evangelicals such as those in Evangelicals Concerned aren't *really* evangelicals."[132]

Conclusion

An Identity in Crisis?

From its earliest emergence on the historical scene, evangelicalism has consistently been almost comically hard to define. Lacking the institutional specificity of a denomination, absent a universally revered founding figure, and without a clearly established guarantor of continuity, the evangelical tradition has often moved like the wind. It has cropped up in a host of times and places, moved in and through a variety of more discrete theological traditions, and been embodied in a diverse range of historical groups and figures. According to many historians, it was prevalent in post-Reformation Europe, evident in historical British Protestantism, perceptible throughout colonial America, and discernible most anywhere that missionaries from those times and places eventually went. In light of its tendency toward contagion, some observers have suggested that Catholics and even non-Christians have occasionally taken part as well.

Evangelicalism's inherent nebulousness has consistently meant that any and all attempts at pinning it down are inevitably scrutinized, critiqued, discussed, debated, and eventually often qualified and revised. Its capacity for periodic shape-shifting, perennial adaptation, and frequent realignment has furthermore given rise to a host of both descriptive attempts to capture what kind of thing it actually is and prescriptive efforts to suggest what it should be. Outside observers and inside participants have varyingly called it a tradition, a subculture, a style, an aesthetic, a worldview, a faith, a tradition, a cult, a social group, a belief structure, a spirit, a coalition, and a movement.

Over the years, a number of observers, participants, and participant-observers have made the same point—that the irreducible evangelical essence is notoriously difficult to pinpoint—in a few different ways. Some have suggested that there is neither an evangelical Vatican nor an evangelical pope. Others have argued that the label connotes more than it denotes and that what it connotes shifts and moves with time. Still others have defended and debated its fundamental nature, reinforced and relitigated its most important associations, and tracked and retraced its historical meanings. Some have also questioned its coherence, bemoaned its misusage, and challenged its imprecision. They have proposed a number of core essentials, delineated a short list of emphases, and argued for a variety of unifying, overarching themes. The resulting discourse has been rife with new questions and old answers, recurrent debates and fresh takes, as well as innovative interpretations and timeworn clichés. In spite of the yet ongoing debates, most insiders, outsiders, laypersons, and leaders nonetheless agree that, whatever it is, evangelicalism indeed names something, and that something has to do with a particular way of being Christian. In fact, although evangelicalism may evade easy description, there is at least some consensus that it is actually not so hard to recognize once you get a feel for it. Like the judge said about pornography, perhaps you just know it when you see it.

Over the course of the twentieth century, the particularly US American version of it gave rise to a religious identity profoundly shaped by the vision of an entrepreneurial group of early to midcentury evangelical leaders who effectively built a coalitional network of flagship institutions that thenceforth defined what it meant to be an official evangelical. Their version of evangelical identity became the mainstream version. It began with the neo-evangelical effort to channel fundamentalist theology into a less sectarian stream that would attract conservative Christians of all kinds, which required defining liberal evangelicals out of the tradition for good. It was always a near-universally white project, built by conservative white Protestant men with conservative white Protestant men in mind. Intentionally or otherwise, it nonetheless often included a variety of Black, Brown, Asian American, Latinx, and various other nonwhite and non-American peoples and peoples of color—but only as long as they could tolerate the overwhelmingly white cultural expectations baked into most mainstream evangelical circles. From the outset, it was also a politically conservative project. Theological conservatism was always important, but political conservatism was more important and became most important of all as time went on. After some twentieth-century evangelical women (and a few men) began suggesting that it also included egalitarians and feminists, gender-essentialist hierarchies in the church and the family became default doctrinal requirements. For gay evangelicals, its price of admission was almost always willingness to try to change.

Throughout the entire story, there were always other kinds of evangelicals, of course. Some never bothered with the mainstream version. But others, like many of those discussed herein, tried to carve out space in the mainstream evangelical world only to be rewarded for their efforts with derision, scorn, and occasionally excommunication. In the process, evangelicalism's mostly fundamentalistic, theologically and politically conservative, white, straight, and male-headship-affirming claimants successfully formed twentieth-century evangelical identity in their own image. By the dawn of the twenty-first century, this is what US American evangelicalism looked like. This version arguably now represents what it means to be an official capital-E Evangelical. Even so, definitional debates over the true essence of evangelicalism continue apace. If anything, in recent years, they have actually sped up.

Once More to the Polls

In 2014, the Pew Research Group conducted an extensive survey of a representative slice of the country's population and published their findings in a 2015 report titled, "America's Changing Religious Landscape." Based on Pew's research at the time, contemporary evangelicalism could be accurately described as a religious tradition in which

- religion is viewed as an extremely important aspect of life and as the most important source for guidance about what is right and what is wrong;
- Bible study is frequent, attendance at religious services regular, and prayer is often daily;
- Scripture is understood as the word of God, which should be taken literally;
- belief in heaven and hell are almost universal;
- conservative is the most common political ideology, and Republican the most frequent party affiliation;

- smaller government is understood as better than larger government, and government aid to the poor is thought of as doing more harm than good;
- abortion would preferably be illegal in all or most cases;
- homosexuality is discouraged, and same-sex marriage strongly opposed;
- humankind is thought to have always existed in its present form rather than to have evolved over time.[1]

But before identifying some of evangelicals' most common characteristics, beliefs, and practices, the organization first needed to decide what it is that makes someone an evangelical. For Pew, the process was simple. According to their rubric, there are three major varieties of American Protestantism: evangelical, mainline, and historically Black. Evangelicals, by extension, were the group of Christians who specifically identified with one of the historically evangelical denominations. Protestants with a vague denominational identity, in Pew's schema, were sorted into one of the three groups based either on race or self-affiliation. Black respondents with a vague denominational identity belonged in the historically Black Protestant tradition. White Protestants with a vague denominational identity were counted either as evangelicals if they identified as born again/evangelical, or mainline if they did not.[2]

As was so often the case with previous studies from organizations like Gallup and Barna, whether the evangelicals identified in the 2014 Pew study were really the true evangelicals or whether the organization's denominational tradition and self-identification metric was actually insufficiently selective for determining who the real evangelicals were quickly became a lively discussion topic among evangelical and nonevangelical commentators alike. Aiming to settle the perennial debate once and for all, the National Association of Evangelicals (NAE) intervened the following year. After two years of research and development in conjunction with LifeWay Research, the flagship evangelical parachurch organization announced that they were finally ready to debut a new metric that would more accurately and consistently "identify people who hold evangelical beliefs regardless of affiliation or behavior."[3]

Lamenting the fact that inconsistent research methods were leading to some widespread misunderstandings about evangelicals, in a 2015 press release, NAE president Leith Anderson explained that the organization's new belief-based rubric would help clear things up. According to the press release, polls that relied exclusively on self-identification or denominational affiliation tended to identify evangelicals "more by political demographics than religious characteristics." In Anderson's judgment, the problem and the solution were obvious. "Evangelicals," he suggested, "are people of faith and should be defined by their beliefs, not by their politics or race." And who better to determine evangelicals' most crucial defining beliefs than the NAE. As LifeWay Research executive director Ed Stetzer went on to explain, "just as Native Americans might best define who is a Native American, we think evangelicals can best define evangelicals."[4]

Toward that end, the NAE/LifeWay team had consulted with a group of evangelical leaders from institutions like Fuller Seminary and the Moody Bible Institute to come up with a list of seventeen questions that would determine whether someone held evangelical beliefs. After field-testing the questions, the team had eventually narrowed the list down to four crucial statements:

1. The Bible is the highest authority for what I believe.
2. It is very important for me personally to encourage non-Christians to trust Jesus Christ as their Savior.
3. Jesus Christ's death on the cross is the only sacrifice that could remove the penalty of my sin.
4. Only those who trust in Jesus Christ alone as their Savior receive God's free gift of eternal salvation.[5]

Only those who strongly agreed with all four statements would be sorted into the evangelical column.

The team put the definition to the test in a September 2015 survey that yielded some surprising results. According to the NAE/LifeWay study, around 30 percent of the broader US American public qualified as truly evangelical in terms of belief, but only 59 percent of Protestants who self-identified as such met the criteria. When it came to the racial breakdown, the press release explained, the results were even more surprising. Twenty-nine percent of white Americans apparently held evangelical beliefs, for instance, and 62 percent of those who did also considered themselves evangelicals. But Black Americans were an entirely different story. Although

44 percent of Black Americans held evangelical beliefs, only 25 percent of those who did self-identified as evangelical.[6]

The following year, Leith Anderson and Ed Stetzer reported, explained, and interpreted the NAE/LifeWay study's results in the April 2016 issue of *Christianity Today*. Opening with the tagline, "It's not about politics. It's not even about self-identification. What the *E word* is really about," the article defended the study's innovative approach and highlighted its important implications. "These days," Anderson and Stetzer pointed out, "everyone wants to know what evangelicals believe—especially about political issues." And understandably so. Evangelicals were an undeniably influential voting bloc after all, the article continued, "But who is an evangelical? Many pollsters and journalists assume that evangelicals are white, suburban, American, Southern, and Republican, when millions of self-identifying evangelicals fit none of these descriptions. . . . The desire to survey white evangelicals to determine their political interests inadvertently ends up conveying two ideas that are not true: that 'evangelical' means 'white' and that evangelicals are primarily defined by their politics."[7]

The problem with so many previous studies of evangelicalism, Anderson and Stetzer explained, came down to an overemphasis on *belonging* while neglecting to consider *belief* and *behavior*. Measuring solely by self-identification with the broader evangelical tradition, for instance, obscured the fact that many self-identified evangelicals don't actually hold evangelical beliefs, while many who don't call themselves evangelical actually do. Since there were mainline Pentecostals and evangelical Episcopalians, they furthermore noted, denominational identification was similarly insufficient for finding the real evangelicals with truly evangelical beliefs. Polls based exclusively on self-identification, in Anderson and Stetzer's judgment, missed these crucial distinctions and thereby gave a false impression of who "the evangelicals" really were. With their "new research-driven definition," the article explained, the NAE/LifeWay team had finally begun addressing "the gap between belief and belonging" that had long bedeviled previous studies. In Anderson and Stetzer's telling, the results were already clarifying. When defined by "classic evangelical beliefs," for example, it was abundantly clear that evangelicals were far more diverse than most other surveys suggested. Researchers quite obviously needed a better rubric, and this belief-based definition offered exactly that. "More important," they concluded, "we

hope that as this tool is used, more Americans will see through the unfortunate cultural and political stereotypes and recognize evangelicals as a diverse
people of faith who have given their lives to Jesus Christ as their Savior."[8]

As an explicit attempt to overturn some prevailing perceptions of evangelicals, the rollout of the NAE/LifeWay criteria was timely. The subtext of
the *Christianity Today* article covering the study wasn't even subtext; it was
right there in the opening paragraph. Tucked between an acknowledgment
of pollsters' understandable fixation on evangelical political behavior and
an explanation of why that fixation unfairly stereotyped all evangelicals
as white Republicans, Anderson and Stetzer nodded to the elephant in the
room. White self-identified evangelicals voted, they voted often, and they
voted Republican when they did. "So it's no surprise that Donald Trump
recently proclaimed, 'I am an evangelical,'" they noted.[9]

The 81 Percent

Published in the midst of the media firestorm inspired by Trump's success
in numerous state-level Republican primaries, the *Christianity Today* article
reminding readers that evangelical was not a political identity and encouraging researchers to define evangelicals by belief rather than self-identification
was responding at least in part to the controversy surrounding evangelicals'
role in the ongoing 2016 election cycle. An earlier, online version of the same
article had already been published with both a title, "Defining Evangelicals
in an Election Year," and an editorial introduction effectively admitting as
much. In her introduction to the digital version, *Christianity Today* print
managing editor Katelyn Beaty noted the widespread media coverage of
evangelicals' strong support for Trump, acknowledged that self-identified
evangelicals had indeed played an outsized role in Super Tuesday states, and
went on to highlight what became one of the most widely discussed developments of the 2016 election. The evangelical laity's apparent preference for
Trump, Beaty observed, was particularly striking given that "many evangelical leaders are criticizing him and even vowing to abandon the 'e' word.'"[10]

Beginning with Trump's June 2015 announcement that he would be
running for president and continuing through the early months of 2016, a
handful of evangelical leaders had indeed gone on record as opposing him.
Among the most surprising examples was Russell Moore, president of the

Southern Baptist Convention's Ethics and Religious Liberty Convention (ERLC), who had already become one of Trump's most vocal evangelical critics. Writing as an op-ed contributor for the *New York Times* in September 2015, Moore questioned whether "evangelicals who support Trump [have] lost their values." Among other things, he pointed out, Trump's "personal lack of a moral compass" made the fact that "some self-identified evangelicals" were supporting him both surprising and disappointing. Judging that Trump's support among social conservatives more broadly and evangelicals in particular was illogical—especially for those who had once castigated Bill Clinton for matters of personal morality—Moore furthermore argued that "to back Mr. Trump, these voters must repudiate everything they believe."[11]

By early 2016, Moore had seen enough. In a February op-ed for the *Washington Post*, he confessed that he had recently "stopped describing myself to people as an 'evangelical.'" According to Moore, the label was not only becoming meaningless but indeed had begun "subverting the gospel of Jesus Christ." In his telling, the recent devolution of the evangelical name could be traced in large part to two main sources. Like the NAE/LifeWay team, Moore similarly argued that the first issue had to do with inaccurate polling measures. "Part of the problem," he explained, "is that more secular people have for a long time misunderstood the meaning of 'evangelical,' seeing us almost exclusively in terms of election-year voting blocs or our most buffoonish television personalities. That's especially true when media don't distinguish in election exit polls between churchgoers and those who merely self-identify as 'born again' or 'evangelical.'" Just because lots of people told pollsters that they were evangelicals, in other words, by no means made it so. For Moore, the second problem was even more disturbing than the first: evangelical leaders who had long emphasized the pivotal importance of a candidate's character were now minimizing and excusing a laundry list of the very sins they once railed against. Even though he was not quite ready to give up on the label entirely, he therefore concluded, "you will forgive me if, at least until this crazy campaign year is over, I choose just to say that I'm a gospel Christian."[12]

Although Moore was not entirely alone among the ranks of never-Trump evangelical leaders, his persistent criticisms of the soon-to-be president earned him few friends and plenty of enemies. In diametric opposition to Moore's stance, a cadre of high-profile evangelical figures—including some from Moore's own denomination—in fact became Trump's most outspoken and undyingly loyal supporters. As it became increasingly clear that Trump would be the Republican nominee, it simultaneously became all the more obvious that much of the evangelical populace were following suit and enthusiastically so. When all was said and done, with exit polls ultimately indicating that Donald Trump had been carried to the presidency in part by the support of 81 percent of white evangelical voters, the results were likely even grimmer than Moore had imagined.

In the postmortem analyses of the November 2016 presidential election, evangelicals' role in general and the 81 percent statistic in particular became some of the most widely discussed and hotly debated topics among evangelical insiders and outsiders alike. In relatively short order, evangelical thinkers with diverging interpretations of the results by and large began coalescing into a few general camps that could accurately be described as the still-Trump evangelicals, the still-*never*-Trump evangelicals, and the not-all evangelicals.

Those who had enthusiastically supported him all along, the still-Trump evangelicals, unsurprisingly viewed his election and the overwhelming evangelical support that he received as clear-cut victories. In their view, evangelicals made the right choice, they helped the country make the right choice, and that was that. With Trump in office, evangelicals could rest assured that their conservative political interests would be protected, and anyone who suggested otherwise probably wasn't really an evangelical.

For the never-Trump evangelicals, the results were devastating. Some began interrogating their own place in the evangelical world and their complicity in what it had become. Others kept their anti-Trump sentiments to themselves for legitimate fear of reprisal. Some were driven out of evangelical communities with little tolerance for dissent. Others voluntarily walked away from a movement they no longer recognized.

Another group, which undoubtedly overlapped with the never-Trump evangelicals, reacted to the 2016 election with bewilderment, confusion, and disbelief. Some in this group, the not-all evangelicals, quickly began trying to question or qualify the numbers. Surely, they suggested, something had gone awry with the polling. It simply could not be the case that 81 percent of evangelicals had actually voted for someone so crassly and openly immoral. Some pointed out that the 81 percent statistic referred to *white* evangelical voters, that the exit polls had inappropriately included all "born-again" voters when not all born-again Christians were real evangelicals, that a portion of the evangelical population had not voted, and therefore that "the actual number of evangelical Trump voters" was arguably closer to the range of 35 to 40 percent.[13] Others noted that self-identified evangelicals and evangelicals by belief were not necessarily the same group, that a sizeable percentage of the actual evangelical populace had voted *against* another candidate rather than *in favor* of their own, and that evangelicals were by no means single-issue voters.[14]

Still Evangelical?

In addition to the celebrations, laments, and qualifications, some evangelicals interpreted the 2016 election results as an invitation for some much-needed soul-searching about the state of evangelicalism. After discussing the possibility with a number of people at the February 2018 funeral of Billy Graham, honorary Lausanne Movement chair Doug Birdsall helped spearhead efforts to convene a gathering of evangelical leaders for precisely that purpose. As former *Christianity Today* managing editor Katelyn Beaty later reported, Birdsall's ultimate goal for the meeting "would be to revitalize Graham's original mission and to discuss the future of the faith." With the help of *Christianity Today* president Harold Smith, North Carolina pastor Claude Alexander, and Wheaton College president Philip Ryken, Birdsall's plans came to fruition on April 16 when fifty or so evangelical leaders traveled to Wheaton College for a private consultation at the Billy Graham Center. Cochaired by World Relief vice president of advocacy and policy Jenny Yang and National Latino Evangelical Coalition president Gabriel Salguero, the two-day, closed-door gathering drew a veritable who's who of contemporary evangelical leaders—including influential pastors like Timothy Keller and John Ortberg, evangelical college and seminary presidents such as Fuller's Mark Labberton, a smattering of evangelical leaders from outside the United States, and at least one eminent evangelical historian, Mark Noll.[15]

It was clear from the outset that the evangelical alignment with Trump was simultaneously a major impetus for the meeting and the constant elephant in the room. In Beaty's telling, early correspondence had initially suggested that one of the goals involved drafting a "pastoral letter" aimed at distancing the evangelical label from its association with right-wing partisanship and set to be released before an upcoming June meeting between the president and a large group of evangelical leaders. In the final few days before the gathering, however, the participants received notification that the Wheaton summit should *not* be understood as an oppositional reaction to the meeting in June. "Organizers seemed to be getting nervous that their efforts would be seen as partisan and anti-Trump," Beaty noted.[16]

Their fears were quickly confirmed. On the first day of the meeting, One NewsNow.com published an article, "Pro-Trump Evangelicals 'Personae Non Gratae,'" describing the event as an effort to rescue evangelicalism from its association with Trump. The article went on to cite Southern Evangelical Seminary's Richard Land—who had previously been the head of the Southern Baptist Convention's ERLC—as arguing that the event's guest list in particular "betrays their real purpose: marginalizing evangelicals who support President Trump."[17] Such reactions would have come as little surprise to the Wheaton gathering. As Beaty later recounted, everyone in attendance was fully aware of the potential repercussions associated with broader evangelical perceptions of the meeting. But some of the organizers grew even cagier as the event progressed. Although they had initially suggested that the conference would include a mixture of on-record and off-record conversations, Beaty explained, "after I tweeted quotes from several on-the-record sessions on the first day, I was asked to stop." Things only got thornier from there.[18]

When it came to the question of the current state and future direction of evangelicalism, it was abundantly clear to Beaty that the participants held drastically different visions that diverged at least in part along generational lines. "With a few exceptions," she observed, "the older, white cohort stressed civility and unity. What the movement needed, they said, was a gentler evangelicalism that reached across partisan aisles for the common good. Others, especially the leaders of color, stressed repentance; there could be no real unity without white evangelicals explicitly confronting the ways in which they had participated in the degradation of persons of color and women. They contended that white evangelical churches and organizations had for decades supported a political agenda that deemed unborn lives more sacred than living black lives." By the second day, she furthermore reported, numbers were down, and at least a couple of the exits were in protest of the event's anti-Trump tone.[19]

When the discussion finally turned to the proposed pastoral letter, the fault lines in the room became all the more apparent. "Several younger speakers urged that the statement had to include a tone of repentance for complicity in racism and sexism," Beaty pointed out. "Others in the room balked. One long-time leader of an evangelical umbrella group said that he had already received calls from donors for merely attending the meeting, and that asking them to repent for racism would be seen as too political. A few participants wondered aloud why they had come to the gathering at Wheaton in the first place." In the end, the internal tensions and external pressures proved too much. The meeting concluded, the group left, and no statement was ever produced.[20]

Though the Wheaton gathering never released a joint statement, at least one of the keynote addresses from the event was made public shortly thereafter. In an April 20 posting on the school's website, Fuller Theological Seminary published an edited transcript of president Mark Labberton's presentation from the conference. In it, Labberton made no bones about what he believed was the direness of the situation. "The central crisis facing us," he observed, "is that the gospel of Jesus Christ has been betrayed and shamed by an evangelicalism that has violated its own moral and spiritual integrity."[21]

The evangelical crisis, Labberton explained, was not external but internal. It was not caused by "Trump, or Hillary, or Obama, or the electoral college, or Comey, or Mueller, or abortion, or LGBTQIA+ debates, or Supreme Court appointees," but it had been occasioned instead by evangelicals' willingness to engage such issues via collusion with all manner of "insidious racist, misogynistic, materialistic, and political power." The evangelical crisis, he argued, was neither recent nor sequestered within a specific evangelical denomination, subtradition, or geographical region. In his judgment, the evangelical crisis also had little to do with the evangelical label, debates over who can define it, whether it was redeemable, or even whether to continue identifying as such. "It is legitimate and important to debate if and how the term 'evangelical' can currently be used in the United States to mean anything more than white, theologically and politically conservative," Labberton acknowledged. "But that is not itself the crisis. The crisis is not at the level of our lexicon, but of our lives and a failure to embody the gospel we preach."[22]

From there, the president of evangelicalism's flagship seminary went on to highlight four concrete areas in which evangelicalism was currently failing to live up to its own professed standards.

The first issue had to do with the ongoing legacy of twentieth-century evangelicalism's complicated relationship to *power*. Evangelicalism, Labberton explained, had sometimes viewed itself as marginalized and unheard; other times, it curried favor with and imitated worldly powers. "An evangelical dance with political power," he pointed out, "has been going on from the time of Billy Graham, through the Moral Majority and the religious right, to the Tea Party, and most recently with the white evangelical vote." So many contemporary social debates— ranging from mass incarceration and police brutality to #MeToo—were fundamentally about the use and abuse of power, Labberton furthermore noted. The evangelical crisis, in his view, similarly could be traced in part to the movement's attraction to the wrong kinds of power, the domineering, controlling, win-at-all-costs kinds of power, which were fundamentally at odds with the example of Jesus. [23]

The second area of evangelical failure had to do with *race*. In Labberton's telling, the heart of the matter came down to the historical responsibility and ongoing complicity of white evangelicals in the nation's violent oppression of people of color. White evangelicals, he explained, had told themselves sanitized fairy tales about American history and their place in it for far too long, white evangelical racism remained an "unreckoned-with reality" permeating contemporary life, and white evangelicals' recent triumphalist celebrations of the president despite his racist rhetoric was a clear message to people of color that theirs was a "racist gospel."[24]

A third area in which Labberton felt that evangelicalism had embarrassed itself, *nationalism*, was similarly a problem mainly among white evangelicals. In a complex modern world, he argued, nationhood was a legitimate idea worth supporting, and pluralistic nations could and should debate the best approach to questions such as immigration policy. But white evangelicals too often embraced an idolatrous kind of nationalism that revered America above all else, endorsed self-interested rhetoric that came at the expense of the other, and thereby revealed that "our central commitments do not reflect Jesus Christ, but rather a cold, white heart."[25]

The fourth and final problem, in Labberton's judgment, involved white evangelicals' prevailing positions on *economics*. Acknowledging that there ought to be room for debating the precise ins and outs of "social support for the vulnerable in our society," he nonetheless indicted white evangelicals for the times when their positions seemed to further prop up the wealthy and secure at the expense of the poor and the vulnerable. "When white evangelicals in prominent and wealthy places speak about what is fair and beneficial for society," Labberton noted, "but then pass laws and tax changes that create more national indebtedness and elevate the top 1% even higher—while cutting services and provisions for children, the disabled, and the poor that are castigated as disgusting 'entitlements'—one has to ask how this is reconciled with being followers of Jesus."[26]

As editor of the 2018 essay collection *Still Evangelical?*, Labberton used the book's introduction to reiterate his sentiment that evangelicalism was in the midst of a serious crisis. "Evangelicalism in America has cracked, split on the shoals of the 2016 presidential election and its aftermath, leaving many wondering whether they want to be in or out of the evangelical tribe," he began. Although he echoed his previous judgment that the election revealed in stark relief some long-standing evangelical problems, this time around, Labberton primarily lamented the increasing polarization of intraevangelical political debates, which he believed were a sign that evangelicals were being driven primarily by social, cultural, and ideological forces rather than by their common theological commitments.[27]

In Labberton's view, the wildly divergent evangelical reactions to the 2016 election could not be traced solely to theological differences. When it came to the widening gap between progressive and conservative evangelicals, he argued, any underlying disagreements over "God, Jesus, the Bible, conversion, and the afterlife" were simply too small to explain the emerging divide. Despite holding similar views on everything from the authority of the Bible to salvation, evangelicals had somehow become as polarized as the broader culture. "Of course, being evangelical typically means belief in theology as the bedrock, not our frame," he observed. "But what the 2016 US presidential election exposed so vividly is the reverse. Evangelicals can affirm that faith commitments and their implications are essential to discerning values; but when evangelicals who affirm the same baseline of faith reach radically opposing social and political opinions, we have to ask what else is at play." Drastic political and social disagreements among evangelicals, according to Labberton, were only explicable in light of the fact that evangelicals on both sides of the divide had allowed their "social locations, personal experience, and spiritual conviction" to take primacy over their common commitment to the gospel. The current evangelical crisis was not even about theology at all, in other words, and that was precisely the problem. In Labberton's view, then, the post-2016 evangelical crisis had next to nothing to do with the "set of primary theological commitments" at the heart of evangelical identity and almost everything to do with the polarization that inevitably resulted when evangelicals let their common faith take a back seat to social and cultural influences.[28]

The *Other* Evangelicals

The idea that US American evangelicalism is currently in the midst of an identity crisis is both spot on and dead wrong. Due in no small part to the fallout from the 2016 election, on the one hand, there does seem to be a contingent of white, nonwhite, self-identified, and defined-by-belief evangelicals who have begun reconsidering their place in the evangelical world. Some have already left, and more will probably leave. Some are currently deconstructing their faith, while others are trying desperately to reconstruct their faith. Some now consider themselves ex-evangelical, or postevangelical, or formerly evangelical. Others have become atheists or agnostics. Still others don't know what they are. But then on the other hand, by many indications, the current crop of evangelical exiles is likely smaller than it seems, some were probably already on their way out, and others likely never considered themselves in anyway.

The idea that the contemporary evangelical crisis is the product of a hyperpartisan struggle between two warring factions furthermore represents a false equivalency at best. From a purely statistical perspective, the likelihood that political partisanship will split post-2016 evangelicalism into two major parties—a "blue evangelicalism" and a "red evangelicalism"—is next to nil.[29] At least when it comes to *white* evangelicals, support for the Trump administration never really wavered and consistently remained far higher than any other religious group. Despite what some evangelical thinkers tried to suggest, the idea that such support came primarily from the kinds of "evangelicals-in-name-only" who might not take their faith as seriously as true evangelicals became increasingly implausible as time went on.[30] Some surveys in fact indicated that evangelicals who attended church more often were even more likely to approve of the president's performance than the infrequent attenders.[31] Further still, if the LifeWay/Billy Graham research was any indication, white evangelicals defined by belief were actually even *likelier* than those who merely self-identified as evangelical to have voted for Trump in the first place.[32] The idea of a two-party evangelicalism in the post-2016 era is predicated, in other words, on some dubious contemporary assumptions.

It's also based on some historically untenable conclusions. Division among contemporary evangelicals may indeed be a problem. But to imagine that a wide swath of the current evangelical world is in equal danger of becoming as closely aligned with the Democratic Party as mainstream evangelicalism has long been aligned with the Republican Party is to minimize the ongoing legacy of a much longer history of evangelical partisanship. At least for the time being, contemporary evangelicalism is in precious little danger of a cataclysmic schism along political lines. By almost any criteria of evangelicalness, US American evangelicals remain an overwhelmingly one-party bunch.

Coming from a group of evangelical leaders that remains almost universally white, an attempt to qualify this reality by suggesting that the significant percentages of nonwhite Christians who hold evangelical beliefs but don't identify as such should nonetheless be counted in the evangelical tallies furthermore seems like disingenuous number-padding. It is certainly true that not all evangelicals voted for Trump. It is also true that far fewer nonwhite voters with classically evangelical beliefs voted for him than their white counterparts. But when predominantly white evangelical gatekeepers emphasize the splendid diversity of evangelicalism by retroactively grafting Christians of color with evangelical beliefs onto the official evangelical roster, they do a profound injustice to many who want nothing to do with the label and what it represents.

Whether various groups of Black, Brown, and other nonwhite Christians with evangelical beliefs should be grouped among *the* evangelicals is a fraught question with complex historical and contemporary implications. But when those who believe evangelically—be they Black, Brown, or even white—are decidedly uninterested in the evangelical name, perhaps a better question is *why*. Labberton's diagnosis of the four failures of contemporary evangelicalism offers a clue. The perception that mainstream evangelicalism has problems with power, or race, or nationalism, or economics has undeniably led some insiders to reconsider their relationship to the evangelical name and many outsiders to steer clear altogether. But, again, the insiders who see no problem with the way that evangelicals have responded to such questions in the past likely outnumber those who no longer find the standard evangelical answers acceptable by a great deal. The chances of a looming mass defection from the evangelical name over mainstream evangelicalism's position on such issues remains thin for now.

One of the main reasons that a massive decampment from the evangelical ranks is currently unlikely has to do with the fact that diagnoses like Labberton's may be timely, but they're also often historically myopic. Many recent analyses of the apparent evangelical crisis insightfully identify some of the crucial ways in which "evangelicalism" has become a four-letter word while simultaneously failing to recognize that the self-same issues featured in countless earlier debates over the nature and limits of evangelical identity. The "evangelical tribe" to which Labberton refers did not come from nowhere, for instance, and many of those who historically dared to challenge prevailing evangelical sentiments either were cast out or simply walked away long ago.

The suggestion that the crisis of evangelicalism is not about the *word* itself but is instead about *power* furthermore misses entirely the historical relationship between the two. Contemporary US American evangelicalism has been shaped by a history in which those with *the power to define the word* set the terms and limits of the kinds of debates that leaders like Labberton believe are currently threatening to tear the evangelical world asunder. Over the course of the twentieth century, a host of evangelicals made similar diagnoses of evangelicalism's many problems, only to be told that their views on race, or science, or politics, or economics, or nationalism, or misogyny were out of bounds and unevangelical. Just ask the evangelical feminists, the Black evangelicals, the progressive evangelicals, or the gay evangelicals.

In the fallout of the 2016 election, some evangelical leaders see an evangelicalism that has become unmoored from the central theological consensus that historically united its diverse constituents and that is now being battered about by evangelicals' competing political, social, cultural, and ideological preferences and commitments. In their view, the emerging division among evangelicals is due in large part to the influence of broader cultural partisanship. Such debates, in their judgment, cannot possibly be about theology because the distinctions between evangelicals' theologies are too few and minor to count. But here, too, leaders like Labberton take a shortsighted and unjustifiably rosy view of the underlying stability of evangelical theological identity. Ask the evangelical liberals, or the Barthian evangelicals, or the noninerrantist evangelicals whether their confessed allegiance to the evangel was enough of a unifying thread to keep them safely within the limits of the minor differences among evangelicals.

In a real sense, the story of twentieth-century evangelicalism is a story about a variety of Christians who all considered themselves committed to the gospel, faithful to the evangel, or loyal to the good news, discovering that their understandings of what it meant to be an evangelical were by no means shared by everyone who claimed the name. Sometimes, this realization involved certain evangelicals finding out that the core theological commitments that they believed made them evangelical were different from those that their fellow evangelicals believed made them evangelical. Other times, it came in the form of two groups of evangelicals agreeing about their consensus theological commitments but then disagreeing either about the actual implications of those commitments or about the range of legitimately evangelical implications of those commitments. When debates reached a boiling point, the uncomfortable reality of internal evangelical pluralism often resulted in an implicit or explicit ruling from the unofficial evangelical gatekeepers that one or the other core commitment, or interpretation of a core commitment, or implication of a core commitment was the preferred evangelical option.

Over time, these sometimes provisional and ad hoc and other times binding and official decisions increasingly added up to an evermore specific set of implicit and explicit parameters for determining what was safely inside and dangerously outside the evangelical circle. In the process, what might once have been a short list of common theological commitments gained an assortment of accoutrements spelling out in detail not only what an official evangelical believed but what they thought, voted, and looked like as well. By the dawn of the twenty-first century, the most evangelically acceptable version of US American evangelical identity, for instance, was someone who believed like an antimodernist antiliberal inerrantist, thought like an antifeminist antigay complementarian, and voted like a white Republican.

This religious identity might indeed be in crisis. In the past few years, the realization that this version of evangelical identity is effectively what it means to be an official evangelical has led some insiders to the conclusion that the theological commitments they thought they shared with their fellow evangelicals are not enough. But whether such reconsiderations will result in a significant reimagining of what it means to be evangelical remains to be seen.

On the one hand, those with the power to police the borders of evangelicalness are redoubling their efforts to ensure that evangelicalism remains what it has become, and many on the inside are perfectly content with the way things are. In the immediate future, neither a wholesale shake-up nor a mass exodus seems likely on their watch.

But then on the other hand, within the span of a generation or so, the possibility of a massive wave of evangelical expatriates could certainly change the calculus. There does seem to be an emerging generational unease, for instance, with many of what have become the most determinative characteristics of contemporary evangelical identity. On the whole, younger evangelicals who may accept what they have been told are the community's most crucial theological commitments appear more likely than their forebearers to openly reject the racism, sexism, and white nationalism that they have discovered coming along with them.

Some might stay and fight for change. Others may give up the ghost and shake the dust from their sandals. Those who leave may face a lonely road, but those who stay will face an uphill battle that grows steeper by the day. But whether they stay or go, whether they push to expand what it can mean to be evangelical or wash their hands of the word, they won't be the first.

Notes

Prologue

1. Quotations, respectively, from Evangelical Theological Society, "ETS Constitution" (Article III: Doctrinal Basis), https://www.etsjets.org/about/constitution #A3; National Association of Evangelicals, "What Is an Evangelical?," https://www.nae.net/what-is-an-evangelical/; Fuller Theological Seminary, "What We Believe and Teach," https://www.fuller.edu/about/mission-and-values/what-we-believe-and-teach/; Alan Wolfe, *The Transformation of American Religion: How We Actually Live Our Faith* (Chicago: University of Chicago Press, 2003), 36.

Introduction

1. For a historical overview of the estimates, see Robert Wuthnow, *Inventing American Religion: Polls, Surveys, and the Tenuous Quest for a Nation's Faith* (New York: Oxford University Press, 2015), 95–98.

2. For more on Carter, Gallup, and the year of the evangelical, see Wuthnow, *Inventing American Religion*, 95–128; and D. G. Hart, *Deconstructing Evangelicalism* (Grand Rapids: Baker Academic, 2004), 85–106.

3. For more on Gallup, see Wuthnow, *Inventing American Religion*, 103–12, quotation on 107.

4. All quotations in this paragraph from Russell Chandler, "50 Million 'Born Again' in U.S.," *Los Angeles Times*, 23 September 1976, B3; for more on coverage of the announcement, see Wuthnow, *Inventing American Religion*, 103–6.

5. Chandler, "50 Million 'Born Again' in U.S."

6. "Counting Souls," *Time*, 4 October 1976, 79.

7. Kenneth L. Woodward, "Born Again!," *Newsweek*, 25 October 1976, 68.

8. Wuthnow, *Inventing American Religion*, 96.

9. Wuthnow, *Inventing American Religion*, 98.

10. For more on Marsden's role in contemporary evangelical studies, see Barry Hankins, "We're All Evangelicals Now: The Existential and Backward Historiography of Twentieth-Century Evangelicalism," in *American Denominational History: Perspectives on the Past, Prospects for the Future*, ed. Keith Harper (Tuscaloosa: University of Alabama Press, 2008), 196–220; and Kenneth J. Collins, *The Evangelical Moment: The Promise of an American Religion* (Grand Rapids: Baker, 2005), 64–70.

11. All quotations in this paragraph from George M. Marsden, *The Evangelical Mind and the New School Presbyterian Experience* (Eugene, OR: Wipf & Stock, 1970), ix.

12. See Barry Hankins, "In Defense of the Academy," *Fides et Historia* 46 (2014): 45–49; and Hankins, "We're All Evangelicals Now," 207.

13. George M. Marsden, *Fundamentalism and American Culture*, 2nd ed. (New York: Oxford University Press, 2006), 3.

14. Marsden, *Fundamentalism and American Culture*, 4.

15. Marsden, *Fundamentalism and American Culture*, 5.

16. For the discussion of Marsden by a later evangelical historian, see Hankins, "We're All Evangelicals Now"; for reference to Marsden's status as dean of evangelical historians, see Collins, *Evangelical Moment*, 64.

17. See Leonard I. Sweet, "Wise as Serpents, Innocent as Doves: The New Evangelical Historiography," *Journal of the American Academy of Religion* 56 (1988): 397.

18. See Sweet, "Wise as Serpents," 402.

19. See Sweet, "Wise as Serpents," 407.

20. See Sweet, "Wise as Serpents," 404, 413.

21. For helpful discussions of the debate, see Collins, *Evangelical Moment*, 64–70; and Hankins, "We're All Evangelicals Now"; also Douglas A. Sweeney, "The Essential Evangelicalism Dialectic: The Historiography of the Early Neoevangelical Movement and the Observer-Participant Dilemma," *Church History* 60 (1991): 70–84; and George M. Marsden, *Reforming Fundamentalism: Fuller Seminary and the New Evangelicalism* (Grand Rapids: Eerdmans, 1987).

22. See Donald W. Dayton, "The Search for the Historical Evangelicalism: George Marsden's History of Fuller Seminary as a Case Study," *Christian Scholar's Review* 23 (1993): 12–33.

23. George Marsden, "Response to Don Dayton," *Christian Scholar's Review* 23 (1993): 34–40.

24. Joel A. Carpenter, "The Scope of American Evangelicalism: Some Comments on the Dayton-Marsden Exchange," *Christian Scholar's Review* 23 (1993): 53–61.

25. Carpenter, "Scope of American Evangelicalism"; Marsden, "Response to Don Dayton."

26. See Doulas A. Sweeney, "Historiographical Dialectics: On Marsden, Dayton, and the Inner Logic of Evangelical History," *Christian Scholar's Review* 23 (1993): 48; see also Sweeney, "Essential Evangelicalism Dialectic," 70–84.

27. See George Gallup Jr. and Jim Castelli, *The People's Religion: American Faith in the 90's* (New York: Macmillan, 1989), 92–93; and George Gallup Jr. and D. Michael Lindsay, *Surveying the Religious Landscape* (Harrisburg, PA: Morehouse, 1999), 65–67.

28. See "The Christianity Today-Gallup Poll: An Overview," *Christianity Today*, 21 December 1979, 12.

29. "Christianity Today-Gallup Poll"; see also *George Gallup Polls America on Religion: A Compilation of Articles from* Christianity Today *with Complete Technical Appendix* (Carol Stream, IL: Christianity Today, 1981).

30. "Christianity Today-Gallup Poll."

31. "We Poll the Pollster: An Interview with George Gallup, Jr.," *Christianity Today*, 21 December 1979, 10.

32. See Wuthnow, *Inventing American Religion*, 113–16; and Hart, *Deconstructing Evangelicalism*, 99–103.

33. George Barna and William Paul MacKay, *Vital Signs: Emerging Social Trends and the Future of American Christianity* (Westchester, IL: Crossway, 1984), 104–5, quotation on 105.

34. See George Barna, *The Barna Report 1992–1993: An Annual Survey of Life-Styles, Values and Religious Views* (Ventura, CA: Regal Books, 1992), 78; Barna, *The Frog in the Kettle: What Christians Need to Know about Life in the 21st Century* (Ventura, CA: Regal Books, 1990), 122; and "Holding Steady," *Christianity Today*, 5 March 1990, 36.

35. Barna, *Barna Report 1992–1993*, 81–84, quotation on 81.

36. For a helpful breakdown of these distinctions, see Conrad Hackett and D. Michael Lindsay, "Measuring Evangelicalism: Consequences of Different Operationalization Strategies," *Journal for the Scientific Study of Religion* 47 (2008): 499–514.

37. See James Davison Hunter, *American Evangelicalism: Conservative Religion and the Quandary of Modernity* (New Brunswick, NJ: Rutgers University Press,

1983), 49-72, quotations on 69; and James Davison Hunter, *Evangelicalism: The Coming Generation* (Chicago: University of Chicago Press, 1987).

38. Christian Smith, *American Evangelicalism: Embattled and Thriving* (Chicago: University of Chicago Press, 1998), 1-26, 75-82, 233-47.

39. Smith, *American Evangelicalism*, 1-19, quotation on 15.

40. Smith, *American Evangelicalism*, 218.

41. Wuthnow, *Inventing American Religion*, 128.

42. Wuthnow, *Inventing American Religion*, 124.

43. See Donald W. Dayton, "Some Doubts about the Usefulness of the Category 'Evangelical,'" in *The Variety of American Evangelicalism*, ed. Donald W. Dayton and Robert K. Johnston (Eugene, OR: Wipf & Stock, 1991), 245-51; and Donald W. Dayton, "An Autobiographical Response," in *From the Margins: A Celebration of the Theological Work of Donald W. Dayton*, ed. Christian T. Collins Winn (Eugene, OR: Pickwick, 2007), 408.

44. Hart, *Deconstructing Evangelicalism*, 17.

45. Hart, *Deconstructing Evangelicalism*, 83.

46. Hart, *Deconstructing Evangelicalism*, quotations on 196 and 32, respectively.

47. Sweeney, "Essential Evangelicalism Dialectic," 81, 83.

Chapter One

1. For the earliest origins of the "two-party" language, see Martin E. Marty, *Righteous Empire: The Protestant Experience in America* (New York: Dial, 1970); also Martin E. Marty, "The Shape of American Protestantism: Are There Two Parties Today?," in *Reforming the Center: American Protestantism, 1900 to the Present*, ed. Douglas Jacobsen and William Vance Trollinger Jr. (Grand Rapids: Eerdmans, 1998), 91-108.

2. See James DeForest Murch, *Cooperation without Compromise: A History of the National Association of Evangelicals* (Grand Rapids: Eerdmans, 1956), 48-61, quotations on vii and 19.

3. Murch, *Cooperation without Compromise*, 59.

4. Murch, *Cooperation without Compromise*, 64.

5. Murch, *Cooperation without Compromise*, 65-66.

6. See George Marsden, *Reforming Fundamentalism: Fuller Seminary and the New Evangelicalism* (Grand Rapids: Eerdmans, 1987), 13-17.

7. For the authoritative account of Fuller's early history, see Marsden, *Reforming Fundamentalism*, 13.

8. See Marsden, *Reforming Fundamentalism*, 54–56.

9. John Wiseman, "The Evangelical Theological Society: Yesterday and Today," *Journal of the Evangelical Theological Society* 28 (1982): 9.

10. Clarence Bouma, "Orthodox Theological Scholarship," *Calvin Forum* 15 (1950): 131, as quoted in Wiseman, "Evangelical Theological Society," 8.

11. Evangelical Theological Society, "ETS Constitution" (Article III: Doctrinal Basis), https://www.etsjets.org/about/constitution#A3.

12. See Marsden, *Reforming Fundamentalism*, 157–61, Smith quotation on 158.

13. Billy Graham, *Just as I Am: The Autobiography of Billy Graham*, rev. and updated 10th anniversary ed. (New York: HarperCollins, 2007), 285.

14. Graham, *Just as I Am*, 284.

15. See Marsden, *Reforming Fundamentalism*, 157–71.

16. "Why 'Christianity Today'?," *Christianity Today*, 15 October 1956, 20.

17. For more on the rivalry between the two magazines, see Elesha J. Coffman, *The Christian Century and the Rise of the Protestant Mainline* (New York: Oxford University Press, 2013), 182–216.

18. Letter as quoted in Gary Dorrien, *The Making of American Liberal Theology: Imagining Progressive Religion, 1805–1900* (Louisville: Westminster John Knox, 2001), 341.

19. Charles Briggs, *Biblical Study: Its Principles, Methods, and History*, 3rd ed. (New York: Scribner's Sons, 1890), 162; see also Mark S. Massa, *Charles Augustus Briggs and the Crisis of Historical Criticism* (Minneapolis: Fortress, 1990), 37–46.

20. See Charles Briggs, *The Authority of Holy Scripture: An Inaugural Address*, 2nd ed. (New York: Scribner's Sons, 1891); Dorrien, *Making of American Liberal Theology, 1805–1900*, 352–61; and Massa, *Charles Augustus Briggs*, 53–90.

21. Briggs, *Authority of Holy Scripture*, 85, 35.

22. See Dorrien, *Making of American Liberal Theology, 1805–1900*, 361–70.

23. See Charles Briggs, *Whither? A Theological Question for the Times* (New York: Scribner's Sons, 1889), 7, 267.

24. As quoted in Massa, *Charles Augustus Briggs*, 44.

25. As quoted in Dorrien, *Making of American Liberal Theology, 1805–1900*, 343.

26. See Dorrien, *Making of American Liberal Theology, 1805–1900*, 369–70.

27. Charles Briggs, *The Fundamental Christian Faith: The Origin, History and Interpretation of the Apostles' and Nicene Creeds* (New York: Scribner's Sons, 1913), vii.

28. Briggs, *Biblical Study*, 370, 135, 246, 200, 136.

29. Briggs, *Biblical Study*, 173, 171, 359, 362; see also Dorrien, *Making of American Liberal Theology, 1805–1900*, 352–58.

30. Briggs, *Whither?*, 85.

31. See Gary Dorrien, *The Making of American Liberal Theology: Idealism, Realism, and Modernity, 1900–1950* (Louisville: Westminster John Knox, 2003), 181–85, quotation on 183.

32. See Shailer Mathews, *New Faith for Old: An Autobiography* (New York: Macmillan, 1936), 51; and Dorrien, *Making of American Liberal Theology, 1900–1950*, 181–85.

33. Shailer Mathews, *The Social Teaching of Jesus* (New York: Macmillan, 1902), 40, 54; see also Dorrien, *Making of American Liberal Theology, 1900–1950*, 185–90.

34. See Shailer Mathews, "Unrepentant Liberalism," *American Scholar* 7 (1938): 302.

35. See Dorrien, *Making of American Liberal Theology, 1900–1950*, 14, 203–8.

36. Shailer Mathews, *The Faith of Modernism* (New York: Macmillan, 1924), 23.

37. See Reuben Archer Torrey, *Will Christ Come Again? An Exposure of the Foolishness, Fallacies and Falsehoods of Shailer Mathews* (Los Angles: Bible Institute of Los Angeles, 1918), 25.

38. Mathews, *Faith of Modernism*, 21–22, 35.

39. Mathews, *Faith of Modernism*, 34–36.

40. Shailer Mathews, *The Church and the Changing Order* (New York: Macmillan, 1907), 34, 85, 86, 87, 89.

41. Dorrien, *Making of American Liberal Theology, 1900–1950*, 14.

42. See Mathews, "Unrepentant Liberalism."

43. See Harry Emerson Fosdick, *The Living of These Days: An Autobiography* (New York: Harper & Brothers, 1956), 55, 57, 66; see also Dorrien, *Making of American Liberal Theology, 1900–1950*, 357–60.

44. Fosdick, *Living of These Days*, 78.

45. See Harry Emerson Fosdick, *The Meaning of Prayer* (New York: Association Press, 1915); Fosdick, *The Meaning of Faith* (New York: Association Press, 1917); Fosdick, *The Meaning of Service* (New York: Association Press, 1920); and Dorrien, *Making of American Liberal Theology, 1900–1950*, 363–64, 372.

46. See Dorrien, *Making of American Liberal Theology, 1900–1950*, 371–75, 383.

47. Harry Emerson Fosdick, "Shall the Fundamentalists Win?," in *The Riverside Preachers*, ed. Paul H. Sherry (New York: Pilgrim, 1978), 29.

48. Fosdick, "Shall the Fundamentalists Win?," 29, 30.

49. See Robert Moats Miller, *Harry Emerson Fosdick: Preacher, Pastor, Prophet* (New York: Oxford University Press, 1985), 116.

50. Fosdick, "Shall the Fundamentalists Win?," 38; see also Miller, *Harry Emerson Fosdick*, 117–22; and Dorrien, *Making of American Liberal Theology, 1900–1950*, 375–83.

51. Fosdick, *Living of These Days*, 244; see also Dorrien, *Making of American Liberal Theology, 1900–1950*, 378–79; and Miller, *Harry Emerson Fosdick*, 172–73.

52. See Miller, *Harry Emerson Fosdick*, 335–37.

53. Harry Emerson Fosdick, "The Church Must Go beyond Modernism," in Sherry, *Riverside Preachers*, 39–48.

54. See Dorrien, *Making of American Liberal Theology, 1900–1950*, 378–79, 387–90, 433–34; and Miller, *Harry Emerson Fosdick*, 389–93.

55. Fosdick, "Shall the Fundamentalists Win?," 32.

56. Clarence E. Macartney, "Shall Unbelief Win?," in *Sermons in American History: Selected Issues in the American Pulpit 1630–1967*, ed. Dewitte Holland (Nashville: Abingdon, 1971), 350, 352.

57. For quotations from both of Fosdick's other critics, see Matthew Burton Bowman, *The Urban Pulpit: New York City and the Fate of Liberal Evangelicalism* (New York: Oxford University Press, 2014), 267.

58. As quoted in Bowman, *Urban Pulpit*, 258, 259.

59. As quoted in Miller, *Harry Emerson Fosdick*, 336.

60. See Dorrien, *Making of American Liberal Theology, 1900–1950*, 16.

61. See Dorrien, *Making of American Liberal Theology, 1900–1950*, 10–20.

62. For more on the history of these distinctions, as well as the argument that they are overwrought, see Dorrien, *Making of American Liberal Theology, 1900–1950*, 10–20, quotation on 14.

63. See Dorrien, *Making of American Liberal Theology, 1900–1950*, 1–72.

64. See Henry Sloane Coffin, *The Practical Aims of a Liberal Evangelicalism* (New York: Union Theological Seminary, 1915).

65. Henry P. Van Dusen, *The Vindication of Liberal Theology: A Tract for the Times* (New York: Scribner's Sons, 1963), 38.

66. As quoted in Dorrien, *Making of American Liberal Theology, 1900–1950*, 548.

67. See Van Dusen, *Vindication of Liberal Theology*, 41.

68. As quoted in Fosdick, *Living of These Days*, 166.

69. See Dorrien, *Making of American Liberal Theology, 1900–1950*, 549.

70. See Dorrien, *Making of American Liberal Theology, 1900-1950*, 435-549.

71. For more on Barth's rebellion as the founding narrative, see Gary Dorrien, *The Barthian Revolt in Modern Theology: Theology without Weapons* (Louisville: Westminster John Knox, 2000), 1-13.

72. See Eberhard Busch, *Karl Barth: His Life from Letters and Autobiographical Texts*, trans. John Bowden (London: SCM, 1976), 81-98.

73. Karl Barth, "The Strange New World within the Bible," in *The Word of God and the Word of Man*, trans. Douglas Horton (New York: Harper & Row, 1957), 28-50.

74. For attribution of the infamous "bomb on the playground" quotation to a 1926 article by Karl Adam, see Colin E. Gunton, *Revelation and Reason: Prolegomena to Systematic Theology* (New York: T&T Clark, 2008), 164.

75. See Dorrien, *Barthian Revolt*, 1-2, 111-16.

76. Albert C. Knudson, "German Fundamentalism," *Christian Century*, 14 June 1928, 762-65; see also Dorrien, *Making of American Liberal Theology, 1900-1950*, 327-28, 348-49.

77. Dorrien, *Barthian Revolt*, 8.

78. Reinhold Niebuhr, "Barth—Apostle of the Absolute," *Christian Century*, 13 December 1928, 1523-34, as quoted in Dorrien, *Making of American Liberal Theology, 1900-1950*, 460.

79. Dorrien, *Barthian Revolt*, 6.

80. See Dorrien, *Barthian Revolt*, 1-13, 131-67.

81. See Phillip R. Thorne, *Evangelicalism and Karl Barth* (Allison Park, PA: Pickwick, 1995), 33-41.

82. See Cornelius Van Til, "Karl Barth on Scripture," *Presbyterian Guardian*, 9 January 1937, 137.

83. Cornelius Van Til, *The New Modernism* (Philadelphia: Presbyterian and Reformed, 1947), 3; see also John R. Muether, *Cornelius Van Til: Reformed Apologist and Churchman* (Phillipsburg, NJ: P&R, 2008), 123-24.

84. Van Til, *New Modernism*, 376.

85. Cornelius Van Til, *Christianity and Barthianism* (Philadelphia: Presbyterian and Reformed, 1962), vii; see also Thorne, *Evangelicalism and Karl Barth*, 31-39.

86. Van Til, *Christianity and Barthianism*, 446.

87. See Muether, *Cornelius Van Til*, 91-118; and D. G. Hart, "Beyond the Battle for the Bible: What Evangelicals Missed in Van Til's Critique of Barth," in *Karl Barth and American Evangelicalism*, ed. Bruce L. McCormack and Clifford B. Anderson (Grand Rapids: Eerdmans, 2011), 42-70.

88. See Bernard Ramm, *After Fundamentalism: The Future of Evangelical Theology* (San Francisco: Harper & Row, 1982), 23.

89. Béla Vassady, *Limping Along . . . Confessions of a Pilgrim Theologian* (Grand Rapids: Eerdmans, 1985), 20.

90. Vassady, *Limping Along*, 21.

91. For more on Vassady's accomplishments, see Marsden, *Reforming Fundamentalism*, 98–99.

92. See Vassady, *Limping Along*, 71–94, 96–99, 111, 122–23.

93. Vassady, *Limping Along*, 125; see also Marsden, *Reforming Fundamentalism*, 97–99.

94. See Marsden, *Reforming Fundamentalism*, 101–2.

95. Béla Vassady, "A Theology of Hope for the Philosophy of Despair," *Theology Today* 5 (1948): 169.

96. See Marsden, *Reforming Fundamentalism*, 101–3.

97. See Vassady, *Limping Along*, 61, 69, quotation on 122.

98. See Marsden, *Reforming Fundamentalism*, 101–3.

99. Carl McIntire, "Caught in the Middle," *Christian Beacon*, 6 October 1949, as quoted in Vassady, *Limping Along*, 131.

100. See Marsden, *Reforming Fundamentalism*, 102–16.

101. Fuller statement of faith as quoted in Robert K. Johnston, *Evangelicals at an Impasse: Biblical Authority in Practice* (Atlanta: John Knox), 32.

102. For the entire story of Vassady's ouster, see Marsden, *Reforming Fundamentalism*, 109–15.

103. Vassady, *Limping Along*, 132–33.

104. See Vassady, *Limping Along*, 132; and Marsden, *Reforming Fundamentalism*, 114.

105. Vassady, *Limping Along*, 138.

106. For a prime example, see Fuller Seminary's website, which to this day includes a section defining "Fuller in Contrast to Neo-orthodoxy," https://www.fuller.edu/about/mission-and-values/what-we-believe-and-teach/.

107. Precisely as Marsden has argued, *Reforming Fundamentalism*, 114–15.

Chapter Two

1. See "The Trans-Atlantic Slave Trade Database," *SlaveVoyages*, http://www.slavevoyages.org/estimates/BIUEGjQz; and "1860 Census: Population of the

United States," United States Census Bureau, https://www.census.gov/library /publications/1864/dec/1860a.html.

2. For more on early missionary colonization and Christianization efforts, as well as debates over slave conversion, see Albert J. Raboteau, *African-American Religion* (New York: Oxford University Press, 1999), 21–22; and Raboteau, *Slave Religion: The "Invisible Institution" in the Antebellum South*, updated ed. (New York: Oxford University Press, 2004), 96–103; on Protestant and Catholic divergences, see Stephen C. Finley and Torin Alexander, *African American Religious Cultures*, ed. Anthony B. Pinn (Santa Barbara: ABC-CLIO, 2009), xxvii.

3. See Finley and Alexander, *African American Religious Cultures*, xxviii.

4. See William Pannell, "The Religious Heritage of Blacks," in *The Evangelicals*, ed. David F. Wells and John D. Woodbridge (Grand Rapids: Baker, 1977), 116–27.

5. Raboteau, *African-American Religion*, 27.

6. For more on the idea of an antebellum evangelical "theological consensus," see George Marsden, *Fundamentalism and American Culture*, 2nd ed. (New York: Oxford University Press, 2006), 6; and Marsden, *Understanding Fundamentalism and Evangelicalism* (Grand Rapids: Eerdmans, 1991), 12; for discussion of Black and white evangelical divergences, see Mark A. Noll, *American Evangelical Christianity* (Malden, MA: Blackwell, 2001), 73–76; see also Albert J. Raboteau, "The Black Experience in American Evangelicalism: The Meaning of Slavery," in *The Evangelical Tradition in America*, ed. Leonard I. Sweet (Macon, GA: Mercer University Press, 1984), 181–98.

7. For a few notable exceptions, see Ronald C. Potter, "The New Black Evangelicals," in *Black Theology: A Documentary History, 1966–1979*, ed. Gayraud S. Wilmore and James H. Cone (Maryknoll, NY: Orbis Books, 1979), 1:302–9; and Soong-Chan Rah, "In Whose Image: The Emergence, Development, and Challenge of African-American Evangelicalism" (PhD diss., Divinity School of Duke University, 2016); also Albert G. Miller, "The Rise of African-American Evangelicalism in American Culture," in *Perspectives on American Religion and Culture*, ed. Peter W. Williams (Malden, MA: Blackwell, 1999), 259–69. Potter's essay was dropped from the second edition of the Wilmore and Cone volume, however.

8. See Miller, "Rise of African-American Evangelicalism"; and Milton G. Sernett, "Black Religion and the Question of Evangelical Identity," in *The Variety of American Evangelicalism*, ed. Donald W. Dayton and Robert K. Johnston (Eugene, OR: Wipf & Stock, 1998), 135–47; for a controversial early example of historiographical wrangling over such debates, see Joseph Washington Jr., *Black Religion:*

The Negro and Christianity in the United States (Boston: Beacon, 1964); see also Edward J. Blum, "Religion, Race, and African American Life," in *The Columbia Guide to Religion in American History*, ed. Paul Harvey and Edward Blum (New York: Columbia University Press, 2012), 213–35.

9. See Noll, *American Evangelical Christianity*, 73.

10. See Miller, "Rise of African-American Evangelicalism"; and Raboteau, "Black Experience in American Evangelicalism."

11. See William Bentley, "Bible Believers in the Black Community," in Wells and Woodbridge, *Evangelicals*, 128–41; and Miller, "Rise of African-American Evangelicalism"; also Noll, *American Evangelical Christianity*, 37.

12. See Bentley, "Bible Believers in the Black Community," 130; also George Marsden, ed., *Evangelicalism and Modern America* (Grand Rapids: Eerdmans, 1984), xv; as well as Noll, *American Evangelical Christianity*, 75.

13. See Mary Beth Swetnam Mathews, *Doctrine and Race: African American Evangelicals and Fundamentalism between the Wars* (Tuscaloosa: University of Alabama Press, 2017); and Daniel R. Bare, *Black Fundamentalists: Conservative Christianity and Racial Identity in the Segregation Era* (New York: New York University Press, 2021). See also Miller's argument that the influential Black Plymouth Brethren leader B. M. Nottage was theologically fundamentalist ("Rise of African-American Evangelicalism," 261–63).

14. For further discussion of racism as a hallmark of white fundamentalism, see Matthew Avery Sutton, *American Apocalypse: A History of Modern Evangelicalism* (Cambridge: Belknap Press of Harvard University Press, 2014), 109–12.

15. See Sutton, *American Apocalypse*, 133–37; as well as William Bell Riley, *The Conflict of Christianity with Its Counterfeits* (Minneapolis: Irene Woods, 1940), 106; and Barry Hankins, *God's Rascal: J. Frank Norris and the Beginnings of Southern Fundamentalism* (Lexington: University Press of Kentucky, 2010), 162–63; also Markku Ruotsila, *Fighting Fundamentalist: Carl McIntire and the Politicization of American Fundamentalism* (New York: Oxford University Press, 2016), 142–47.

16. See Mark Noll's argument, for instance, that the "Curse of Ham" continued to enjoy "considerable currency" among the members of the Christian populace well into the twentieth century (*God and Race in American Politics: A Short History* [Princeton: Princeton University Press, 2008], 133); see also Miles S. Mullin II, "Postwar Evangelical Social Concern: Evangelical Identity and the Modes and Limits of Social Engagement, 1945–1960" (PhD diss., Vanderbilt University, 2009), 412.

17. For discussion of the Federal Council of Churches' record on interracial marriage, for example, see Ruotsila, *Fighting Fundamentalist*, 147; see also Barbara Dianne Savage, *Your Spirits Walk Beside Us: The Politics of Black Religion* (Cambridge: Belknap Press of Harvard University Press, 2008), 210–13.

18. See Douglas A. Sweeney, "Fundamentalism and the Neo-evangelicals," *Fides et Historia* 24 (1992): 81–96; also Marsden, *Reforming Fundamentalism*.

19. For extensive coverage of the Montgomery bus boycott, see Gary Dorrien, *Breaking White Supremacy: Martin Luther King Jr. and the Black Social Gospel* (New Haven: Yale University Press, 2018), 288–301.

20. See Miles S. Mullin II, "Neoevangelicalism and the Problem of Race in Postwar America," in *Christians and the Color Line: Race and Religion after Divided by Faith*, ed. J. Russell Hawkins and Phillip Luke Sinitiere (New York: Oxford University Press, 2013), 15–35.

21. For an in-depth exploration of the various racial views espoused in numerous different evangelical periodicals of the era, including the presence of some antisegregation sentiments at places like Wheaton College and the NAE, see Mullin, "Neoevangelicalism and the Problem of Race," 15–35.

22. See "Race Tensions and Social Change," *Christianity Today*, 19 January 1959, 20–23; for more on the responses of the NAE, *Christianity Today*, and the development of the "evangelical moderate" position, see Sutton, *American Apocalypse*, 306–7, 333–35; and John W. Oliver Jr., "Evangelical Campus and Press Meet Black America's Quest for Civil Rights, 1956–1959: Malone College and Christianity Today," *Fides et Historia* 8 (1975): 54–70; as well as Curtis J. Evans, "White Evangelical Protestant Responses to the Civil Rights Movement," *Harvard Theological Review* 102 (2009): 245–73.

23. For an example of condemnations of "forced integration," see "The Church and the Race Problem," *Christianity Today*, 18 March 1957, 20–21.

24. For analyses of the evangelical position, see Sutton, *American Apocalypse*, 333–35; Mullin, "Neoevangelicalism and the Problem of Race"; Evans, "White Evangelical Protestant Responses"; and Dennis Hollinger, *Individualism and Social Ethics: An Evangelical Syncretism* (Lanham, MD: University Press of America, 1983), 197.

25. For discussion of the mythos around Graham's relationship to King, see Steven P. Miller, *Billy Graham and the Rise of the Republican South* (Philadelphia: University of Pennsylvania Press, 2011), 91–96.

26. Billy Graham, *World Aflame* (Garden City, NY: Doubleday, 1965), 39.

27. Billy Graham, "Billy Graham Makes Plea for an End to Intolerance," *Life*, 1 October 1956, 146.

28. See Carl F. H. Henry, *The Uneasy Conscience of Modern Fundamentalism* (Grand Rapids: Eerdmans, 1947), 17, 78; and "Race Tensions and Social Change," 21, 22; see also "Desegregation and Regeneration," *Christianity Today*, 29 September 1958, 20–21.

29. See Sernett, "Black Religion," 142–43, quotation on 137; and Sutton, *American Apocalypse*, 286–87.

30. See James DeForest Murch, *Cooperation without Compromise: A History of the National Association of Evangelicals* (Grand Rapids: Eerdmans, 1956), 64, 196.

31. See Sernett, "Black Religion," 143.

32. See Mullin, "Neoevangelicalism and the Problem of Race," 20–22.

33. See Edward Gilbreath, *Reconciliation Blues: A Black Evangelical's Inside View of White Christianity* (Downers Grove, IL: InterVarsity Press, 2006), 14.

34. See Lauralee Farrer, "A Legacy of Steadfast Belief," *Fuller Focus Magazine*, Fall 2007, https://fullerstudio.fuller.edu/a-legacy-of-steadfast-belief/; and Farrer, "This Is Then, That Was Now," *Fuller Studio*, https://fullerstudio.fuller.edu/this-is-then-that-was-now/.

35. See Potter, "New Black Evangelicals," 302–3.

36. Potter, "New Black Evangelicals," 303.

37. See Howard O. Jones and Edward Gilbreath, *Gospel Trailblazer: An African-American Preacher's Historic Journey across Racial Lines* (Chicago: Moody, 2003), 24–28, 37–42, 45–48.

38. See Jones and Gilbreath, *Gospel Trailblazer*, 51, 53, 25.

39. See Jones and Gilbreath, *Gospel Trailblazer*, 69–72, quotations on 59.

40. See Jones and Gilbreath, *Gospel Trailblazer*, 76.

41. See Jones and Gilbreath, *Gospel Trailblazer*, 91–92, 95, 100–101, 106–7.

42. See Jones and Gilbreath, *Gospel Trailblazer*, 115–29, quotation on 127.

43. See Jones and Gilbreath, *Gospel Trailblazer*, 133–40, quotation on 124.

44. See Jones and Gilbreath, *Gospel Trailblazer*, 139–46.

45. See Jones and Gilbreath, *Gospel Trailblazer*, 140, 151–52, 161–72, 207, 211–18.

46. Jones and Gilbreath, *Gospel Trailblazer*, 207, 211–18.

47. See William H. Bentley and Ruth Lewis Bentley, "Reflections on the Scope and Function of a Black Evangelical Black Theology," in *Evangelical Affirmations*, ed. Kenneth S. Kantzer and Carl F. H. Henry (Grand Rapids: Academie Books, 1990),

299–333; and Miller, "Rise of African-American Evangelicalism," 267; also Kenan Heise, "Pentecostals' Rev. William Bentley," *Chicago Tribune*, 22 May 1993, https://www.chicagotribune.com/news/ct-xpm-1993-05-22-9305220099-story.html.

48. See Bentley and Bentley, "Reflections on the Scope," 300.

49. See Ronald C. Potter, "Editorial: Thinking for Ourselves," *The Other Side*, July–August 1975, 56.

50. See Albert G. Miller, "National Black Evangelical Association," *Encyclopedia of African American Culture and History*, ed. Colin A. Palmer, 2nd ed. (Detroit: Macmillan, 2006), 4:1606–7; and William H. Bentley, *The National Black Evangelical Association* (Chicago: William H. Bentley, 1979), 10–16; also Bentley and Bentley, "Reflections on the Scope," 301.

51. See Bentley, *National Black Evangelical Association*, 10; also Miller, "National Black Evangelical Association," 1606; and Bentley and Bentley, "Reflections on the Scope," 325.

52. See Bentley, *National Black Evangelical Association*, 10–16, 54, quotation on 10–11.

53. See Bentley, *National Black Evangelical Association*, 53–55, quotation on 53.

54. See Bentley, *National Black Evangelical Association*, 55–56; see also Bentley and Bentley, "Reflections on the Scope," 304–5.

55. See Bentley, *National Black Evangelical Association*, 110–16.

56. See Bentley, *National Black Evangelical Association*, 16–26, 27–33, 110–16; also Miller, "National Black Evangelical Association," 1606–7.

57. See William E. Pannell, *My Friend, the Enemy* (Waco, TX: Word, 1968), 17–18, 39, 48; and "T1. Oral History Interview with William E. Pannell, 25 May 1995," Collection 498 Oral History Interviews with William E. Pannell, CN-498, Billy Graham Center Archives, https://archives.wheaton.edu/repositories/4/resources/448/collection_organization.

58. See Pannell, *My Friend, the Enemy*, 39, 18, 48.

59. See Pannell, *My Friend, the Enemy*, 48, 51–52, 50.

60. See Pannell, *My Friend, the Enemy*, 55–57; also "T2. Oral History Interview with William E. Pannell, 21 April 1998"; and "T3. Oral History Interview with William E. Pannell, 21 April 1998."

61. See Pannell, *My Friend, the Enemy*, 55–57.

62. See "T3. Oral History Interview with William E. Pannell, 21 April 1998"; "T4. Oral History Interview with William E. Pannell, 28 February 2000"; "T6. Oral History Interview with William E. Pannell, 18 August 2003."

63. See Tom Skinner, *Black and Free* (Grand Rapids: Zondervan, 1968), 22–47, quotations on 45, 29; and Edward Gilbreath, "A Prophet Out of Harlem," *Christianity Today*, 16 September 1996, 36–43.

64. See Skinner, *Black and Free*, 29.

65. See Tom Skinner, "The U.S. Racial Crisis and World Evangelism," in *Christ the Liberator: Urbana 70*, ed. John R. W. Stott (Downers Grove, IL: InterVarsity Press, 1971), 189–209, quotations on 197, 202.

66. See Skinner, *Black and Free*, 54–64, quotations on 62–63.

67. See Skinner, *Black and Free*, 66–75, quotation on 67.

68. See Skinner, *Black and Free*, 74–87, quotations on 53, 75.

69. See Skinner, *Black and Free*, 88–104, 124–28, quotation on 88; and McCandlish Phillips, "Evangelist Finds Harlem Vineyard," *New York Times*, 16 August 1964.

70. See Potter, "Thinking for Ourselves"; and Potter, "New Black Evangelicals"; for "dream team" reference, see Gilbreath, "Prophet Out of Harlem," 39.

71. Pannell, *My Friend, the Enemy*, 7.

72. Pannell, *My Friend, the Enemy*, 13–20, 61–75, quotations on 13, 63.

73. Pannell, *My Friend, the Enemy*, 65.

74. See "Books: Social Issues Top Most Significant List," *Eternity*, December 1968, 49–50.

75. See "T4. Oral History Interview with William E. Pannell, 28 February 2000"; "T5. Oral History Interview with William E. Pannell, 28 February 2000"; and "T6. Oral History Interview with William E. Pannell, 18 August 2003."

76. See "Controversial Black Preacher Putting Stress on Social Issues," *New York Times*, 2 September 1973, 38.

77. See Potter, "New Black Evangelicals," 304.

78. See Gilbreath, "Prophet Out of Harlem," 40.

79. See Bentley, *National Black Evangelical Association*, 18–21, quotation on 20.

80. See Potter, "New Black Evangelicals," 304; also Potter, "Editorial: Thinking for Ourselves"; and Bentley, *National Black Evangelical Association*, 34.

81. See Gilbreath, "Prophet Out of Harlem," 36.

82. Gilbreath, "Prophet Out of Harlem," 37.

83. See Gilbreath, "Prophet Out of Harlem," 41.

84. See Skinner, "U.S. Racial Crisis," 190, 191, 192.

85. Skinner, "U.S. Racial Crisis," 193, 200.

86. Skinner, "U.S. Racial Crisis," 194, 196, 199.

87. Skinner, "U.S. Racial Crisis," 199.

88. Skinner, "U.S. Racial Crisis," 204.

89. Skinner, "U.S. Racial Crisis," 208–9.

90. See Gilbreath, "Prophet Out of Harlem," 41, 42.

91. See Potter, "New Black Evangelicals"; and "Tenth Anniversary Issue: The New Black Evangelicals," *The Other Side*, July–August 1975.

92. For discussion of "reverse racism" charges, see Bentley, *National Black Evangelical Association*, 20.

93. See William H. Bentley, "Reflections," in *The Chicago Declaration*, ed. Ronald J. Sider (Carol Stream, IL: Creation House, 1974), 135–36, quotations on 136.

94. See Bentley, "Bible Believers in the Black Community"; and William H. Bentley, *The Relevance of a Black Evangelical Black Theology for American Theology* (Chicago: BECN, 1981), 21–24, 34–35; also Miller, "National Black Evangelical Association"; and Jimmy Locklear, "Theology-Culture Rift Surfaces among Black Evangelicals," *Christianity Today*, 23 May 1980, 44; as well as John Maust, "The NBEA: Striving to Be Both Black and Biblical," *Christianity Today*, 27 June 1980, 58–59.

95. See Gilbreath, "Prophet Out of Harlem," 36–43.

96. See Gilbreath, "Prophet Out of Harlem," 36–43; and "T8. Oral History Interview with William E. Pannell, 27 March 2007."

97. For more on Perkins's work and legacy, see John M. Perkins, *With Justice for All* (Ventura, CA: Regal Books, 1982); and Charles Marsh and John M. Perkins, *Welcoming Justice: God's Movement toward Beloved Community* (Downers Grove, IL: InterVarsity Press, 2009); as well as Peter Slade, Charles Marsh, and Peter Goodwin Heltzel, eds., *Mobilizing for the Common Good: The Lived Theology of John M. Perkins* (Jackson: University Press of Mississippi, 2013).

98. See Farrer, "This Is Then, That Was Now"; and Farrer, "Legacy of Steadfast Belief"; also Lewis V. Baldwin, "Black Church Studies as an Academic Interest and Initiative," in *The Black Church Studies Reader*, ed. Alton B. Pollard III and Carol B. Duncan (New York: Palgrave Macmillan, 2016), 31–55; for discussion of Pannell's legacy, see Reggie Williams, "Pannell, Fuller, and the African American Student," Public Address, https://www.youtube.com/watch?v=YVnS9G9foNs.

99. Gilbreath, *Reconciliation Blues*, 33–41.

100. See Gilbreath, *Reconciliation Blues*, 9–21, quotations on 19, 20.

101. See Gilbreath, *Reconciliation Blues*, 7.

102. Gilbreath, *Reconciliation Blues*, 127.

103. Gilbreath, *Reconciliation Blues*, 127.

104. Gilbreath, *Reconciliation Blues*, 139.

105. See Michael O. Emerson and Christian Smith, *Divided by Faith: Evangelical Religion and the Problem of Race in America* (New York: Oxford University Press, 2000), 18–19, 169; for discussion of the book's success, see J. Russell Hawkins and Phillip Luke Sinitiere, eds., *Christians and the Color Line: Race and Religion after Divided by Faith* (New York: Oxford University Press, 2014), 2–3.

106. Gilbreath, *Reconciliation Blues*, 173.

107. Emerson and Smith, *Divided by Faith*, 170.

108. See Emerson and Smith, *Divided by Faith*, 170.

109. Gilbreath, *Reconciliation Blues*, 173–74.

110. See Gilbreath, *Reconciliation Blues*, 18.

Chapter Three

1. See Bill J. Leonard, *Baptists in America* (New York: Columbia University Press, 2005), 117; and H. Leon McBeth, *The Baptist Heritage: Four Centuries of Baptist Witness* (Nashville: Broadman, 1987), 755–59.

2. See Kyle Cleveland, "The Politics of Jubilee: Ideological Drift and Organizational Schism in a Religious Sect" (PhD diss., Temple University, 1990), 47–52; and David R. Swartz, *Moral Minority: The Evangelical Left in an Age of Conservatism* (Philadelphia: University of Pennsylvania Press, 2012), 26–30.

3. See John Alexander, "God's Preferential Option for the Poor," *The Other Side*, March–April 1990, 49.

4. For more on the Alexanders' evolution, see Swartz, *Moral Minority*, 28–29; see also Mark Olson, "John Alexander: Taking Jesus Seriously," *The Other Side*, October 1985, 10–15.

5. See Alexander, "God's Preferential Option for the Poor," 50.

6. See Fred Alexander, "Something Big," *Freedom Now*, August 1965, 3; and John Alexander, "Our Name," *Freedom Now*, August 1965, 4; see also Cleveland, "Politics of Jubilee," 47.

7. See John Alexander, "I'm All Fired Up," *Freedom Now*, October 1965, 3.

8. For discussion of the shifting audience, see Cleveland, "Politics of Jubilee," 47–58, 122–24; as well as Swartz, *Moral Minority*, 29–31.

9. See Swartz, *Moral Minority*, 31–38; and Cleveland, "Politics of Jubilee," 49–54; also Phillip Harnden, "Remembering John," *The Other Side*, September–October 2001, 9–10, 9.

10. See Cleveland, "Politics of Jubilee," 49-54, 75-76, 96-98; for all quotations, see also "The Other Side," *Freedom Now*, September-October 1969, 31, as quoted in Cleveland, "Politics of Jubilee," 49-50.

11. See "The Other Side," as quoted in Cleveland, "Politics of Jubilee," 49-50.

12. See Cleveland, "Politics of Jubilee," 58-63, 75-76, 96-98; and Swartz, *Moral Minority*, 47; for more on his wrestling with just war and pacifism, see John Alexander, "God and the Poor, Part 2," *The Other Side*, May-June 1990, 51-53; see also Olson, "John Alexander," 11.

13. See Joel Fetzer and Gretchen S. Carnes, "Dr. Ron Sider: Mennonite Environmentalist on the Evangelical Left," in *Religious Leaders and Faith-Based Politics: Ten Profiles*, ed. Jo Renee Formicola and Hubert Morken (Lanham, MD: Rowman & Littlefield, 2001), 159.

14. See Ronald J. Sider, *Evangelism and Social Action* (London: Hodder & Stoughton, 1993), 12-23, quotations on 16.

15. See Fetzer and Carnes, "Dr. Ron Sider," 160; see also Jeffrey McClain Jones, "Ronald Sider and Radical Evangelical Political Theology" (PhD diss., Northwestern University, 1990), 9-12; and Tim Stafford, "Ron Sider's Unsettling Crusade," *Christianity Today*, 27 April 1992, 18-22.

16. See Stafford, "Ron Sider's Unsettling Crusade," 20; and Sider, *Evangelism and Social Action*, 16-18, quotations on 16, 17.

17. See Sider, *Evangelism and Social Action*, 17; see also Jones, "Ronald Sider," 405-37.

18. Jones, "Ronald Sider," 406.

19. See Kathleen Hayes, "Ron Sider: Working for Kingdom Values," *The Other Side*, October 1986, 11; also Sider, *Evangelism and Social Action*, 17-18.

20. Sider, *Evangelism and Social Action*, 18.

21. See Sider, *Evangelism and Social Action*, 18; also Stafford, "Ron Sider's Unsettling Crusade," 20.

22. See Jim Wallis, *Faith Works: Lessons from the Life of an Activist Preacher* (New York: Random House, 2000), 3-4.

23. See Jim Wallis, *The Call to Conversion* (New York: Harper & Row, 1981), xv; see also Jim Wallis, *Revive Us Again: A Sojourner's Story* (Nashville: Abingdon, 1983), 46.

24. Wallis, *Faith Works*, 10.

25. See Wallis, *Faith Works*, 12; also Wallis, *Call to Conversion*, xv; and Wallis, *Revive Us Again*, 56.

26. See Wallis, *Revive Us Again*, 52–75; Wallis, *Call to Conversion*, xv–xvi; and Wallis, *Faith Works*, 12.

27. Wallis, *Call to Conversion*, xvi.

28. Wallis, *Revive Us Again*, 77.

29. Wallis, *Call to Conversion*, xvi–xvii.

30. Wallis, *Revive Us Again*, 77.

31. See Wallis, *Revive Us Again*, 76–91, quotations on 82.

32. See Wallis, *Revive Us Again*, 76–91, quotations on 83, 84.

33. See Wallis, *Revive Us Again*, 84.

34. See John G. Turner, *Bill Bright and Campus Crusade for Christ: The Renewal of Evangelicalism in Postwar America* (Chapel Hill: University of North Carolina Press, 2008), 144.

35. Wallis, *Revive Us Again*, 85.

36. Wallis, *Revive Us Again*, 92–93.

37. Wallis, *Revive Us Again*, 16; see also Mark G. Toulouse, "Sojourners," in *Popular Religious Magazines of the United States*, ed. P. Mark Fackler and Charles H. Lippy (Westport, CT: Greenwood, 1995), 444–51; and Randall Balmer, "Jim Wallis," in *Encyclopedia of Evangelicalism*, rev. and exp. ed. (Waco, TX: Baylor University Press, 2004), 715–16.

38. See "Who Are We?," *Post-American*, Fall 1971.

39. See Jim Wallis, "Post-American Christianity," *Post-American*, Fall 1971, 2–3, as quoted in Wallis, *Revive Us Again*, 92–93; see also Boyd T. Reese Jr., "Resistance and Hope: The Interplay of Theological Synthesis, Biblical Interpretation, Political Analysis, and Praxis in the Christian Radicalism of 'Sojourners' Magazine" (PhD diss., Temple University, 1991), 45, 212–13.

40. See Wallis, *Revive Us Again*, 13–18, 92–93, quotation on 93; for discussion of subscription numbers, see Swartz, *Moral Minority*, 54–56.

41. For a detailed account of Graham's direct involvement with Nixon, see Steven P. Miller, *Billy Graham and the Rise of the Republican South* (Philadelphia: University of Pennsylvania Press, 2011), 124–54; for further discussions of Graham's meetings with Nixon's aides, see Daniel K. Williams, *God's Own Party: The Making of the Christian Right* (New York: Oxford University Press, 2010), 98–99.

42. See Miller, *Billy Graham*, 150–53; and Williams, *God's Own Party*, 98–99.

43. For background on Campus Crusade, Explo, and Nixon's telegram, see Turner, *Bill Bright*, 141–46, quotations on 144.

44. See Miller, *Billy Graham*, 152–53; see also, Williams, *God's Own Party*, 99;

for both quotations, see Billy Graham, Letter to Richard Nixon, 4 August 1972, https://www.nixonlibrary.gov/virtuallibrary/documents/donated/080472_graham.pdf.

45. See Barrie Doyle, "The Religious Campaign: Backing Their Man," *Christianity Today*, 17 October 1972, 38–39, as quoted in Swartz, *Moral Minority*, 174.

46. See Miller, *Billy Graham*, 153.

47. For statistics on the evangelical vote that year, see Lyman Kellstedt et al., "Faith Transformed: Religion and American Politics from FDR to George W. Bush," in *Religion and American Politics: From the Colonial Period to the Present*, ed. Mark A. Noll and Luke E. Harlow (New York: Oxford University Press, 2007), 272–73.

48. See Fetzer and Carnes, "Dr. Ron Sider," 160.

49. See Swartz, *Moral Minority*, 171–78; Jones, "Ronald Sider," 405–7; and James Alan Patterson, "Evangelicals and the Presidential Elections of 1972, 1976, and 1980," *Fides et Historia* 18 (1986): 44–62, quotation on 45–46.

50. Stafford, "Ron Sider's Unsettling Crusade," 21.

51. See Charles P. Henderson Jr., "The {Social} Gospel according to 1. Richard Nixon 2. George McGovern," *Commonweal*, 29 September 1972, 521.

52. See Patterson, "Evangelicals and the Presidential Elections," 46–48.

53. For discussion of broader progressive evangelical support for McGovern, including the kinds of views expressed in magazines like *The Other Side*, see Swartz, *Moral Minority*, 171–75.

54. See Richard J. Mouw, "Evangelicals and Political Activism," *Christian Century*, 27 December 1972, 1316.

55. Stephen Charles Mott, "An Evangelical McGovern at Wheaton," *Qoheleth*, 25 October 1972, 1, 7–8, as quoted in Patterson, "Evangelicals and the Presidential Elections," 59.

56. See Swartz, *Moral Minority*, 175–77; Williams, *God's Own Party*, 100–102; and Patterson, "Evangelicals and the Presidential Elections," 45–48.

57. See Arthur P. Holmes, "Evangelicals, Morality and Politics," *Reformed Journal* 22, no. 9 (November 1972): 3.

58. See Nicholas Wolterstorff, "McGovern at Wheaton," *Reformed Journal* 22, no. 9 (November 1972): 4.

59. See Fetzer and Carnes, "Dr. Ron Sider," 160.

60. See "The Evangelical Vote," *Newsweek*, October 1972, 93.

61. For more on Sider's plans and letters, see Swartz, *Moral Minority*, 178; also Fetzer and Carnes, "Dr. Ron Sider," 160–61.

62. See Ronald J. Sider, "A Reflection," Evangelicals for Social Action, https://web.archive.org/web/20180727215659/http://www.evangelicalsforsocialaction.org/about-esa/history/.

63. See Ronald J. Sider, "Introduction: An Historic Moment for Biblical Social Concern," in *The Chicago Declaration*, ed. Ronald J. Sider (Carol Stream, IL: Creation House, 1974), 21–22.

64. Sider, "Introduction," 22.

65. For discussion of the complexities related to the gathering's diverse constituencies, see Swartz, *Moral Minority*, 178–83, quotation on 182.

66. See Sider, "Introduction," 24.

67. For discussion of Alexander and Gabelein's reactions, see Swartz, *Moral Minority*, 179–80.

68. See Sider, "Introduction," 27.

69. See Sider, "Introduction," 28–31; as well as Swartz, *Moral Minority*, 179–81.

70. For all quotations, see "The Chicago Declaration," in *The Chicago Declaration*, ed. Ronald J. Sider (Carol Stream, IL: Creation House, 1974), cover, 1–2.

71. Sider, "Introduction," 29.

72. Roy Larson, "Historic Workshop: Evangelicals Do U-turn, Take on Social Problems," *Chicago Sun-Times*, 1 December 1973.

73. George Cornell, Religion Today, Associated Press, 30 November 1973, a319.

74. Marjorie Hyer, "Evangelicals: Tackling the Gut Issues," *Christian Century*, 19 December 1973, 1244–45.

75. For a helpful rundown of the variety of media responses to the Chicago Declaration, see Martin E. Marty, "Needed: Revised Social Gospel," *Context*, 15 March 1974, 1–6; see also Sider, "Introduction," 32–35; and Swartz, *Moral Minority*, 181–83.

76. National Council of Churches Unit Committee of Division of Church and Society, "A Response to a Declaration of Evangelical Concern," *Post-American*, March 1975, https://sojo.net/magazine/march-1975/response-declaration-evangelical-concern.

77. See Bob Jones, editorial, *Faith for the Family*, September–October 1974, 2, as quoted in Fetzer and Carnes, "Dr. Ron Sider," 161.

78. For further discussion of criticisms and negative reactions, see Axel R. Schäfer, *Countercultural Conservatives: American Evangelicalism from the Postwar Revival to the New Christian Right* (Madison: University of Wisconsin Press, 2011), 84–86; see also Swartz, *Moral Minority*, 182.

79. See Billy Graham, "Watergate," *Christianity Today*, 4 January 1974, 9-19; for discussion of Graham's reluctance and its source, see Swartz, *Moral Minority*, 181-83; as well as Wesley Granberg-Michaelson, *Unexpected Destinations: An Evangelical Pilgrimage to World Christianity* (Grand Rapids: Eerdmans, 2011), 77; for quotations from the document, see "The Chicago Declaration," cover, 1-2.

80. See Sider, "Reflection"; as well as Schäfer, *Countercultural Conservatives*, 80-90; and Swartz, *Moral Minority*, 187-88.

81. For discussion of ESA's early growth, travails, and change, see Schäfer, *Countercultural Conservatives*, 80-90; also see Swartz, *Moral Minority*, 187-88.

82. See *The Other Side*, May-June 1976; and John Alexander, "Homosexuality: It's Not That Clear," *The Other Side*, June 1978, 8-6.

83. See L. Aubrey F. McGann, Letters, *The Other Side*, September-October 1972, 5; and A. E. Michelsen, Letters, *The Other Side*, September-October 1972, 5; as well as Jewel E. Duke, Letters, *The Other Side*, May-June 1972, 7.

84. See Gordon H. Clark, Letters, *The Other Side*, July-August 1972, 6.

85. See William Varner, Letters, *The Other Side*, September-October 1976, 3; see also William S. Barker, Letters, *The Other Side*, September-October 1976, 7; and Paul Woolley, Letters, *The Other Side*, September-October 1976, 7.

86. See Francis Schaeffer, Letters, *The Other Side*, September-October 1976, 6.

87. See Cleveland, "Politics of Jubilee," 104-15, 123-25; and Swartz, *Moral Minority*, 44-45.

88. See Vernon C. Grounds, Letters, *The Other Side*, September-October 1976, 79.

89. See Wallis, *Revive Us Again*, 94.

90. For additional discussion of the evolution of the community, see Swartz, *Moral Minority*, 60-66; see also Toulouse, "Sojourners."

91. See Wallis, *Revive Us Again*, 81-82; as well as James Alden Hedstrom, "Evangelical Program in the United States: The Morphology of Establishment, Progressive, and Radical Platforms" (PhD diss., Vanderbilt University, 1982), 418.

92. See Mark Hatfield, *Between a Rock and a Hard Place* (Waco, TX: Word, 1976), 25; also Swartz, *Moral Minority*, 56.

93. See Wallis, *Revive Us Again*, 92-108, quotations on 99, 102.

94. For more on the community's early demonstrations, see Robert K. Johnston, *Evangelicals at an Impasse* (Atlanta: John Knox, 1979), 106-7; see also Swartz, *Moral Minority*, 60-66.

95. See Toulouse, "Sojourners," 448.

96. See Richard Quebedeaux, *The Worldly Evangelicals* (San Francisco: Harper & Row, 1978), 149-51.

97. See Carl F. H. Henry, "Revolt on Evangelical Frontiers," *Christianity Today*, 26 April 1974, 4–8.

98. Jim Wallis, "'Revolt on Evangelical Frontiers': A Response," *Christianity Today*, 21 June 1974, 20–21, as quoted in Reese, "Resistance and Hope," 258.

99. For discussion of the Marxism charges, see Reese, "Resistance and Hope," 257–71.

100. See Richard Quebedeaux, *The Young Evangelicals* (New York: Harper & Row, 1974).

101. See Quebedeaux, *Worldly Evangelicals*, 152, 150, xii.

102. See Fetzer and Carnes, "Dr. Ron Sider," 162–63; also Stafford, "Ron Sider's Unsettling Crusade."

103. See Ronald J. Sider, *Rich Christians in an Age of Hunger: A Biblical Study* (New York: Paulist, 1977), 189, 223.

104. See Sider, *Rich Christians*, 57, 128.

105. For a sampling of early reviews, see C. D. Freudenberger, review of *Rich Christians in an Age of Hunger*, by Ronald J. Sider, *Occasional Bulletin of Missionary Research* 1 (1977): 34–35; and John W. Gladwin, review of *Rich Christians in an Age of Hunger*, by Ronald J. Sider, *Churchman* 93 (1979): 181–84; also John P. Tiemstra, review of *Rich Christians in an Age of Hunger*, by Ronald J. Sider, *Fides et Historia* 12 (1979): 89–93; for statistics on the book, see Fetzer and Carnes, "Dr. Ron Sider," 163; also see Ronald J. Sider, *Rich Christians in an Age of Hunger: Moving from Affluence to Generosity*, 5th ed. (Nashville: Thomas Nelson, 2005).

106. See George Mavrodes, "On Helping the Hungry," *Christianity Today*, 30 December 1977, 46.

107. See "Books of the Century," *Christianity Today*, 24 April 2000, 92–94; and David Neff, "The Top 50 Books That Have Shaped Evangelicals," *Christianity Today*, October 2006, 51–55.

108. For a more thorough and detailed account of this era, including the argument that the movement resisting Reagan's foreign policy represented the peak of the evangelical left, see the brilliant work of historian David Swartz (*Moral Minority*, 233–43).

109. See Christian Smith, *Resisting Reagan: The U.S. Central America Peace Movement* (Chicago: University of Chicago Press, 1996), 17–56.

110. See Swartz, *Moral Minority*, 234–35.

111. See Swartz, *Moral Minority*, 234–38.

112. Swartz, *Moral Minority*, 237.

113. Swartz, *Moral Minority*, 238.

114. See Smith, *Resisting Reagan*, 78–86.

115. See Swartz, *Moral Minority*, 238–43, quotation on 239.

116. See Francis Schaeffer, *The Great Evangelical Disaster* (Westchester, IL: Crossway, 1984); also Swartz, *Moral Minority*, 233–34.

117. See Isaac B. Sharp, review of *Evangelicalism and the Decline of American Politics*, by Jan G. Linn, *Reading Religion*, http://readingreligion.org/books/evangelicalism-and-decline-american-politics.

118. See Schäfer, *Countercultural Conservatives*, 3–14, 69–71, 111–21, 151–55, quotation on 6.

119. See Brantley W. Gasaway, *Progressive Evangelicals and the Pursuit of Social Justice* (Chapel Hill: University of North Carolina Press, 2014), 3–22, 270–77.

120. See Swartz, *Moral Minority*, 1–9, 170–212, 250–54, 255–66, quotation on 6.

121. Schäfer, Gasaway, and Swartz have done invaluable work on a woefully underacknowledged chapter of twentieth-century evangelicalism, and this chapter is indebted to their groundbreaking contributions. With a few qualifications here and there, I find their respective arguments compelling and largely persuasive. Rather than proposing any major revisions, then, I offer this final section as a sort of gloss with a tweak on their enormously helpful accounts.

122. For an in-depth exploration of reconstructionist theology, see Julie J. Ingersoll, *Building God's Kingdom: Inside the World of Christian Reconstruction* (New York: Oxford University Press, 2015).

123. See Gary North, "What Is the ICE?," https://www.garynorth.com/free books/whatsice.htm; see also Mark Oppenheimer, "'Christian Economics' Meets the Antiunion Movement," *New York Times*, 30 April 2011, A19.

124. See Gary North, "The Background of 'Productive Christians,'" in David Chilton, *Productive Christians in an Age of Guilt-Manipulators*, 3rd ed. (Tyler, TX: Institute for Christian Economics, 1990), 351, 352.

125. See Chilton, *Productive Christians*, 7, 8, 9, 39.

126. See North, "Background," 362; and North, "What Is the ICE?"

127. See North, "Background," 362, 363; and North, "What Is the ICE?"

128. See Harold Lindsell, *Free Enterprise: A Judeo-Christian Defense* (Wheaton, IL: Tyndale House, 1982), 30, 31, 32.

129. For a summary of *The Sojourners File* and its attack on Sojourners, see Reese, "Resistance and Hope," 262–68, quotation on 264; see also Joan Harris, *The Sojourners File* (Washington, DC: New Century Foundation, 1983).

130. See "Mad Hatter . . . Tales from the Washington Tea Party," *Conservative Digest*, October 1983, 6.

131. See Reese, "Resistance and Hope," 267.

132. See Lloyd Billingsley, *The Generation That Knew Not Josef: A Critique of Marxism and the Religious Left* (Portland: Multnomah, 1985), 143; see also Billingsley, "First Church of Christ Socialist," *National Review*, 28 October 1983, 1339.

133. Ronald Nash, *Social Justice and the Christian Church* (Lanham, MD: University Press of America, 1990), 158.

134. Ronald H. Nash, *Evangelicals in America: Who They Are, What They Believe* (Nashville: Abingdon, 1987), 10, 108.

135. See Ronald H. Nash, *Why the Left Is Not Right: The Religious Left; Who They Are and What They Believe* (Grand Rapids: Zondervan, 1996), 84–99, quotations on 56, 141, 59.

136. See Sharon Anderson, "Sanctity of Life Issues Bring a Variety of Demonstrators to Washington, D.C.," *Christianity Today*, 12 July 1985, 40, 42.

137. See George E. Curry, "248 Seized in Capital in Day of Protests," *Chicago Tribune*, 30 May 1985, 5.

138. See Ann Monroe, "Devout Dissidents: Radical Evangelicals Are Gaining Influence Protesting U.S. Policy," *Wall Street Journal*, 24 May 1985, 1, 10, quotation on 1.

139. See Anderson, "Sanctity of Life Issues," 42.

140. See "Morality and the Presidential Election," NPR, 13 July 2004, https://www.npr.org/templates/story/story.php?storyId=3354001; see also Angela M. Lahr, *Millennial Dreams and Apocalyptic Nightmares: The Cold War Origins of Political Evangelicalism* (New York: Oxford University Press, 2007), 5; and Benjamin T. Lynerd, *Republican Theology: The Civil Religion of American Evangelicals* (New York: Oxford University Press, 2014), 194; and Bob Allen, "Falwell Says Wallis Isn't an Evangelical," *Ethicsdaily.com*, 20 July 2004, http://www.ethicsdaily.com/falwell-says-wallis-isnt-an-evangelical-cms-4470.

Chapter Four

1. See Ann Braude, "Women's History *Is* American Religious History," in *Retelling U.S. Religious History*, ed. Thomas A. Tweed (Berkeley: University of California Press, 1997), 87–107.

2. See Nancy Hardesty, *Women Called to Witness: Evangelical Feminism in the Nineteenth Century* (Nashville: Abingdon, 1984); and Jane Harris, "America's Evangelical Women: More Than Wives and Mothers—Reformers, Ministers, and Leaders," in *Encyclopedia of Women and Religion in North America*, ed. Rosemary

Skinner Keller, Rosemary Radford Ruether, and Marie Cantlon (Bloomington: Indiana University Press, 2006), 1:447-57; and Gary Dorrien, *The New Abolition: W. E. B. Dubois and the Black Social Gospel* (New Haven: Yale University Press, 2015); as well as Sarah L. Silkey, *Black Woman Reformer: Ida B. Wells, Lynching, and Transatlantic Activism* (Athens: University of Georgia Press, 2015).

3. See Margaret Lamberts Bendroth, *Fundamentalism and Gender: 1875 to the Present* (New Haven: Yale University Press, 1993), 120, 96; and Betty A. DeBerg, *Ungodly Women: Gender and the First Wave of American Fundamentalism* (Minneapolis: Fortress, 1990); also Margaret L. Bendroth, "Fundamentalism," in *Encyclopedia of Women and Religion in North America*, 1:439-47.

4. See John R. Rice, *Bobbed Hair, Bossy Wives, and Women Preachers* (Wheaton, IL: Sword of the Lord, 1941); and Bendroth, *Fundamentalism and Gender*, 73-117; also Bendroth, "Fundamentalism," 446.

5. For discussion of women's ordination and Christian feminism in the United States, see Rosemary Radford Ruether, "Feminism in World Christianity," in *Feminism and World Religions*, ed. Arvind Sharma and Katherine K. Young (Albany: State University of New York Press, 1999), 217-47; for further discussion of fundamentalism and evangelicalism's lack of female leadership, see Margaret Lamberts Bendroth, "Fundamentalism and Femininity: Points of Encounter between Religious Conservatives and Women, 1919-1935," *Church History* 61 (1992): 221-33.

6. See George Marsden, *Reforming Fundamentalism: Fuller Seminary and the New Evangelicalism* (Grand Rapids: Eerdmans, 1987), 158.

7. For discussion of women in the NAE, see Bendroth, *Fundamentalism and Gender*, 94-95, quotations on 94; see also Bendroth, "Fundamentalism," 445.

8. See Bendroth, "Fundamentalism"; and Bendroth, *Fundamentalism and Gender*, 73-96.

9. See Bendroth, "Fundamentalism," 445; and Bendroth, *Fundamentalism and Gender*, 94.

10. See Arlin C. Migliazzo, "'She Must Be a Proper Exception': Females, Fuller Seminary, and the Limits of Gender Equity among Southern California Evangelicals, 1947-1952," *Fides et Historia* 45 (2013): 1-19; and Marsden, *Reforming Fundamentalism*, 123-28.

11. Marsden, *Reforming Fundamentalism*, 127.

12. See Migliazzo, "'She Must Be a Proper Exception,'" 6-7, quotations on 7.

13. See Migliazzo, "'She Must Be a Proper Exception,'" 8-17, quotations on 8, 10, 12; see also Marsden, *Reforming Fundamentalism*, 127-28.

14. See Sandra Sue Geeting Horner, "Becoming All We're Meant to Be: A Social History of the Contemporary Evangelical Feminist Movement; A Case Study of the Evangelical and Ecumenical Women's Caucus" (PhD diss., Northwestern University, 2000), 342–44; also Randall Balmer, "Letha Dawson Scanzoni," in *Encyclopedia of Evangelicalism*, rev. and exp. ed. (Waco, TX: Baylor University Press, 2004), 603.

15. Horner, "Becoming All We're Meant to Be," 343–45.

16. See Letha Dawson Scanzoni, "Backstory: Woman's Place—Silence or Service?," *Letha's Calling: A Christian Feminist Voice* (blog), 25 March 2010, https://www.lethadawsonscanzoni.com/2010/03/backstory-womans-placesilence-or-service/.

17. See Letha Dawson Scanzoni and Nancy A. Hardesty, *All We're Meant to Be: Biblical Feminism for Today*, 3rd rev. ed. (Grand Rapids: Eerdmans, 1992), ix; see also Balmer, "Letha Dawson Scanzoni," 603.

18. See Scanzoni, "Backstory: Woman's Place."

19. See Letha Dawson Scanzoni, "Woman's Place: Silence or Service?," *Letha's Calling: A Christian Feminist Voice* (blog), https://lethadawsonscanzoni.com/womens-place-silence-or-service/.

20. See Scanzoni, "Backstory: Woman's Place."

21. See Letha Dawson Scanzoni, "Backstory: 'Elevate Marriage to Partnership' (1968 Eternity article)," *Letha's Calling: A Christian Feminist Voice* (blog), 14 April 2010, https://www.lethadawsonscanzoni.com/2010/04/backstory-elevate-marriage-to-partnership1968-eternity-article/.

22. See Scanzoni, "Backstory: 'Elevate Marriage to Partnership.'"

23. See Scanzoni, "Backstory: 'Elevate Marriage to Partnership.'"

24. See Horner, "Becoming All We're Meant to Be," 322–24; and Randall Balmer, "Hardesty, Nancy A(nn) (1941–)," in *Encyclopedia of Evangelicalism*, rev. and exp. ed. (Waco, TX: Baylor University Press, 2004), 321; also Alison J. Killeen, "Nancy A. Hardesty Papers: Finding Aid," The Archive of Women in Theological Scholarship, The Burke Library, Union Theological Seminary, https://library.columbia.edu/content/dam/libraryweb/locations/burke/fa/awts/ldpd_6163424.pdf.

25. Horner, "Becoming All We're Meant to Be," 324.

26. See Letha Dawson Scanzoni, "Part 1. Coauthoring 'All We're Meant to Be'—The Beginning," *Letha's Calling: A Christian Feminist Voice* (blog), 7 January 2011, https://www.lethadawsonscanzoni.com/2011/01/part-1-coauthoring-all-were-meant-to-be-the-beginning/.

27. See Letha Dawson Scanzoni and Nancy A. Hardesty, *All We're Meant to Be: A Biblical Approach to Women's Liberation* (Waco, TX: Word, 1974), 9.

28. See Scanzoni, "Part 1."

29. See Letha Dawson Scanzoni, "Part 4. Coauthoring 'All We're Meant to Be'—The Writing Process," *Letha's Calling: A Christian Feminist Voice* (blog), 3 March 2011, https://www.lethadawsonscanzoni.com/2011/03/part-4-coauthoring-all-were-meant-to-bethe-writing-process/.

30. See Letha Dawson Scanzoni, "Part 5. Coauthoring 'All We're Meant to Be'—Getting Published," *Letha's Calling: A Christian Feminist Voice* (blog), 21 March 2011, https://www.lethadawsonscanzoni.com/2011/03/part-5-coauthoring-all-were-meant-to-be-getting-published/; and Letha Dawson Scanzoni, "Part 6. Coauthoring 'All We're Meant to Be'—Exciting Times in 1973!," *Letha's Calling: A Christian Feminist Voice* (blog), 31 March 2011, https://www.lethadawsonscanzoni.com/2011/03/part-6-coauthoring-all-were-meant-to-be-exciting-times-in-1973/.

31. For more on *Christianity Today*'s coverage of feminism in the early 1970s, see Sally K. Gallagher, "The Marginalization of Evangelical Feminism," *Sociology of Religion* 65 (2004): 215–37; see also "Eve's Second Apple," *Christianity Today*, 21 August 1970, 29, as quoted in Gallagher, "Marginalization of Evangelical Feminism," 223.

32. See Billy Graham, "Jesus and the Liberated Woman," *Ladies' Home Journal*, December 1970, 40, 42, 44, 114, quotations on 42, 114.

33. See Mary Bouma, "Liberated Mothers," *Christianity Today*, 7 May 1971, 4–6, as quoted in Brantley W. Gasaway, *Progressive Evangelicals and the Pursuit of Social Justice* (Chapel Hill: University of North Carolina Press, 2014), 105.

34. See Ruth A. Schmidt, "Second-Class Citizenship in the Kingdom of God," *Christianity Today*, 1 January 1971, 13–14.

35. See Nancy A. Hardesty, "Women: Second Class Citizens?," *Eternity*, January 1971, 14–16.

36. See Horner, "Becoming All We're Meant to Be," 337–38.

37. See Virginia Ramey Mollenkott, "Virginia Ramey Mollenkott: Founding Member, Evangelical Women's Caucus," in *Transforming the Faiths of Our Fathers: Women Who Changed American Religion*, ed. Ann Braude (New York: Palgrave Macmillan, 2004), 55–72.

38. See Mollenkott, "Virginia Ramey Mollenkott," 57–58, quotations on 58.

39. See Mollenkott, "Virginia Ramey Mollenkott," 58–60, quotation on 59.

40. See David Stiver, "Inventory of the Virginia Ramey Mollenkott Papers," Graduate Theological Union Archives, Graduate Theological Union, http://pdf.oac.cdlib.org/pdf/gtu/mollenkott.pdf; see also Mollenkott, "Virginia Ramey Mollenkott," 64–66.

41. See Mollenkott, "Virginia Ramey Mollenkott," 60–62.

42. See Horner, "Becoming All We're Meant to Be," 335–38.

43. See Horner, "Becoming All We're Meant to Be," 335–38; also Stiver, "Inventory," 2; and Mollenkott, "Virginia Ramey Mollenkott," 68.

44. See Marabel Morgan, *The Total Woman* (Old Tappan, NJ: Revell, 1973), as excerpted in Matthew Avery Sutton, *Jerry Falwell and the Rise of the Religious Right: A Brief History with Documents* (Boston: Bedford/St. Martin's, 2013), 110–14, quotations on 114, 111, 112.

45. See Daisy Maryles, "The Stakes Rise for Chart Toppers," *Publishers Weekly*, 22 March 2004, https://www.publishersweekly.com/pw/print/20040322/26495 -the-stakes-rise-for-chart-toppers.html; and Susan Donaldson James, "Christians Promote Holy, Hot Sex in Marriage," *ABC News*, 9 May 2008, http://abcnews.go .com/US/story?id=4651272&page=1.

46. See Elisabeth Elliot Leitch, "Feminism or Femininity?," *Cambridge Fish*, Winter 1975–1976, 6, as quoted in Virginia Ramey Mollenkott, "Evangelicalism: A Feminist Perspective," *Union Seminary Quarterly Review* 32 (1977): 96; and Elisabeth Elliot, "Why I Oppose the Ordination of Women," *Christianity Today*, 6 June 1975, 12–14; also Elliot, *Let Me Be a Woman: Notes to My Daughter on the Meaning of Womanhood* (Wheaton, IL: Tyndale House, 1976); as well as Elliot, "The Bible and Women 1975," *Interlit*, December 1975, 6; and Elliot, "The Essence of Femininity: A Personal Perspective," in *Recovering Biblical Manhood and Womanhood*, ed. John Piper and Wayne Grudem (Wheaton, IL: Crossway, 1991), 400–404; see also Horner, "Becoming All We're Meant to Be," 176–77.

47. See Reta Halteman Finger and S. Sue Horner, "Euro-American Evangelical Feminism," in *Encyclopedia of Women and Religion in North America*, 1:467–76; see also Nancy A. Hardesty, "Blessed the Waters That Rise and Fall to Rise Again," Evangelical and Ecumenical Women's Caucus, https://eewc.com/blessed-the -waters/; as well as Horner, "Becoming All We're Meant to Be," 167–69.

48. See Scanzoni and Hardesty, *All We're Meant to Be*, 18.

49. See Gallagher, "Marginalization of Evangelical Feminism," 223; and Pamela D. H. Cochran, *Evangelical Feminism: A History* (New York: New York University Press, 2005), 25; as well as David R. Swartz, *Moral Minority: The Evangelical Left in an Age of Conservatism* (Philadelphia: University of Pennsylvania Press, 2012), 199; see also C. E. Cerling Jr., review of *All We're Meant to Be*, by Letha Dawson Scanzoni and Nancy A. Hardesty, *Journal of the Evangelical Theological Society* 18

(1975): 292–95; and "The Top Books That Have Shaped Evangelicals," *Christianity Today*, 6 October 2006, 51–55.

50. See Hardesty, "Blessed the Waters"; and Horner, "Becoming All We're Meant to Be," 167–69; as well as Gasaway, *Progressive Evangelicals*, 106–8.

51. See Cochran, *Evangelical Feminism*, 12–13, quotation on 13.

52. See Nancy Hardesty, "Reflection," in *The Chicago Declaration*, ed. Ronald J. Sider (Carol Stream, IL: Creation House, 1974), 123–26; and Marjorie Hyer, "Evangelicals: Tackling the Gut Issues," *Christian Century*, 19 December 1973, 1244–45; also Ronald J. Sider, "Introduction: An Historic Moment for Biblical Social Concern," in *Chicago Declaration*, 11–42; as well as Horner, "Becoming All We're Meant to Be," 159–67; see also Sider, *Chicago Declaration*, quotation from declaration on 2; for discussion of Graham's reaction, see Hardesty, "Blessed the Waters."

53. See Gasaway, *Progressive Evangelicals*, 106–8; and Horner, "Becoming All We're Meant to Be," 167–69.

54. See Hardesty, "Blessed the Waters."

55. See Finger and Horner, "Euro-American Evangelical Feminism," 470; as well as Horner, "Becoming All We're Meant to Be," 170–72.

56. See Finger and Horner, "Euro-American Evangelical Feminism," 470; and Hardesty, "Blessed the Waters."

57. See Mollenkott, "Virginia Ramey Mollenkott," 70; and Horner, "Becoming All We're Meant to Be," 175.

58. See Mollenkott, "Evangelicalism," 96.

59. See Horner, "Becoming All We're Meant to Be," 175–76.

60. See Finger and Horner, "Euro-American Evangelical Feminism," 470.

61. See "Women in Transition: The First Evangelical Women's Caucus Conference (1975)," *Christian Feminism Today*, https://eewc.com/the-first-evangelical -womens-caucus-conference/.

62. See Horner, "Becoming All We're Meant to Be," 178–94; and Cochran, *Evangelical Feminism*, 37–40.

63. See Paul K. Jewett, *Man as Male and Female: A Study in Sexual Relationships from a Theological Point of View* (Grand Rapids: Eerdmans, 1975).

64. For more on Clark and his influence, see Doug J. Douma, *The Presbyterian Philosopher: The Authorized Biography of Gordon H. Clark* (Eugene, OR: Wipf & Stock, 2016), 199–203; for discussion of Jewett's arrival at Fuller, including the comparison to Charles Hodge, see Marsden, *Reforming Fundamentalism*, 146, 280–82.

65. See Jewett, *Man as Male and Female*, 112–19, 134–35, quotations on 119, 135.

66. See Jewett, *Man as Male and Female*, 14; as well as Virginia Mollenkott, foreword to *Man as Male and Female*, by Jewett, 7–12.

67. Mollenkott, "Evangelicalism," 97.

68. See Mollenkott, "Virginia Ramey Mollenkott," 63; and Mollenkott, foreword to *Man as Male and Female*, by Jewett, 7–12; see also Virginia Ramey Mollenkott, *Women, Men, and the Bible* (Nashville: Abingdon, 1977).

69. See Mollenkott, *Women, Men, and the Bible*, 32, 105, 106.

70. Mollenkott, "Evangelicalism," 98.

71. See Harold Lindsell, *The Battle for the Bible* (Grand Rapids: Zondervan, 1976).

72. See Lindsell, *Battle for the Bible*, 116–21, 210, quotations on 116, 120–21.

73. See Harold Lindsell, "Egalitarianism and Scriptural Infallibility," *Christianity Today*, 26 March 1976, 45–46, as quoted in Sally K. Gallagher, *Evangelical Identity and Gendered Family Life* (New Brunswick, NJ: Rutgers University Press, 2003), 50.

74. See Patricia Gundry, *Woman Be Free: The Clear Message of Scripture* (Grand Rapids: Zondervan, 1977), 37.

75. See Gundry, *Woman Be Free*, 60, 57.

76. See Gundry, *Woman Be Free*, 38, 12, 11.

77. See Gundry, *Woman Be Free*, 84, 60.

78. See Russ Williams, "Truth . . . and Consequences: How Pat Gundry Discovered Biblical Feminism," *The Other Side*, October 1980, 15–19, quotations on 16, 17, 18.

79. For an overview, see Gallagher, *Evangelical Identity*, 47–55; also see Larry Christensen, *The Christian Family* (Minneapolis: Bethany Fellowship, 1970); and James Dobson, *Straight Talk to Men and Their Wives* (Waco, TX: Word, 1980); as well as Dobson, *What Wives Wish Their Husbands Knew about Women* (Wheaton, IL: Tyndale House, 1975); and Tim and Beverly LaHaye, *The Act of Marriage* (Grand Rapids: Zondervan, 1976); also Beverly LaHaye, *The Spirit-Controlled Woman* (Irvine, CA: Harvest House, 1976); and Tim LaHaye, *Understanding the Male Temperament* (Old Tappan, NJ: Revell, 1977).

80. See Horner, "Becoming All We're Meant to Be," 178–94; and Cochran, *Evangelical Feminism*, 37–40.

81. See Phyllis E. Alsdurf, "Evangelical Feminists: Ministry Is the Issue," *Christianity Today*, 21 July 1978, 46–47.

82. For a summary and overview of the speeches, see Horner, "Becoming All We're Meant to Be," 194–200; for discussion of Mollenkott's sermon, see Claire K. Wolterstorff, "Encouragement and Unanswered Questions: Evangelicals Discuss Women's Issues," *Reformed Journal* 28 (1978): 16–19.

83. See Letha Scanzoni, "Marching On!," in *Women and the Ministries of Christ*, ed. Roberta Hestenes and Lois Curley (Pasadena, CA: Fuller Theological Seminary, 1979), 131, 130, 133.

84. See "Statement of Faith," in Hestenes and Curley, *Women and the Ministries of Christ*, 356; also see Horner, "Becoming All We're Meant to Be," 201–2.

85. See Alsdurf, "Evangelical Feminists," 46; for more on Roberta Hestenes and her history at Fuller, see Roberta Hestenes, "Stained Glass Ceilings and Sticky Floors," *Fuller Magazine* 3 (2015): 58–62.

86. See Horner, "Becoming All We're Meant to Be," 179, 207–33; as well as Finger and Horner, "Euro-American Evangelical Feminism," 470.

87. See Letha Dawson Scanzoni and Virginia Ramey Mollenkott, *Is the Homosexual My Neighbor? Another Christian View* (San Francisco: Harper & Row, 1978), ix–x; as well as Scanzoni and Mollenkott, *Is the Homosexual My Neighbor? A Positive Christian Response*, rev. and updated ed. (San Francisco: HarperSanFrancisco, 1994), vi–xix.

88. See Scanzoni and Mollenkott, *Is the Homosexual My Neighbor? Another Christian View*, ix; see also Horner, "Becoming All We're Meant to Be," 193–94; as well as Cochran, *Evangelical Feminism*, 77.

89. See Don Williams, "Shall We Revise the Homosexual Ethic?," *Eternity*, May 1978, 46–48; and Tim Stafford, "Issue of the Year," *Christianity Today*, 5 May 1978, 36; as well as Kay Lindskoog, review of *Is the Homosexual My Neighbor?*, by Letha Dawson Scanzoni and Virginia Ramey Mollenkott, *Wittenburg Door*, October–November 1977, 35–36.

90. See Mollenkott, "Virginia Ramey Mollenkott," 70.

91. See Finger and Horner, "Euro-American Evangelical Feminism," 470; as well as Hardesty, "Blessed the Waters."

92. See Horner, "Becoming All We're Meant to Be," 188–238; and Finger and Horner, "Euro-American Evangelical Feminism," 471.

93. See Horner, "Becoming All We're Meant to Be," 233–38; as well as Finger and Horner, "Euro-American Evangelical Feminism," quotation from resolution on 470; see also Cochran, *Evangelical Feminism*, 93.

94. See Horner, "Becoming All We're Meant to Be," 239–53, quote from resolution on 242–43; as well as Cochran, *Evangelical Feminism*, 91–97.

95. See Horner, "Becoming All We're Meant to Be," 250–58; and Cochran, *Evangelical Feminism*, 102–3; for further discussion of Kroeger's role in the new organization, see Julie Ingersoll, *Evangelical Christian Women: War Stories in the Gender Battles* (New York: New York University Press, 2003), 33–46; see also Beth Spring, "Gay Rights Resolution Divides Membership of Evangelical Women's Caucus," *Christianity Today*, 3 October 1986, 40–41, 43, as referenced in Finger and Horner, "Euro-American Evangelical Feminism," 471.

96. For discussion of CBE's founding, see Finger and Horner, "Euro-American Evangelical Feminism," 471; as well as CBE International, "History of CBE," https://www.cbeinternational.org/content/cbes-history; see also "New Organization Incorporated," *Priscilla Papers*, Fall 1987, 1–3, quotations from founding statement on 2; for further discussion of CBE's development and alignment with the NAE, see Ingersoll, *Evangelical Christian Women*, 37.

97. See Fred Zaspel, "Interview with Wayne Grudem, author of *Evangelical Feminism and Biblical Truth*," *Books at a Glance*, 5 August 2014, https://www.booksataglance.com/author-interviews/interview-with-wayne-grudem-author-of-evangelical-feminism-and-biblical-truth/.

98. See Wayne Grudem, "Personal Reflections on the History of CBMW and the State of the Gender Debate," *Journal for Biblical Manhood and Womanhood* 14 (2009): 12–17, quotations on 12.

99. See Simon J. Kistemaker, "Thirty-Eighth Annual Meeting," *Journal of the Evangelical Theological Society* 30 (1987): 121–24.

100. See Grudem, "Personal Reflections," 13.

101. See "Our History," The Council on Biblical Manhood and Womanhood, https://cbmw.org/about/history/.

102. See Grudem, "Personal Reflections," 13–14, quotation on 13.

103. Grudem, "Personal Reflections," 14.

104. See "Council on Biblical Manhood and Womanhood," *Christianity Today*, 13 January 1989.

105. For all quotations, see "The Danvers Statement," as printed in *Christianity Today*, 13 January 1989; see also Grudem, "Personal Reflections," 14–15.

106. See John Piper and Wayne Grudem, eds., *Recovering Biblical Manhood and Womanhood: A Response to Evangelical Feminism* (Wheaton, IL: Crossway, 1991), 10.

107. See Piper and Grudem, *Recovering*, 405, 421, quotations on 405.

108. For a sampling of Grudem's (ongoing) work fighting feminism, see Wayne Grudem, ed., *Biblical Foundations for Manhood and Womanhood* (Wheaton, IL: Crossway, 2002); and Wayne Grudem and Dennis Rainey, eds., *Pastoral Lead-*

ership for Manhood and Womanhood (Wheaton, IL: Crossway, 2002); as well as Grudem, *Evangelical Feminism and Biblical Truth* (Sisters, OR: Multnomah, 2004); also Wayne Grudem and Vern Poythress, *The TNIV and the Gender-Neutral Bible Controversy* (Nashville: Broadman & Holman, 2004); and Grudem, *Evangelical Feminism: A New Path to Liberalism?* (Wheaton, IL: Crossway, 2006); as well as Grudem, *What's Wrong with Gender-Neutral Bible Translations?* (Libertyville, IL: Council on Biblical Manhood and Womanhood, 1997); and Grudem, *Countering the Claims of Evangelical Feminism* (Sisters, OR: Multnomah, 2006).

109. For a thorough historical account of the sway that masculinist ideology has long held over US American evangelicals, see the brilliant Kristin Kobes Du Mez, *Jesus and John Wayne: How White Evangelicals Corrupted a Faith and Fractured a Nation* (New York: Liveright, 2020).

110. For the major published history that uses this framing, see Cochran, *Evangelical Feminism*, 147-48, 178-91, quotations on 148, 182.

111. See Cochran, *Evangelical Feminism*, 71, 178-91, quotation on 71.

112. See Virginia Mollenkott, *Speech, Silence, Action! The Cycle of Faith* (Nashville: Abingdon, 1980), 25-29, quotations on 25, 26.

113. See Virginia Ramey Mollenkott, *Sensuous Spirituality: Out from Fundamentalism* (New York: Crossroad, 1992), 33.

114. See Virginia Ramey Mollenkott, "Interreligious Dialogue: A Pilgrimage," in *The Wisdom of Daughters: Two Decades of the Voice of Christian Feminism*, ed. Reta Halteman Finger and Kari Sandhaas (Philadelphia: Innisfree, 2001), 105-8, quotations on 107.

115. See Virginia Ramey Mollenkott, "Cochran's Evangelical Feminism—Yet Once More," *EEWC Update*, October-December 2005, https://eewc.com/evangelical-feminism/.

116. See Virginia Ramey Mollenkott, foreword to *Desperate for Authenticity: A Critical Analysis of the Feminist Theology of Virginia Ramey Mollenkott*, by Patricia Hawley (Lanham, MD: University Press of America, 2010), 2-5, quotation on 4.

117. See Mollenkott, foreword to *Desperate for Authenticity*, by Hawley, 4.

Chapter Five

1. A note about terminology: For a variety of reasons—ranging from its origins as a pathologizing term to its insufficiently inclusive meanings—most contemporary LGBTQ people reject the label "homosexual." The use of terms and phrases

like "homosexuality," "homosexuals," "homosexuality debates," and "homosexual persons" herein should be understood only as a reflection of the historical context of the "homosexuality debates" in twentieth-century US American Christianity and in no way signify an endorsement of such language. References to categories like "gay" and "gay rights" similarly reflect common contextual usage and should not be interpreted as a statement about their appropriateness.

2. N.B. Although they will no longer necessarily appear in quotes for the remainder of the chapter, "homosexuality" and "homosexuality debates" are in scare quotes one last time in this paragraph for at least two reasons: (1) to indicate once more that I am using them contextually and by no means endorsing them, and (2) to suggest that such debates were never exclusively about "homosexuality."

3. See Chris Glaser, "The Love That Dare Not Pray Its Name: The Gay and Lesbian Movement in America's Churches," in *Homosexuality in the Church: Both Sides of the Debate*, ed. Jeffrey S. Siker (Louisville: Westminster John Knox, 1994), 151.

4. Be on the lookout for forthcoming work on the history of gay evangelical activism during the 1970s and 1980s by Princeton PhD candidate William Stell.

5. See Tanya Erzen, *Straight to Jesus: Sexual and Christian Conversions in the Ex-gay Movement* (Berkeley: University of California Press, 2006), 79–83, quotation on 79.

6. See Ralph Blair, "Looking Back: Evangelicals and Homosexuality," *Record: Newsletter of Evangelicals Concerned, Inc.*, Fall 2015, 2–3; as well as Erzen, *Straight to Jesus*, 79–83.

7. See Blair, "Looking Back," 2–3, 5; as well as Erzen, *Straight to Jesus*, 79–83.

8. See Blair, "Looking Back," 2–4.

9. See Blair, "Looking Back," 2–4, quotations on 4.

10. See Ralph Blair, *Holier-Than-Thou Hocus-Pocus and Homosexuality* (New York: Homosexual Community Counseling Center, 1977), 4.

11. See Randall Balmer, "Blair, Ralph," in *Encyclopedia of Evangelicalism*, rev. and exp. ed. (Waco, TX: Baylor University Press, 2004), 83.

12. See Blair, "Looking Back," 2–5; as well as Erzen, *Straight to Jesus*, 79–83; also Ralph Blair, *The Best of Both Worlds: A Brief History of Evangelicals Concerned, Inc.* (New York: Evangelicals Concerned, 2000).

13. See Blair, "Looking Back," 5, 12; also Erzen, *Straight to Jesus*, 79–83.

14. See Evangelicals Concerned, untitled newsletter, 20 April 1977, in Foster Gunnison Jr. Papers, Institute for Social Ethics Archives, University of Connecticut: Connecticut Digital Archive, http://hdl.handle.net/11134/20002:860296712.

15. See Letha Scanzoni, "Conservative Christians and Gay Civil Rights," *Christian Century*, 13 October 1976, 861.

16. See Ralph Blair, "Evangelicals Concerned: Urbana Report," 1977, 1–2, quotations on 1, in Foster Gunnison Jr. Papers, Institute for Social Ethics Archives, University of Connecticut: Connecticut Digital Archive, http://hdl.handle.net /11134/20002:860296712.

17. See Ralph Blair, "Attention!," 4 January 1977, 1–4, quotations on 1–2, in Foster Gunnison Jr. Papers, Institute for Social Ethics Archives, University of Connecticut: Connecticut Digital Archive, http://hdl.handle.net/11134/20002:860296712.

18. See Ralph Blair, *One Foolishness or Another: The Gospel and Foolish Galatians, Gays and Lesbians* (New York: Evangelicals Concerned, 1999).

19. See Ralph Blair, *Evangelicals (?!) Concerned* (New York: Evangelicals Concerned, 1982), 29.

20. Blair, "Evangelicals Concerned: Urbana Report," 2.

21. See Tom Minnery, "Homosexuals Can Change," *Christianity Today*, 6 February 1981, 36–41, quotation on 39.

22. For more on the founding of LIA, see Erzen, *Straight to Jesus*, 22–31.

23. See Kent Philpott, *The Third Sex? Six Homosexuals Tell Their Stories* (Plainfield, NJ: Logos International, 1975), 169–80, quotation on 172.

24. See Erzen, *Straight to Jesus*, 27–28; also see Tom Waidzunas, *The Straight Line: How the Fringe Science of Ex-gay Therapy Reoriented Sexuality* (Minneapolis: University of Minnesota Press, 2015), 77–80.

25. See Erzen, *Straight to Jesus*, 31–33, quotation on 33.

26. See Chuck Stewart, "Sexual Orientation Change Efforts," in *Proud Heritage: People, Issues, and Documents of the LGBT Experience*, ed. Chuck Stewart (Santa Barbara: ABC-CLIO, 2014), 1:306–11, quotations on 307; also see Stewart, "Exodus International," in Stewart, *Proud Heritage*, 1:159–62.

27. As quoted in Erzen, *Straight to Jesus*, 33.

28. For more on the early years of Exodus, see Erzen, *Straight to Jesus*, 33–35.

29. See Blair, *Holier-Than-Thou Hocus-Pocus*.

30. For more on the demedicalization process in mainstream psychology and its relationship to ex-gay organizations, see Waidzunas, *Straight Line*, 67–112.

31. See Blair, "Looking Back," 12.

32. See News Brief, *Episcopal News Service*, 28 July 1977, Archives of the Episcopal Church, https://www.episcopalarchives.org/cgi-bin/ENS/ENSpress_release .pl?pr_number=77248/.

33. See Guy Charles, "The Church and the Homosexual," in *The Secrets of Our Sexuality: Role Liberation for the Christian*, ed. Gary R. Collins (Waco, TX: Word, 1976), 117–31.

34. See Blair, "Looking Back," 12.

35. See "Liberation Closes Fairfax Homosexual Ministry," *Integrity Forum: A Journal for Gay Episcopalians and Their Friends*, October 1977; also Ralph Blair, *Ex-gay* (New York: HCCC, 1982), 6–7.

36. Blair, *Ex-gay*, 7.

37. See Blair, *Holier-Than-Thou Hocus-Pocus*, 26, 36.

38. See Blair, *Holier-Than-Thou Hocus-Pocus*, 20, 32.

39. See Minnery, "Homosexuals Can Change," 41.

40. For more on Bussee and Cooper's story see Erzen, *Straight to Jesus*, 34–35; as well as the interview with the two men in the documentary *One Nation under God*, directed and produced by Francine Rzeznik and Teodoro Maniaci (New York: First Run Features, 1993).

41. See Robert K. Johnston, *Evangelicals at an Impasse: Biblical Authority in Practice* (Atlanta: John Knox, 1979), 113–45, quotations on 121, 115.

42. See Johnston, *Evangelicals at an Impasse*, 2–7.

43. See Johnston, *Evangelicals at an Impasse*, 113–21; for the original typology that Johnston followed, which was originally developed based on nonevangelical thinkers, see James B. Nelson, "Homosexuality and the Church," *Christianity and Crisis*, 4 April 1977, 63–69.

44. See Johnston, *Evangelicals at an Impasse*, 121; for virulently antigay quotes from Falwell and Wyrtzen, see Tom Mathews, "Battle over Gay Rights," *Newsweek*, 6 June 1977, 16–26.

45. See Johnston, *Evangelicals at an Impasse*, 121–23; also Don Williams, *The Bond That Breaks: Will Homosexuality Split the Church?* (Los Angeles: BIM, 1978); as well as Richard F. Lovelace, *Homosexuality and the Church* (Old Tappan, NJ: Revell, 1978), quotation on 125.

46. See Johnston, *Evangelicals at an Impasse*, 125, 128, 126, 127; see also Lewis B. Smedes, *Sex for Christians* (Grand Rapids: Eerdmans, 1976); as well as Helmut Thielicke, *The Ethics of Sex*, trans. John W. Doberstein (New York: Harper & Row, 1964), 271, 285.

47. See Johnston, *Evangelicals at an Impasse*, 128–32, quotations on 129.

48. See Johnston, *Evangelicals at an Impasse*, 128–32, quotations on 131.

49. See Johnston, *Evangelicals at an Impasse*, 132–45, quotations on 135.

50. See Blair, *Evangelicals (?!)*, 3–4, 17, quotation on 17.

51. For discussion of Pattison's influence, see Waidzunas, *Straight Line*, 79–80; see also Richard H. Cox, "E. Mansell Pattison, M.D.," *Pastoral Psychology* 20 (1969): 4, 66; see also E. Mansell Pattison, "Forbidden Love: A Homosexual Looks for Help and Understanding," *Christianity Today*, 12 May 1972, 20–21; and Pattison, "Positive Though Inaccurate," *Journal of the American Scientific Affiliation* 29 (1977): 106–8; as well as Pattison, "Confusing Concepts about the Concept of Homosexuality," *Psychiatry* 37 (1974): 340–49.

52. Pattison, "Positive Though Inaccurate," 107.

53. See Pattison, "Confusing Concepts," 348, 341.

54. See "Journal Interviews . . . Christian Answers on Homosexuality," *Journal of the American Scientific Affiliation* 31 (1979): 50.

55. See Pattison, "Positive Though Inaccurate," 107.

56. See E. M. Pattison and Myrna Loy Pattison, "'Ex-gays': Religiously Mediated Change in Homosexuals," *American Journal of Psychiatry* 137 (1980): 1553, 1555, 1559, 1561.

57. See Waidzunas, *Straight Line*, 79–80.

58. See Enos D. Martin and Ruth Keener Martin, "Developmental and Ethical Issues in Homosexuality: Pastoral Implications," *Journal of Psychology and Theology* 9 (1981): 58–68; and Robert K. Johnston, "Homosexuality: Can It Be 'Cured'?," *Reformed Journal* 31 (1981): 9–12; as well as E. Mansell Pattison, "Good Thinking: How Homosexuality Happens," *Eternity*, May 1982, 34–35.

59. See "Homosexuality: Biblical Guidance through a Moral Morass," *Christianity Today*, 18 April 1980, 12–13, quotations on 13.

60. See Minnery, "Homosexuals Can Change," 36, 37, 41.

61. See Minnery, "Homosexuals Can Change," 37, 38, 41.

62. See Johnston, "Homosexuality," 11–12.

63. See Ralph Blair, "Homosexuality: Letter to the Editor," *Christianity Today*, 27 March 1981, 9; and Blair, "Changing the Homosexual?," *Reformed Journal* 31 (1981): 6–7.

64. See Blair, "Changing the Homosexual?," 6–7, quotations on 7.

65. See Warren Throckmorton, "Participant Discredits the Original Ex-gay Study," *Religion Dispatches*, 10 November 2011, http://religiondispatches.org/participant-discredits-the-original-ex-gay-study/.

66. See Kenneth S. Kantzer, "Homosexuals in the Church," *Christianity Today*, 22 April 1983, 8–9, quotations on 9.

67. See Beth Spring, "These Christians Are Helping Gays Escape from Homosexual Lifestyles," *Christianity Today*, 21 September 1984, 56–58, quotations on 57, 58.

68. See Randy Frame, "The Homosexual Lifestyle: Is There a Way Out?," *Christianity Today*, 9 August 1985, 32–36, quotations on 32, 33, 34.

69. See Frame, "Homosexual Lifestyle," 33.

70. See Elizabeth R. Moberly, *Homosexuality: A New Christian Ethic* (Cambridge: James Clarke, 1983), 1–16, 27–28, quotations on 8, 9, 28.

71. See Moberly, *Homosexuality*, 27; for more on Moberly's role in the ex-gay movement, see Erzen, *Straight to Jesus*, 142–48; and Waidzunas, *Straight Line*, 79–81; as well as Jack Drescher, "Sexual Conversion ('Reparative') Therapies: History and Update," in *Mental Health Issues in Lesbian, Gay, Bisexual, and Transgender Communities*, ed. Billy E. Jones and Marjorie J. Hill (Washington, DC: American Psychiatric), 71–91.

72. See Ralph Blair, "Does 'Ex-gay' Equal Heterosexual? Letter to the Editor," *Christianity Today*, 20 September 1985, 6.

73. See John R. W. Stott, "Homosexual 'Marriage,'" *Christianity Today*, 22 November 1985, 21–28, quotations on 28.

74. See, for example, Russell Chandler, "Christian Activists Help Kill a California Gay Rights Bill," *Christianity Today*, 20 April 1984, 42.

75. See "National Association of Evangelicals: Statement on Homosexuality (1985)," in *The Churches Speak on Homosexuality*, ed. J. Gordon Melton (Detroit: Gale, 1991), 141–42.

76. See "National Association of Evangelicals: Statement on Homosexuality," 142.

77. For "gay plague" and "a definite form" quotations, see Sue Cross, "Jerry Falwell Calls AIDS a 'Gay Plague,'" *Washington Post*, 6 July 1983, B3; for "lethal judgment" quotation, see Jerry Falwell, "AIDS: The Judgment of God," *Liberty Report*, 5 April 1987, 5, as quoted in Albert Jonsen and Earl Shelp, "Religion and Religious Groups," in *The Social Impact of AIDS in the United States*, ed. Albert R. Jonsen and Jeff Stryker (Washington, DC: National Academy, 1993), 131; though Falwell eventually denied/recanted the "wrath of God" statement, numerous sources reference reporters hearing him say it. For example, see William Martin, *With God on Our Side: The Rise of the Religious Right in America* (New York: Broadway Books, 1996), 242; and Robert S. McElvaine, *Grand Theft Jesus: The Hijacking of Religion in America* (New York: Crown, 2007), 35; see also Dennis Altman, *AIDS in the Mind of America* (Garden City, NY: Doubleday, 1986), 67.

78. For a detailed history of the development of religious reactions and rhetoric about AIDS, including evangelical responses and the influence of the Religious Right, see the indispensable Anthony M. Petro, *After the Wrath of God: AIDS, Sexuality, and American Religion* (New York: Oxford University Press, 2015), 24–34.

79. See Cornelius Plantinga Jr., "The Justification of Rock Hudson," *Christianity Today*, 18 October 1985, 16–17, quotations on 16.

80. See Billy Graham, "AIDS, Herpes, Sex, and the Bible," Tallahassee, Florida, 6 November 1986, https://billygraham.org/audio/aids-herpes-sex-and-the-bible-part-1/.

81. See John Godges, "Religious Groups Meet the San Francisco AIDS Challenge," *Christian Century*, 10–17 September 1986, 771–75, quotation on 772.

82. See "Southern Baptist Convention: Resolution No. 8—On AIDS (1987)," in *The Churches Speak on AIDS: Official Statements from Religious Bodies and Ecumenical Organizations*, ed. J. Gordon Melton (Detroit: Gale, 1989), 130.

83. See David Chilton, *Power in the Blood: A Christian Response to AIDS* (Brentwood, TN: Wolgemuth & Hyatt, 1987), 16; for more on Chilton as an example of conservative evangelical rhetoric around AIDS, see Petro, *After the Wrath of God*, 26–28.

84. See "National Association of Evangelicals: Statement on AIDS (1988)," in *The Churches Speak on AIDS: Official Statements from Religious Bodies and Ecumenical Organizations*, ed. J. Gordon Melton (Detroit: Gale, 1989), 114.

85. See Ronald J. Sider, "AIDS: An Evangelical Perspective," *Christian Century*, 6–13 January 1988, 11–14, quotations on 11, 12.

86. See Tony Campolo, *20 Hot Potatoes Christians Are Afraid to Touch* (Dallas: Word, 1988), 105, 110, 112.

87. See Campolo, *20 Hot Potatoes*, 111, 113.

88. See Randy Frame, "Homosexuality: Campolo's Views Challenged," *Christianity Today*, 8 September 1989, 43.

89. See Stanton L. Jones, "Homosexuality according to Science," *Christianity Today*, 18 August 1989, 26–29.

90. See Colin Cook, "I Found Freedom," *Christianity Today*, 18 August 1989, 22–24, quotations on 22.

91. See Tim Stafford, "Coming Out," *Christianity Today*, 18 August 1989, 16–21, quotations on 19.

92. See Stafford, "Coming Out," 20, 21.

93. See Ralph Blair, *Review* 14, no. 4 (Fall 1989).

94. For a sampling of *Christianity Today*'s ongoing coverage, see Randy Frame, "Homosexuality: The Evangelical Closet," *Christianity Today*, 5 November 1990, 56–57; and David Neff, "The New Ex-gay Agenda," *Christianity Today*, 9 March 1992, 21; also Joe Dallas, "Born Gay?," *Christianity Today*, 22 June 1992, 20–23; as well as David Neff, "Two Men Don't Make a Right," *Christianity Today*, 19 July 1993, 14–15; and Stanton L. Jones, "The Loving Opposition," *Christianity Today*, 19 July 1993, 18–25.

95. See Erzen, *Straight to Jesus*, 183–215, Worthen quotation on 188.

96. See Erzen, *Straight to Jesus*, 183–215.

97. See Erzen, *Straight to Jesus*, 202–4, quotations on 203.

98. See Tim Stafford, "An Older, Wiser Ex-gay Movement: The 30-Year-Old Ministry Now Offers Realistic Hope for Homosexuals," *Christianity Today*, October 2007, 48–51, quotations on 49.

99. See Erzen, *Straight to Jesus*, 183–204.

100. See Stafford, "Older, Wiser," 49.

101. See John W. Kennedy, "Homosexuality: Ad Campaign Ignites Firestorm," *Christianity Today*, 7 September 1998, 19; as well as Erzen, *Straight to Jesus*, 183–89.

102. See John Leland and Mark Miller, "Can Gays Convert?," *Newsweek*, 17 August 1988, 46, 48–50.

103. See Erzen, *Straight to Jesus*, 185–86, quotations on 185.

104. See "Homosexuality: Falwell Tames His Rhetoric," *Christianity Today*, 6 December 1999, 29.

105. For statistics on the organization's growth, see Michelle Wolkomir, *"Be Not Deceived": The Sacred and Sexual Struggles of Gay and Ex-gay Christian Men* (New Brunswick, NJ: Rutgers University Press, 2006), 28–32; as well as Jonathan Merritt, "The Downfall of the Ex-gay Movement," *Atlantic*, 6 October 2015, https://www.theatlantic.com/politics/archive/2015/10/the-man-who-dismantled -the-ex-gay-ministry/408970/; for more on Exodus's political advocacy, see Erzen, *Straight to Jesus*, 184–90; and Waidzunas, *Straight Line*, 116–20.

106. For more on the backlash and scrutiny of the movement, see Waidzunas, *Straight Line*, 116–20, "anti-reorientation" descriptor on 116.

107. See Douglas LeBlanc, "Ex-gay Sheds the Mocking Quote Marks: An Interview with Bob Davies," *Christianity Today*, 7 January 2002, 52–55, quotation on 52; see also Jason Cianciotto and Sean Cahill, *Youth in the Crosshairs: The Third Wave of Ex-gay Activism* (New York: National Gay and Lesbian Task Force Policy Institute, 2006).

108. See American Psychological Association, Task Force on Appropriate Therapeutic Responses to Sexual Orientation, *Report of the American Psychological Association Task Force on Appropriate Therapeutic Responses to Sexual Orientation* (Washington, DC: APA, 2009), https://www.apa.org/pi/lgbt/resources/therapeutic-response.pdf.

109. See Joel Lawson, "Ex-gay Leader Confronted in Gay Bar," *Southern Voice*, 21 September 2000; as well as Evangelical Press and Jody Veenker, "Ex-gay Leader Disciplined for Gay Bar Visit," *Christianity Today*, 1 October 2000.

110. See Alan Chambers, *My Exodus: From Fear to Grace* (Grand Rapids: Zondervan, 2015), 191, 196, 199.

111. See Weston Gentry, "Exodus from Exodus," *Christianity Today*, 1 December 2012, 17–18; and Erik Eckholm, "Rift Forms in Movement as Belief in Gay 'Cure' Is Renounced," *New York Times*, 7 July 2012, A9, A11; for "the oldest and largest" quotation, see "Exodus International to Shut Down," Exodus International, 19 June 2013, https://web.archive.org/web/20220124162057/http://exodusinternational.org/2013/06/exodus-international-to-shut-down/.

112. See Sarah Pulliam Bailey, "Evangelical Leader Russell Moore Denounces Ex-gay Therapy," *Religion News Service*, 28 October 2014, https://religionnews.com/2014/10/28/evangelical-leader-russell-moore-denounces-ex-gay-therapy/.

113. See Bailey, "Evangelical Leader."

114. See Sarah Pulliam Bailey, "Gay, Christian and . . . Celibate: The Changing Face of the Homosexuality Debate," Religion News Service, 4 August 2014, https://religionnews.com/2014/08/04/gay-christian-celibate-changing-face-homosexuality-debate/.

115. See "Justin Lee," in *Gale Literature: Contemporary Authors* (Farmington Hills, MI: Gale, 2014), Gale in Context: Biography; and Lillian Daniel, "Evangelical and Gay," *Christian Century*, 20 March 2013, 36; as well as "'Torn': Living as an Openly Gay Christian," *All Things Considered*, NPR, 9 December 2012, https://www.npr.org/2012/12/09/165276593/torn-living-as-an-openly-gay-christian; see also Justin Lee, *Torn: Rescuing the Gospel from the Gays-vs.-Christians Debate* (New York: Jericho Books, 2012).

116. See Neela Banerjee, "Gay and Evangelical, Seeking Paths of Acceptance," *New York Times*, 12 December 2006, https://www.nytimes.com/2006/12/12/us/12evangelical.html.

117. See Douglas Quenqua, "Turned Away, He Turned to the Bible," *New York Times*, 14 September 2012, https://www.nytimes.com/2012/09/16/fashion/matthew-vines-wont-rest-in-defending-gay-christians.html.

118. See Matthew Vines, *God and the Gay Christian: The Biblical Case in Support of Same-Sex Relationships* (New York: Convergent Books, 2014).

119. See Christopher Yuan, "Why 'God and the Gay Christian' Is Wrong about the Bible and Same-Sex Relationships," *Christianity Today*, 9 June 2014, https://www.christianitytoday.com/ct/2014/june-web-only/why-matthew-vines-is-wrong-about-bible-same-sex-relationshi.html.

120. See R. Albert Mohler Jr., "God, the Gospel and the Gay Challenge: A Response to Matthew Vines," in *God and the Gay Christian? A Response to Matthew Vines*, ed. R. Albert Mohler Jr. (Louisville: SBTS Press, 2014), 11.

121. See Mohler, "God, the Gospel," 17.

122. See Owen Strachan, "Have Christians Been Wrong All Along? What Has the Church Believed and Taught?," in Mohler, *God and the Gay Christian?*, 66.

123. See Denny Burk, "Suppressing the Truth in Unrighteousness: Matthew Vines Takes on the New Testament," in Mohler, *God and the Gay Christian?*, 54–55.

124. See Jacqueline L. Salmon, "Evangelical Leader Quits over Gay Union Remark," *Washington Post*, 12 December 2008, http://www.washingtonpost.com/wp-dyn/content/article/2008/12/11/AR2008121103578_pf.html.

125. See Sarah Pulliam Bailey, "No 'Poster Boy': Rick Warren Draws Criticism for Distancing Himself from Proposition 8," *Christianity Today*, June 2009, 14–15.

126. See Celeste Gracey and Jeremy Weber, "World Vision: Why We're Hiring Gay Christians in Same-Sex Marriages," *Christianity Today*, 24 March 2014, https://www.christianitytoday.com/ct/2014/march-web-only/world-vision-why-hiring-gay-christians-same-sex-marriage.html.

127. See Celeste Gracey and Jeremy Weber, "World Vision Reverses Decision to Hire Christians in Same-Sex Marriages," *Christianity Today*, 26 March 2014, https://www.christianitytoday.com/ct/2014/march-web-only/world-vision-reverses-decision-gay-same-sex-marriage.html.

128. See David P. Gushee, "When the Evangelical Establishment Comes after You," Religion News Service, 17 July 2017, https://religionnews.com/2017/07/17/lgbtq-equality-evangelical-rejection/; as well as Gushee, *Changing Our Mind* (Canton, MI: David Crumm Media, 2014).

129. See David P. Gushee, *Still Christian: Following Jesus Out of American Evangelicalism* (Louisville: Westminster John Knox, 2017), viii, 142.

130. See Sarah Pulliam Bailey, "From Franklin Graham to Tony Campolo, Some Evangelical Leaders Are Splitting over Gay Marriage," *Washington Post*, 9 June 2015, https://www.washingtonpost.com/news/acts-of-faith/wp/2015/06/09/from

-franklin-graham-to-tony-campolo-some-evangelical-leaders-are-dividing-over
-gay-marriage/?utm_term=.24df226f18f7.

131. See Mark Galli, "Breaking News: 2 Billion Christians Believe in Traditional Marriage; And So Do We," *Christianity Today*, 9 June 2015, https://www
.christianitytoday.com/ct/2015/june-web-only/breaking-news-2-billion-christian
-believe-in-traditional-ma.html.

132. See Blair, "Looking Back," 8.

Conclusion

1. See Benjamin Wormald, "U.S. Public Becoming Less Religious," Pew Research Center, 3 November 2015, https://www.pewforum.org/2015/11/03/u-s-public
-becoming-less-religious/.

2. See Benjamin Wormald, "America's Changing Religious Landscape," Pew Research Center, 12 May 2015, https://www.pewforum.org/2015/05/12/americas
-changing-religious-landscape/.

3. See National Association of Evangelicals, "Press Release: NAE, LifeWay Research Publish Evangelical Beliefs Research Definition," 19 November 2015, https://
www.nae.net/evangelical-beliefs-research-definition/.

4. See National Association of Evangelicals, "Press Release: NAE, LifeWay."

5. See National Association of Evangelicals, "Press Release: NAE, LifeWay."

6. See National Association of Evangelicals, "Press Release: NAE, LifeWay"; as well as Leith Anderson and Ed Stetzer, "A New Way to Define Evangelicals," *Christianity Today*, April 2016, 52–55.

7. See Anderson and Stetzer, "New Way to Define," 53, 54.

8. See Anderson and Stetzer, "New Way to Define," 54, 55.

9. See Anderson and Stetzer, "New Way to Define," 53.

10. See Leith Anderson and Ed Stetzer, "Research: Defining Evangelicals in an Election Year," *Christianity Today*, 2 March 2016, https://www.christianitytoday
.com/ct/2016/april/defining-evangelicals-in-election-year.html.

11. See Russell Moore, "Have Evangelicals Who Support Trump Lost Their Values?," *New York Times*, 17 September 2015, https://www.nytimes.com/2015/09/17
/opinion/have-evangelicals-who-support-trump-lost-their-values.html?_r=0.

12. See Russell Moore, "Why This Election Makes Me Hate the Word 'Evangelical,'" *Washington Post*, 29 February 2016, https://www.washingtonpost.com/news
/acts-of-faith/wp/2016/02/29/russell-moore-why-this-election-makes-me-hate
-the-word-evangelical/?noredirect=on.

13. See Joe Carter, "No, the Majority of American Evangelicals Did Not Vote for Trump," *Gospel Coalition*, 15 November 2016, https://www.thegospelcoalition .org/article/no-the-majority-of-american-evangelicals-did-not-vote-for-trump/.

14. See Ed Stetzer, "Debunking the 81 Percent," *Christianity Today*, October 2018, 21–24.

15. See Katelyn Beaty, "At a Private Meeting in Illinois, a Group of Evangelicals Tried to Save Their Movement from Trumpism," *New Yorker*, 26 April 2018, https://www.newyorker.com/news/on-religion/at-a-private-meeting-in-illinois-a -group-of-evangelicals-tried-to-save-their-movement-from-trumpism.

16. See Beaty, "At a Private Meeting in Illinois."

17. See Steve Jordahl, "Pro Trump Evangelicals 'Personae Non Gratae,'" One NewsNow.com, 16 April 2018, https://web.archive.org/web/20210420033107 /https://onenewsnow.com/church/2018/04/16/pro-trump-evangelicals-personae -non-gratae/.

18. See Beaty, "At a Private Meeting in Illinois."

19. See Beaty, "At a Private Meeting in Illinois."

20. See Beaty, "At a Private Meeting in Illinois."

21. See Mark Labberton, "Political Dealing: The Crisis of Evangelicalism," Fuller Theological Seminary, 20 April 2018, https://www.fuller.edu/posts/politi cal-dealing-the-crisis-of-evangelicalism.

22. See Labberton, "Political Dealing."

23. See Labberton, "Political Dealing."

24. See Labberton, "Political Dealing."

25. See Labberton, "Political Dealing."

26. See Labberton, "Political Dealing."

27. See Mark Labberton, "Introduction," in *Still Evangelical?*, ed. Mark Labberton (Downers Grove, IL: InterVarsity Press, 2018), 1.

28. See Labberton, "Introduction," 5, 6, 10, 3.

29. See Emily MacFarlan Miller, "There's a 'Red Evangelicalism and a Blue Evangelicalism': Faith Leaders Gather to Discuss Their Common Future," *Washington Post*, 18 April 2018, https://www.washingtonpost.com/news/acts-of-faith/wp/2018/04/18 /theres-a-red-evangelicalism-and-a-blue-evangelicalism-faith-leaders-gather-to-dis cuss-evangelical-future/?noredirect=on&utm_term=.968fcc97e749.

30. See Jemar Tisby, "White Evangelical Support for Trump Comes from Churchgoers, Not EINOs," Religion News Service, 19 March 2019, https://reli gionnews.com/2019/03/19/white-evangelical-support-for-trump-comes-from -churchgoers-not-einos/.

31. See Philip Schwadel and Gregory A. Smith, "Evangelical Approval of Trump Remains High, but Other Religious Groups Are Less Supportive," Pew Research Center, 18 March 2019, https://www.pewresearch.org/fact-tank/2019/03/18/evangelical-approval-of-trump-remains-high-but-other-religious-groups-are-less-supportive/.

32. See Stetzer, "Debunking the 81 Percent"; as well as LifeWay Research, "Evangelical and Non-evangelical Voting and Political Views," 19 October 2018, https://lifewayresearch.com/2018/10/19/evangelical-and-non-evangelical-voting-and-political-views/.

Works Cited

Alexander, Fred. "Something Big." *Freedom Now*, August 1965.

Alexander, John. "God and the Poor, Part 2." *The Other Side*, May–June 1990.

——. "God's Preferential Option for the Poor." *The Other Side*, March–April 1990.

——. "Homosexuality: It's Not That Clear." *The Other Side*, June 1978.

——. "I'm All Fired Up." *Freedom Now*, October 1965.

——. "Our Name." *Freedom Now*, August 1965.

Allen, Bob. "Falwell Says Wallis Isn't an Evangelical." *Ethicsdaily.com*, 20 July 2004. http://www.ethicsdaily.com/falwell-says-wallis-isnt-an-evangelical-cms-4470.

Alsdurf, Phyllis E. "Evangelical Feminists: Ministry Is the Issue." *Christianity Today*, 21 July 1978.

Altman, Dennis. *AIDS in the Mind of America*. Garden City, NY: Doubleday, 1986.

American Psychological Association, Task Force on Appropriate Therapeutic Responses to Sexual Orientation. *Report of the American Psychological Association Task Force on Appropriate Therapeutic Responses to Sexual Orientation*. Washington, DC: APA, 2009. https://www.apa.org/pi/lgbt/resources/therapeutic-response.pdf.

Anderson, Leith, and Ed Stetzer. "A New Way to Define Evangelicals." *Christianity Today*, April 2016.

——. "Research: Defining Evangelicals in an Election Year." *Christianity Today*, 2 March 2016. https://www.christianitytoday.com/ct/2016/april/defining-evangelicals-in-election-year.html.

Anderson, Sharon. "Sanctity of Life Issues Bring a Variety of Demonstrators to Washington, D.C." *Christianity Today*, 12 July 1985.

Bailey, Sarah Pulliam. "Evangelical Leader Russell Moore Denounces Ex-gay Therapy." Religion News Service, 28 October 2014. https://religionnews .com/2014/10/28/evangelical-leader-russell-moore-denounces-ex-gay -therapy/.

——. "From Franklin Graham to Tony Campolo, Some Evangelical Leaders Are Splitting over Gay Marriage." *Washington Post*, 9 June 2015. https://www .washingtonpost.com/news/acts-of-faith/wp/2015/06/09/from-franklin -graham-to-tony-campolo-some-evangelical-leaders-are-dividing-over -gay-marriage/?utm_term=.24df226f18f7.

——. "Gay, Christian and . . . Celibate: The Changing Face of the Homosexuality Debate." Religion News Service, 4 August 2014. https://religionnews.com /2014/08/04/gay-christian-celibate-changing-face-homosexuality-debate/.

——. "No 'Poster Boy': Rick Warren Draws Criticism for Distancing Himself from Proposition 8." *Christianity Today*, June 2009.

Baldwin, Lewis V. "Black Church Studies as an Academic Interest and Initiative." Pages 31–55 in *The Black Church Studies Reader*. Edited by Alton B. Pollard III and Carol B. Duncan. New York: Palgrave Macmillan, 2016.

Balmer, Randall. "Blair, Ralph." Page 83 in *Encyclopedia of Evangelicalism*. Rev. and exp. ed. Waco, TX: Baylor University Press, 2004.

——. "Hardesty, Nancy A(nn) (1941–)." Page 321 in *Encyclopedia of Evangelicalism*. Rev. and exp. ed. Waco, TX: Baylor University Press, 2004.

——. "Jim Wallis." Pages 715–16 in *Encyclopedia of Evangelicalism*. Rev. and exp. ed. Waco, TX: Baylor University Press, 2004.

——. "Letha Dawson Scanzoni." Page 603 in *Encyclopedia of Evangelicalism*. Rev. and exp. ed. Waco, TX: Baylor University Press, 2004.

Banerjee, Neela. "Gay and Evangelical, Seeking Paths of Acceptance." *New York Times*, 12 December 2006. https://www.nytimes.com/2006/12/12/us/12evan gelical.html.

Bare, Daniel R. *Black Fundamentalists: Conservative Christianity and Racial Identity in the Segregation Era*. New York: New York University Press, 2021.

Barker, William S. Letters. *The Other Side*, September–October 1976.

Barna, George. *The Barna Report 1992–1993: An Annual Survey of Life-Styles, Values and Religious Views*. Ventura, CA: Regal Books, 1992.

—. The Frog in the Kettle: What Christians Need to Know about Life in the 21st Century. Ventura, CA: Regal Books, 1990.

——. *The Frog in the Kettle: What Christians Need to Know about Life in the 21st Century.* Ventura, CA: Regal Books, 1990.

Barna, George, and William Paul MacKay. *Vital Signs: Emerging Social Trends and the Future of American Christianity.* Westchester, IL: Crossway, 1984.

Barth, Karl. "The Strange New World within the Bible." Pages 28–50 in *The Word of God and the Word of Man.* Translated by Douglas Horton. New York: Harper & Row, 1957.

Beaty, Katelyn. "At a Private Meeting in Illinois, a Group of Evangelicals Tried to Save Their Movement from Trumpism." *New Yorker,* 26 April 2018. https://www.newyorker.com/news/on-religion/at-a-private-meeting-in-illinois-a-group-of-evangelicals-tried-to-save-their-movement-from-trumpism.

Bendroth, Margaret Lamberts. "Fundamentalism." Pages 439–47 in vol. 1 of *Encyclopedia of Women and Religion in North America.* Edited by Rosemary Skinner Keller, Rosemary Radford Ruether, and Marie Cantlon. Bloomington: Indiana University Press, 2006.

——. "Fundamentalism and Femininity: Points of Encounter between Religious Conservatives and Women, 1919–1935." *Church History* 61 (1992): 221–33.

——. *Fundamentalism and Gender: 1875 to the Present.* New Haven: Yale University Press, 1993.

Bentley, William H. "Bible Believers in the Black Community." Pages 128–41 in *The Evangelicals.* Edited by David F. Wells and John D. Woodbridge. Grand Rapids: Baker, 1977.

——. *The National Black Evangelical Association.* Chicago: William H. Bentley, 1979.

——. "Reflections." Pages 135–36 in *The Chicago Declaration.* Edited by Ronald J. Sider. Carol Stream, IL: Creation House, 1974.

——. *The Relevance of a Black Evangelical Black Theology for American Theology.* Chicago: BECN, 1981.

Bentley, William H., and Ruth Lewis Bentley. "Reflections on the Scope and Function of a Black Evangelical Black Theology." Pages 299–333 in *Evangelical Affirmations.* Edited by Kenneth S. Kantzer and Carl F. H. Henry. Grand Rapids: Academie Books, 1990.

Billingsley, Lloyd. "First Church of Christ Socialist." *National Review,* 28 October 1983.

——. *The Generation That Knew Not Josef: A Critique of Marxism and the Religious Left.* Portland: Multnomah, 1985.

Blair, Ralph. "Attention!" 4 January 1977. Foster Gunnison Jr. Papers. Institute
    for Social Ethics Archives. University of Connecticut: Connecticut Digital
    Archive. http://hdl.handle.net/11134/20002:860296712.

———. *The Best of Both Worlds: A Brief History of Evangelicals Concerned, Inc.* New
    York: Evangelicals Concerned, 2000.

———. "Changing the Homosexual?" *Reformed Journal* 31 (1981): 6–7.

———. "Does 'Ex-gay' Equal Heterosexual? Letter to the Editor." *Christianity Today*,
    20 September 1985.

———. *Evangelicals (?!) Concerned.* New York: Evangelicals Concerned, 1982.

———. "Evangelicals Concerned: Urbana Report." 1977. Foster Gunnison Jr. Papers.
    Institute for Social Ethics Archives. University of Connecticut: Connecti-
    cut Digital Archive. http://hdl.handle.net/11134/20002:860296712.

———. *Ex-gay.* New York: HCCC, 1982.

———. *Holier-Than-Thou Hocus-Pocus and Homosexuality.* New York: Homosexual
    Community Counseling Center, 1977.

———. "Homosexuality: Letter to the Editor." *Christianity Today*, 27 March 1981.

———. "Looking Back: Evangelicals and Homosexuality." *Record: Newsletter of Evan-
    gelicals Concerned, Inc.*, Fall 2015.

———. *One Foolishness or Another: The Gospel and Foolish Galatians, Gays and Lesbi-
    ans.* New York: Evangelicals Concerned, 1999.

———. *Review* 14, no. 4 (Fall 1989).

Blum, Edward J. "Religion, Race, and African American Life." Pages 213–35 in *The
    Columbia Guide to Religion in American History.* Edited by Paul Harvey and
    Edward Blum. New York: Columbia University Press, 2012.

"Books of the Century." *Christianity Today*, 24 April 2000.

"Books: Social Issues Top Most Significant List." *Eternity*, December 1968.

Bouma, Clarence. "Orthodox Theological Scholarship." *Calvin Forum* 15 (1950): 131.

Bouma, Mary. "Liberated Mothers." *Christianity Today*, 7 May 1971.

Bowman, Matthew Burton. *The Urban Pulpit: New York City and the Fate of Liberal
    Evangelicalism.* New York: Oxford University Press, 2014.

Braude, Ann. "Women's History *Is* American Religious History." Pages 87–107
    in *Retelling U.S. Religious History.* Edited by Thomas A. Tweed. Berkeley:
    University of California Press, 1997.

Briggs, Charles. *The Authority of Holy Scripture: An Inaugural Address.* 2nd ed.
    New York: Scribner's Sons, 1891.

——. *Biblical Study: Its Principles, Methods, and History.* 3rd ed. New York: Scribner's Sons, 1890.

——. *The Fundamental Christian Faith: The Origin, History and Interpretation of the Apostles' and Nicene Creeds.* New York: Scribner's Sons, 1913.

——. *Whither? A Theological Question for the Times.* New York: Scribner's Sons, 1889.

Burk, Denny. "Suppressing the Truth in Unrighteousness: Matthew Vines Takes on the New Testament." Pages 43–57 in *God and the Gay Christian? A Response to Matthew Vines.* Edited by R. Albert Mohler Jr. Louisville: SBTS Press, 2014.

Busch, Eberhard. *Karl Barth: His Life from Letters and Autobiographical Texts.* Translated by John Bowden. London: SCM, 1976.

Campolo, Tony. *20 Hot Potatoes Christians Are Afraid to Touch.* Dallas: Word, 1988.

Carpenter, Joel A. "The Scope of American Evangelicalism: Some Comments on the Dayton-Marsden Exchange." *Christian Scholar's Review* 23 (1993): 53–61.

Carter, Joe. "No, the Majority of American Evangelicals Did Not Vote for Trump." *Gospel Coalition*, 15 November 2016. https://www.thegospelcoalition.org/article/no-the-majority-of-american-evangelicals-did-not-vote-for-trump/.

CBE International. "History of CBE." https://www.cbeinternational.org/content/cbes-history.

Cerling, C. E., Jr. Review of *All We're Meant to Be,* by Letha Dawson Scanzoni and Nancy A. Hardesty. *Journal of the Evangelical Theological Society* 18 (1975): 292–95.

Chambers, Alan. *My Exodus: From Fear to Grace.* Grand Rapids: Zondervan, 2015.

Chandler, Russell. "Christian Activists Help Kill a California Gay Rights Bill." *Christianity Today*, 20 April 1984.

——. "50 Million 'Born Again' in U.S." *Los Angeles Times*, 23 September 1976.

Charles, Guy. "The Church and the Homosexual." Pages 117–31 in *The Secrets of Our Sexuality: Role Liberation for the Christian.* Edited by Gary R. Collins. Waco, TX: Word, 1976.

"The Chicago Declaration." Cover and pages 1–2 in *The Chicago Declaration.* Edited by Ronald J. Sider. Carol Stream, IL: Creation House, 1974.

Chilton, David. *Power in the Blood: A Christian Response to AIDS.* Brentwood, TN: Wolgemuth & Hyatt, 1987.

——. *Productive Christians in an Age of Guilt-Manipulators.* 3rd ed. Tyler, TX: Institute for Christian Economics, 1990.

Christensen, Larry. *The Christian Family*. Minneapolis: Bethany Fellowship, 1970.

"The Christianity Today-Gallup Poll: An Overview." *Christianity Today*, 21 December 1979.

"The Church and the Race Problem." *Christianity Today*, 18 March 1957.

Cianciotto, Jason, and Sean Cahill. *Youth in the Crosshairs: The Third Wave of Ex-gay Activism*. New York: National Gay and Lesbian Task Force Policy Institute, 2006.

Clark, Gordon H. Letters. *The Other Side*, July-August 1972.

Cleveland, Kyle. "The Politics of Jubilee: Ideological Drift and Organizational Schism in a Religious Sect." PhD diss., Temple University, 1990.

Cochran, Pamela D. H. *Evangelical Feminism: A History*. New York: New York University Press, 2005.

Coffin, Henry Sloane. *The Practical Aims of a Liberal Evangelicalism*. New York: Union Theological Seminary, 1915.

Coffman, Elesha J. *The Christian Century and the Rise of the Protestant Mainline*. New York: Oxford University Press, 2013.

Collins, Kenneth J. *The Evangelical Moment: The Promise of an American Religion*. Grand Rapids: Baker, 2005.

"Controversial Black Preacher Putting Stress on Social Issues." *New York Times*, 2 September 1973.

Cook, Colin. "I Found Freedom." *Christianity Today*, 18 August 1989.

Cornell, George. Religion Today. *Associated Press*, 30 November 1973.

"Council on Biblical Manhood and Womanhood." *Christianity Today*, 13 January 1989.

"Counting Souls." *Time*, 4 October 1976.

Cox, Richard H. "E. Mansell Pattison, M.D." *Pastoral Psychology* 20 (1969): 4, 66.

Cross, Sue. "Jerry Falwell Calls AIDS a 'Gay Plague.'" *Washington Post*, 6 July 1983.

Curry, George E. "248 Seized in Capital in Day of Protests." *Chicago Tribune*, 30 May 1985.

Dallas, Joe. "Born Gay?" *Christianity Today*, 22 June 1992.

Daniel, Lillian. "Evangelical and Gay." *Christian Century*, 20 March 2013.

"The Danvers Statement." *Christianity Today*, 13 January 1989.

Dayton, Donald W. "An Autobiographical Response." Pages 383-426 in *From the Margins: A Celebration of the Theological Work of Donald W. Dayton*. Edited by Christian T. Collins Winn. Eugene, OR: Pickwick, 2007.

——. "The Search for the Historical Evangelicalism: George Marsden's History of Fuller Seminary as a Case Study." *Christian Scholar's Review* 23 (1993): 12–33.

——. "Some Doubts about the Usefulness of the Category 'Evangelical.'" Pages 245–51 in *The Variety of American Evangelicalism.* Edited by Donald W. Dayton and Robert K. Johnston. Eugene, OR: Wipf & Stock, 1998.

DeBerg, Betty A. *Ungodly Women: Gender and the First Wave of American Fundamentalism.* Minneapolis: Fortress, 1990.

"Desegregation and Regeneration." *Christianity Today,* 29 September 1958.

Dobson, James. *Straight Talk to Men and Their Wives.* Waco, TX: Word, 1980.

——. *What Wives Wish Their Husbands Knew about Women.* Wheaton, IL: Tyndale House, 1975.

Dorrien, Gary. *The Barthian Revolt in Modern Theology: Theology without Weapons.* Louisville: Westminster John Knox, 2000.

——. *Breaking White Supremacy: Martin Luther King Jr. and the Black Social Gospel.* New Haven: Yale University Press, 2018.

——. *The Making of American Liberal Theology: Idealism, Realism, and Modernity, 1900–1950.* Louisville: Westminster John Knox, 2003.

——. *The Making of American Liberal Theology: Imagining Progressive Religion, 1805–1900.* Louisville: Westminster John Knox, 2001.

——. *The New Abolition: W. E. B. DuBois and the Black Social Gospel.* New Haven: Yale University Press, 2015.

Douma, Doug J. *The Presbyterian Philosopher: The Authorized Biography of Gordon H. Clark.* Eugene, OR: Wipf & Stock, 2016.

Doyle, Barrie. "The Religious Campaign: Backing Their Man." *Christianity Today,* 17 October 1972.

Drescher, Jack. "Sexual Conversion ('Reparative') Therapies: History and Update." Pages 71–91 in *Mental Health Issues in Lesbian, Gay, Bisexual, and Transgender Communities.* Edited by Billy E. Jones and Marjorie J. Hill. Washington, DC: American Psychiatric, 2002.

Duke, Jewel E. Letters. *The Other Side,* May–June 1972.

Du Mez, Kristin Kobes. *Jesus and John Wayne: How White Evangelicals Corrupted a Faith and Fractured a Nation.* New York: Liveright, 2020.

Eckholm, Erik. "Rift Forms in Movement as Belief in Gay 'Cure' is Renounced." *New York Times,* 7 July 2012.

"1860 Census: Population of the United States." United States Census Bureau. https://www.census.gov/library/publications/1864/dec/1860a.html.

Elliot, Elisabeth. "The Bible and Women 1975." *Interlit*, December 1975.

——. "The Essence of Femininity: A Personal Perspective." Pages 400–404 in *Recovering Biblical Manhood and Womanhood*. Edited by John Piper and Wayne Grudem. Wheaton, IL: Crossway, 1991.

——. *Let Me Be a Woman: Notes to My Daughter on the Meaning of Womanhood*. Wheaton, IL: Tyndale House, 1976.

——. "Why I Oppose the Ordination of Women." *Christianity Today*, 6 June 1975.

Emerson, Michael O., and Christian Smith. *Divided by Faith: Evangelical Religion and the Problem of Race in America*. New York: Oxford University Press, 2000.

Erzen, Tanya. *Straight to Jesus: Sexual and Christian Conversions in the Ex-gay Movement*. Berkeley: University of California Press, 2006.

Evangelical Press and Jody Veenker. "Ex-gay Leader Disciplined for Gay Bar Visit." *Christianity Today*, 1 October 2000.

Evangelicals Concerned. Untitled Newsletter. 20 April 1977. Foster Gunnison Jr. Papers. Institute for Social Ethics Archives. University of Connecticut: Connecticut Digital Archive. http://hdl.handle.net/11134/20002:860296712.

Evangelical Theological Society. "ETS Constitution" (Article III: Doctrinal Basis). https://www.etsjets.org/about/constitution#A3.

"The Evangelical Vote." *Newsweek*, 30 October 1972.

Evans, Curtis J. "White Evangelical Protestant Responses to the Civil Rights Movement." *Harvard Theological Review* 102 (2009): 245–73.

"Eve's Second Apple." *Christianity Today*, 21 August 1970.

"Exodus International to Shut Down." Exodus International. 19 June 2013. https://web.archive.org/web/20220124162057/http://exodusinternational.org/2013/06/exodus-international-to-shut-down/.

Falwell, Jerry. "AIDS: The Judgment of God." *Liberty Report*, 5 April 1987.

Farrer, Lauralee. "A Legacy of Steadfast Belief." *Fuller Focus Magazine*, Fall 2007. https://fullerstudio.fuller.edu/a-legacy-of-steadfast-belief/.

——. "This Is Then, That Was Now." *Fuller Studio*. https://fullerstudio.fuller.edu/this-is-then-that-was-now/.

Fetzer, Joel, and Gretchen S. Carnes. "Dr. Ron Sider: Mennonite Environmentalist on the Evangelical Left." Pages 159–74 in *Religious Leaders and Faith-Based Politics: Ten Profiles*. Edited by Jo Renee Formicola and Hubert Morken. Lanham, MD: Rowman & Littlefield, 2001.

Finger, Reta Halteman, and S. Sue Horner. "Euro-American Evangelical Feminism." Pages 467–76 in vol. 1 of *Encyclopedia of Women and Religion in North America*. Edited by Rosemary Skinner Keller, Rosemary Radford Ruether, and Marie Cantlon. Bloomington: Indiana University Press, 2006.

Finley, Stephen C., and Torin Alexander. *African American Religious Cultures*. Edited by Anthony B. Pinn. Santa Barbara: ABC-CLIO, 2009.

Fosdick, Harry Emerson. "The Church Must Go beyond Modernism." Pages 39–48 in *The Riverside Preachers*. Edited by Paul H. Sherry. New York: Pilgrim, 1978.

———. *The Living of These Days: An Autobiography*. New York: Harper & Brothers, 1956.

———. *The Meaning of Faith*. New York: Association Press, 1917.

———. *The Meaning of Prayer*. New York: Association Press, 1915.

———. *The Meaning of Service*. New York: Association Press, 1920.

———. "Shall the Fundamentalists Win?" Pages 27–38 in *The Riverside Preachers*. Edited by Paul H. Sherry. New York: Pilgrim, 1978.

Frame, Randy. "Homosexuality: Campolo's Views Challenged." *Christianity Today*, 8 September 1989.

———. "Homosexuality: The Evangelical Closet." *Christianity Today*, 5 November 1990.

———. "The Homosexual Lifestyle: Is There a Way Out?" *Christianity Today*, 9 August 1985.

Freudenberger, C. D. Review of *Rich Christians in an Age of Hunger*, by Ronald J. Sider. *Occasional Bulletin of Missionary Research* 1 (1977): 34–35.

Fuller Theological Seminary. "Fuller in Contrast to Neo-orthodoxy." http://fuller .edu/about/mission-and-values/what-we-believe-and-teach/.

———. "What We Believe and Teach." http://fuller.edu/about/mission-and-values /what-we-believe-and-teach/.

Gallagher, Sally K. *Evangelical Identity and Gendered Family Life*. New Brunswick, NJ: Rutgers University Press, 2003.

———. "The Marginalization of Evangelical Feminism." *Sociology of Religion* 65 (2004): 215–37.

Galli, Mark. "Breaking News: 2 Billion Christians Believe in Traditional Marriage; And So Do We." *Christianity Today*, 9 June 2015. https://www.christian itytoday.com/ct/2015/june-web-only/breaking-news-2-billion-christian -believe-in-traditional-ma.html.

Gallup, George, Jr., and D. Michael Lindsay. *Surveying the Religious Landscape*. Harrisburg, PA: Morehouse, 1999.

Gallup, George, Jr., and Jim Castelli. *The People's Religion: American Faith in the 90's*. New York: Macmillan, 1989.

Gasaway, Brantley W. *Progressive Evangelicals and the Pursuit of Social Justice*. Chapel Hill: University of North Carolina Press, 2014.

Gentry, Weston. "Exodus from Exodus." *Christianity Today*, 1 December 2012.

George Gallup Polls America on Religion: A Compilation of Articles from Christianity Today *with Complete Technical Appendix*. Carol Stream, IL: Christianity Today, 1981.

Gilbreath, Edward. "A Prophet Out of Harlem." *Christianity Today*, 16 September 1996.

———. *Reconciliation Blues: A Black Evangelical's Inside View of White Christianity*. Downers Grove, IL: InterVarsity Press, 2006.

Gladwin, John W. Review of *Rich Christians in an Age of Hunger*, by Ronald J. Sider. *Churchman* 93 (1979): 181–84.

Glaser, Chris. "The Love That Dare Not Pray Its Name: The Gay and Lesbian Movement in America's Churches." Pages 150–57 in *Homosexuality in the Church: Both Sides of the Debate*. Edited by Jeffrey S. Siker. Louisville: Westminster John Knox, 1994.

Godges, John. "Religious Groups Meet the San Francisco AIDS Challenge." *Christian Century*, 10–17 September 1986.

Gracey, Celeste, and Jeremy Weber. "World Vision Reverses Decision to Hire Christians in Same-Sex Marriages." *Christianity Today*, 26 March 2014. https://www.christianitytoday.com/ct/2014/march-web-only/world-vision-reverses-decision-gay-same-sex-marriage.html.

———. "World Vision: Why We're Hiring Gay Christians in Same-Sex Marriages." *Christianity Today*, 24 March 2014. https://www.christianitytoday.com/ct/2014/march-web-only/world-vision-why-hiring-gay-christians-same-sex-marriage.html.

Graham, Billy. "AIDS, Herpes, Sex, and the Bible." Tallahassee, Florida. 6 November 1986. https://billygraham.org/audio/aids-herpes-sex-and-the-bible-part-1/.

———. "Billy Graham Makes Plea for an End to Intolerance." *Life*, 1 October 1956.

———. "Jesus and the Liberated Woman." *Ladies' Home Journal*, December 1970.

———. *Just as I Am: The Autobiography of Billy Graham*. Rev. and updated 10th anniversary ed. New York: HarperCollins, 2007.

———. Letter to Richard Nixon. 4 August 1972. https://www.nixonlibrary.gov/vir tuallibrary/documents/donated/080472_graham.pdf.

———. "Watergate." *Christianity Today*, 4 January 1974.

———. *World Aflame*. Garden City, NY: Doubleday, 1965.

Granberg-Michaelson, Wesley. *Unexpected Destinations: An Evangelical Pilgrimage to World Christianity*. Grand Rapids: Eerdmans, 2011.

Grounds, Vernon C. Letters. *The Other Side*, September–October 1976.

Grudem, Wayne, ed. *Biblical Foundations for Manhood and Womanhood*. Wheaton, IL: Crossway, 2002.

Grudem, Wayne. *Countering the Claims of Evangelical Feminism*. Sisters, OR: Multnomah, 2006.

———. *Evangelical Feminism and Biblical Truth*. Sisters, OR: Multnomah, 2004.

———. *Evangelical Feminism: A New Path to Liberalism?* Wheaton, IL: Crossway, 2006.

———. "Personal Reflections on the History of CBMW and the State of the Gender Debate." *Journal for Biblical Manhood and Womanhood* 14 (2009): 12–17.

———. *What's Wrong with Gender-Neutral Bible Translations?* Libertyville, IL: Council on Biblical Manhood and Womanhood, 1997.

Grudem, Wayne, and Dennis Rainey, eds. *Pastoral Leadership for Manhood and Womanhood*. Wheaton, IL: Crossway, 2002.

Grudem, Wayne, and Vern Poythress. *The TNIV and the Gender-Neutral Bible Controversy*. Nashville: Broadman & Holman, 2004.

Gundry, Patricia. *Woman Be Free: The Clear Message of Scripture*. Grand Rapids: Zondervan, 1977.

Gunton, Colin E. *Revelation and Reason: Prolegomena to Systematic Theology*. New York: T&T Clark, 2008.

Gushee, David P. *Changing Our Mind*. Canton, MI: David Crumm Media, 2014.

———. *Still Christian: Following Jesus Out of American Evangelicalism*. Louisville: Westminster John Knox, 2017.

———. "When the Evangelical Establishment Comes after You." Religion News Service, 17 July 2017, https://religionnews.com/2017/07/17/lgbtq-equality -evangelical-rejection/.

Hackett, Conrad, and D. Michael Lindsay. "Measuring Evangelicalism: Consequences of Different Operationalization Strategies." *Journal for the Scientific Study of Religion* 47 (2008): 499–514.

Hankins, Barry. *God's Rascal: J. Frank Norris and the Beginnings of Southern Fundamentalism*. Lexington: University Press of Kentucky, 2010.

———. "In Defense of the Academy." *Fides et Historia* 46 (2014): 45–49.

———. "We're All Evangelicals Now: The Existential and Backward Historiography of Twentieth-Century Evangelicalism." Pages 196–220 in *American Denominational History: Perspectives on the Past, Prospects for the Future*. Edited by Keith Harper. Tuscaloosa: University of Alabama Press, 2008.

Hardesty, Nancy A. "Blessed the Waters That Rise and Fall to Rise Again." Evangelical and Ecumenical Women's Caucus. https://eewc.com/blessed-the-waters/.

———. "Reflection." Pages 123–26 in *The Chicago Declaration*. Edited by Ronald J. Sider. Carol Stream, IL: Creation House, 1974.

———. *Women Called to Witness: Evangelical Feminism in the Nineteenth Century*. Nashville: Abingdon, 1984.

———. "Women: Second Class Citizens?" *Eternity*, January 1971.

Harnden, Phillip. "Remembering John." *The Other Side*, September–October 2001.

Harris, Jane. "America's Evangelical Women: More Than Wives and Mothers—Reformers, Ministers, and Leaders." Pages 447–57 in vol. 1 of *Encyclopedia of Women and Religion in North America*. Edited by Rosemary Skinner Keller, Rosemary Radford Ruether, and Marie Cantlon. Bloomington: Indiana University Press, 2006.

Harris, Joan. *The Sojourners File*. Washington, DC: New Century Foundation, 1983.

Hart, D. G. "Beyond the Battle for the Bible: What Evangelicals Missed in Van Til's Critique of Barth." Pages 42–70 in *Karl Barth and American Evangelicalism*. Edited by Bruce L. McCormack and Clifford B. Anderson. Grand Rapids: Eerdmans, 2011.

———. *Deconstructing Evangelicalism*. Grand Rapids: Baker Academic, 2004.

Hatfield, Mark. *Between a Rock and a Hard Place*. Waco, TX: Word, 1976.

Hawkins, J. Russell, and Phillip Luke Sinitiere, eds. *Christians and the Color Line: Race and Religion after Divided by Faith*. New York: Oxford University Press, 2013.

Hayes, Kathleen. "Ron Sider: Working for Kingdom Values." *The Other Side*, October 1986.

Hedstrom, James Alden. "Evangelical Program in the United States: The Morphology of Establishment, Progressive, and Radical Platforms." PhD diss., Vanderbilt University, 1982.

Heise, Kenan. "Pentecostals' Rev. William Bentley." *Chicago Tribune*, 22 May 1993. https://www.chicagotribune.com/news/ct-xpm-1993-05-22-9305220099 -story.html.

Henderson, Charles P., Jr. "The {Social} Gospel according to 1. Richard Nixon 2. George McGovern." *Commonweal*, 29 September 1972.

Henry, Carl F. H. "Revolt on Evangelical Frontiers." *Christianity Today*, 26 April 1974.

——. *The Uneasy Conscience of Modern Fundamentalism*. Grand Rapids: Eerdmans, 1947.

Hestenes, Roberta. "Stained Glass Ceilings and Sticky Floors." *Fuller Magazine* 3, 2015.

"Holding Steady." *Christianity Today*, 5 March 1990.

Hollinger, Dennis. *Individualism and Social Ethics: An Evangelical Syncretism*. Lanham, MD: University Press of America, 1983.

Holmes, Arthur P. "Evangelicals, Morality and Politics." *Reformed Journal* 22, no. 9 (November 1972): 3.

"Homosexuality: Biblical Guidance through a Moral Morass." *Christianity Today*, 18 April 1980.

"Homosexuality: Falwell Tames His Rhetoric." *Christianity Today*, 6 December 1999.

Horner, Sandra Sue Geeting. "Becoming All We're Meant to Be: A Social History of the Contemporary Evangelical Feminist Movement; A Case Study of the Evangelical and Ecumenical Women's Caucus." PhD diss., Northwestern University, 2000.

Hunter, James Davison. *American Evangelicalism: Conservative Religion and the Quandary of Modernity*. New Brunswick, NJ: Rutgers University Press, 1983.

——. *Evangelicalism: The Coming Generation*. Chicago: University of Chicago Press, 1987.

Hyer, Marjorie. "Evangelicals: Tackling the Gut Issues." *Christian Century*, 19 December 1973.

Ingersoll, Julie J. *Building God's Kingdom: Inside the World of Christian Reconstruction*. New York: Oxford University Press, 2015.

——. *Evangelical Christian Women: War Stories in the Gender Battles*. New York: New York University Press, 2003.

James, Susan Donaldson. "Christians Promote Holy, Hot Sex in Marriage." *ABC News*, 9 May 2008. http://abcnews.go.com/US/story?id=4651272&page=1.

Jewett, Paul K. *Man as Male and Female: A Study in Sexual Relationships from a Theological Point of View*. Grand Rapids: Eerdmans, 1975.

Johnston, Robert K. *Evangelicals at an Impasse: Biblical Authority in Practice*. Atlanta: John Knox, 1979.

———. "Homosexuality: Can It Be 'Cured'?" *Reformed Journal* 31 (1981): 9–12.

Jones, Bob. Editorial. *Faith for the Family*, September–October 1974.

Jones, Howard O., and Edward Gilbreath. *Gospel Trailblazer: An African-American Preacher's Historic Journey across Racial Lines*. Chicago: Moody, 2003.

Jones, Jeffrey McClain. "Ronald Sider and Radical Evangelical Political Theology." PhD diss., Northwestern University, 1990.

Jones, Stanton L. "Homosexuality according to Science." *Christianity Today*, 18 August 1989.

———. "The Loving Opposition." *Christianity Today*, 19 July 1993.

Jonsen, Albert, and Earl Shelp. "Religion and Religious Groups." Pages 115–57 in *The Social Impact of AIDS in the United States*. Edited by Albert R. Jonsen and Jeff Stryker. Washington, DC: National Academy, 1993.

Jordahl, Steve. "Pro-Trump Evangelicals 'Personae Non Gratae.'" OneNewsNow .com, 16 April 2018. https://web.archive.org/web/20210420033107/https: /onenewsnow.com/church/2018/04/16/pro-trump-evangelicals-personae -non-gratae/.

"Journal Interviews . . . Christian Answers on Homosexuality." *Journal of the American Scientific Affiliation* 31 (1979): 48–53.

"Justin Lee." In *Gale Literature: Contemporary Authors*. Farmington Hills, MI: Gale, 2014. Gale in Context: Biography.

Kantzer, Kenneth S. "Homosexuals in the Church." *Christianity Today*, 22 April 1983.

Kellstedt, Lyman, John Green, Corwin Smidt, and James Guth. "Faith Transformed: Religion and American Politics from FDR to George W. Bush." Pages 272–73 in *Religion and American Politics: From the Colonial Period to the Present*. Edited by Mark A. Noll and Luke E. Harlow. New York: Oxford University Press, 2007.

Kennedy, John W. "Homosexuality: Ad Campaign Ignites Firestorm." *Christianity Today*, 7 September 1998.

Killeen, Alison J. "Nancy A. Hardesty Papers: Finding Aid." The Archive of Women in Theological Scholarship, The Burke Library, Union Theologi-

cal Seminary. https://library.columbia.edu/content/dam/libraryweb/loca
tions/burke/fa/awts/ldpd_6163424.pdf.

Kistemaker, Simon J. "Thirty-Eighth Annual Meeting." *Journal of the Evangelical Theological Society* 30 (1987): 121–24.

Knudson, Albert C. "German Fundamentalism." *Christian Century*, 14 June 1928.

Labberton, Mark. "Introduction." Pages 1–17 in *Still Evangelical?* Edited by Mark Labberton. Downers Grove, IL: InterVarsity Press, 2018.

———. "Political Dealing: The Crisis of Evangelicalism." Fuller Theological Seminary. 20 April 2018. https://www.fuller.edu/posts/political-dealing-the -crisis-of-evangelicalism.

LaHaye, Beverly. *The Spirit-Controlled Woman*. Irvine, CA: Harvest House, 1976.

LaHaye, Tim. *Understanding the Male Temperament*. Old Tappan, NJ: Revell, 1977.

LaHaye, Tim, and Beverly LaHaye. *The Act of Marriage*. Grand Rapids: Zondervan, 1976.

Lahr, Angela M. *Millennial Dreams and Apocalyptic Nightmares: The Cold War Origins of Political Evangelicalism*. New York: Oxford University Press, 2007.

Larson, Roy. "Historic Workshop: Evangelicals Do U-turn, Take on Social Problems." *Chicago Sun-Times*, 1 December 1973.

Lawson, Joel. "Ex-gay Leader Confronted in Gay Bar." *Southern Voice*, 21 September 2000.

LeBlanc, Douglas. "Ex-gay Sheds the Mocking Quote Marks: An Interview with Bob Davies." *Christianity Today*, 7 January 2002.

Lee, Justin. *Torn: Rescuing the Gospel from the Gays-vs.-Christians Debate*. New York: Jericho Books, 2012.

Leitch, Elisabeth Elliot. "Feminism or Femininity?" *Cambridge Fish*, Winter 1975–1976.

Leland, John, and Mark Miller. "Can Gays Convert?" *Newsweek*, 17 August 1988.

Leonard, Bill J. *Baptists in America*. New York: Columbia University Press, 2005.

"Liberation Closes Fairfax Homosexual Ministry." *Integrity Forum: A Journal for Gay Episcopalians and Their Friends*, October 1977.

LifeWay Research. "Evangelical and Non-Evangelical Voting and Political Views." 19 October 2018. https://lifewayresearch.com/2018/10/19/evangelical-and -non-evangelical-voting-and-political-views/.

Lindsell, Harold. *The Battle for the Bible*. Grand Rapids: Zondervan, 1976.

———. "Egalitarianism and Scriptural Infallibility." *Christianity Today*, 26 March 1976.

——. *Free Enterprise: A Judeo-Christian Defense*. Wheaton, IL: Tyndale House, 1982.

Lindskoog, Kay. Review of *Is the Homosexual My Neighbor?*, by Letha Dawson Scanzoni and Virginia Ramey Mollenkott. *Wittenburg Door*, October–November 1977.

Locklear, Jimmy. "Theology-Culture Rift Surfaces among Black Evangelicals." *Christianity Today*, 23 May 1980.

Lovelace, Richard F. *Homosexuality and the Church*. Old Tappan, NJ: Revell, 1978.

Lynerd, Benjamin T. *Republican Theology: The Civil Religion of American Evangelicals*. New York: Oxford University Press, 2014.

Macartney, Clarence E. "Shall Unbelief Win?" Pages 349–64 in *Sermons in American History: Selected Issues in the American Pulpit 1630–1967*. Edited by Dewitte Holland. Nashville: Abingdon, 1971.

"Mad Hatter . . . Tales from the Washington Tea Party." *Conservative Digest*, October 1983.

Marsden, George, ed. *Evangelicalism and Modern America*. Grand Rapids: Eerdmans, 1984.

Marsden, George. *The Evangelical Mind and the New School Presbyterian Experience*. Eugene, OR: Wipf & Stock, 1970.

——. *Fundamentalism and American Culture*. 2nd ed. New York: Oxford University Press, 2006.

——. *Reforming Fundamentalism: Fuller Seminary and the New Evangelicalism*. Grand Rapids: Eerdmans, 1987.

——. "Response to Don Dayton." *Christian Scholar's Review* 23 (1993): 34–40.

——. *Understanding Fundamentalism and Evangelicalism*. Grand Rapids: Eerdmans, 1991.

Marsh, Charles, and John M. Perkins. *Welcoming Justice: God's Movement toward Beloved Community*. Downers Grove, IL: InterVarsity Press, 2009.

Martin, Enos D., and Ruth Keener Martin. "Developmental and Ethical Issues in Homosexuality: Pastoral Implications." *Journal of Psychology and Theology* 9 (1981): 58–68.

Martin, William. *With God on Our Side: The Rise of the Religious Right in America*. New York: Broadway Books, 1996.

Marty, Martin E. "Needed: Revised Social Gospel." *Context*, 15 March 1974.

——. *Righteous Empire: The Protestant Experience in America*. New York: Dial, 1970.

——. "The Shape of American Protestantism: Are There Two Parties Today?" Pages

91–108 in *Reforming the Center: American Protestantism, 1900 to the Present.* Edited by Douglas Jacobsen and William Vance Trollinger Jr. Grand Rapids: Eerdmans, 1998.

Maryles, Daisy. "The Stakes Rise for Chart Toppers." *Publishers Weekly*, 22 March 2004. https://www.publishersweekly.com/pw/print/20040322/26495-the -stakes-rise-for-chart-toppers.html.

Massa, Mark S. *Charles Augustus Briggs and the Crisis of Historical Criticism.* Minneapolis: Fortress, 1990.

Mathews, Mary Beth Swetnam. *Doctrine and Race: African American Evangelicals and Fundamentalism between the Wars.* Tuscaloosa: University of Alabama Press, 2017.

Mathews, Shailer. *The Church and the Changing Order.* New York: Macmillan, 1907.

———. *The Faith of Modernism.* New York: Macmillan, 1924.

———. *New Faith for Old: An Autobiography.* New York: Macmillan, 1936.

———. *The Social Teaching of Jesus.* New York: Macmillan, 1902.

———. "Unrepentant Liberalism." *American Scholar* 7 (1938): 296–308.

Mathews, Tom. "Battle over Gay Rights." *Newsweek*, 6 June 1977.

Maust, John. "The NBEA: Striving to Be Both Black and Biblical." *Christianity Today*, 27 June 1980.

Mavrodes, George. "On Helping the Hungry." *Christianity Today*, 30 December 1977.

McBeth, H. Leon. *The Baptist Heritage: Four Centuries of Baptist Witness.* Nashville: Broadman, 1987.

McElvaine, Robert S. *Grand Theft Jesus: The Hijacking of Religion in America.* New York: Crown, 2007.

McGann, L. Aubrey F. Letters. *The Other Side*, September–October 1972.

McIntire, Carl. "Caught in the Middle." *Christian Beacon*, 6 October 1949.

Merritt, Jonathan. "The Downfall of the Ex-gay Movement." *Atlantic*, 6 October 2015. https://www.theatlantic.com/politics/archive/2015/10/the-man-who -dismantled-the-ex-gay-ministry/408970/.

Michelsen, A. E. Letters. *The Other Side*, September–October 1972.

Migliazzo, Arlin C. "'She Must Be a Proper Exception': Females, Fuller Seminary, and the Limits of Gender Equity among Southern California Evangelicals, 1947–1952." *Fides et Historia* 45 (2013): 1–19.

Miller, Albert G. "National Black Evangelical Association." Pages 1606–7 in vol. 4

of *Encyclopedia of African American Culture and History*. Edited by Colin A. Palmer. 2nd ed. Detroit: Macmillan, 2006.

———. "The Rise of African-American Evangelicalism in American Culture." Pages 259–69 in *Perspectives on American Religion and Culture*. Edited by Peter W. Williams. Malden, MA: Blackwell, 1999.

Miller, Emily MacFarlan. "There's a 'Red Evangelicalism and a Blue Evangelicalism': Faith Leaders Gather to Discuss Their Common Future." *Washington Post*, 18 April 2018. https://www.washingtonpost.com/news/acts-of-faith /wp/2018/04/18/theres-a-red-evangelicalism-and-a-blue-evangelicalism -faith-leaders-gather-to-discuss-evangelical-future/?noredirect=on&u tm_term=.968fcc97e749.

Miller, Robert Moats. *Harry Emerson Fosdick: Preacher, Pastor, Prophet*. New York: Oxford University Press, 1985.

Miller, Steven P. *Billy Graham and the Rise of the Republican South*. Philadelphia: University of Pennsylvania Press, 2011.

Minnery, Tom. "Homosexuals Can Change." *Christianity Today*, 6 February 1981.

Moberly, Elizabeth R. *Homosexuality: A New Christian Ethic*. Cambridge: James Clarke, 1983.

Mohler, R. Albert, Jr. "God, the Gospel and the Gay Challenge: A Response to Matthew Vines." Pages 9–23 in *God and the Gay Christian? A Response to Matthew Vines*. Edited by R. Albert Mohler Jr. Louisville: SBTS Press, 2014.

Mollenkott, Virginia Ramey. "Virginia Ramey Mollenkott: Founding Member, Evangelical Women's Caucus." Pages 55–72 in *Transforming the Faiths of Our Fathers: Women Who Changed American Religion*. Edited by Ann Braude. New York: Palgrave Macmillan, 2004.

———. "Cochran's Evangelical Feminism—Yet Once More." *EEWC Update*, October–December 2005. https://eewc.com/evangelical-feminism/.

———. "Evangelicalism: A Feminist Perspective." *Union Seminary Quarterly Review* 32 (1977): 95–103.

———. Foreword to *Desperate for Authenticity: A Critical Analysis of the Feminist Theology of Virginia Ramey Mollenkott*, by Patricia Hawley, 2–5. Lanham, MD: University Press of America, 2010.

———. Foreword to *Man as Male and Female*, by Paul K. Jewett, 7–12. Grand Rapids: Eerdmans, 1975.

———. "Interreligious Dialogue: A Pilgrimage." Pages 105–8 in *The Wisdom of*

Daughters: Two Decades of the Voice of Christian Feminism. Edited by Reta Halteman Finger and Kari Sandhaas. Philadelphia: Innisfree, 2001.

———. *Sensuous Spirituality: Out from Fundamentalism.* New York: Crossroad, 1992.

———. *Speech, Silence, Action! The Cycle of Faith.* Nashville: Abingdon, 1980.

———. *Women, Men, and the Bible.* Nashville: Abingdon, 1977.

Monroe, Ann. "Devout Dissidents: Radical Evangelicals Are Gaining Influence Protesting U.S. Policy." *Wall Street Journal,* 24 May 1985.

Moore, Russell. "Have Evangelicals Who Support Trump Lost Their Values?" *New York Times,* 17 September 2015. https://www.nytimes.com/2015/09/17/opin ion/have-evangelicals-who-support-trump-lost-their-values.html?_r=0.

———. "Why This Election Makes Me Hate the Word 'Evangelical.'" *Washington Post,* 29 February 2016. https://www.washingtonpost.com/news/acts-of -faith/wp/2016/02/29/russell-moore-why-this-election-makes-me-hate -the-word-evangelical/?noredirect=on.

"Morality and the Presidential Election." NPR, 13 July 2004. https://www.npr.org /templates/story/story.php?storyId=3354001.

Morgan, Marabel. *The Total Woman.* Old Tappan, NJ: Revell, 1973.

Mott, Stephen Charles. "An Evangelical McGovern at Wheaton." *Qoheleth,* 25 October 1972.

Mouw, Richard J. "Evangelicals and Political Activism." *Christian Century,* 27 December 1972.

Muether, John R. *Cornelius Van Til: Reformed Apologist and Churchman.* Phillipsburg, NJ: P&R, 2008.

Mullin, Miles S., II. "Neoevangelicalism and the Problem of Race in Postwar America." Pages 15–35 in *Christians and the Color Line: Race and Religion after Divided by Faith.* Edited by J. Russell Hawkins and Phillip Luke Sinitiere. New York: Oxford University Press, 2013.

———. "Postwar Evangelical Social Concern: Evangelical Identity and the Modes and Limits of Social Engagement, 1945–1960." PhD diss., Vanderbilt University, 2009.

Murch, James DeForest. *Cooperation without Compromise: A History of the National Association of Evangelicals.* Grand Rapids: Eerdmans, 1956.

Nash, Ronald H. *Evangelicals in America: Who They Are, What They Believe.* Nashville: Abingdon, 1987.

———. *Social Justice and the Christian Church.* Lanham, MD: University Press of America, 1990.

——. *Why the Left Is Not Right: The Religious Left; Who They Are and What They Believe*. Grand Rapids: Zondervan, 1996.

National Association of Evangelicals. "Press Release: NAE, LifeWay Research Publish Evangelical Beliefs Research Definition." 19 November 2015. https://www.nae.net/evangelical-beliefs-research-definition/.

"National Association of Evangelicals: Statement on AIDS (1988)." Pages 114–15 in *The Churches Speak on AIDS: Official Statements from Religious Bodies and Ecumenical Organizations*. Edited by J. Gordon Melton. Detroit: Gale, 1989.

"National Association of Evangelicals: Statement on Homosexuality (1985)." Pages 141–42 in *The Churches Speak on Homosexuality*. Edited by J. Gordon Melton. Detroit: Gale, 1991.

National Association of Evangelicals. "What Is an Evangelical?" https://www.nae.net/what-is-an-evangelical/.

National Council of Churches Unit Committee of Division of Church and Society. "A Response to a Declaration of Evangelical Concern." *Post-American*, March 1975. https://sojo.net/magazine/march-1975/response-declaration-evangelical-concern.

Neff, David. "The New Ex-gay Agenda." *Christianity Today*, 9 March 1992.

——. "The Top 50 Books That Have Shaped Evangelicals." *Christianity Today*, October 2006.

——. "Two Men Don't Make a Right." *Christianity Today*, 19 July 1993.

Nelson, James B. "Homosexuality and the Church." *Christianity and Crisis*, 4 April 1977.

"New Organization Incorporated." *Priscilla Papers*, Fall 1987.

News Brief. *Episcopal News Service*, 28 July 1977. Archives of the Episcopal Church. https://www.episcopalarchives.org/cgi-bin/ENS/ENSpress_release.pl?pr_number=77248/.

Niebuhr, Reinhold. "Barth—Apostle of the Absolute." *Christian Century*, 13 December 1928.

Noll, Mark. *American Evangelical Christianity*. Malden, MA: Blackwell, 2001.

——. *God and Race in American Politics: A Short History*. Princeton: Princeton University Press, 2008.

North, Gary. "The Background of 'Productive Christians.'" Pages 347–65 in David Chilton, *Productive Christians in an Age of Guilt-Manipulators*. 3rd ed. Tyler, TX: Institute for Christian Economics, 1990.

——. "What Is the ICE?" https://www.garynorth.com/freebooks/whatsice.htm.

Oliver, John W., Jr. "Evangelical Campus and Press Meet Black America's Quest for Civil Rights, 1956–1959: Malone College and Christianity Today." *Fides et Historia* 8 (1975): 54–70.

Olson, Mark. "John Alexander: Taking Jesus Seriously." *The Other Side*, October 1985.

Oppenheimer, Mark. "'Christian Economics' Meets the Antiunion Movement." *New York Times*, 30 April 2011.

"The Other Side." *Freedom Now*, September–October 1969.

The Other Side, May–June 1976.

"Our History." The Council on Biblical Manhood and Womanhood. https://cbmw .org/about/history/.

Pannell, William E. *My Friend, the Enemy*. Waco, TX: Word, 1968.

———. "The Religious Heritage of Blacks." Pages 116–27 in *The Evangelicals*. Edited by David F. Wells and John D. Woodbridge. Grand Rapids: Baker, 1977.

Patterson, James Alan. "Evangelicals and the Presidential Elections of 1972, 1976, and 1980." *Fides et Historia* 18 (1986): 44–62.

Pattison, E. Mansell. "Confusing Concepts about the Concept of Homosexuality." *Psychiatry* 37 (1974): 340–49.

———. "Forbidden Love: A Homosexual Looks for Help and Understanding." *Christianity Today*, 12 May 1972.

———. "Good Thinking: How Homosexuality Happens." *Eternity*, May 1982.

———. "Positive Though Inaccurate." *Journal of the American Scientific Affiliation* 29 (1977): 106–8.

Pattison, E. M., and Myrna Loy Pattison. "'Ex-gays': Religiously Mediated Change in Homosexuals." *American Journal of Psychiatry* 137 (1980): 1553–62.

Perkins, John M. *With Justice for All*. Ventura, CA: Regal Books, 1982.

Petro, Anthony M. *After the Wrath of God: AIDS, Sexuality, and American Religion*. New York: Oxford University Press, 2015.

Phillips, McCandlish. "Evangelist Finds Harlem Vineyard." *New York Times*, 16 August 1964.

Philpott, Kent. *The Third Sex? Six Homosexuals Tell Their Stories*. Plainfield, NJ: Logos International, 1975.

Piper, John, and Wayne Grudem, eds. *Recovering Biblical Manhood and Womanhood: A Response to Evangelical Feminism*. Wheaton, IL: Crossway, 1991.

Plantinga, Cornelius, Jr. "The Justification of Rock Hudson." *Christianity Today*, 18 October 1985.

Potter, Ronald C. "Editorial: Thinking for Ourselves." *The Other Side*, July–August 1975.

———. "The New Black Evangelicals." Pages 302–9 in vol. 1 of *Black Theology: A Documentary History, 1966–1979*. Edited by Gayraud S. Whitmore and James H. Cone. Maryknoll, NY: Orbis Books, 1979.

Quebedeaux, Richard. *The Worldly Evangelicals*. San Francisco: Harper & Row, 1978.

———. *The Young Evangelicals*. New York: Harper & Row, 1974.

Quenqua, Douglas. "Turned Away, He Turned to the Bible." *New York Times*, 14 September 2012. https://www.nytimes.com/2012/09/16/fashion/matthew-vines-wont-rest-in-defending-gay-christians.html.

Raboteau, Albert J. *African-American Religion*. New York: Oxford University Press, 1999.

———. "The Black Experience in American Evangelicalism: The Meaning of Slavery." Pages 181–98 in *The Evangelical Tradition in America*. Edited by Leonard I. Sweet. Macon, GA: Mercer University Press, 1984.

———. *Slave Religion: The "Invisible Institution" in the Antebellum South*. Updated ed. New York: Oxford University Press, 2004.

"Race Tensions and Social Change." *Christianity Today*, 19 January 1959.

Rah, Soong-Chan. "In Whose Image: The Emergence, Development, and Challenge of African-American Evangelicalism." PhD diss., Divinity School of Duke University, 2016.

Ramm, Bernard. *After Fundamentalism: The Future of Evangelical Theology*. San Francisco: Harper & Row, 1982.

Reese, Boyd T., Jr. "Resistance and Hope: The Interplay of Theological Synthesis, Biblical Interpretation, Political Analysis, and Praxis in the Christian Radicalism of 'Sojourners' Magazine." PhD diss., Temple University, 1991.

Rice, John R. *Bobbed Hair, Bossy Wives, and Women Preachers*. Wheaton, IL: Sword of the Lord, 1941.

Riley, William Bell. *The Conflict of Christianity with Its Counterfeits*. Minneapolis: Irene Woods, 1940.

Ruether, Rosemary Radford. "Feminism in World Christianity." Pages 217–47 in *Feminism and World Religions*. Edited by Arvind Sharma and Katherine K. Young. Albany, NY: State University of New York Press, 1999.

Ruotsila, Markku. *Fighting Fundamentalist: Carl McIntire and the Politicization of American Fundamentalism*. New York: Oxford University Press, 2016.

Rzeznik, Francine, and Teodoro Maniaci, dirs. *One Nation under God*. New York: First Run Features, 1993.

Salmon, Jacqueline L. "Evangelical Leader Quits over Gay Union Remark." *Washington Post*, 12 December 2008. http://www.washingtonpost.com/wp-dyn /content/article/2008/12/11/AR2008121103578_pf.html.

Savage, Barbara Dianne. *Your Spirits Walk Beside Us: The Politics of Black Religion*. Cambridge: Belknap Press of Harvard University Press, 2008.

Scanzoni, Letha Dawson. "Backstory: 'Elevate Marriage to Partnership' (1968 Eternity article)." *Letha's Calling: A Christian Feminist Voice* (blog), 14 April 2010. https://www.lethadawsonscanzoni.com/2010/04/backstory-elevate -marriage-to-partnership1968-eternity-article/.

———. "Backstory: Woman's Place—Silence or Service?" *Letha's Calling: A Christian Feminist Voice* (blog), 25 March 2010. https://www.lethadawsonscanzoni .com/2010/03/backstory-womans-placesilence-or-service/.

———. "Conservative Christians and Gay Civil Rights." *Christian Century*, 13 October 1976.

———. "Marching On!" Pages 126–34 in *Women and the Ministries of Christ*. Edited by Roberta Hestenes and Lois Curley. Pasadena, CA: Fuller Theological Seminary, 1979.

———. "Part 1. Coauthoring 'All We're Meant to Be'—The Beginning." *Letha's Calling: A Christian Feminist Voice* (blog), 7 January 2011. https://www.letha dawsonscanzoni.com/2011/01/part-1-coauthoring-all-were-meant-to-be -the-beginning/.

———. "Part 4. Coauthoring 'All We're Meant to Be'—The Writing Process." *Letha's Calling: A Christian Feminist Voice* (blog), 3 March 2011. https://www .lethadawsonscanzoni.com/2011/03/part-4-coauthoring-all-were-meant -to-bethe-writing-process/.

———. "Part 5. Coauthoring 'All We're Meant to Be'—Getting Published." *Letha's Calling: A Christian Feminist Voice* (blog), 21 March 2011. https://www.letha dawsonscanzoni.com/2011/03/part-5-coauthoring-all-were-meant-to-be -getting-published/.

———. "Part 6. Coauthoring 'All We're Meant to Be'—Exciting Times in 1973!" *Letha's Calling: A Christian Feminist Voice* (blog), 31 March 2011. https://www.letha dawsonscanzoni.com/2011/03/part-6-coauthoring-all-were-meant-to-be -exciting-times-in-1973/.

———. "Woman's Place: Silence or Service?" *Letha's Calling: A Christian Feminist*

Voice (blog). https://lethadawsonscanzoni.com/womens-place-silence-or
-service/.

Scanzoni, Letha Dawson, and Nancy A. Hardesty. *All We're Meant to Be: A Biblical Approach to Women's Liberation*. Waco, TX: Word, 1974.

———. *All We're Meant to Be: Biblical Feminism for Today*. 3rd rev. ed. Grand Rapids: Eerdmans, 1992.

Scanzoni, Letha Dawson, and Virginia Ramey Mollenkott. *Is the Homosexual My Neighbor? Another Christian View*. San Francisco: Harper & Row, 1978.

———. *Is the Homosexual My Neighbor? A Positive Christian Response*. Rev. and updated ed. San Francisco: HarperSanFrancisco, 1994.

Schaeffer, Francis. *The Great Evangelical Disaster*. Westchester, IL: Crossway, 1984.

———. Letters. *The Other Side*, September–October 1976.

Schäfer, Axel R. *Countercultural Conservatives: American Evangelicalism from the Postwar Revival to the New Christian Right*. Madison: University of Wisconsin Press, 2011.

Schmidt, Ruth A. "Second-Class Citizenship in the Kingdom of God." *Christianity Today*, 1 January 1971.

Schwadel, Philip, and Gregory A. Smith. "Evangelical Approval of Trump Remains High, but Other Religious Groups Are Less Supportive." Pew Research Center. 18 March 2019. https://www.pewresearch.org/fact-tank/2019/03/18 /evangelical-approval-of-trump-remains-high-but-other-religious-groups -are-less-supportive/.

Sernett, Milton G. "Black Religion and the Question of Evangelical Identity." Pages 135–47 in *The Variety of American Evangelicalism*. Edited by Donald W. Dayton and Robert K. Johnston. Eugene, OR: Wipf & Stock, 1998.

Sharp, Isaac B. Review of *Evangelicalism and the Decline of American Politics*, by Jan G. Linn. *Reading Religion*. http://readingreligion.org/books/evangeli calism-and-decline-american-politics.

Sider, Ronald J. "AIDS: An Evangelical Perspective." *Christian Century*, 6–13 January 1988.

———. *Evangelism and Social Action*. London: Hodder & Stoughton, 1993.

———. "Introduction: An Historic Moment for Biblical Social Concern." Pages 11–42 in *The Chicago Declaration*. Edited by Ronald J. Sider. Carol Stream, IL: Creation House, 1974.

———. "A Reflection." Evangelicals for Social Action. https://web.archive.org /web/20180727215659/http://www.evangelicalsforsocialaction.org/about -esa/history/.

——. *Rich Christians in an Age of Hunger: A Biblical Study*. New York: Paulist, 1977.

——. *Rich Christians in an Age of Hunger: Moving from Affluence to Generosity*. 5th ed. Nashville: Thomas Nelson, 2005.

Silkey, Sarah L. *Black Woman Reformer: Ida B. Wells, Lynching, and Transatlantic Activism*. Athens: University of Georgia Press, 2015.

Skinner, Tom. *Black and Free*. Grand Rapids: Zondervan, 1968.

——. "The U.S. Racial Crisis and World Evangelism." Pages 189-209 in *Christ the Liberator: Urbana 70*. Edited by John R. W. Stott. Downers Grove, IL: InterVarsity Press, 1971.

Slade, Peter, Charles Marsh, and Peter Goodwin Heltzel, eds. *Mobilizing for the Common Good: The Lived Theology of John M. Perkins*. Jackson: University Press of Mississippi, 2013.

Smedes, Lewis B. *Sex for Christians*. Grand Rapids: Eerdmans, 1976.

Smith, Christian. *American Evangelicalism: Embattled and Thriving*. Chicago: University of Chicago Press, 1998.

——. *Resisting Reagan: The U.S. Central America Peace Movement*. Chicago: University of Chicago Press, 1996.

"Southern Baptist Convention: Resolution No. 8—On AIDS (1987)." Pages 129-30 in *The Churches Speak on AIDS: Official Statements from Religious Bodies and Ecumenical Organizations*. Edited by J. Gordon Melton. Detroit: Gale, 1989.

Spring, Beth. "Gay Rights Resolution Divides Membership of Evangelical Women's Caucus." *Christianity Today*, 3 October 1986.

——. "These Christians Are Helping Gays Escape from Homosexual Lifestyles." *Christianity Today*, 21 September 1984.

Stafford, Tim. "Coming Out." *Christianity Today*, 18 August 1989.

——. "Issue of the Year." *Christianity Today*, 5 May 1978.

——. "An Older, Wiser Ex-gay Movement: The 30-Year-Old Ministry Now Offers Realistic Hope for Homosexuals." *Christianity Today*, October 2007.

——. "Ron Sider's Unsettling Crusade." *Christianity Today*, 27 April 1992.

"Statement of Faith." Page 356 in *Women and the Ministries of Christ*. Edited by Roberta Hestenes and Lois Curley. Pasadena, CA: Fuller Theological Seminary, 1979.

Stetzer, Ed. "Debunking the 81 Percent." *Christianity Today*, October 2018.

Stewart, Chuck. "Exodus International." Pages 159-62 in vol. 1 of *Proud Heritage: People, Issues, and Documents of the LGBT Experience*. Edited by Chuck Stewart. Santa Barbara: ABC-CLIO, 2014.

——. "Sexual Orientation Change Efforts." Pages 306-11 in vol. 1 of *Proud Heri-*

tage: People, Issues, and Documents of the LGBT Experience. Edited by Chuck Stewart. Santa Barbara: ABC-CLIO, 2014.

Stiver, David. "Inventory of the Virginia Ramey Mollenkott Papers." Graduate Theological Union Archives. http://pdf.oac.cdlib.org/pdf/gtu/mollenkott.pdf.

Stott, John R. W. "Homosexual 'Marriage.'" *Christianity Today*, 22 November 1985.

Strachan, Owen. "Have Christians Been Wrong All Along? What Has the Church Believed and Taught?" Pages 59–75 in *God and the Gay Christian? A Response to Matthew Vines*. Edited by R. Albert Mohler Jr. Louisville: SBTS Press, 2014.

Sutton, Matthew Avery. *American Apocalypse: A History of Modern Evangelicalism*. Cambridge: Belknap Press of Harvard University Press, 2014.

———. *Jerry Falwell and the Rise of the Religious Right: A Brief History with Documents*. Boston: Bedford/St. Martin's, 2013.

Swartz, David R. *Moral Minority: The Evangelical Left in an Age of Conservatism*. Philadelphia: University of Pennsylvania Press, 2012.

Sweeney, Douglas A. "The Essential Evangelicalism Dialectic: The Historiography of the Early Neo-evangelical Movement and the Observer-Participant Dilemma." *Church History* 60 (1991): 70–84.

———. "Fundamentalism and the Neo-evangelicals." *Fides et Historia* 24 (1992): 81–96.

———. "Historiographical Dialectics: On Marsden, Dayton, and the Inner Logic of Evangelical History." *Christian Scholar's Review* 23 (1993): 48–52.

Sweet, Leonard I. "Wise as Serpents, Innocent as Doves: The New Evangelical Historiography." *Journal of the American Academy of Religion* 56 (1988): 397–416.

"T1. Oral History Interview with William E. Pannell, 25 May 1995." Collection 498 Oral History Interviews with William E. Pannell, CN-498. Billy Graham Center Archives. https://archives.wheaton.edu/repositories/4/resources/448/collection_organization.

"T2. Oral History Interview with William E. Pannell, 21 April 1998." Collection 498 Oral History Interviews with William E. Pannell, CN-498. Billy Graham Center Archives. https://archives.wheaton.edu/repositories/4/resources/448/collection_organization.

"T3. Oral History Interview with William E. Pannell, 21 April 1998." Collection 498 Oral History Interviews with William E. Pannell, CN-498. Billy Graham Center Archives. https://archives.wheaton.edu/repositories/4/resources/448/collection_organization.

"T4. Oral History Interview with William E. Pannell, 28 February 2000." Collection 498 Oral History Interviews with William E. Pannell, CN-498. Billy Graham Center Archives. https://archives.wheaton.edu/repositories/4/resources/448/collection_organization.

"T5. Oral History Interview with William E. Pannell, 28 February 2000." Collection 498 Oral History Interviews with William E. Pannell, CN-498. Billy Graham Center Archives. https://archives.wheaton.edu/repositories/4/resources/448/collection_organization.

"T6. Oral History Interview with William E. Pannell, 18 August 2003." Collection 498 Oral History Interviews with William E. Pannell, CN-498. Billy Graham Center Archives. https://archives.wheaton.edu/repositories/4/resources/448/collection_organization.

"T8. Oral History Interview with William E. Pannell, 27 March 2007." Collection 498 Oral History Interviews with William E. Pannell, CN-498. Billy Graham Center Archives. https://archives.wheaton.edu/repositories/4/resources/448/collection_organization.

"Tenth Anniversary Issue: The New Black Evangelicals." *The Other Side*, July–August 1975.

Thielicke, Helmut. *The Ethics of Sex*. Translated by John W. Doberstein. New York: Harper & Row, 1964.

Thorne, Phillip R. *Evangelicalism and Karl Barth*. Allison Park, PA: Pickwick, 1995.

Throckmorton, Warren. "Participant Discredits the Original Ex-gay Study." *Religion Dispatches*, 10 November 2011. http://religiondispatches.org/participant-discredits-the-original-ex-gay-study/.

Tiemstra, John P. Review of *Rich Christians in an Age of Hunger*, by Ronald J. Sider. *Fides et Historia* 12 (1979): 89–93.

Tisby, Jemar. "White Evangelical Support for Trump Comes from Churchgoers, Not EINOs." Religion News Service, 19 March 2019. https://religionnews.com/2019/03/19/white-evangelical-support-for-trump-comes-from-churchgoers-not-einos/.

"The Top Books That Have Shaped Evangelicals." *Christianity Today*, 6 October 2006.

"'Torn': Living as an Openly Gay Christian." *All Things Considered*. NPR, 9 December 2012. https://www.npr.org/2012/12/09/165276593/torn-living-as-an-openly-gay-christian.

Torrey, Reuben Archer. *Will Christ Come Again? An Exposure of the Foolishness,*

Fallacies and Falsehoods of Shailer Mathews. Los Angeles: Bible Institute of Los Angeles, 1918.

Toulouse, Mark G. "Sojourners." Pages 444–51 in *Popular Religious Magazines of the United States*. Edited by P. Mark Fackler and Charles H. Lippy. Westport, CT: Greenwood, 1995.

"The Trans-Atlantic Slave Trade Database." *SlaveVoyages*. http://www.slavevoyages.org/estimates/BIUEGjQz.

Turner, John G. *Bill Bright and Campus Crusade for Christ: The Renewal of Evangelicalism in Postwar America*. Chapel Hill: University of North Carolina Press, 2008.

Van Dusen, Henry P. *The Vindication of Liberal Theology: A Tract for the Times*. New York: Scribner's Sons, 1963.

Van Til, Cornelius. *Christianity and Barthianism*. Philadelphia: Presbyterian and Reformed, 1962.

———. "Karl Barth on Scripture." *Presbyterian Guardian*, 9 January 1937.

———. *The New Modernism*. Philadelphia: Presbyterian and Reformed, 1947.

Varner, William. Letters. *The Other Side*, September–October 1976.

Vassady, Béla. *Limping Along . . . Confessions of a Pilgrim Theologian*. Grand Rapids: Eerdmans, 1985.

———. "A Theology of Hope for the Philosophy of Despair." *Theology Today* 5 (1948): 158–73.

Vines, Matthew. *God and the Gay Christian: The Biblical Case in Support of Same-Sex Relationships*. New York: Convergent Books, 2014.

Waidzunas, Tom. *The Straight Line: How the Fringe Science of Ex-gay Therapy Reoriented Sexuality*. Minneapolis: University of Minnesota Press, 2015.

Wallis, Jim. *The Call to Conversion*. New York: Harper & Row, 1981.

———. *Faith Works: Lessons from the Life of an Activist Preacher*. New York: Random House, 2000.

———. "Post-American Christianity." *Post-American*, Fall 1971.

———. *Revive Us Again: A Sojourner's Story*. Nashville: Abingdon, 1983.

———. "'Revolt on Evangelical Frontiers': A Response." *Christianity Today*, 21 June 1974.

Washington, Joseph, Jr. *Black Religion: The Negro and Christianity in the United States*. Boston: Beacon, 1964.

"We Poll the Pollster: An Interview with George Gallup, Jr." *Christianity Today*, 21 December 1979.

"Who Are We?" *Post-American*, Fall 1971.

"Why 'Christianity Today'?" *Christianity Today*, 15 October 1956.

Williams, Daniel K. *God's Own Party: The Making of the Christian Right*. New York: Oxford University Press, 2010.

Williams, Don. *The Bond That Breaks: Will Homosexuality Split the Church?* Los Angeles: BIM, 1978.

———. "Shall We Revise the Homosexual Ethic?" *Eternity*, May 1978.

Williams, Reggie. "Pannell, Fuller, and the African American Student." Public Address. https://www.youtube.com/watch?v=YVnS9G9foNs.

Williams, Russ. "Truth . . . and Consequences: How Pat Gundry Discovered Biblical Feminism." *The Other Side*, October 1980.

Wiseman, John. "The Evangelical Theological Society: Yesterday and Today." *Journal of the Evangelical Theological Society* 28 (1982): 5–24.

Wolfe, Alan. *The Transformation of American Religion: How We Actually Live Our Faith*. Chicago: University of Chicago Press, 2003.

Wolkomir, Michelle. *"Be Not Deceived": The Sacred and Sexual Struggles of Gay and Ex-gay Christian Men*. New Brunswick, NJ: Rutgers University Press, 2006.

Wolterstorff, Claire K. "Encouragement and Unanswered Questions: Evangelicals Discuss Women's Issues." *Reformed Journal* 28 (1978): 16–19.

Wolterstorff, Nicholas. "McGovern at Wheaton." *Reformed Journal* 22, no. 9 (November 1972): 3–5.

"Women in Transition: The First Evangelical Women's Caucus Conference (1975)." *Christian Feminism Today*. https://eewc.com/the-first-evangelical-womens-caucus-conference/.

Woodward, Kenneth L. "Born Again!" *Newsweek*, 25 October 1976.

Woolley, Paul. Letters. *The Other Side*, September–October 1976.

Wormald, Benjamin. "America's Changing Religious Landscape." Pew Research Center. 12 May 2015. https://www.pewforum.org/2015/05/12/americas-changing-religious-landscape/.

———. "U.S. Public Becoming Less Religious." Pew Research Center. 3 November 2015. https://www.pewforum.org/2015/11/03/u-s-public-becoming-less-religious/.

Wuthnow, Robert. *Inventing American Religion: Polls, Surveys, and the Tenuous Quest for a Nation's Faith*. New York: Oxford University Press, 2015.

Yuan, Christopher. "Why 'God and the Gay Christian' Is Wrong about the Bible and Same-Sex Relationships." *Christianity Today*, 9 June 2014. https://

www.christianitytoday.com/ct/2014/june-web-only/why-matthew-vines -is-wrong-about-bible-same-sex-relationshi.html.

Zaspel, Fred. "Interview with Wayne Grudem, author of *Evangelical Feminism and Biblical Truth.*" *Books at a Glance*, 5 August 2014. https://www.books ataglance.com/author-interviews/interview-with-wayne-grudem-author -of-evangelical-feminism-and-biblical-truth/.

Index

of Christ," 190–92; Scanzoni and, 183, 191–92; statement of faith, 192
Evans, Elizabeth, 166–67
EWC. *See* Evangelical Women's Caucus (EWC)
Ex-Active-Gay-Liberated-Externally (EAGLE), 218
Ex-gay Intervention Team (EXIT), 215–16, 218, 228, 230–31
ex-gay movement, evangelical, 211, 215–19, 224–47; Blair's response, 216–19, 224, 229–31, 233–34, 240–42; *Christianity Today* coverage, 219, 220–21, 226, 228–29, 231–34, 239–42, 244, 245, 246; and the "ex-ex-gay phenomenon," 219, 246; Ex-gay Intervention Team (EXIT), 215–16, 218, 228, 230–31; Exodus International, 216, 219, 225–26, 231–32, 238, 239, 241, 244–45, 246–47; fall of, 245–48; Love in Action (LIA), 215, 218, 229; minors and sexual orientation change efforts (SOCE), 246; Pattison study, 226–28, 229–31; and psychological community on homosexuality and reorientation efforts, 217, 218, 225–31, 233, 246; and the Religious Right, 242–45. *See also* gay evangelicals
"'Ex-gays': Religiously Mediated Change in Homosexuals" (Pattison), 228
existentialism, 72
Exodus International, 216, 219, 225–26, 231–32, 238, 239, 241, 242, 244–45, 246–47
Explo '72 conference (Campus Crusade for Christ), 129–30, 132

Faith Bible Center (Cleveland, Ohio), 120, 121
Faith for the Family (Bob Jones University magazine), 140
Faith of Modernism, The (Mathews), 52–55, 56–57
Falwell, Jerry: and AIDS epidemic, 236, 237; conservative antigay agenda, 221, 224, 225, 231, 236, 237, 245; and Wallis, 160–61
Family Research Council, 243
Farber, Barry, 217
Farrakhan, Louis, 109

Federal Council of Churches, 36–37, 39, 40
feminist biblical scholarship, 177, 180–81, 183, 184–87, 200, 203–5
feminist movement, secular, 163, 175, 178, 197
feminists, evangelical, 31–32, 163–206, 209; biblical scholarship, 177, 180–81, 183, 184–87, 200, 203–5; the conservative antifeminist backlash against, 165, 187–88, 190, 196–200, 201–2; and conservative biblical manhood and womanhood movement, 31, 165, 197–200; emergence from within mainstream evangelicalism, 169–79; evangelical feminist organizations today, 201; Evangelical Women's Caucus (EWC), 183–84, 190–96, 203; growth and peak of the movement, 190–93; Hardesty, 32, 172–76, 178, 180–84, 200; homosexuality controversy and fracture of the movement, 193–96, 209, 222–23; "Jewett-Mollenkott view of Scripture," 184–87; Jewett's *Man as Male and Female*, 184–87; Mollenkott, 32, 176–78, 183, 186–87, 193–94, 200, 203–5, 222–24; Scanzoni, 32, 169–75, 178, 180–81, 183, 191, 193–94, 200, 222–24; Scanzoni and Hardesty's *All We're Meant to Be*, 180–81, 184, 186; and sexual complementarianism, 165, 198–200, 202; and sexual egalitarianism, 165, 178, 186–88, 196–200, 201–2; Thanksgiving Workshop (1973) and progressive Chicago Declaration, 138, 181–82. *See also* women and mainstream evangelicalism
feminist theology, radical, 178
Focus on the Family, 243–45
Fort Wayne Bible Institute, 94–95
Fosdick, Harry Emerson, 30, 55–60, 61, 70, 74; defense of modernism, 59; and evangelical liberalism, 61, 63; and the fundamentalist-modernist controversies, 56–59; popular writings and sermons, 56, 58; "Shall the Fundamentalists Win?" (1922 sermon), 57–59
Frame, Randy, 232–33
Freedom Now (periodical), 121–22

Index

shop (1973), 136–41, 181–82; Wallis, 31, 126–31, 143–46, 149, 151, 158–61. *See also* feminists, evangelical
Progressive Evangelicals and the Pursuit of Social Justice (Gasaway), 154–55
Promise Keepers, 113, 201
Puritans, 11

Quebedeaux, Richard, 146
Quest Learning Center, 240

"racial reconciliation" movement, 83, 109–11, 113–14
racism, white evangelical, 31, 77, 78, 81, 85–86, 89–91, 99–100, 101, 105–6, 108, 110–15, 264–66. *See also* white evangelicals
Ramm, Bernard, 74
Rauschenbusch, Walter, 133
Reagan, Ronald: and ascent of the Religious Right, 7, 117, 149, 150; and the evangelical left, 149–52, 161; foreign policy in Central America, 149–52
Reconciliation Blues: A Black Evangelical's View of White Christianity (Gilbreath), 111–12, 115
Recovering Biblical Manhood and Womanhood: A Response to Evangelical Feminism (Piper and Grudem), 199–200
Reformed Journal, 135, 139, 229
Reformed Theological Seminary (Florida), 159
Reformed tradition, xviii, 10–13, 23, 66–67, 70. *See also* Calvinists
Reforming Fundamentalism: Fuller Seminary and the New Evangelicalism (Marsden), 10–12, 41
Religious Right, 31, 117–19, 149, 152–62; and AIDS crisis, 236; antifeminism, 201–2; antigay prejudice and denunciation of homosexuality, 221, 225, 236, 242–45; attacks on Sider's *Rich Christians in an Age of Hunger*, 148, 156–58; attacks on Wallis and *Sojourners*, 158–61; and the ex-gay movement, 242–45; and the progressive evangelical left, 31, 117–19, 149, 152–62; Reagan and, 7, 117, 149, 150;

and the Republican Party, 31, 117, 118–19, 154, 155
Republican Party: Billy Graham and Nixon campaign, 131–33; and the Religious Right, 31, 117–19, 154, 155; Trump and the 2016 election, 260–64, 269
Restored Hope Network, 247
Rian, Joseph, 93
Rice, Jim, 151
Rice, John R., 80
Rich Christians in an Age of Hunger (Sider), 146–48, 156–58
Riley, William Bell, 80, 167
Roberts, Oral, 132
Robertson, Carole, 96
Roe v. Wade, 117
Roman Catholic Church, 76, 158, 161, 183
Roosevelt University, 90
Rushdoony, R. J., 156, 232
Ryken, Philip, 263
Ryrie, Charles C., 171

Salguero, Gabriel, 263
Salley, Columbus, 102
same-sex marriage, 210, 247–48, 250–52, 257
Scanzoni, Letha Dawson, 32, 169–75, 178, 180–81, 183, 191, 193–94, 200, 222–24; *All We're Meant to Be* (1974), 180–81, 184, 186; early life, evangelical education, and writing career, 169–71; on egalitarian marriage, 172–73; *Eternity* articles on women in the church, 171–73; and the evangelical feminist controversy over homosexuality, 193–94, 222–23; and EWC, 183, 191; and Hardesty, 172–75, 180–81; *Is the Homosexual My Neighbor?* (1978), 193–94, 222–23
Schaeffer, Francis, 142, 153
Schäfer, Axel R., 154, 155
Schmidt, Ruth A., 175
Scopes trial, 116
secular humanism, 153
Sensuous Spirituality (Mollenkott), 204
Sex for Christians (Smedes), 221
sexual orientation change efforts (SOCE),